# Empire's Children

Between 1869 and 1967, government-funded British charities sent nearly 100,000 underprivileged children to start new lives in the settler empire. This pioneering study tells the story of the rise and fall of child emigration to Canada, Australia, New Zealand, and Southern Rhodesia. In the mid-Victorian period, the book reveals, the concept of a global British race had a profound impact on the practice of charity work, the evolution of child welfare, and the experiences of poor children. During the twentieth century, however, rising nationalism in the dominions, alongside the emergence of new, psychological theories of child welfare, eroded faith in the "British world" and brought child emigration into question. Combining archival sources with original oral histories, *Empire's Children* not only explores the powerful influence of empire on child-centered social policy, it also uncovers how the lives of ordinary children and families were forever transformed by imperial forces and settler nationalism.

ELLEN BOUCHER is Assistant Professor of History at the Department of History, Amherst College, Massachusetts.

# Empire's Children

*Child Emigration, Welfare, and the Decline of
the British World, 1869–1967*

Ellen Boucher

CAMBRIDGE
UNIVERSITY PRESS

# CAMBRIDGE
## UNIVERSITY PRESS

University Printing House, Cambridge CB2 8BS, United Kingdom

Cambridge University Press is part of the University of Cambridge.

It furthers the University's mission by disseminating knowledge in the pursuit of education, learning and research at the highest international levels of excellence.

www.cambridge.org
Information on this title: www.cambridge.org/9781316620304

First published 2014
First paperback edition 2016

*A catalogue record for this publication is available from the British Library*

*Library of Congress Cataloguing in Publication data*
Boucher, Ellen, 1978–
Empire's children : child emigration, welfare, and the decline of the British
world, 1869–1967 / Ellen Boucher.
    pages   cm
Includes bibliographical references and index.
ISBN 978-1-107-04138-7 (hardback)
1. Child welfare–Great Britain–Colonies–History–20th
century.   2. Unaccompanied immigrant children–Great Britain–Colonies–
History–20th century.   3. Great Britain–Colonies–Emigration and
immigration–History–20th century.   4. Group identity–Great
Britain–Colonies–History–20th century.   I. Title.
HV751.A6B66 2014
362.709171′24109041–dc23
2013039678

ISBN 978-1-107-04138-7 Hardback
ISBN 978-1-316-62030-4 Paperback

# Contents

# Illustrations and table

## Illustrations

## Table

# Acknowledgments

I accumulated many debts in the process of researching and writing this book, and it is my great pleasure to be able to acknowledge here the people and institutions that made this work possible. First and foremost, my sincere thanks to the men and women who graciously shared with me their memories of growing up in child migrant farm schools and institutions. Their rich, perceptive, and candid insights informed every aspect of my thinking, deepening my engagement with the archive in unexpected ways. Although I have not been able to use material from all of their interviews in the text that follows, their influence has shaped every page. I am grateful as well to Peter Gould, Bill Hoyles, Mervyn Humphreys, Dennis Silver, and Pam Wilson for their assistance in making contact with potential interviewees. Vivian Finn's astute comments on early drafts were extremely helpful, and I thank him for many stimulating conversations along the way.

This work began life as my dissertation at Columbia University under the direction of Susan Pedersen, whose advice, encouragement, humor, and support were unfailing throughout the many years of this project. I deeply appreciate her continued mentorship, and owe her more than I will ever be able to repay. Marcia Wright and Lisa Tiersten were wonderful mentors as well; they offered challenging and incisive comments on multiple drafts, and were always generous with their time and guidance. I would also like to thank Frank Mort for encouraging the early development of this project while he was a visiting professor at Columbia, as well as Lynn Lees and Ellen Ross for their thought-provoking suggestions on an earlier version of the manuscript.

I am grateful to the numerous institutions that provided funding for the research and writing of this book, including the Council on Library and Information Resources, the Doris Quinn Foundation, the Mellon Foundation, Columbia University, Furman University, and Amherst College. Numerous archivists and librarians went out of their way to answer my questions and to help me locate sources, particularly Adrian Allan at the University of Liverpool, Jim Andrighetti at the Mitchell

Library, and Rachel Rowe at the University of Cambridge. My thanks to Barnardo's, the Fairbridge Society, and the National Children's Home for kindly granting me permission to access their archives. I have not included any specific identification details of child migrants in these records in order to protect their anonymity, and these charities bear no responsibility for this publication.

Many friends and colleagues offered invaluable feedback during the process of writing this book. Monica Black, Victoria Blake, Charlotte Boucher, Brian DeVore, Allison Hurst, Laura Lovett, and Joni Tevis read drafts of the manuscript at critical points in its development, and their comments were immensely helpful in shaping my thinking. Marianne Bessy, Mehmet Dosemeci, Victoria Durrer, Marilyn Lake, Jeffrey Saletnik, Michal Shapira, Penny Sinanaglou, Jennifer Thomson, Andrew Vagg, and Theresa Ventura – alongside many, many others – offered insights, support, and good cheer across numerous continents, for which I am incredibly grateful. The two anonymous readers of the manuscript for Cambridge University Press provided wonderful advice that pushed me to refine or expand my ideas in numerous places. In particular, Reader A helped clarify my thinking about the history of child emigration to Canada, while Reader B encouraged me to delve deeper into the lasting legacies of the programs. My thanks to them both for their critical attention and their excellent comments; any errors that remain in the text are, of course, my responsibility alone. I would also like to thank the members of the Five-College History Faculty Seminar as well as the Valley Victorianists Group for making Amherst such a welcoming and inspiring place to work. I have learned a tremendous amount from my colleagues in the History department at Amherst College, and before that Furman University, and am indebted to them all for their encouragement and assistance. Kate Barton lovingly read the entire manuscript, which is much improved thanks to her sharp editorial eye. I also appreciate the hard work Destiny Casillas contributed to tracking down references and compiling the bibliography. My thanks as well to Michael Watson at Cambridge University Press for making the daunting process of publication so straightforward and stress free.

Finally, throughout the process of writing this book, I have been reminded in countless ways of how fortunate I am to have my family. I could not have completed this project without the unswerving faith in my abilities of my parents, Charlotte and Douglas, and my brother, Johnny. In addition, Brian DeVore has enriched every part of my life since he entered it five years ago. His enthusiasm, unstinting praise, steady encouragement, and quick wit have kept me going through the final stages of this book, and I cannot thank him enough for filling my days with joy. Esme DeVore joined our family just as this book was heading to press, and brightened the long hours of revisions and copy editing with her loving presence. Finally, I am so grateful for the love and inspiration of one of my greatest champions – my Granny, another Ellen Boucher. This book is dedicated to her.

Portions of Chapters 1, 2, and 4 have been published before, although in significantly altered form, as: "Developing Empire, Building Children: The Ideology of British Child Emigration, 1918–1939," *Histoires d'enfant, histoires d'enfance (Stories for Children, Histories of Childhood): GRAAT Revue* 36 (June 2007): 261–285; "The Limits of Potential: Race, Welfare, and the Interwar Extension of Child Emigration to Southern Rhodesia," *Journal of British Studies* 48 (October 2009): 914–934.

# Abbreviations

| | |
|---|---|
| ANA | Australian National Archives |
| CAF | Central African Federation |
| CCCW | Canadian Council of Child Welfare |
| CES | Child Emigration Society (later Fairbridge Society) |
| CRO | Commonwealth Relations Office |
| CUL: RCS | Cambridge University Library, Royal Commonwealth Society |
| CVOCE | Council of Voluntary Organisations for Child Emigration |
| EEC | European Economic Community |
| LGB | Local Government Board |
| NCH | National Children's Home |
| NLA | National Library of Australia |
| NSPCC | National Society for the Prevention of Cruelty to Children |
| OSC | Oversea Settlement Committee |
| OVC | Overseas Visitors Club |
| RFMC | Rhodesia Fairbridge Memorial College |
| SAWA: BL | State Archives of Western Australia: Battye Library |
| SLNSW | State Library of New South Wales, Mitchell Library |
| TNA: PRO | The National Archives: Public Record Office (United Kingdom) |
| UDI | Rhodesian Unilateral Declaration of Independence, 1965 |
| ULSCA | University of Liverpool Special Collections and Archives |
| WHO | World Health Organization |

# Introduction

Michael Oldfield was born on May 8, 1936. But he dates the real beginning of his life to ten years later, in September of 1946, when he entered a child welfare home called Folly House run by Barnardo's, Britain's largest children's charity at the time. Of course, he had lived through those earlier years, yet his memory of them is "more or less blank. I really just have very faint ideas that I was there, but nothing more. And it wasn't until I arrived in [Folly House] that I really sort of started to recollect my thoughts as I know them today."[1] Given these gaps in his memory, all that Oldfield knows about his early childhood comes from clues found in his official Barnardo's file, which he received in 1979 after he became curious about his missing years and asked the organization for a copy. He brought this thick manila folder with him when we met in Petersham on the outskirts of Sydney, Australia, on a sunny summer day in 2006. Our conversation began with a great shuffling of papers, as Oldfield sorted through medical reports, school records, and old photos, carefully piecing together his history from the time before it became his memory. As his narrative moved forward chronologically, he grew less dependent on the file, and by the time we reached the late 1940s he had largely placed it aside. Instead, he relied on his trove of memories of events long past but not forgotten, weaving these together to give me a sense of who he is today, and how he came to be that way.

Oldfield's story begins in the maternity ward of London's St. Pancras Hospital, where he and his twin sister Sheila were born during the later years of the Great Depression. His parents were never well off, and struggled to make ends meet. It was perhaps the promise of a steady paycheck that led his father to sign up for the army as soon as the Second World War began, leaving his mother to continue to care for the two children while working full time as a domestic servant. The work was exhausting, and when she received word in 1941 that her husband had been killed in action, it all became too much. On the advice of her employer as well as

---

[1] Author's interview with Michael Oldfield, February 23, 2006.

the local welfare authorities, she decided to place the by-now four-year-old twins with Barnardo's.

Judging by the stack of transfer reports in Oldfield's file, the next few years were a flurry of activity. He and his sister moved from one orphanage to the next to avoid Nazi air raids. In all the commotion, they lost touch with their mother, although the siblings stayed together throughout the war and eventually ended up in a group home in Scotland. Oldfield, though, had always been a sickly child, and, when he contracted an illness so severe that he needed hospitalization, the directors of the home decided that the northern weather was not agreeing with him. Barnardo's sent him south to England and to Folly House, but away from Sheila, who stayed up north. They would meet again several years later, but in a different continent, half a world away. The period in Scotland was the last time that the two were in regular contact with each other.

When Oldfield entered Folly House, it was a large, three-story country home surrounded by farmlands and filled with almost thirty little boys. He settled in easily, joining the local choir and succeeding in his classes. He was voted "boy of the year" three years in a row, an honor for which he won an elegant pinstriped suit that he wore until it was bursting at the seams. Oldfield probably would have continued along happily in Folly House had a man from Barnardo's head office not arrived one day in 1949 to talk to the boys about a unique opportunity available to them. The official told them that the organization often sent parties of children to live in a farm school in Australia. Would any boys from Folly House like to go? The talk struck a chord with Oldfield because he had recently studied the country in his geography class. His first thought was: "Australia, I've just drawn a map of that!" The rest of the discussion was a blur, but Oldfield notes that it must have been "persuasive," since after the meeting ended he asked for his name to be put on the list. A few weeks later, Oldfield received word that he was one of three boys from Folly House accepted for emigration that year. To Barnardo's, he was an ideal candidate: smart, well adjusted, and with no ties to his immediate family. His file indicates that the organization attempted to contact his mother for permission, but there is no record of her response. Perhaps, Oldfield muses, she had simply moved on with her life. There was another reason that he seemed particularly suited for the program. Although he would not know it until the eve of his departure, Barnardo's had already sent Sheila to Australia two years before. The siblings would meet again briefly on the quayside after his arrival in Sydney harbor, two awkward thirteen-year-olds who looked remarkably alike but found they had little to say to each other.

At the time, Oldfield never saw himself as a historical actor, as someone whose life was both shaped by, and was actively shaping, the wider
forces of history around him. Yet in retrospect, his story of family separation, institutional care, and movement across continents has made his
childhood seem atypical, at least in comparison to the majority of those
in the modern West. This sense of historical disjuncture has meant that
although Oldfield has defined himself in a variety of ways throughout his
life – farmer, scholar, Anglican, freemason, world traveler – today others
are more likely to think of him as a member of a distinct and historically
specific group: British child migrants. Oldfield and his sister were two
of the roughly 95,000 boys and girls selected between the years 1869
and 1967 by government-funded British charities for permanent relocation to the settler dominions of Canada, Australia, New Zealand, and
Southern Rhodesia.[2] Like Oldfield, the majority of these children were
between the ages of five and thirteen. Most also came, as he did, from
poor, primarily working-class households in Britain's major cities. Once
overseas, they were groomed for a rural lifestyle and tended to remain
in agricultural careers in the dominions throughout their lives. In more
recent decades, however, large numbers of these former child migrants
have returned to the United Kingdom as adults in search of lost relatives
or to start life over in the land of their birth. Many have spoken openly
about the feelings of pain and dislocation stemming from their removal
from family and birth country, as well as of their experiences of abuse,
neglect, or institutionalization in children's homes and orphanages in the
dominions.[3] At the same time, activist groups in Britain and Australia

---

[2] The exact number of child migrants sent abroad in this period is impossible to tell given
the inadequate nature of the records. The highest estimate cited is 150,000, although
this figure includes "juvenile migrants" – those over the school-leaving age of fourteen –
as well as those sent abroad before the modern child emigration movement began in
the late Victorian period. Recent scholars agree that at least 80,000 went to Canada
from the 1860s through the 1920s; in *Children of the Empire* (London: Weidenfeld and
Nicholson, 1982), 259, Gillian Wagner puts the figure at 88,000. Adding in the slightly
more than 6,000 sent to Australia in the twentieth century, as well as the estimated 500
to New Zealand and 276 to Southern Rhodesia in the postwar period, the total number
of child migrants amounts to around 95,000. For a full discussion, see Marjory Harper
and Stephen Constantine, *Migration and Empire* (Oxford University Press, 2010), 248.

[3] These testimonies have appeared prominently in two government inquiries into the policy
held in Britain and Australia, the reports of which can be found in: House of Commons,
Health Committee, *The Welfare of Former British Child Migrants* (London: Stationery
Office, 1998); Senate Community Affairs References Committee, *Lost Innocents: Righting
the Record – Report on Child Migration* (Canberra: Commonwealth of Australia, 2001). A
number of popular histories have also highlighted the more abusive aspects of the policy.
See in particular: Philip Bean and Joy Melville, *Lost Children of the Empire: The Untold
Story of Britain's Child Migrants* (London: Unwin Hyman, 1989); Margaret Humphreys,
*Empty Cradles* (London: Doubleday, 1994); Alan Gill, *Orphans of the Empire: The Shocking
Story of Child Migration to Australia* (Sydney: Millennium Books, 1997); David Hill, *The*

have done much to raise awareness about the long-term emotional consequences of the initiatives for former child migrants, and to push for compensation.[4] These efforts have not been in vain; in 2009 and 2010, both governments issued formal apologies for their previous sponsorship of the programs. Gordon Brown, the British Prime Minister at the time, called child emigration a "shameful episode of history" that represented Britain's "failure in the first duty of a nation, which is to protect its children."[5]

I spoke with Oldfield three years before these apologies made the history of child emigration international news, but he was already well aware that the general view of the policy was a negative one. He thus took pains to emphasize that his own experience was different. He had only fond memories of his time with Barnardo's, and never felt the trauma and loss that some other former migrants have known. He spoke of his resettlement to Australia as a wonderful adventure, stressing the thrill he felt when boarding an ocean liner in the port of Southampton, as well as his excitement at seeing the "vastness" of the country when he arrived, some six weeks later, at the Barnardo's farm school of Mowbray Park in Picton, New South Wales. Oldfield remembered Mowbray Park as a "beautiful place … grand," with more space to play in than he had ever seen in Britain, and he told me funny stories about adapting to Australian culture. To his horror, on his second night at the school he was served roasted pumpkin, a food that only animals ate back at Folly House. He managed to suffer it down, but never developed much of a taste for it. Even today, the only way he can bear it is baked in a scone. On the whole, though, his transition was smooth. He excelled at the local school, made friends quickly, and enjoyed the training he received in farming and dairying. When Oldfield talked about Mowbray Park, he switched from the first-person singular, "I," to the plural, "we." To him, this was not an isolated institution but a community, "a small village," where he counted as a valued member of the whole. He noted that this sense of connection and camaraderie helped him to become assimilated into the country that is now his home. He has remained in Australia to this day, and has no desire to return to Britain for more than the occasional holiday.

---

*Forgotten Children: Fairbridge Farm School and Its Betrayal of Britain's Child Migrants to Australia* (Sydney: Random House, 2007).

[4] The most prominent advocacy group is the Child Migrants Trust, based in Nottingham, with an additional office in Melbourne. For a description of its work, see the book authored by its founder: Humphreys, *Empty Cradles*.

[5] Great Britain, House of Commons, *Debates* 506, no. 44, 6th series, February 24, 2010, col. 301. For the Australian apology, see Commonwealth of Australia, House of Representatives, *Debates* 17, 1st session, 6th period, November 16, 2009, 11,647–11,650.

As Oldfield told it, his was a tale of successful integration, of crossing oceans to find a place where he belonged. Even so, when I asked how he identified himself – did he feel more British or Australian? – his feelings lay somewhere in between. "I've always associated myself as half English," he said. Noting that his accent had changed little over the years, he told me that, when people asked where he was from, he usually replied that he was an "English gentleman or English fellow. Even though I know – I've been here for fifty years – that I'm Australian. But people still accept me as being English." He joked that he even dressed the part, having kept his penchant for pinstriped suits ever since receiving that first one back at Folly House. He certainly looked smart on the day of our interview, his dark blue suit, Windsor knotted tie, and pocket handkerchief considerably outshining my own graduate-student attire.

Michael Oldfield's migration story, and his comments about feeling simultaneously "Australian" and "half English" provide a helpful reminder, in this era of passport controls and visa restrictions, that the boundaries between nations and national identities have not always been as fixed as they might now appear. On the contrary, it has long been possible for people to imagine themselves as members of multiple and overlapping communities, a fluidity of belonging that was especially prominent among those who lived in the context of empire. As Linda Colley has shown, the notion that individuals could ascribe to several different identities at once lay at the heart of Britain's imperial project from the eighteenth century onward. It was central to the development of a new, overarching sense of "Britishness" that served to unify the disparate inhabitants of England, Ireland, Scotland, and Wales into a coherent nation without destroying their preexisting loyalties.[6] In the nineteenth and early twentieth centuries, as this small island nation came to rule one-quarter of the world's population, this ethic of Britishness was transformed into a truly global identity. It was carried overseas by the roughly 25 million souls who left the United Kingdom for foreign shores between the end of the Napoleonic wars through the 1920s, a massive transfer of people that still stands as one of the largest world migrations in the modern era.[7] The great majority of these Britons chose to live among their "brethren" in the United States and the settler empire. There, like Oldfield, they forged unique local identities but also retained a firm connection to their natal heritage. This complex sense of self became the

---

[6] Linda Colley, *Britons: Forging the Nation, 1707–1837* (New Haven: Yale University Press, 1992).

[7] James Belich, *Replenishing the Earth: The Settler Revolution and the Rise of the Angloworld, 1783–1939* (Oxford University Press, 2009), 126.

hallmark of the territories that made up what recent scholars have termed the "British world" but that contemporaries at the time were more likely to call, simply, "Greater Britain."[8]

Both at home and abroad, Britishness was often viewed as an exceptional spirit, the core part of a person's being that encompassed her "British soul."[9] For Oldfield, this inner nature still found expression in the most basic and unconscious aspects of his personality: how he spoke and carried himself, how he dressed. This notion that all people contain a deep-seated essence reflecting their origins is an old one, dating back in British culture to at least the Enlightenment. In the eighteenth century, writers described it as the natural "bent" or "inclination" that distinguished each individual and that, writ large, tended to separate society into discrete social classes.[10] In the nineteenth century, the idea was reworked in two different yet complementary ways. The first was a growing emphasis on childhood as the most formative stage of life, the time in which every person interacted with their environment to develop an identity that determined how they would think, feel, and behave in adulthood.[11] The second was an argument about the power of heredity, which underwrote a view of the world divided by blood and culture into separate nations, races, and ethnicities.[12] In late Victorian Britain, as the nation rapidly expanded its imperial reach, these ideas combined into the jingoistic ideal that the British people

---

[8] Carl Bridge and Kent Fedorowich, eds., *The British World: Diaspora, Culture, and Identity* (London: Frank Cass, 2003); Philip Buckner and R. Douglas Francis, eds., *Rediscovering the British World* (University of Calgary Press, 2005); Duncan Bell, *The Idea of Greater Britain: Empire and the Future of the World Order, 1860–1900* (Princeton University Press, 2007); Kate Darian-Smith, Patricia Grimshaw, and Stuart Macintyre, eds., *Britishness Abroad: Transnational Movements and Imperial Cultures* (Melbourne University Press, 2008); John Darwin, *The Empire Project: The Rise and Fall of the British World-System, 1830–1970* (Cambridge University Press, 2009).

[9] This quote comes from the original version of "Advance Australia Fair," by the Scottish composer Peter Dodds McCormick (1878), cited in Neville Meaney, "Britishness and Australia: Some Reflections," *Journal of Imperial and Commonwealth History* 31, no. 2 (May 2003): 121–135, 121.

[10] Jenny Davidson, *Breeding: A Partial History of the Eighteenth Century* (New York: Columbia University Press, 2009).

[11] Carolyn Steedman, *Strange Dislocations: Childhood and the Idea of Human Interiority, 1780–1930* (Cambridge, MA: Harvard University Press, 1995).

[12] This hardening of racial attitudes has been most apparent in studies of missionaries, which have traced the waning of an earlier, evangelical faith in the universal brotherhood of man during the middle decades of the nineteenth century and the rise of newer tendencies to essentialize the differences between colonizer and colonized. See especially Catherine Hall, *Civilising Subjects: Metropole and Colony in the English Imagination, 1830–1867* (University of Chicago Press, 2002); Richard Price, *Making Empire: Colonial Encounters and the Making of Imperial Rule in Nineteenth-Century Africa* (Cambridge University Press, 2008).

formed a distinct master race, gifted in the art of liberty and destined
to spread the benefits of their civilization around the globe.[13] Britons, it
seemed, were born with a kernel of this superiority lodged deep within
them. Yet it was the experiences of childhood that determined whether
it would bloom or remain dormant, as well as the particular expression
it would take in adulthood.

Child emigration was a product of this tendency to understand
Britishness as an ethnic and spiritual core that required careful cultivation
to achieve its full potential. While Poor Law authorities and private charities had sporadically resettled child apprentices in the colonies since the
seventeenth century, child emigration first emerged as a coherent movement in 1869, when the philanthropist Maria Rye began sending regular
parties of what she called her "gutter children" to Canada.[14] Like other
"child savers" of her time, Rye was eager to pluck poor children from
the streets of British slums before their malleable constitutions were corrupted through the forces of want, disease, and immorality. Transferred
overseas to the underpopulated yet bountiful dominions, they would live
among those who were, as she assured readers of *The Times*, "bone of
your bone and flesh of your flesh."[15] There, as the children grew fit and
strong from the hearty, outdoor lifestyle, they would also help extend the
reach of British settlement, bringing thousands of new acres of Greater
Britain's dark, rich soil under plow.

This was a vision of mutual development: of needy children made whole
and the settler empire fulfilled. Its effects were significant. In Britain, it
served to justify a more intensive intrusion into the private realm of the
family. At the time, it was not uncommon for social reformers to seek the
removal of children from destitute households in an effort to improve
their life chances and to protect the future stability of the nation. Thomas
Barnardo, the founder of the organization that still bears his name, called
this form of intervention "philanthropic abduction," and he touted it as

[13] The concept found its clearest expression in two extremely popular works of Victorian
literature, Charles Dilke's travelogue, *Greater Britain: A Record of Travel in the English-
Speaking Countries during 1866 and 1867*, 2 vols. (London: Macmillan, 1868), and J.
R. Seeley's bestselling *The Expansion of England: Two Courses of Lectures* (London:
Macmillan, 1883).

[14] On the earlier history of child emigration, see Wagner, *Children of the Empire*, 1–35;
Elaine Hadley, "Natives in a Strange Land: The Philanthropic Discourse of Juvenile
Emigration in Mid-Nineteenth-Century England," *Victorian Studies* 33, no. 3 (Spring
1990): 411–439; Barry Coldrey, "'A Thriving and Ugly Trade': The First Phase of Child
Migration, 1617–1757," *History of Education Society Bulletin* 58 (Autumn 1996): 4–14;.
On Rye's life and work, see Marion Diamond, *Emigration and Empire: The Life of Maria S.
Rye* (New York: Garland, 1999); Lisa Chilton, *Agents of Empire: British Female Migration
to Canada and Australia, 1860s–1930* (University of Toronto Press, 2007).

[15] Maria S. Rye, "Our Gutter Children," *The Times*, March 29, 1869, 8.

one of the most laudable aspects of his work.[16] In this respect, child emigration was no different from a host of late nineteenth-century initiatives that placed the collective interests of society over the claims of poor parents. Its ideology was mirrored in the "orphan trains" that trundled some 250,000 boys and girls across the United States from the 1850s to the 1920s, most of whom were foundlings from New York City sent to live with farming families in the American West.[17] This vision also appeared in the public and charitable institutions that sprang up across Europe to take in the children of paupers.[18]

Setting child emigration apart from these other schemes was its emphasis on the settler empire as a redemptive space for the British race. Like many in the dominions, emigration proponents defined these territories not as mere replicas of the mother country but as "Better Britains," egalitarian regions that lacked the entrenched class hierarchies and social problems that plagued the homeland.[19] This concept underlay their insistence that resettlement would allow destitute children to attain a higher degree of social mobility than if they remained in Britain. While most metropolitan reformers aimed to promote their wards into the ranks of the respectable working class, emigration enthusiasts aimed higher, imagining that even the lowest "gutter child" could become an independent property owner or a member of the professions. This promise of future advancement provided a powerful justification for a program that often severed the children's links to the people and places they had formerly known. In Britain, as Lydia Murdoch has shown, many struggling parents placed their young in charitable homes and Poor Law institutions only temporarily. They often maintained contact with their children and exercised a degree of control over their fate.[20] Emigration, on the other hand, was intended to be permanent. It understood children

---

[16] Thomas Barnardo, "Is Philanthropic Abduction Ever Justifiable?" *Night and Day* (November 1885): 149–150.

[17] Stephen O'Connor, *Orphan Trains: The Story of Charles Loring Brace and the Children He Saved and Failed* (New York: Houghton Mifflin, 2001), xvii. See also Marilyn Holt, *The Orphan Trains: Placing Out in America* (Lincoln: University of Nebraska Press, 1992); Jeanne F. Cook, "A History of Placing-Out: The Orphan Trains," *Child Welfare* 74, no. 1 (January–February 1995): 181–197; Linda Gordon, *The Great Arizona Orphan Abduction* (Cambridge, MA: Harvard University Press, 1999).

[18] Rachel Fuchs, *Abandoned Children: Foundlings and Child Welfare in Nineteenth Century France* (Albany: State University of New York Press, 1984); Lydia Murdoch, *Imagined Orphans: Poor Families, Child Welfare, and Contested Citizenship in London* (New Brunswick: Rutgers University Press, 2006).

[19] Buckner and Francis, "Introduction," *Rediscovering the British World*, 15. On the concept of the dominions as "Better Britains," see also James Belich, *Paradise Reforged: A History of the New Zealanders from the 1880s to the Year 2000* (Honolulu: University of Hawaii Press, 2001).

[20] Murdoch, *Imagined Orphans*, 92–119.

to be less the product of their biological families than the embodiment of an imperial race destined for greatness.

In articulating this expanded and seemingly classless vision of British children's potential in the empire, and by employing it to reconfigure the conventional boundaries of parental rights, child emigration left a significant imprint on late Victorian culture, even though the actual number of children resettled during these years was a fraction of the total in care.[21] As such, the policy stands as another example of how the growth of British imperialism shaped the ideologies, practices, and institutions of metropolitan life during the final decades of the nineteenth century. In this instance, Britain's status as an imperial nation inspired reformers to think in fresh ways about the social value of poor children, and offered new possibilities for their care.[22] In recent years, the task of illuminating the influence of empire "at home" in Britain has become a major concern of historians and literary scholars, with the majority of their scholarship focusing on the networks of power and authority that connected the nation to its colonies in Africa and Asia.[23] Yet the case of child emigration suggests that, within the emerging realm of child welfare, it was not the formal empire, marked by clear notions of racial and cultural difference, that dominated the minds of British social reformers. Rather, it was the "kith and kin" territories, defined through the bonds of spiritual and ethnic "sameness," that had the most effect. Expanding the analysis to take this other imperial terrain into account is important, for it provides a new perspective on the role imperialism played in determining what it meant to be "British" in the late nineteenth century. For many Victorians, the idea of a pan-Britannic race freely occupying a larger British world resonated more strongly and more personally in their lives than the less

[21] As Murdoch points out, the proportion of child migrants sent overseas in the Victorian era was always much lower than the number of children receiving indoor relief in Britain. In just one year, 1884–1885, for example, over 54,000 boys and girls under the age of sixteen were living in Poor Law institutions in England and Wales. Ibid, 170, note 24.

[22] On the impact of imperialism on the development of British child welfare more generally, see Anna Davin, "Imperialism and Motherhood," in *Tensions of Empire: Colonial Cultures in a Bourgeois World*, ed. Frederick Cooper and Ann Stoler (Berkeley: University of California Press, 1997), 87–151.

[23] Essential introductions to this now considerable literature include: Catherine Hall, ed., *Cultures of Empire, a Reader: Colonizers in Britain and the Empire in the Nineteenth and Twentieth Centuries* (Manchester University Press, 2000); Antoinette Burton, ed., *After the Imperial Turn: Thinking With and Through the Nation* (Durham: Duke University Press, 2003); Kathleen Wilson, ed., *A New Imperial History: Culture, Identity and Modernity in Britain and the Empire, 1660–1840* (Cambridge University Press, 2004); Andrew Thompson, *The Empire Strikes Back? The Impact of Imperialism on Britain from the Mid-Nineteenth Century* (New York: Pearson Longman, 2005); Catherine Hall and Sonya Rose, eds., *At Home with the Empire: Metropolitan Culture and the Imperial World* (Cambridge University Press, 2006).

familiar and sometimes alarming visions that were associated with the empire of domination.[24]

While more work is needed to explore just how deeply the concept of Greater Britain permeated British society and culture, its effect overseas is clearer. The decades surrounding the turn of the twentieth century were a period of tremendous growth in local patriotisms across the settler empire, as nationalists in each of the dominions sought to define the qualities and characteristics that they felt were unique to their countrymen.[25] The rise of these local identities did little to challenge the central place of Britishness within the settler imagination, however.[26] On the contrary, the notion of a global community of Britons arguably meant more in the settler territories during these years than it did in Britain itself, for it invested these emerging nations with the potent notions of White racial superiority and civilizational pride that underpinned the wider imperial mission. Such sentiments were clearly on display in the popular enthusiasm at the turn of the twentieth century for the South African War, a conflict that was much less controversial in Australia or New Zealand than it was in the mother country.[27] And they received another boost from the movement toward self-government across the settler empire, a trend that was effectively completed by 1931 when the Statute of Westminster recognized the dominions' legislative autonomy and equal status to Britain. Instead of weakening the bonds of imperial belonging throughout the British world, these constitutional changes

---

[24] Stuart Ward, "Echoes of Empire," *History Workshop Journal* 62, no. 1 (October 2006): 264–278.

[25] John Eddy and Deryck Schreuder, eds., *The Rise of Colonial Nationalism: Australia, New Zealand, Canada, and South Africa First Assert Their Nationalities, 1880–1914* (Sydney and Boston: Allen and Unwin, 1988). The use of the gendered term "countrymen" is intentional, for this was in many ways a masculine enterprise. In Australia, for instance, as the male-centric notions of "mateship" and the frontier became central to the national imagination, they served to conscribe women's role in society. The fact that these ideals were equally defined in terms of a restrictive brand of "Whiteness" also allowed for the continued subordination of Indigenous peoples and exclusion of non-British immigrants. Patricia Grimshaw, Marilyn Lake, Ann McGrath, and Marian Quartly, *Creating a Nation* (Ringwood: McPhee Gribble, 1994).

[26] Douglas Cole, "The Problem of 'Nationalism' and 'Imperialism' in British Settlement Colonies," *Journal of British Studies* 10, no. 2 (May 1971): 160–182.

[27] Craig Wilcox, *Australia's Boer War: The War in South Africa, 1899–1902* (Oxford University Press, 2002); John Crawford and Ian McGibbon, eds., *One Flag, One Queen, One Tongue: New Zealand and the South African War, 1899–1902* (Auckland University Press, 2003). The Canadian response was more muted on account of Francophone opposition to the country's involvement in a British imperial war. Here too, however, the government contributed a military contingent, and the war served as a focal point for affirming Anglo-Canadian race patriotism. Jacques Monet, "Canadians, Canadiens, and Colonial Nationalism, 1896–1914: The Thorn in the Lion's Paw," in *The Rise of Colonial Nationalism*, 160–191.

only strengthened them, for they upheld a romantic view of the empire as a progressive enterprise that respected the sovereignty of all civilized peoples. This persistent faith in the imperial ties of blood and kinship sustained the expansion of British and dominion state funding for migration initiatives during the interwar period.[28] These schemes not only supported the transfer of some two million Britons overseas but also helped the child emigration movement extend from Canada to Australia and later to Southern Rhodesia and New Zealand. Throughout the first half of the twentieth century, when looking to swell their country's populations with assimilable new migrants, dominion nationalists unfailingly followed the ethic that British was best.

Still, if the public and political faith in the British world remained solid in the early twentieth century, how and when did these attachments break apart? The issue was first raised in 1979 by Australian historian Jim Davidson, who wondered how the end of empire had affected a country like his, where Britishness had formed such a crucial part of the national identity. At the time, Davidson's call for scholars to trace the "gradual change that occurred in assumptions" alongside the "often quite dramatic shifts in self-perception" that marked the demise of the settler empire – a process he termed "de-dominionisation" – went largely unanswered.[29] Scholarly interest in Britain centered on the more dramatic story of the struggle against colonial oppression in Africa and Asia. In the dominions, national histories tended to focus on internal themes, such as labor or urban history, which minimized the significance of the British connection.[30] Nonetheless, the question remains a valuable one, for it helps us understand the eclipse of the imperial era not simply in terms of political and economic shifts but also as a series of profound cultural dislocations that changed the ways that ordinary people conceived the world and defined their place within it. Significantly, when I asked Michael Oldfield to comment on his feelings of "Britishness," he unconsciously switched to the more narrowly defined term "English" in his response. For Oldfield, as for many other members of the old dominions, the more globalized and imperial sense of Britishness that originally underwrote child emigration has ceased to be a meaningful way of understanding his identity. Examining how this shift in subjectivity came

---

[28] Stephen Constantine, ed., *Emigrants and Empire: British Settlement in the Dominions between the Wars* (Manchester University Press, 1990).

[29] Jim Davidson, "The De-dominionisation of Australia," *Meanjin* 38, no. 2 (July 1979): 139–153, 139. See also his "De-dominionisation Revisited," *Australian Journal of Politics and History* 51, no. 1 (March 2005): 108–113.

[30] A. G. Hopkins, "Rethinking Decolonization," *Past and Present* 200 (August 2008): 211–247, 213–214.

to pass, as well as exploring its continuing legacies, are central aims of this book.

In the past few years, a number of historians have started integrating the dominions into the wider narratives of decolonization in an effort to account for how the momentous changes of the 1960s and 1970s played out across the settler territories.[31] In general, this literature has presented the eclipse of the British world as part and parcel of the wider postwar processes of globalization. Particular attention has been paid to the rise of an international ethic of multiculturalism, the reorientation of the British economy toward Europe, and the establishment of the United States as the Western world's foremost defensive partner.[32] Combined, these trends not only reduced the political and economic viability of the ties connecting Britain and its dominions but also made obsolete the older notions about the glory and sanctity of the British race. Throughout the postwar decades, they chipped away at the unity of Greater Britain, reducing, by the later 1970s, this once coherent sphere to an "empire of irreconcilable interests."[33]

These are persuasive arguments, but the story I wish to tell here is at once more gradual, more localized, and more intimate. When viewed from too high a vantage point, the end of empire appears almost as an inevitability, instead of the product of intense struggle and contestation. We risk losing sight of how the political debates over the nature and limits of the imperial relationship reverberated through the lives of the people who experienced these changes first hand, altering their social

---

[31] Stuart Ward has taken the lead in this effort. See his "The End of Empire and the Fate of Britishness," in *History, Nationhood, and the Question of Britain*, ed. Helen Brocklehurst and Robert Phillips (New York: Palgrave, 2004), 242–258; "The 'New Nationalism' in Australian, Canada and New Zealand: Civic Culture in the Wake of the British World," in Darian-Smith et al., *Britishness Abroad*, 231–263. On Australia, see also James Curran and Stuart Ward, *The Unknown Nation: Australia after Empire* (Melbourne University Press, 2010) as well as Ward's *Australia and the British Embrace: The Demise of the Imperial Ideal* (Melbourne University Press, 2001) and the collection of essays on "Post-Imperial Australia" edited by Ward in the *Australian Journal of Politics and History* 51, no. 1 (2005); David Goldsworthy, *Losing the Blanket: Australia and the End of Britain's Empire* (Melbourne University Press, 2002); and Meaney, "Britishness and Australia." The other focus of research has been Canada: Phillip Buckner, ed., *Canada and the End of Empire* (Vancouver: University of British Columbia Press, 2005); José Igartua, *The Other Quiet Revolution: National Identities in English Canada, 1945–1971* (Vancouver: University of British Columbia Press, 2006); Phillip Buckner, "Canada and the End of Empire, 1939–1982," in *Canada and the British Empire*, ed. Phillip Buckner (Oxford University Press, 2008), 107–126.

[32] These arguments about the forces of globalization appear in various forms throughout this scholarship but are presented most succinctly in Hopkins, "Rethinking Decolonization."

[33] Stuart Ward, "Imperial Identities Abroad," in *The British Empire: Themes and Perspectives*, ed. Sarah Stockwell (Oxford: Blackwell, 2008), 219–245, 234.

realities and adjusting the terms on which they could conceive themselves as actors in the world. Shifting the focus to the realm of child welfare, and exploring these changes through the lens of an imperial social policy like child emigration, helps bring this other terrain into view.

As scholars of childhood have long shown, the young have often occupied a central place within the political imagination. The sentimental figure of the child as youthful, flawless, and still in the process of growing offered politicians and reformers a universally recognizable and politically neutral emblem onto which they could project their national vision into the future.[34] No wonder that the first flourishing of public and state interest in child welfare occurred amid the wave of nationalism that swept across Europe at the end of the nineteenth century. At a time when ethnic affiliations remained contested or ambiguous, the act of setting explicit standards about how children should be raised – what values they should exhibit, what identities they should perform – provided a powerful means to demarcate the boundaries of the nation.[35] This same impulse underlay the early political enthusiasm for child emigration, which arose in the period when Britain's imperial power was at its height and when its borders had suddenly expanded to encompass large swathes of the world. The great strength of the policy was its ability to condense the abstract qualities of the now global British race into a tangible form. The ideals of imperial Britishness found institutional expression in the training and educational programs provided to child migrants, and supporters could take heart that the schemes were cementing the foundations of the empire for generations to come. These beliefs held firm until the middle decades of the twentieth century, when developments both in Britain and the dominions began to expose a sizable gap between the realities of life on the ground and the larger image of Greater Britain. As the political faith in the bonds of British belonging began to waver, child emigration transformed from a crucible of lasting imperial power into a site of negotiation over the boundaries between British authority and the dominions' national sovereignty. In the shift to a postimperial era, child welfare again provided a means of defining new forms of nationhood both in Britain and overseas. Yet these emerging identities no longer centered on an ethic of shared British ethnicity or a trust in the endurance of the imperial connection.

[34] Nick Frost and Mike Stein, *The Politics of Child Welfare: Inequality, Power and Change* (New York: Harvester Wheatsheaf, 1989); Harry Hendrick, *Child Welfare: Historical Dimensions, Contemporary Debates* (Bristol: Policy Press, 2003).

[35] A point beautifully demonstrated by Tara Zahra in *Kidnapped Souls: National Indifference and the Battle for Children in the Bohemian Lands, 1900–1948* (Ithaca: Cornell University Press, 2008).

These fault lines first began to appear in the decades surrounding the First World War, with the most potent strains involving racial issues. Marilyn Lake and Henry Reynolds have highlighted the rise of political anxiety throughout the early twentieth-century Anglophone world over the vulnerability of the White race. These worries were especially intense in countries such as Australia, that far-flung outpost of European civilization that seemed under threat from Asian expansionism, and the United States, where the inflowing stream of migrants appeared to be darkening at an alarming rate. In the early decades of the century, these and the other self-styled "White men's countries" of Canada, South Africa, and New Zealand led an international campaign to safeguard the global purity and status of the race. The first step was to create vigorous new immigration controls along the lines of the "White Australia" policy.[36] As politicians constructed a scaffold of restrictive visa requirements and quotas – a process largely completed by the end of the 1920s – they also turned their attention inward, seeking to employ the latest scientific knowledge to improve the vitality of their national populations. This concern with demographic fitness arose at different times throughout the dominions. It came earlier in Canada than in Australia, for instance. But, by the early 1920s and accelerating in the 1930s, government officials across the settler territories were implementing a rush of eugenics-inspired social legislation, much of which focused especially on the young.[37] Whereas prior settler attempts to promote "Whiteness" had remained within a conceptual framework that presented all native-born Britons as indisputably "White," now dominion authorities began to assert distinct standards of race. The trend provoked immigration officers, first in Canada and then in Australia and Southern Rhodesia, to examine the physical and mental "fitness" of child migrants with an unprecedented scrutiny. By the 1930s, these local officials had abandoned their practice of accepting almost all British boys and girls without question. Instead, they had begun denying entry to whole classes of children. They had also become quick to repatriate any child whose racial health appeared suspect, a category that came to include many boys and girls who had been living in these countries for years.

[36] Marilyn Lake and Henry Reynolds, *Drawing the Global Colour Line: White Men's Countries and the International Challenge of Racial Equality* (Cambridge University Press, 2008).

[37] Angus McLaren, *Our Own Master Race: Eugenics in Canada, 1885–1945* (Oxford University Press, 1990); Warwick Anderson, *The Cultivation of Whiteness: Science, Health and Racial Destiny in Australia* (New York: Basic Books, 2003). On parallel developments in Europe, see Mark Mazower, *Dark Continent: Europe's Twentieth Century* (New York: Vintage, 1998), 76–103.

In highlighting how the assumption of a unified British ethnicity came under challenge during the interwar period, the case of child emigration provides a further example of the flexibility of racial classifications in the empire. As scholars such as Dane Kennedy, Elizabeth Buettner, Ann Stoler, and Satoshi Mizutani have demonstrated, colonial standards of "Whiteness" were fluid, open to reinterpretation, and never a matter of skin color alone.[38] The example of child emigration adds to this literature by illustrating how these divergent, local variants came to function in opposition to, rather than within, the ideology of Britishness. By following the flow of children from Britain to the dominions and sometimes back again, all the while listening to the conversations held between reformers, politicians, and medical experts about their care, I have sought to uncover the ways in which settler authorities articulated and asserted independent national selves. This method, which views the empire as a web of connections stretching between Britain and the dominions, across these imperial sites, as well as outside the empire, helps illuminate the new ideas and processes that made Greater Britain appear less the setting for the redemption of the imperial race than a collection of exclusive territories in which not all Britons were fit for admission.[39] In what follows, although I trace the rise and fall of the child emigration movement as a whole, I pay particular attention to the initiatives that sent boys and girls to Australia and Southern Rhodesia. These regions formed the focus of the policy in the crucial decades when child emigration became a government-funded project, thereby illuminating most clearly the transimperial political debates about which British children would count as members of the settler nation and which would not. They also offered a particularly compelling point of comparison, revealing the distinct articulations of Whiteness that emerged across two late imperial sites: an "old" dominion that proudly espoused itself as being

[38] Dane Kennedy, *Islands of White: Settler Society and Culture in Kenya and Southern Rhodesia, 1890–1939* (Durham: Duke University Press, 1987); Elizabeth Buettner, *Empire Families: Britons and Late Imperial India* (Oxford University Press, 2004); Ann Stoler, *Carnal Knowledge and Imperial Power: Race and the Intimate in Colonial Rule* (Berkeley: University of California Press, 2010, originally 2002); Satoshi Mizutani, *The Meaning of White: Race, Class, and the "Domiciled Community" in British India, 1858–1930* (Oxford University Press, 2011).

[39] On the concept of the empire as a web, see Tony Ballantyne, *Orientalism and Race: Aryanism in the British Empire* (New York: Palgrave, 2002). Other works of transnational history that have particularly influenced my approach are: Lake and Reynolds, *Drawing the Global Colour Line*; Ann Curthoys and Marilyn Lake, eds., *Connected Worlds: History in Transnational Perspective* (Canberra: ANU E-Press, 2005); Mrinalini Sinha, *Specters of Mother India: The Global Restructuring of an Empire* (Durham: Duke University Press, 2006); Kevin Grant, Philippa Levine, and Frank Trenmann, eds., *Beyond Sovereignty: Britain, Empire and Transnationalism, 1880–1950* (New York: Palgrave Macmillan, 2007).

"95 percent British" and a self-governing colony in which Black Africans consistently outnumbered Europeans by a factor of twenty to one.

Key to these transformations in the meaning of Britishness was the growing influence of child psychology. The mental sciences of childhood first arose in the United States around the turn of the twentieth century, and by the 1920s the field was slowly becoming professionalized in Britain, Europe, and throughout the settler empire.[40] In the dominions, the growing impact of psychological ideas provided authorities with useful new tools to define the standards of mental fitness that qualified a person for membership of the nation. In Australia, the criteria were predominantly (but not exclusively) eugenic in character. Immigration personnel used IQ tests to isolate individuals whom they judged to have been "feebleminded," "subnormal," or "pathological" from birth. In Southern Rhodesia on the other hand, the emphasis centered on a child's cultural upbringing. Medical representatives there were more likely to view all boys or girls who had grown up in poverty as emotionally damaged, and to question their ability to become productive members of society. In making these assessments, local officials were, somewhat ironically, aided by child psychology's status as a general science, grounded in a set of developmental norms that seemingly applied across the divides of race, ethnicity, and nation. By defining their selection policies in reference to this universal scale of mental and emotional fitness, dominion authorities could set higher standards for their own "unique" populations than were typical in Britain. While a double-digit IQ score, a tendency to stutter, or a curiosity about sex might have been cause for concern among parents and reformers back in the United Kingdom, overseas they were reasons for a child's exclusion from the national community. Whether defined through blood or environment, the effect of these psychological measures was to outline a model of "Australian" or "Rhodesian" mentality that had less and less to do with the ideal of a collective British inheritance. In the late empire, the universal language of psychology became a means for expressing the differences between national populations rather than for transcending them.

The process could cut both ways, however. In the postwar period, a disparate understanding of child development began gaining ground within British medical and welfare circles. Associated with the work of prominent British psychologists such as John Bowlby and Susan Isaacs,

---

[40] Mathew Thomson offers a comprehensive analysis of the penetration of psychological concepts in British society in his *Psychological Subjects: Identity, Culture and Health in Twentieth-Century Britain* (Oxford University Press, 2006); on child-centered psychology, see especially 109–139.

this "maternal deprivation theory" stressed that all children needed a stable home and an emotional connection with a mother or mother figure for lasting mental health.[41] Unsurprisingly, this view achieved its greatest influence in the 1950s, a period in which, Wendy Webster has argued, British culture became "domesticated," drawing back from the increasingly menacing realm of the empire to focus on a more restricted national vision that centered on the imagery of hearth, home, and family.[42] As this model of "little England" displaced the older imperial notions about the global British race, the ideal of Greater Britain as an intimately connected ethnic community began to fade from the metropolitan imagination much as it had already started to do so overseas. These changing cultural dynamics on the eve of the decolonization era encouraged British reformers to think about children's needs in more generalized terms, and without reference to their supposed innate "Britishness." All boys and girls, they argued, needed a stable home life, whether they lived at home, in the empire, or further afield.

The fact that child emigration was at odds with this trend did not long escape the notice of the newly formed Children's Department of the Home Office.[43] In 1955, the bureau launched a vigorous critique of the policy that focused on the roughly three dozen welfare homes that were still receiving child migrants in Australia. Even though these British representatives couched their criticisms in the scientific authority of child psychology, their intervention appeared to many in the Australian government as a persistent form of cultural domination, one that jarred with the political realities of the postwar empire. The resulting dispute over which country had the right to determine the care of child migrants provided Australian officials with another opportunity to assert their national sovereignty. Earlier in the century the politics of empire had significantly shaped the ways that reformers and politicians understood the needs of the young, but now the reverse proved true. During the last breath of the imperial era, discussions over children's "best interests" opened a space for dominion officials to contest the continued legitimacy of British power in a postwar world.

It would be easy to view these debates as mere political posturing, the bluster and swagger of politicians eager to enhance their claim to authority. Nevertheless, throughout the long history of child emigration,

---

[41] Denise Riley, *War in the Nursery: Theories of the Child and Mother* (London: Virago, 1983).

[42] Wendy Webster, *Englishness and Empire, 1939–1965* (Oxford University Press, 2007).

[43] Stephen Constantine, "The British Government, Child Welfare, and Child Migration to Australia after 1945," *Journal of Imperial and Commonwealth History* 30, no. 1 (2002): 99–132.

discussions about the nature of Britishness, of White racial identity, and of national belonging in the empire had important consequences for the lives of child migrants. These shifting ideas became embedded in the policies and practices of emigration charities, and were reflected in the daily routines of dominion orphanages and children's institutions. Throughout this book, I have sought to capture these echoes of the  changing imperial relationship in the lived realities of child migrants' lives. This goal led me to pay close attention to the structures that governed life in Australian and Rhodesian farm schools, from the types of education on offer to the ways children spent their free time. It also pushed me beyond the historian's traditional realm of the archive into the messier world of oral history. During the initial research for this book in 2005 and 2006, I conducted thirty-seven interviews with former child migrants in the United Kingdom and Australia. Three years later, I did nine more, five of which were follow-up sessions with people I had spoken to before and four of which were with new contacts in Australia and South Africa.

The majority of these interviewees were active in child migrant reunion associations, which meant that many, if certainly not all, had fairly positive views on the policy. Some were eager to talk with me because they felt that the typical portrayal of the history was inaccurate, or that it defined the policy too unilaterally as abusive. Others volunteered because they wanted to tell their own painful story of family loss and institutionalization, which often remained profoundly upsetting decades later. Throughout the interviewing process, I was struck by how, even when the people I spoke with had a clear reason for wanting to share their experiences, their memories were still nuanced, wide ranging, and insightful. To balance any particular viewpoint that may have emerged from the methods I used to locate interviewees, however, I also supplemented my own interviewing with research in the excellent collections of oral histories with former child migrants that are housed in the Battye Library in Perth, the State Library of New South Wales in Sydney, and the National Library of Australia in Canberra.

In the past thirty years or so, oral history has become a well-established academic discipline, with several peer-reviewed journals, regular international conferences, and scores of theory and method courses within college curricula around the world. Yet this vibrant field continues to exist alongside the mainstream of historical scholarship, and only rarely does a historical study based primarily on written documents also integrate interviews. Undoubtedly, not every historical question can be explored using oral histories. But many can, and the effect of sidelining the discipline is not simply to overlook a potentially valuable new vein of information; it also threatens to make the always fuzzy line between "history" and "memory" appear deceptively clear.[44]

My aim has been to use oral history interviews in two complementary ways. The first is to gain an impression of what it was like to grow up in Australian or Rhodesian child migrant farm schools at various points in time between the First World War and the 1960s. As adults, we tend to forget just how observant children are as they puzzle out their worlds. Years later, many of the experiences former migrants had during their youth remained vivid in their minds. In this respect, the interviews shed light on aspects of institutional life that were hidden or obscured in the archival records. Former migrants frequently described in rich detail the nature and severity of the punishments meted out, the extent to which children were able to maintain contact with relatives back in Britain, or the unique cultures they created out of adult sight: the games they played, the rituals they followed, the rules they flouted. These adult memories of the past cannot, of course, be taken as a direct reflection of the child's historical perspective transported to the present day. But they do support an understanding of child migrants not simply as objects but as subjects of history. While institutional records painted a picture of uniformity and of the cold, hard fairness of life in farm schools, where every child was treated alike, the interviews evoked a wholly different portrait of the children as individuals who interacted with their own, albeit circumscribed, worlds in distinct, original, and unintended ways.

This desire to recover a sense of child migrants as historical actors in their own right underpins the second way that I have used oral interviews in this study: as a lens on some of the broader legacies of empire in the postimperial era. The boys and girls who grew up in imperial farm schools were originally conceived as representatives of the global British race and of the future of Greater Britain. As they aged, however, these concepts rapidly lost their meaning. For many former migrants today, as for others who still live in what was once the British world, the empire appears as a vanished land, a relic from the past that survives only in their recollections. This is especially true for the somewhat less than 300 child migrants sent to Rhodesia from the late 1940s through the early 1960s, a large number of whom stayed in the country through its 1965 Unilateral Declaration of Independence (UDI) from the British empire and subsequent violent transition from settler colony into the nation

---

[44] Paula Hamilton and Linda Shopes, "Introduction: Building Partnerships between Oral History and Memory Studies," in *Oral History and Public Memory*, ed. Hamilton and Shopes (Philadelphia: Temple University Press, 2008), vii–xvii.

of Zimbabwe. Unlike Australian culture, which continues to adapt to the modern world and is slowly coming to terms with its imperial past, Rhodesia no longer exists in any concrete form. It is a nation frozen in time, unable to move beyond its last, defiant stance for White racial superiority. The colony's demise has thus created a profound ideological problem for those people whose subjectivities were first formed there. Either they can renounce all that Rhodesia once stood for and in so doing cast aside many of their childhood memories, or they can use their personal experiences to challenge the current, largely negative media portrayal of the colony. The fact that this latter option often leads them to reject today's ethic of multiculturalism offers a powerful illustration of how the memory of empire can determine political choices in the present.

The complexities of the Rhodesian case serve as a reminder that memories are influential, living things – the binding glue of our individual selves – that are perhaps most commanding when inflected by feelings of loss to become nostalgia, that mode of reminiscing that juxtaposes an idealized past against a less satisfactory present.[45] Similar forms of nostalgia are present among former migrants to Australia as well, although they are usually expressed in different ways. During my initial interview with Michael Oldfield, for instance, he dedicated a lot of time to the story of his first trip back to Britain in 1980, when he logged long hours in a rental car, using his Barnardo's file to track down the addresses of the places he had once lived. Haphazardly and almost miraculously, he uncovered some of his former relatives, a few of whom had never known of his or his sister's existence. As Oldfield told it, the story was an example of his continued connection to Britain. After all those years in Australia, his British roots remained. Despite the excitement of finding a lost family, though, it was his visit back to Folly House that he remembered most clearly. It was "a sad thing for me to do," he said, for he arrived as the home was in the process of being closed. Once filled with scurrying children, it now housed only about half a dozen boys, and was beginning to look run down. The local church in which Oldfield had been confirmed and had sung in the choir was "locked up like a tombstone," the minister nowhere in sight.[46] The vibrant community life of his childhood, he intimated, had undergone a serious decline, and the faded, secular, postimperial Britain

---

[45] George Behlmer, "Introduction," in *Singular Continuities: Tradition, Nostalgia, and Identity in Modern British Culture*, ed. George Behlmer and Fred Leventhal (Stanford University Press, 2000), 7.

[46] Oldfield interview.

of today bore little resemblance to the dynamic and venerable nation he had once known.

In these and countless other ways, former migrants carry the memories of their imperial childhoods with them as they continue to leave their imprint on the world. They often make their past experiences of empire a tangible part of the present, using them to inform everything from their voting patterns to the newspapers they read and the choices they make as consumers. The strength of oral histories is their ability to illuminate how these personal narratives interact with current media and academic representations to keep alive not only a certain vision of the imperial past but also the attitudes and worldviews that were initially forged in the empire. The foundations of Greater Britain have long since crumbled, but its spirit still haunts many of those who once lived in its borders and who continue to play a vital role in defining the collective memory of their societies.[47]

At its most basic level, therefore, *Empire's Children* uses the history of the child emigration movement as a lens to illuminate the rise, reconfiguration, and lasting effects of the concept of imperial Britishness within the modern era. Chapters 1 and 2 chart the origins of the policy from the Victorian period to the early 1920s, exploring how the ideal of a global British race came to influence the care of needy children in Britain and to redefine their political value throughout the settler empire. Chapter 3 examines how the growth of racial nationalism across Australia in the interwar years both amplified the political importance of the imperial connection and imposed significant restrictions on the upbringing and opportunities offered to child migrants. Chapters 4 and 5 trace the fragmentation of the concept of Greater Britain from the 1930s to the 1960s, during which time national cultures in the dominions grew more firmly associated with distinct brands of Whiteness, and the philosophy of child welfare became profoundly influenced by psychological theory. As the faith in the unity of the British world faded, the structures and policies of farm schools grew progressively "nationalized" to reflect the seemingly distinct character of settler communities in the late empire, a trend that is explored in Chapter 6 through a comparison of postwar child migrant institutions in Australia and Southern Rhodesia. The book concludes with an elaboration of the complex subjectivities of former migrants in the postimperial era. By following the return journeys of

---

[47] For an illuminating analysis of the concept of haunting, see Avery Gordon, *Ghostly Matters: Haunting and the Sociological Imagination* (Minneapolis: University of Minnesota Press, 2008).

many former migrants "home" to Britain in search of family or a more general sense of belonging, it illuminates the myriad ways that particular, and often nostalgic, conceptions of the imperial past live on into the present, inflecting dominant understandings of Britishness long after the empire's official end.

# 1 Poverty and possibility in the era of Greater Britain

In June of 1909, William Baker, the executive director of Barnardo's Homes, the charity founded nearly forty years earlier by the evangelical reformer Thomas Barnardo, received a disturbing letter. The manager of the organization's flagship Stepney mission in London's East End, Adam Fowler, had written to pass along an inquiry from a "respectable widow" about her son. The boy in question was a former Barnardo's ward who had emigrated to Canada a few months previously, and his mother was hoping for any news that Fowler might have about his progress. Such requests were routine. At the time, the charity was sheltering nearly 7,000 boys and girls in its branch homes across the United Kingdom, as well as sending an additional 1,100 to Canada each year.[1] The parents of these children often sought to remain in contact with them, and Stepney provided a stable address for the exchange of letters and information. This case was unique, though, because, unbeknownst to the mother, her child had returned from Canada the week before and was a patient in the local hospital. His story was tragic. Fowler wrote:

[The boy] alleges he was given work to do in the fields which made his back ache, and that when he rested he was beaten with an India rubber strap. One night last November he went out and hid himself under a barn. A report from Canada states that he "ran away"; the barn, however, under which he was found formed, I understand, a part of the farm on which he lived. When found, he was made to walk back to the house (so the boy says) although his limbs had, by that time, become black, as the result of frost-bite. Not until two days later, the boy asserts, was any doctor brought to see him. When seen by the doctor he was ordered to a hospital, where, soon afterwards, both his legs were amputated. One of his arms is now in such a condition that it may also have to be removed.[2]

Fowler went on to acknowledge the obvious fact that the child had not been well placed. Since 1882, when Barnardo's first joined the then-

---

[1] In 1908, Barnardo's reported having 6,736 children in care in Britain; the previous year, it sent 1,082 boys and girls to Canada. Barnardo's, Council Minutes, January 22, 1908, D.239/B1/2/4, ULSCA.

[2] Fowler to Baker, June 23, 1909, D.239/C1/1/1, ULSCA.

burgeoning child emigration movement, the organization's policy had been to send boys and girls to live with farming families along the Canadian frontier. Its directors accepted that many of these children would work for their keep by performing light duties around the house, but the family that had taken in this boy had given him an excessive amount of work for his age. Although "only twelve last September," he had been required to do tasks that usually were the preserve of hired servants, such as milking cows, plowing, and making breakfast. "If his story is true," Fowler noted, this work was not in keeping with the definition of "merely 'nominal' employment" that the organization allowed. Equally troubling was the devastating lack of communication from the Barnardo's representatives in Canada. Not only had the Toronto office failed to keep track of the child's wellbeing but they had also neglected to inform Stepney of the situation until the boy had arrived back in Britain, a full seven months after the amputations had occurred. In the intervening period, the child had recovered alone in his hospital bed, and no Barnardo's official had visited him until the eve of his return journey. This long silence from Canada now placed Fowler in a difficult situation with the mother, who "cannot have heard anything of the terrible misfortune that has befallen [her son] ... She has certainly had no notice from Stepney, for we knew nothing, and could, therefore, tell her nothing."[3]

From there, the record falls silent. The case of "the boy" – his name was never mentioned – was not considered at the next meetings of Barnardo's Council or Executive Committees. If Baker wrote back to Fowler about the situation, his letter did not make it into the archive. No legal action appears to have been taken, and the episode did not provoke any change in or interruption to the organization's emigration program. In fact, only two years later the Council expressed its delight at the receipt of a £10,000 contribution toward its Canadian initiatives.[4] The money went to fund a publicity campaign that pasted thousands of Barnardo's advertisements in railway carriages throughout Britain, offering a "new start in life to ... young emigrants."[5] As for the boy himself, the lack of basic information about his identity makes it impossible to do more than speculate. Perhaps he returned to the care of his mother, although, given the difficulties of providing for disabled children at the turn of the century, it seems more likely that he remained in one of Barnardo's

[3] Ibid.
[4] Barnardo's, Council Minutes, April 24, 1912, D.239/B1/2/4, ULSCA.
[5] This quote comes from a typical Barnardo's advertisement of the period, published in *The Quiver* 34, no. 6 (May 1909), 22.

specialized homes for "crippled" boys and girls. There, he would have received training in a manual skill in the hope that despite his missing limbs he might still make an independent life for himself.[6]

Instances of extreme abuse like this one are rare in the archive, and, given the inadequate nature of inspections and record keeping in the period, it is impossible to know how common they were in reality. Nevertheless, the case sheds light on the kinds of hardships that child migrants faced during the Victorian and Edwardian eras. The rapid expansion of the child emigration movement in the four decades before the First World War, during which period over a dozen agencies sent more than 80,000 boys and girls to Canada, created widespread problems of supervision and placement.[7] In the words of one early critic, the system amounted to "nothing more than just scattering the children broadcast here and there, and losing sight of them."[8] Child migrants' isolation could also be amplified through a loss of contact with their families in Britain. As Fowler's reference to the respectability of the mother makes clear, judgments about the validity of a family's connection were enmeshed with subjective assessments of character and morality. Middle-class and elite reformers rarely took seriously the opinions of those they deemed the "undeserving poor," and they often explicitly attempted to sever family ties. In a careful study of Barnardo's case files from the years 1882 through 1908, Joy Parr found that, while parents signed their consent to the possibility of emigration when they admitted their child into the Homes, only one in every three migrant girls' guardians were notified when their daughter was actually scheduled to leave the country; of these, two-thirds of the parents described as "respectable" received advanced notification. Forty-two percent were informed only after their daughter had sailed, and one

---

[6] On the limited assistance provided to disabled children and their parents in this period, see Ellen Ross, *Love and Toil: Motherhood in Outcast London, 1870–1918* (Oxford University Press, 1993), 180–181; Seth Koven, "Remembering and Dismemberment: Crippled Children, Wounded Soldiers, and the Great War in Britain," *American Historical Review* 99, no. 4 (October 1994): 1167–1202.

[7] Overviews of the early development of the movement can be found in Gillian Wagner, *Children of the Empire* (London: Weidenfeld and Nicolson, 1982); Joy Parr, *Labouring Children: British Immigrant Apprentices to Canada, 1869–1924* (University of Toronto Press, 1994, originally 1980); Kenneth Bagnell, *The Little Immigrants: The Orphans Who Came to Canada* (Toronto: Dundurn Press, 2001, originally 1980); Marjorie Kohli, *The Golden Bridge: Young Immigrants to Canada, 1833–1939* (Toronto: Natural Heritage, 2003); Roger Kershaw and Janet Sacks, *New Lives for Old* (Kew: The National Archives, 2008); Roy Parker, *Uprooted: The Shipment of Poor Children to Canada, 1867–1917* (Vancouver: University of British Columbia Press, 2008).

[8] "The Emigration of Pauper Children," *The Times*, June 11, 1875, 4. This was the finding of a Local Government Board inquiry. For a summary of the full investigation, see Andrew Doyle, "Report to the President of the Local Government Board ... as to the Emigration of Pauper Children to Canada," *Parliamentary Papers* LXVII (1875).

in four received no notice at all.[9] Moreover, caregivers almost always disregarded the views of children outright, as shown by the numerous qualifications and asides – "so the boy says," "if his story is true" – that littered Fowler's letter. As such, episodes like this one underscore the relative powerlessness of needy parents and children at the turn of the century, a time in which one in ten child migrants was sent to Canada without the expressed permission of their guardians.[10]

That is a significant, and disturbing, proportion. Yet the fact that the majority of parents who grappled with the agonizing decision to allow their child's resettlement gave their assent suggests that child emigration was an acceptable, if desperate, option for poor families in the late nineteenth and early twentieth centuries. From the vantage point of the present day, it can be difficult to fathom the former vibrancy of a practice that now so jars with twenty-first-century ideals of child welfare and the family, and easier to dismiss it as another example of the victimization of poor families by an overly zealous charitable sector.[11] Recent historians of nineteenth-century philanthropy, however, have done much to refute the stereotype of the omnipotent and interventionist "Lady Bountiful." Although voluntary campaigns were frequently condescending and hierarchical, they could also offer a space for working-class men and women to participate in civil society, to engage in the culture of respectability, and to advocate for the needs of their communities at a time when most Britons remained excluded from active citizenship.[12] The challenge is to understand how child emigration made sense to a generation of Britons – rich and poor alike – who were swept up by the possibilities of a new life overseas. In an era of growing concern that chronic, industrial

---

[9] Parr, *Labouring Children*, 71.

[10] The power to emigrate children against the wishes of their parents was officially granted to the Home Secretary under the 1894 Prevention of Cruelty to Children Act, but many charities had been exercising the practice for some time. Parr identified 100 out of a total of 997 Barnardo boys and girls who had been sent to Canada without their parents' consent or under court order by the Home Secretary. Ibid, 67.

[11] An emphasis on the victimization of poor parents dominates the popular literature on child emigration, which has contended that most guardians throughout the history of the movement did not consent to their children's emigration. Philip Bean and Joy Melville, for instance, claimed that "parents, when they gave their child(ren) into the care of an institution or society, generally had no idea that the children would end up being sent to the other side of the world." Philip Bean and Joy Melville, *Lost Children of the Empire: The Untold Story of Britain's Child Migrants* (London: Unwin Hyman, 1989), 4. For a critique, see Barry Coldrey, *Child Migration: Consent of Parents to their Children's Emigration, the Legal and Moral Dimension* (Altrincham: Tamanaraik Press, 1996).

[12] Frank Prochaska, *Christianity and Social Service in Modern Britain: The Disinherited Spirit* (Oxford University Press, 2006). On the agency of poor parents within the Victorian child welfare sector, see Lydia Murdoch, *Imagined Orphans: Poor Families, Child Welfare, and Contested Citizenship in London* (New Brunswick: Rutgers University Press, 2006).

poverty was stifling the potential of thousands of British children, the vision of a more wholesome life to be found in the farmlands of Greater Britain appealed widely, from the elevated tier of elite reformers to the most struggling of poor parents. Exploring how this came to be is the focus of this chapter.

## Britons overseas

During the long nineteenth century, Britons were a people on the move. From the conclusion of the Napoleonic wars through the Great War a hundred years later, the country witnessed a series of emigration booms that propelled millions of English, Irish, Welsh, and Scottish across the seas. In 1815, when the trend was just beginning, some 2,000 people left the British Isles. By mid century this number had risen to 250,000 people per year.[13] During the early 1900s, over 1,670,000 men, women, and children left the country. And in one remarkable year – 1913 – nearly 400,000 poured forth.[14] To put this figure into perspective, it roughly equaled the size of one of Britain's larger cities, as if all of the residents of Leeds or Bristol had suddenly departed for foreign shores.[15]

Not all of these people went to the empire. During the mid-Victorian period the majority traveled to locales outside Greater Britain, particularly the United States. Yet the settler colonies of Canada, Australia, New Zealand, and South Africa grew steadily in popularity, and by the early 1900s they were attracting nearly two-thirds of all British migrants.[16] As James Belich has argued, this sustained period of emigration was nothing less than a "settler revolution." By the end of Victoria's reign in 1901, it had ushered forth a new world entity, the "British West," which contained some 24 million people and rivaled the power and energy of the more famed American frontier.[17]

The effects of this expanded emigration were far reaching. Most noticeably, it led to a tremendous increase in the public awareness of the colonies

[13] Eric Richards, *Britannia's Children: Emigration from England, Scotland, Wales and Ireland since 1600* (London: Hambledon and London, 2004), 118.

[14] Stephen Constantine, "British Emigration to the Empire-Commonwealth since 1880: From Overseas Settlement to Diaspora?" in *The British World: Diaspora, Culture and Identity*, ed. Carl Bridge and Kent Fedorowich (London: Frank Cass, 2003), 16–35, 19.

[15] In 1911, the population of Leeds was 445,500 while that of Bristol was 357,048. Frank Moore Colby, *The New International Year Book for the Year 1914* (New York: Dodd, Mead, and Co., 1915), 314.

[16] Marjorie Harper and Stephen Constantine, *Migration and Empire* (Oxford University Press, 2010), 3.

[17] James Belich, *Replenishing the Earth: The Settler Revolution and the Rise of the Angloworld, 1783–1939* (Oxford University Press, 2009), 85.

within metropolitan culture. The revolution in communications technology that occurred during the second half of the nineteenth century did much to facilitate this process, allowing idealized images of settler life to saturate all levels of society. The creation of an undersea network of telegraph and cable lines secured a prominent spot for news from the British world in the pages of the national and penny press, while the rapid development of the postal service helped sustain contacts between migrants and their loved ones.[18] Also important was the rise of "booster literature" that aimed to encourage emigration, particularly following the "hungry forties," when large numbers of philanthropists became convinced that resettlement offered the best means to restore independence to starving paupers.[19] In the wake of that decade, a growing number of charities and civic groups and (from 1886) the government's own Emigrants' Information Office issued cheap pamphlets and posters extolling the benefits of the settler territories.[20] Perhaps the most powerful source of knowledge about life in the empire, however, came from return migrants. Between 1860 and 1914, an estimated one-third of English settlers traveled back home, especially from Canada, which was relatively close by and well serviced by steam-powered ocean liners.[21] Back in Britain, the period of time spent overseas gave return migrants added cache in their old neighborhoods, where many were eager to share their experiences.[22] In sum, during the late nineteenth century the paths conveying information about the settler colonies to Britain were diverse and well trodden. This influx of news, personal stories, and adventure tales made the rural empire a living concept in the minds of most Victorians. It also helped remove the stigma that had once been attached to emigration. By the end of the century, resettlement no longer appeared as an unhappy fate reserved for convicts and castoffs but as a respectable life decision available to all walks of life.[23]

The heightened cultural conversation about the settler world extended the mental frameworks in which ordinary Britons contemplated their

---

[18] Simon Potter, "Communication and Integration: The British and Dominions Press and the British World, 1876–1914," in *The British World*, ed. Bridge and Fedorowich, 190–206, 196. See also Simon Potter, *News and the British World: The Emergence of an Imperial Press System, 1876–1922* (New York: Oxford University Press, 2003). In 1839, Britons sent an average of four letters per capita, but by the 1870s they were sending thirty-two. Belich, *Replenishing the Earth*, 122.

[19] Hilary Carey, *God's Empire: Religion and Colonialism in the British World, 1801–1908* (Cambridge University Press, 2011), 332.

[20] Constantine, "British Emigration," 20.

[21] Richards, *Britannia's Children*, 169.

[22] On this phenomenon, see Marjory Harper, ed., *Emigrant Homecomings: The Return Movement of Emigrants, 1600–2000* (Manchester University Press, 2005).

[23] Belich, *Replenishing the Earth*, 153–165.

lives. Its impact was soon felt within the broader national discussion of issues such as urban poverty, joblessness, and overcrowding. Public concern about these problems, which commentators tended to lump together under the heading of "the social question," was especially intense during the later years of the nineteenth century, when the prolonged economic downturn of 1873–1896 made destitution appear more entrenched and visible than ever before. Ironically, this perception of a worsening social crisis came at a time of rising real wages and declining family sizes, which together helped usher in an overall improvement in the standard of living.[24] Yet these trends did little to alleviate the plight of the unemployed or of those who labored in areas such as agriculture and dock work, where jobs remained scarce, poorly paid, and often temporary. The debate about the social question thus focused less on the matter of generalized poverty than on what the reformer Charles Booth called the "residuum" of society: the subsection of chronically destitute people who appeared to be mired in a state of perpetual need.[25]

Opinion remained divided about how, or even if, the problem could be solved. Many "public moralists" saw pauperism as a product of a sinful character in need of salvation.[26] This belief had deep roots within the eighteenth-century evangelical tradition, which continued to dominate philanthropic circles in the Victorian period.[27] In the post-Darwinian era, however, its persuasiveness was fading. From the 1870s onward, it became increasingly common to understand poverty less in personal terms, as the product of moral flaws, than in systemic terms, as having resulted from "chains of causation outside the individual."[28] The rise of data-driven forms of social investigation, like Booth's mammoth seventeen-volume study *Life and Labour of the People in London*,

---

[24] The rates of those receiving poor relief as a percentage of the total population continued to fall throughout these years from a high of between 80 and 100 people per 1,000 in the 1840s to 25 per 1,000 in 1900. Lynn Lees, *The Solidarity of Strangers: The English Poor Laws and the People, 1700–1948* (Cambridge University Press, 1998), 239 and 295.

[25] Gareth Stedman Jones, *Outcast London: A Study in the Relationship between Classes in Victorian Society* (Oxford: Clarendon Press, 1971); Jose Harris, "Between Civic Virtue and Social Darwinism: The Concept of the Residuum," in *Retrieved Riches: Social Investigation in Britain, 1840–1914*, ed. David Englander and Rosemary O'Day (Aldershot: Scolar Press, 1995), 67–87.

[26] Stefan Collini, *Public Moralists: Political Thought and Intellectual Life in Britain, 1850–1930* (Oxford: Clarendon Press, 1991).

[27] Boyd Hilton, *Age of Atonement: The Influence of Evangelicalism on Social and Economic Thought, 1796–1865* (New York: Clarendon Press, 1988); Prochaska, *Christianity and Social Service*.

[28] Lees, *The Solidarity of Strangers*, 243.

and Seebohm Rowntree's analysis of York, added "scientific" authority to this view.[29] Rowntree's work was especially influential in this regard. By defining the concept of the "poverty cycle," he focused awareness on the structures that trapped whole communities in destitution, defined economic need as a problem rather than a state of being, and helped spur the "New Liberal" social legislation of the early twentieth century.[30]

The importance of the idea of Greater Britain to these discussions was that it held out the hope that change was possible. By the late nineteenth century, the iconography of the settler empire had matured into a set repertoire that emphasized natural abundance and productivity. An 1886 *Times* editorial on Canada was typical. It drew readers' attention to the "long reaches of river, great expanses of lake and plain, lofty mountain ranges, illimitable wheatland, populous cities, and railways running on and on for thousands of miles" with which the region had become synonymous.[31] In part, these notions of boundless imperial fertility took hold because they fit neatly within the broader "pastoral impulse" of late Victorian culture.[32] Juxtaposed against the "metaphors [of] the swamp, the forest, and the labyrinth" that dominated descriptions of the urban landscape at home, they invoked nostalgic conceptions of a simpler, rural, preindustrial Britain.[33] This idealized vision of the dominions as naturally rich but "empty" lands also appealed within the settler societies, which were at the time engaged in their own imperial wars against Indigenous peoples for control of the frontier.[34] Throughout the nineteenth century, Canadian settlers steadily encroached on Aboriginal "reserved lands," ignoring a 1763 Proclamation that protected Indigenous rights to territory that had not been purchased by the Crown. Following Confederation in 1867, the new federal government moved aggressively to extinguish Aboriginal title. Administrators were greatly aided in this effort by the simultaneous disappearance of the buffalo from the western plains, which forced Indigenous leaders to enter into one-sided treaties

[29] Charles Booth, *Life and Labour of the People in London*, 17 vols. (London: Macmillan, 1889–1903); Seebohm Rowntree, *Poverty: A Study of Town Life* (London: Macmillan, 1901).

[30] Jose Harris, *Private Lives and Public Spirit: A Social History of Britain, 1870–1914* (Oxford University Press, 1993), 230–241.

[31] "Canadian Tour," *The Times*, September 16, 1886, 7.

[32] Jan Marsh, *Back to the Land: The Pastoral Impulse in England from 1880 to 1914* (New York: Quartet Books, 1982).

[33] Felix Driver, *Geography Militant: Cultures of Exploration and Empire* (Oxford: Blackwell, 2001), 180.

[34] Philip Buckner, "The Creation of the Dominion of Canada, 1860–1901," in *Canada and the British Empire*, ed. Phillip Buckner (Oxford University Press, 2008), 66–86, 74–75.

that ceded control of their land in exchange for food and supplies.[35] As westward expansion picked up pace in the latter half of the century, and as the total number of Aboriginal peoples fell to under 1 percent of the population, the politically expedient vision of Indigenous peoples as a "dying race" whose decline would leave the prairies open for the taking came to dominate Canadian society, much as it had in other settler sites, such as Australia.[36]

What made the rhetoric of open spaces and natural wealth so compelling was its forward momentum. The settler territories were not simply idyllic representations of the past transported to the present; they were also portrayed as inherently modern, located on the cusp of the future.[37] This temporal complexity was evident in commentators' frequent tendency to describe the settler colonies using a mix of tenses that jostled together past, present, and future.[38] A 1903 *Monthly Review* editorial, again on Canada, noted that the territory was premodern and untouched, absent "those signs of age-long conflict with the forces of Nature so visible in every acre of trim and well-kempt England." Yet at the same time, it was progressing swiftly forward, aided by its "widespread potentialities" and "preternaturally extended vision."[39] To metropolitan Britons, the rural empire was much more than a throwback to a bygone era. It represented an alternative modernity, one in which social advancement did not depend on the immiseration of the poor and in which economic prosperity did not necessarily produce an urban wasteland.

Complementing this vision were the well-established ties of religious faith and Christian community that united the British world. Hilary Carey has demonstrated how eagerly nineteenth-century metropolitan Anglican,

[35] Sarah Carter, "Aboriginal People of Canada and the British Empire," in *Canada and the British Empire*, ed. Phillip Buckner, 200–219.

[36] Canada's Indigenous peoples constituted at least one-fifth of the population in 1815. But the influx of new settlers in the later decades of the century, accompanied by the ravages of disease and starvation within Aboriginal communities, cut their total population in half. By 1911, Indigenous peoples numbered around 100,000, which was under 1 percent of the country's total. Ged Martin, "Canada from 1815," in *The Oxford History of the British Empire*, vol. III, ed. Andrew Porter (Oxford University Press, 1999), 522–545, 533.

[37] David Hamer, *New Towns in the New World: Images and Perceptions of the Nineteenth Century Urban Frontier* (Columbia University Press, 1990), especially 163–183. This rhetoric found parallels in the "nostalgic modernism" espoused by a range of conservationists and reformers in the United States. On this concept, see Laura Lovett, *Conceiving the Future: Pronatalism, Reproduction, and the Family in the United States, 1890–1938* (Chapel Hill: University of North Carolina Press, 2007), 10–12.

[38] A complexity that Peter Mandler has also identified in Victorian discussions of the British countryside, "Against 'Englishness': English Culture and the Limits to Rural Nostalgia, 1850–1940," *Transactions of the Royal Historical Society* 7 (1996): 155–175.

[39] Arnold Haultain, "Who Should Emigrate to Canada?" *Monthly Review* 11, no. 33 (June 1903): 91–108, 92.

Nonconformist, and Catholic authorities looked to the settler empire to extend their influence. Bolstered by the concerted spread of clergy, missionary societies, and cheaply produced tracts throughout the colonies, the overseas branches of certain denominations, such as Methodism and Presbyterianism, grew dramatically. By the beginning of the twentieth century, both had outstripped Anglicanism, becoming the leading Protestant churches in British North America.[40] At the same time, religious leaders in Britain became active promoters of emigration, whether through organizations such as the Emigrants' Spiritual Aid Fund (1849) and the Church Emigration Society (1886) or simply by lauding the spiritual merits of the settler territories in their sermons. The outcome of this activism was to make the "Christian empire" a vibrant, multidenominational terrain, much less homogenous than Anglican-dominated, Protestant Britain.[41] The strength of religious fellowship throughout the settler world helped cement its reputation as a locus of Britannic liberty and moral virtue in the minds of many Britons, both "at home" and overseas.

In a period of widespread anxiety that chronic destitution was sapping the strength of the nation, therefore, Greater Britain held out a promise of renewal. As the Prince of Wales put it in 1901, the colonies offered ordinary men and women an escape from the "almost hopeless struggle for existence ... in the old country" and an opportunity to create better lives for themselves through hard work.[42] The essential assumption underlying such statements was that paupers *were* redeemable, that destitution was not a fixed caste or a life sentence. In this respect, the portrayals of the rural empire as a locus of progressive British individualism helped undercut Social Darwinist arguments that explained societal disorders in terms of inherited mental or physical defects. Instead, they supported the mainstream interpretation that "the stock" was sound and that any seeming "degeneration" of the national character was the fault of unhealthy slum environments and unnatural city lifestyles, not heredity.[43] The success of the common man in the settler territories offered living proof of the continued power of the British race. Greater Britain

[40] Carey, *God's Empire*, 60.
[41] Ibid, 82.
[42] Quoted in Urquhart A. Forbes, "Overcrowding and Emigration," *London Quarterly Review* 8, no. 2 (October 1902): 236–252, 252.
[43] This view was officially sanctioned by the 1904 Interdepartmental Committee on Physical Deterioration. See "Report of the Inter-Departmental Committee on Physical Deterioration," *Parliamentary Papers* XXXII, Cmd. 2,175, 1904. On the limited influence of Social Darwinism and the eugenics movement in late nineteenth-century Britain, see Harris, "Between Civic Virtue and Social Darwinism"; Lucy Bland and Lesley Hall, "Eugenics in Britain: The View from the Metropole," in *The Oxford Handbook of the History of Eugenics*, ed. Alison Bashford and Philippa Levine (Oxford University Press, 2010), 213–227.

helped sustain the nation's faith that lasting and definitive reform was achievable.

By the end of the century, many reformers were suggesting that the solution to the social question was to be found through an expanded reliance on the resources of the British world. Assisted emigration initiatives, which local authorities had quietly and sporadically used since the 1830s, were given new life by prominent figures such as Edward Gibbon Wakefield, who spent most of the 1830s and 1840s urging the state to fund the resettlement of poor men and women in Australia, New Zealand, and Canada.[44] Later, religious leaders such as William Booth, one of the founders of the Salvation Army, took up the call. Booth's plan, which was encapsulated in his 1890 treatise, *In Darkest England and the Way Out*, combined an emphasis on personal discipline with a strong faith in the curative power of the countryside.[45] He advocated removing the nation's unemployed first to temporary training colonies across Britain and then on to permanent settlements in the rural empire. Although Booth's vision proved too elaborate and expensive to implement, the book did create a minor sensation after its publication.[46] It provided fuel for the gospel of redemptive emigration by broadcasting the notion that paupers could rise above their origins if they were provided with proper guidance and were placed in the right setting.

The confident tone of *In Darkest England* aside, the question of whether all poor people were available for reform remained a matter of debate. Despite the underlying optimism that individuals were molded by their environments and could be recast in different circumstances, slum poverty nevertheless appeared to be a deforming influence. To Victorians, destitution was like a cancer. If left unchecked, it would seep into people's bones, warping their bodies and distorting their spirits. It followed that those who had grown up in desperate settings could not simply slough off their effects. Most would have permanent physical and spiritual scars, and even the lucky ones who did succeed would have an arduous road ahead of them. In time, these concerns about the lasting impact of urban poverty led many reformers to shift their focus from pauper adults to the seemingly

---

[44] Carey, *God's Empire*, 313–331.

[45] William Booth, *In Darkest England and the Way Out* (London: Salvation Army, 1890).

[46] While Booth's plan was never realized, the Salvation Army did later serve as an emigration agent, resettling between 200,000 and 250,000 poorer Britons in Canada between 1903 and 1930. Myra Rutherdale, "Scrutinizing the 'Submerged Tenth': Salvation Army Immigrants and Their Reception in Canada," in *Canada and the British World: Culture, Migration, and Identity*, ed. Phillip Buckner and R. Douglas Francis (Vancouver: University of British Columbia Press, 2006), 174–198; Desmond Glynn, "'Exporting Outcast London': Assisted Emigration to Canada, 1886–1914," *Histoire Sociale: Social History* 15, no. 29 (May 1982): 209–238.

less tarnished young. By the 1870s, a vibrant "child rescue" movement had taken shape, which united activists across Britain in the effort, as Florence Davenport Hill put it, to provide children with "delivery ... from their terrible environments" before it was too late.[47] And it was here, within this rapidly expanding social crusade, that the idea of Greater Britain had its most profound impact. While the vision of the settler empire made the redemption of the poor first seem possible, it was the targeted reclamation of children that promised to turn that ideal into a reality.

### Imperial potential

Public fervor for child rescue burned brightest during the second half of the nineteenth century, when the rise of celebrated organizations such as Lord Shaftesbury's Ragged School Union (1844), Barnardo's Homes (1870), and the National Society for the Prevention of Cruelty to Children (1889) placed the needs of poor children in the national spotlight.[48] Yet the foundations of this commitment had first been laid a hundred years earlier, when the combined influences of Romanticism and the Enlightenment ushered in a new model of childhood as a distinct stage of life, separate from adulthood, and characterized by the "childlike" traits of innocence, vulnerability, and dependence.[49] Taken up by an increasingly powerful middle class, this novel conception spread throughout British society during the early decades of the nineteenth century. In the 1830s and 1840s, Parliament pushed through a stricter regulation of child labor, and in 1880 it instituted compulsory schooling. These legislative milestones elevated child protection to a national ideal and helped solidify a single cultural standard of childhood across Britain.[50] By the later Victorian era, the notion that the young required nurturing, education, and specialized care to achieve a full and healthy development was widely accepted, and a new field of charitable action, which sought to provide every British boy or girl with a "proper childhood," had been born.

---

[47] Florence Davenport Hill, "Emigration of Children," *The Times*, December 27, 1886, 6.

[48] There is a large literature on the history of child rescue; for a comprehensive overview, see Shurlee Swain and Margot Hillel, *Child, Nation, Race and Empire: Child Rescue Discourse, England, Canada, and Australia, 1850–1915* (Manchester University Press, 2010).

[49] Hugh Cunningham, *Children and Childhood in Western Society since 1500* (New York: Longman, 1995); Carolyn Steedman, *Strange Dislocations: Childhood and the Idea of Human Interiority, 1780–1930* (Cambridge, MA: Harvard University Press, 1995).

[50] Hugh Cunningham, *Children of the Poor: Representations of Childhood Since the Seventeenth Century* (London: Blackwell, 1992); Eric Hopkins, *Childhood Transformed: Working-Class Children in Nineteenth Century England* (Manchester University Press, 1994).

Heavily influenced by evangelical tenets, the principal aim of most self-styled "child savers" was to deliver poor children from sinful influences and place them on the path of righteousness. To these reformers, helping a needy child ensured the spread of Christianity not only by counteracting the hold of vice and immorality on the rising generation but also by training the young to become disciples of the Lord. Echoing a sentiment that permeated the movement, Barnardo's maintained that its "watchword" was that "'children must be saved!' ... saved, that Christ may claim them for his kingdom; saved, that they may *save others*."[51] The best way to bring about this redemption, it followed, was to maintain the seemingly natural divide between the innocent, carefree world of youth and the starker realities of adulthood. The first step was to get boys and girls off the streets and out of the workhouses, since only then could reformers preserve children's inherent purity and protect them from sin. Starting in the 1870s a host of child-centered charities established free shelters for homeless or destitute children across the country. Most of these institutions took the form of "cottage homes," small-scale residences that accommodated between twelve and twenty children under the care of a matron. The idea was to create a more healthy, domestic, and familial setting than could be found in the massive, barrack-style orphanages left over from the 1834 Poor Law, which ranged in size from 174 children to over 1,500.[52] Charities also began to increase their use of foster care, or "boarding out" in the parlance of the time. Barnardo's led the way in both regards. In Essex in 1876, it founded the "Girls' Village Home," a large compound containing dozens of smaller cottages. The organization began boarding out in 1886 and opened a parallel "Boys' Garden City" in 1909.[53] Barnardo's stressed that, in these controlled and homelike environments, destitute children would exchange their former lives of "poor and insufficient food, impure air and unhygienic conditions" for a more structured existence of "good food, early hours, better air and household discipline."[54] Such simple fare was the best way to domesticate the youth of the slums, cutting boys and girls "clean adrift from the evils of the past" and redirecting them toward "a useful, clean and worthy life."[55]

Reformers often used vague phrases such as "the evils of the past" to invoke a host of corruptive forces from which they sought to redeem

---

[51] *My Cottage: A Story of Dr. Barnardo's Village Home for Orphan and Destitute Girls* (London: Shaw and Co., 1885), 38. Emphasis in the original.

[52] Murdoch, *Imagined Orphans*, 53.

[53] On the development of Barnardo's, see Gillian Wagner, *Barnardo* (London: Weidenfeld and Nicolson, 1979).

[54] Barnardo's, Annual Report, 1907, D.239/A3/1/42, ULSCA.

[55] Barnardo's, Annual Report, 1911, D.239/A3/1/46, ULSCA.

children. In practice, their objective was more explicit: to isolate boys and girls from destitute or "immoral" adults, and from families that seemed beyond repair.[56] Child-saving literature usually depicted poor parents as yet another element of the harmful slum environment from which children needed protection, and they used sensationalized imagery to advocate total separation. As one supporter of emigration wrote in *The Times*, placing boys and girls "beyond the ocean" was the only reliable way to make sure they would not be "dragged back into misery and permanent degradation by so-called 'friends,' who, whether relatives or not, are often their worst enemies."[57] Lawmakers sustained reformers' incursions into the private sphere by standardizing a code of parental conduct that, if broken, abnegated guardians' claims to their children. Between 1885 and 1913, Parliament passed more than fifty pieces of legislation pertaining to child welfare, including the landmark 1889 Prevention of Cruelty to Children Act, which empowered local authorities to remove boys and girls from parents convicted of neglect, as well as the 1908 Children and Young Persons Act, which obligated official intervention in such cases.[58] This flurry of lawmaking emboldened many child savers. In a highly publicized 1886 article, Barnardo proudly acknowledged having stolen, bought, or smuggled forty-seven children away from their families.[59] A few years later he boasted having employed a squad of night agents, which the journalist W. T. Stead applauded as "child hunters" and "human wolfhounds," to patrol the streets looking for ragged children to save.[60]

To justify these forms of vigilante behavior, reformers drew on the racialized language of light and dark, salvation and peril that was common across British culture during the era of the new imperialism. They spoke of their efforts to civilize the "street Arabs" and "urban savages"

[56] Swain and Hillel, *Child, Nation, Race and Empire*. The one major exception was the NSPCC, which focused less on the removal of children than on targeted family intervention. George Behlmer, *Child Abuse and Moral Reform in England, 1870–1908* (Stanford University Press, 1982). Nevertheless, the Society did advocate separating parents and children in cases of extreme abuse, and frequently lent its support to emigration initiatives. In 1910, for instance, its director Robert Parr noted that, while he felt "very strongly against the emigration of able-bodied and intelligent children if there is the slightest prospect of their being able to do well at home," the policy was justifiable to "remove a child from the bad influences of undesirable parents." Parr to Undersecretary of State for the Home Office, June 22, 1910, HO 45/10598/188663, TNA: PRO.

[57] William Tallack, "The Emigration of Children," *The Times*, November 26, 1886, 4.

[58] Harry Hendrick, *Child Welfare: Historical Dimensions, Contemporary Debate* (Bristol: Policy Press, 2003), 28–33.

[59] Thomas Barnardo, "Is Philanthropic Abduction Ever Justifiable?" *Night and Day* (November 1885): 149–150.

[60] W. T. Stead, "For All Those Who Love Their Fellow-Men," *Review of Reviews* (December 1901): 670–678, 675.

of the slums, and to illuminate the "rookeries" that concealed "hordes" of unwashed children. This tendency to view metropolitan destitution through the prism of colonial racial categories was widespread at the time, and has been well documented by historians.[61] The comparisons were effective because they aligned the work of rescue organizations with the nation's larger imperial mission, and defined child poverty as an urgent threat to Britain's continued world supremacy. Less noted, yet equally important, is the fact that, alongside these tropes of "otherness," another imperial language – that of Greater Britain – was also at play. Arguably, this alternate rhetoric was more influential, for it directed attention not to the uncomfortable distance that separated rabble from respectable at home but to the power, unity, and shared potential of the global Britannic people.[62] Child savers might have projected stark scenes reminiscent of the colonized world to draw on readers' sympathy, yet they never went so far as to position poor children as a "race apart," as some historians have claimed.[63] Rather, by tapping into a wider conversation about the redemptive effects of the rural empire, they countered the frightening images of urban decay with hopeful portrayals of the heights British boys and girls could reach if placed in more wholesome environments overseas.

This emphasis on the transformative power of the settler colonies permeated child rescue pamphlets and magazines as well as children's books more generally. The popular Scottish author Robert Ballantyne, for instance, set the bulk of his boys' adventure stories in Canada, a territory he had traveled across as a teenager. Many of his novels take the form of emigration tales, which follow the journeys of slum children pursuing success and independence in the empire.[64] A classic example is his 1884 melodrama, *Dusty Diamonds: Cut and Polished*, which centers on the renewal of a Whitechapel scamp, Bobby Frog, in the farmlands of the far

---

[61] Cunningham, *Children of the Poor*, 95–132; Laura Peters, *Orphan Texts: Victorian Orphans, Culture, and Empire* (Manchester University Press, 2000); Murdoch, *Imagined Orphans*, 24–32; Swain and Hillel, *Child, Nation, Race and Empire*, 79–109. On the racialization of the urban poor more generally, see Deborah Epstein Nord, "The Social Explorer as Anthropologist: Victorian Travelers among the Urban Poor," in *Visions of the Modern City: Essays in History, Art, and Literature*, ed. William Sharpe and Leonard Wallock (Baltimore: Johns Hopkins University Press, 1987), 122–134.

[62] Shurlee Swain, "'Brighter Britain': Images of Empire in the International Child Rescue Movement, 1850–1914," in *Empires of Religion*, ed. Hilary Carey (New York: Palgrave Macmillan, 2008), 161–176.

[63] Murdoch, *Imagined Orphans*, 14.

[64] On Ballantyne's work, and the portrayal of Canada in British children's literature more generally, see R. G. Moyles and Doug Owram, *Imperial Dreams and Colonial Realities: British Views of Canada, 1880–1914* (University of Toronto Press, 1988), 37–60.

northwest.[65] Escaping a drunken father and depressed mother, Bobby joins a party of child migrants and soon finds himself in the home of a cheerful Canadian farming family. The majority of the story details how he and two other child migrants are "polished" into "splendid gems" through a combination of loving discipline, honest work, spiritual tutelage, and Nature's bounty.[66] Ballantyne makes clear that the settler environment does the bulk of the work. Under the influence of the hearty rural lifestyle, the lingering traces of the slums quickly fade. Once overseas, Bobby loses his Cockney accent "as if by magic," while merely breathing "the air of Canada" invests him with a strong constitution and "wonderful delicacy of feeling."[67] By the end of the novel, Bobby has become an ideal specimen of British imperial manhood, a "broad-chested, well-made, gentlemanly young man."[68] He has also changed class. Reinvented as Robert Frog, Esquire, his move into the ranks of the propertied is cemented through the purchase of his own farm. In an ultimate sign of Victorian respectability, when the adult Bobby returns to London to visit his (chastened) father's deathbed, a passing policeman unconsciously calls him "Sir."

The central claim of *Dusty Diamonds* is that the solution to Britain's problem of child poverty lay in the connections of the wider British world. Indeed, by styling the charity responsible for Bobby's emigration after the work of a leading child emigration agent, Annie Macpherson, Ballantyne intentionally blurs the lines between fact and fiction in the novel, and suggests that the success the characters find overseas was available to all British children. The mining metaphor reiterates this theme. The book was published in the midst of South Africa's mineral revolution and just after the North American and Australian gold rushes of the 1850s. The references thus immediately pulled readers' imaginations to the settler colonies while invoking the notion that slum children contained hidden value. Such evocative symbolism caught on quickly. By the turn of the century, editorials were describing orphanages as having the "character of an undeveloped mine, full of possibilities of wealth"[69] and needy children as "residual gold" processed from the "tailings of the street."[70]

The spread of these ideals throughout British culture both provoked and sustained an upsurge in child emigration initiatives from the 1870s

---

[65] Robert Ballantyne, *Dusty Diamonds: Cut and Polished* (London: James Nisbet and Co., 1884).

[66] Ibid, 352.    [67] Ibid, 217 and 388.    [68] Ibid, 416.

[69] D. L. Woolmer, "Up the Ladder," *Quiver* 985 (January 1903): 881–887, 882.

[70] Lord Bishop of Glasgow and Galloway, "The Cyanide Process," *Night and Day* 33, no. 252 (1910): 11, quoted in Swain and Hillel, *Child, Nation, Race and Empire*, 66.

onward. Although the notion of sending needy boys and girls to the colonies had a long history – one of the first instances occurred in 1618 when the City of London apprenticed a hundred pauper children in the newly founded settlement of Virginia – these earlier programs tended to be sporadic and short lived, usually running out of funding after a few years.[71] In contrast, the establishment of two separate ventures by reformist women, Maria Rye's 1869 project to send workhouse girls to Canada followed by Annie Macpherson's 1870 initiative that focused on boys, triggered a wave of activism that soon coalesced into a coherent movement.[72] Religious rivalry played an important part in encouraging this rapid development. Because Nonconformists were the dominant force behind the initial schemes, Catholic and Anglican organizations such as the Liverpool Catholic Children's Protection Society (LCCPS) and the Church of England Waifs and Strays Society soon created their own initiatives in order to prevent child migrants of their faiths from being placed in evangelical homes.[73] An equally influential stimulus, however, was the widely held view that the environment of the settler colonies was vital to unlocking poor children's potential. One advocate of emigration, Arnold Haultain, believed there was an "antiseptic property in the air of prairie and veldt and bush" that guaranteed children's transformation. Arguing that the schemes offered a "catch-all cure for hooliganism … and an antidote to many another canker in the State," he called on charities to increase the annual number of child migrants sent to Canada from roughly 2,500 to over 100,000, and pressed the government to consider funding the movement.[74] In a similar vein, Barnardo's reported that, while "all the bacteria of moral disease" were present in the settler territories, the setting was "unfavourable" to their "germination and growth." The regions lacked the "dark and noisome places in which the rank weeds of vice and evil bear their most deadly fruits," as well as the "conditions of squalor and overcrowding" that "enervated

---

[71] On this early history, see Wagner, *Children of the Empire*, 1–35; Barry Coldrey, "'A Thriving and Ugly Trade': The First Phase of Child Migration, 1617–1757," *History of Education Society Bulletin* 58 (Autumn 1996): 4–14; Parker, *Uprooted*, 3–35.

[72] Both women had been influenced by, and to a large extent modeled their schemes after, the American precedent of the "orphan trains," which had begun relocating street children from cities such as New York to western farms in the aftermath of the Civil War. Parker, *Uprooted*, 20. On the orphan trains, see Marilyn Holt, *The Orphan Trains: Placing Out in America* (Lincoln: University of Nebraska Press, 1992); Stephen O'Connor, *Orphan Trains: The Story of Charles Loring Brace and the Children He Saved and Failed* (New York: Houghton Mifflin, 2001).

[73] Between 1881 and 1902, the LCCPS sent 2,400 children to Canada, while the Waifs and Strays Society sent 2,240 to the colony between 1885 and 1914. Parker, *Uprooted*, 94 and 86.

[74] Haultain, "Who Should Emigrate to Canada?," 106.

and emasculated" Britons "in the old country."[75] Underlining the point, the charity's *Night and Day* magazine summarized that the removal of slum children overseas promised to break the poverty cycle once and for all; it served to "*prevent* the pauper and the criminal, and ... *create* the honest workman – often out of very unpromising materials!"[76]

These arguments that the atmosphere of Greater Britain was curative, that it could clean and restore the essence of needy children, allowed reformers to envision futures for child migrants that moved beyond the hierarchies of class that constrained charitable activism at home. The child emigration movement arose at a time when increasing numbers of boys and girls were entering the care of local authorities and charities. By the turn of the century, between 70,000 and 80,000 British children were receiving some kind of residential assistance. Most of this aid remained under the auspices of the Poor Law, yet a sizable proportion of children, some 10,000 to 15,000, were being helped by voluntary organizations.[77] While the specifics of care varied from place to place, on average the education provided in most institutions consisted of vocational skills training coupled with a heavy dose of moral and spiritual instruction.[78] The intent was to prepare children to fill niches in "class-appropriate" jobs such as blacksmithing, carpentry, or domestic service. On the whole, reformers' expectations for their wards were modest. Few believed that they would find a future doctor, lawyer, or prime minister in the backalleys and tenements of the nation's slums. Instead, they gauged success in humbler terms and according to existing societal models. The Ragged School Union, for instance, defined "productive work" as any occupation that would engender discipline and a steady wage, and famously sent its wards scavenging through garbage as members of rag-collecting brigades.[79] The ultimate goal among metropolitan child rescue societies, in short, was to turn Britain's poorest children, those plucked from the lowest rungs on the social ladder, into independent laborers and members of the respectable working class.

In comparison, the settler empire appeared to offer poor children the chance of real upward mobility as well as a more egalitarian attitude toward labor. The colonies were not classless spaces, and they were never broadly perceived as such. But they did contain a more fluid social hierarchy, which meant that, while recognizable differences between

---

[75] Barnardo's, Annual Report, 1908, D.239/A3/1/43, ULSCA.
[76] Barnardo's, "A Gilt-Edged Investment," *Night and Day* 29 (December 1906): 7. Emphasis in the original.
[77] Hendrick, *Child Welfare*, 42.
[78] Murdoch, *Imagined Orphans*, 120–141.
[79] Prochaska, *Christianity and Social Service*, 45.

professionals and laborers remained, these tended to lack the negative connotations of privilege and paternalism that they carried in Britain.[80] Commentators argued that, without the conventional rigid divides of status, children born into poverty could attain a level of achievement that was unthinkable at home. As Maria Rye exclaimed, sending boys and girls to Canada allowed them to become "honourable members of society" and offered the possibility of "a far brighter career than the one which would, most probably, have awaited them had they remained in England."[81] Rapid social advancement seemed especially available to girls, given the empire's long-standing gender imbalances. The Irish philanthropist and prison reform activist Susanna Meredith's observation that settler women "marry soon and have wealth early" led her to champion emigration as a technique for providing desperate girls with "ways of escape … by means of socialities."[82] Transfer overseas appeared an effective method of unleashing poor children's potential, regardless of gender. As one enthusiast summarized, it allowed the "wastrels of our crowded English cities" to find new lives of "independence and prosperity" in the wider terrain of the empire.[83]

It is difficult to tell whether these stories of "hyper-environmental change"[84] were based in fact. Certainly, emigration improved the prospects of many children, and it was indeed true that the stigma of early pauperism was less of a handicap in the settler territories than in Britain.[85] Yet, as the case that opened this chapter illustrates, it was customary for host families to treat child migrants as inexpensive farm workers. The demand for rural labor remained intense throughout the Canadian provinces during the closing decades of the nineteenth century, and this trend goes a long way toward explaining why applications for child migrants always exceeded the available supply, usually by a factor of eight to one.[86] The tendency to view child migrants as a form of unpaid help undercut the children's access to education and limited their opportunities

---

[80] Belich, *Replenishing the Earth*, 157–158.

[81] William Gilbert, "Maria S. Rye," *Good Words* 12 (January 1871): 573–577, 577.

[82] Mrs. Meredith, "Juvenile Emigration," *Sunday at Home* 1369 (July 24, 1880): 477–478, 478. In this vein, proponents of child emigration echoed the claims of reformers active in promoting the resettlement of young, single women as domestic servants and governesses throughout the empire. Some women, such as Rye, were key figures in both movements. Lisa Chilton, *Agents of Empire: British Female Migration to Canada and Australia, 1860s–1930* (University of Toronto Press, 2007).

[83] W. H. W. Pelham, "Emigration of Pauper Children," *The Times*, January 22, 1877, 4.

[84] Swain and Hillel, *Child, Nation, Race and Empire*, 115.

[85] Although the stigma was not erased entirely. For a full discussion, see Stephen Constantine, "Children as Ancestors: Child Migrants and Identity in Canada," *British Journal of Canadian Studies* 16, no. 1 (2003): 150–159.

[86] Parker, *Uprooted*, 135.

for social advancement, although it is important to remember that rates of school attendance among rural, Canadian-born youth also remained low throughout the period.[87] For most migrant boys and girls, the ideal of upward mobility was belied by a reality of long working hours, limited schooling, and social isolation.

Nevertheless, the actualities that structured child migrants' daily lives were always less apparent in Britain, where emigration charities touted success stories and centered publicity drives around tales of boys' and girls' extraordinary upward climbs. Typical editorials featured formerly destitute children whose "good conduct and smartness" had led them to become successful barristers in Canada, or whose moral fortitude had prepared them to take on missionary work battling "cannibalism and barbarism" in the "far Pacific."[88] In a particularly vivid brochure published in 1908, the Barnardo's director of emigration, Alfred Owen, encouraged readers to envision a parade of the 20,000 child migrants the organization had settled in Canada since the 1880s. Once penniless, these boys and girls now held an array of occupations in the country. The procession was led by the professionals: those doctors, lawyers, and ministers "who have pushed themselves through College ... by sheer hard work and unremitting self-denial." Next were the fit and the brave, the "rugged, hard-muscled" railroad workers and firemen, who were accompanied by scores of daintier "married ladies" and "young schoolmistresses." Last but not least came the "great bulk of our family – the farmers and farm boys and girls," who had recently arrived and were just beginning on the road to self-reliance. "Taken as a whole," Owen declared, the migrants were "undeniably and unquestionably a fine body of young lads [and lasses] and a noble asset to any country."[89]

Owen's "march past" highlights how the late Victorian vision of the settler empire opened up new ways of thinking about the potential of poor children. Although an implicit class hierarchy remained – the procession, after all, was organized with the brains at the front and the brawn toward the back – the focus was on the diversity of paths that awaited children in the colonies. In this respect, the brochure underlined the central claim of the resettlement movement: every British child contained the seeds of future greatness. Like young plants, they only needed the proper soil

[87] Across Canada in the 1880s, the average daily attendance rate of children in the rural areas was 46 percent, a figure that does not account for the large numbers of boys and girls who never registered for school. In Ontario, where most child migrants were placed, full-year compulsory schooling was only established in 1891; in Quebec, the province that received the second highest number of child migrants, it was not instituted until 1942. Ibid, 143.

[88] Woolmer, "Up the Ladder," 883.

[89] Alfred Owen, "Our March Past," Barnardo's Homes, 1908, D.239/A3/18/34, ULSCA.

and cultivation to grow strong and upright.[90] In part, this faith in the universal social value of the young was a legacy of the rise and extension of the Victorian cult of childhood. Equally, however, it was a product of the vision of the united British world that infused metropolitan culture in the decades surrounding the turn of the century. In common with other social activists of his day, Owen viewed the settler empire as a site of spiritual and physical redemption, a place where young Britons were not just reformed but remade. These ideas affirmed a wider confidence in the power of the global Britannic race, and they also forecast an end to the problems of domestic poverty once and for all.

Although potent, the image of Greater Britain that underlay this optimism remained abstract. While Britons recognized the general differences between, say, the terrain and lifestyles of Canada and Australia, their overall impression of these places revolved around a series of set tropes. The settler territories were prosperous, productive, and, most importantly, British. This coherent vision of the rural empire was easier to maintain, however, if one had little firsthand experience of the colonies. As Thomas Barnardo found when he attempted to expand his programs into southern Africa at the dawn of the twentieth century, these ideals about the capacity of the imperial landscape to renovate boys and girls beyond the boundaries of class depended on a particular conception of empire that focused myopically on Canada. In a territory such as South Africa, the potential of British children, and even the meaning of "Britishness" itself, was less certain.

### Pauper children for a White South Africa

By the dawn of the twentieth century, Thomas Barnardo's more than three decades of experience "saving" slum children had made him one of Britain's most well-known philanthropists. Yet, despite his fame, he was beleaguered by persistent money troubles that stemmed from his doctrine of never refusing care to a child in need. His charity operated one of the least restrictive admissions policies of its time, and each year thousands of boys and girls poured into the organization's network of orphanages and foster homes. Even with an annual income of over £100,000, Barnardo still struggled to make ends meet. Child emigration offered a straightforward solution, for, while it cost the society £16 per year to

---

[90] Garden metaphors were widespread in child rescue literature at the time, particularly in places such as Canada, where agrarian ideals were central to the burgeoning national ethic. See Xiaobei Chen, *Tending the Gardens of Citizenship: Child Saving in Toronto, 1880s–1920s* (University of Toronto Press, 2005).

feed, clothe, and educate a child in the United Kingdom, sending that same boy or girl to Canada required just a one-time outlay of £10.[91] Barnardo genuinely believed that resettlement benefited poor children, and these economics gave him even more reason to champion the policy. Always on the lookout for opportunities to expand, he was thrilled in the summer of 1902 when the Duke of Argyll, the former Governor General of Canada and then president of the Homes, offered a plot of land in South Africa to use in founding a training institution for child migrants.

It was not the first time that reformers had considered resettling pauper children in the region. Almost sixty years prior, just after the passage of the 1833 act abolishing slavery in the empire, the Children's Friend Society sent 1,300 juvenile apprentices to the Cape. Applauded by the British elite as a way to ease the colony's transition from forced labor, the venture soon became the focus of fierce popular opposition. As Elaine Hadley has argued, the crux of the problem was the initiative's conceptual incoherence, marked by its blurring of the categories of "emigration" and "transportation."[92] In theory the distinction was clear: emigration signified a voluntary relocation in pursuit of better prospects, whereas transportation was a form of expulsion and punishment. In the early days of emancipation, however, many Britons viewed the prospect of sending White boys and girls to work alongside former slaves as degrading. The scheme never escaped public censure. Opponents stoned the governing committee as they walked to a meeting in 1833, and, when the Society's founder died a few years later, reputedly of grief, the remaining members disbanded in disgrace.

More than half a century later, these tensions had long subsided. The government abandoned convict transportation in the late 1860s, just before the child emigration movement to Canada took off. Around the same time, the public had begun to recalibrate its image of the settler empire, recasting these once remote wildernesses as highly-sought-after pioneer destinations. In particular, recent developments in the south of Africa – including the opening up of the diamond fields in the 1870s, the discovery of gold in the 1880s, and the establishment of Southern Rhodesia in 1895 – positioned it as one of the richest sites in the empire. As the Duke of Argyll observed in an editorial in *Nineteenth Century*, the time was ripe for "planting out state children in South Africa." The abundant land was perfect for bringing up "healthy little colonists," and

---

[91] For funding specifics see Wagner, *Barnardo*, 214. A monthly breakdown of costs is also available in the Barnardo's Council Minutes, D.239/B1/2/3–4, ULSCA.

[92] Elaine Hadley, "Natives in a Strange Land: The Philanthropic Discourse of Juvenile Emigration in Mid-Nineteenth-Century England," *Victorian Studies* 33, no. 3 (Spring 1990): 411–439.

he was sure that child migrants "would never wish to leave the country they would regard as their own."[93]

Beyond these philanthropic intentions, there was another, more strictly imperial motive fueling the renewed interest in an African venture. Argyll wrote his editorial in 1900, one year into Britain's South African War against the region's two Boer republics, and at a point when the conflict was escalating into the nation's largest and costliest since the Napoleonic era. When the fighting finally dragged to a halt in May of 1902, the imperial government had spent more than £200 million and mobilized between 250,000 and 450,000 troops to suppress a total Afrikaner force of no more than 88,000. The army had resorted to devastating scorched earth tactics, destroying over 30,000 farmhouses and laying waste to large tracts of land in the Orange Free State and the Transvaal. More than 28,000 Afrikaner civilians, some 22,000 of whom were children, died of disease and starvation in British concentration camps, while another 14,000 African refugees perished in even worse conditions.[94] The three long years of fighting left deep rifts between the British and Afrikaner settler populations. It also provoked strong political unease in Whitehall, having shown the world the weakness of Britain's military control in one of the most vital sectors of the empire.

Even as shots were still being fired, imperial officials were at work strategizing ways to reestablish British supremacy in the territory. Heading up the effort on the ground was South Africa's High Commissioner, Lord Alfred Milner, a self-proclaimed "race patriot" and ardent proponent of the policy of "Anglicization." His plan combined an infusion of state capital into the mining industry with initiatives designed to universalize the English language and culture.[95] This vision hinged on an expansion of British settlement, and throughout his tenure Milner proposed a series of ambitious immigration schemes. Although most of these initiatives failed, Milner's platform nevertheless cast child emigration in a new light. No longer just a humanitarian policy, it equally began to appear as an effective imperial tool, well tuned to the needs of the colonial administration. As one advocate, Francis Stevenson, proposed in another supportive *Nineteenth Century* editorial, the movement had an essential contribution to make to Britain's long-term colonial mission. Using poor children to fill the ranks of a new generation of South African settlers would ease the

[93] Duke of Argyll, "Planting Out State Children in South Africa," *Nineteenth Century* 47, no. 278 (April 1900): 609–611, 611.
[94] Donal Lowry, "Not Just a Teatime War," in *The South African War Reappraised*, ed. Donal Lowry (Manchester University Press, 2000), 1–22.
[95] Shula Marks and Stanley Trapido, "Lord Milner and the South African State," *History Workshop* 8 (October 1979): 50–80.

"wearying task of governing a race that will not readily be reconciled and will be still more difficult to assimilate or amalgamate."[96]

The unruly "race" that Stevenson was referring to was not the colony's African, "Colored," or Asian populations but rather its other "European" element, the Afrikaners. British administrators viewed the racial issue in the region less as a battle between White and Black than as a struggle for ethnic ascendency *within* the settler community. They took as writ that the "Britannic race" was a coherent entity and that "Britishness" encapsulated certain traits (such as respectability, morality, civilization, and progress) that uniquely prepared Britons to rule subject peoples.[97] Indeed, the South African War had reaffirmed this ideal of Britannic solidarity, as more than 30,000 soldiers and nurses from Canada, Australia, and New Zealand poured into the region to support the imperial cause.[98] Applied in the context of early twentieth-century South Africa, this brand of racial thinking presented two complementary options. Either the British heritage should be institutionalized and extended to those who lingered outside its glow, as Milner wanted, or it should be combined with the best qualities of the Afrikaners to create a novel variety of White colonial patriotism, as was the hope of Milner's "Kindergarten," the loyal group of administrators who came to power following his 1905 departure.[99] The connecting thread between these conceptions was a jingoistic faith in the superiority of the British spirit. Britons may have been tested in southern Africa, but they had emerged undefeated.

Back in London, Barnardo was aware that these imperial considerations might complicate his new undertaking. Ever the prudent Victorian, he decided that a full investigation was needed before he could commit himself to the proposal. He commissioned his eldest son Stuart to travel to the four loosely connected colonies that made up preunion South Africa, and to send back his impressions. Armed with letters of introduction from influential officials such as Joseph Chamberlain, the Colonial

---

[96] Francis Stevenson, "Child-Settlers for South Africa," *Nineteenth Century* 50, no. 298 (December 1901): 1020–1029, 1021.

[97] Douglas Lorimer, "From Victorian Values to White Virtues: Assimilation and Exclusion in British Racial Discourse, 1870–1914," in *Rediscovering the British World*, ed. Phillip Alfred Buckner and R. Douglas Francis (University of Calgary Press, 2005), 109–134.

[98] For overviews of the settler participation in the war, see Carman Miller, *Painting the Map Red: Canada and the South African War, 1899–1902* (Montreal: McGill-Queen's University Press, 1992); Craig Wilcox, *Australia's Boer War: The War in South Africa, 1899–1902* (Oxford University Press, 2002); John Crawford and Ian McGibbon, eds., *One Flag, One Queen, One Tongue: New Zealand and the South African War* (Auckland University Press, 2003).

[99] Saul Dubow, "Colonial Nationalism, the Milner Kindergarten, and the Rise of 'South Africanism,' 1902–1910," *History Workshop Journal* 43 (Spring 1997): 53–85.

Secretary, the twenty-eight-year-old Stuart boarded a ship for Cape Town in August of 1902.

He got off to a good start. As luck would have it, on the boat out Stuart chanced upon two members of the South African political elite: Leander Starr Jameson, the leader of the botched 1895 coup against the Transvaal, and his friend and coconspirator Alfred Beit, the mine magnate and philanthropist. Both were intrigued by Barnardo's plan, and gave Stuart their blessing, although they suggested the need for proper safeguards to make sure the children would not compete with "Native labor." Jameson and Beit were the first of many colonial dignitaries that Stuart encountered in his travels, and a constellation of powerful names is scattered through his journal. On arrival, he met with the Governor of the Cape Colony, Sir Hely Hutchinson, who seemed "very keen on getting boy and girl emigrants" but who warned that securing state funding for the scheme would be difficult.[100] In late September, Stuart moved north into the Transvaal for meetings with Milner as well as with the Lieutenant-Governor, Sir Arthur Lawley. He also toured some of the twenty sites Argyll had offered. Stuart wrapped up his trip in Natal, the most "British" of the colonies, where he discussed the proposal with the Premier, Sir Albert Hime. As elsewhere, his reception was cordial but guarded. Hime liked the notion of importing girls to train as servants in the towns, but he was less optimistic about the prospects for boys, arguing that the climate along the coast was altogether "too tropical ... for whites to do any hard manual work in the open."[101]

Hime's advice about the weather confirmed some of the larger concerns that Stuart had started to develop. Summarizing the position for his father, he noted that South Africa was "not an agricultural country like Canada." Farming seemed risky in each of the districts he visited, and Argyll's properties were all located in "very sparsely settled" areas.[102] Moreover, the region labored "under the curse of having almost every known disease and pest which kill the stock and ruin the crops, such as rinderpest, lung sickness, red water and locusts, to say nothing of the universal lack of water at the right seasons."[103] Apparently, Stuart had not become enthralled by the "romance of the veldt" that attracted so many other British men of his age and that appeared memorably in the writings of novelists such as John Buchan.[104] Instead, the majestic landscape

---

[100] Stuart Barnardo, *Journal of a Visit to South Africa*, 1902, 7, D.239/A3/17/42, ULSCA. A detailed summary of Stuart's journey is included in Wagner, *Children of the Empire*, 162–187.

[101] Barnardo, *Journal*, 84.    [102] Ibid, 71 and 83.    [103] Ibid, 140.

[104] Dubow, "Colonial Nationalism," 64; for a full discussion of Buchan's views on empire, see Daniel Gorman, *Imperial Citizenship: Empire and the Question of Belonging* (Manchester University Press, 2006), 77–114.

that most appealed to Stuart was located across the Atlantic in Canada, the country of rich harvests and a vigorous outdoor lifestyle, not in the "most trying ... sub-tropical heat" and humidity of South Africa, whose climate was so oppressive that even those people "who have lived here many years feel it much."[105]

These comments represent some of the cracks and fissures that were beginning to fragment the unified concept of the settler empire in Stuart's mind. He had come to southern Africa anticipating a temperate and restorative land in keeping with the iconography of Greater Britain. But he encountered a territory that looked and felt quite different, where the sun harassed rather than soothed and where the wind came on so fiercely and suddenly that it sometimes sent him scuttling inside for shelter. Beyond the altered landscape, Stuart was also finding that the unique demographics of South Africa, with its ethnically divided White community and African majority, had given rise to a distinct local culture that appeared at odds with Barnardo's aims. To proponents of child emigration, one of the greatest strengths of the settler world was its abundant supply of honest jobs. They believed that steady work endowed poor children with character and discipline, qualities that were widely accepted as essential for social mobility. In southern Africa, however, Stuart found few opportunities for this brand of uplift. He noted that the "racial feeling" between Afrikaner and British was still so "frightfully bitter" that no Boer farmer would employ a child migrant.[106] More to the point, he reminded his father that the "great bulk of the population is black, and the majority of the native races, instead of dying out like the North American Indian, are increasing in numbers very rapidly."[107] There was already more than enough cheap labor to fill the demand for farm hands or rural servants, and the ubiquitous presence of Africans in unskilled or semi-skilled positions had led many Whites to forgo the principles of independence and self-reliance. As Stuart reported, the local motto seemed to be that "honest manual work [was] *infra dig.* and only fit for Kaffirs."[108]

Stuart would hear this last point time and again. The problem with settling young Britons in the territory was that they would climb the social ladder too quickly. Because of the color of their skin, coupled with their British ancestry, poor children would find themselves on arrival in the colony "one step higher in the scale." This sudden advance would naturally cause them to "look down on and refuse to do hard work of the kind they have previously been quite willing to do." Having risen in standing

---

[105] Barnardo, *Journal*, 146.     [106] Ibid, 21.
[107] Ibid, 138–139.     [108] Ibid, 62.

without having had to strive for their position, the majority would then be "very apt to deteriorate morally after being out here a short time," lowering the standard of the British community as a whole.[109] No less a figure than Lord Milner had stressed this danger, warning that if Barnardo brought out "children of the lower class" to do "menial work, which whites do not do, they might fall to the level of natives, a most undesirable state of affairs."[110] Stuart emphasized to his father that the greatest risk of the scheme was of child migrants "getting down to the native level and forgetting they are whites, and consequently the superior race."[111]

This last comment – that destitute boys and girls could "forget" their Whiteness – serves as a striking illustration of the complexities of race in settler societies, which went well beyond the matter of skin color. In colonial South Africa, being "White" connoted prestige, character, and power, traits that also occupied a central place within the global Britannic identity. These attributes were cultural rather than biological. As Vivian Bickford-Smith has described it, "[a]nglicisation was not something that had happened to anyone in the womb."[112] Instead, it was a slow and rigorous, if often unconscious, process whereby individuals learned "a set of affinities" that designated them as colonizers.[113] This definition of Whiteness as a culture that needed to be protected, rather than as a state of being that was innate, underlay the emergence of official concern with "poor Whiteism" in the same period. Yet, at the turn of the century, the problem appeared distinct to the Afrikaner community, especially its subsection of rural *bywoners*, or tenant farmers.[114] Stuart's investigation was revealing the possibility that Britons were not immune to the threat. In South Africa, child migrants would have to earn their membership in the colonial elite, and Stuart remained unsure whether the atmosphere of the colony, with its vigorous "Native" and Afrikaner populations, could provide destitute children with the values and ethics they needed to begin this upward journey.

The issue was severe enough to derail the scheme. Upon receipt of Stuart's report, Barnardo decided to decline Argyll's offer and quietly shelved the idea of extending child emigration outside Canada. It would be over three decades before proponents would again raise the idea of sending children to the south of Africa, and, even then, many of the

---

[109] Ibid, 140.   [110] Ibid, 49–50.   [111] Ibid, 148.

[112] Vivian Bickford-Smith, "Revisiting Anglicisation in the Nineteenth Century Cape Colony," in *The British World*, ed. Bridge and Fedorowich, 82–95.

[113] Saul Dubow, "How British Was the British World? The Case of South Africa," *Journal of Imperial and Commonwealth History* 37, no. 1 (March 2009): 1–27, 19.

[114] Robert Morrell, ed., *White but Poor: Essays on the History of Poor Whites in Southern Africa, 1880–1940* (Pretoria: University of South Africa, 1992).

questions that had plagued Stuart remained unresolved. Barnardo's venture in South Africa was a minor moment in the history of child emigration, but it does illuminate the profound impact of the idea of Greater Britain on turn-of-the-century understandings of child welfare. The revelation that the African empire held little prospect for the redemption of destitute children exposed how closely the idea of children's universal potential relied on a narrow vision of the settler empire that centered on Canada. The lack of a similarly transformative environment in South Africa threw doubt on the ability of working-class children to cast off their social origins and to move beyond the moral and spiritual corruptions of poverty. It thus called into question the common view that Britishness, like Whiteness, was a coherent identity, one that was available to all Britons regardless of class. In South Africa, it seemed, pauper children would likely never count as fully British, or as fully White.

### Conclusion

While the failure of Barnardo's South African initiative exposed the tensions within the British world ideal at the turn of the century, these doubts about the unity of the British race were always more apparent overseas than they were at home. Back in Britain, the romanticized imagery of the settler frontier as a space in which ordinary people could start afresh remained powerful. The vision retained its hold over the metropolitan imagination not only because it sustained public optimism that the poor were in fact redeemable but also because it inspired Britons to think in new ways about the potential of poor children. When placed in the right setting, such as those rural spaces on offer across Greater Britain, pauper children appeared able to cast aside destitution and achieve a prosperous independence. The "kith and kin" connections spanning the settler empire held out the promise of individual rebirth alongside a broader national renewal.

Judging by the rapid growth of the child emigration movement in the decades before the First World War, these ideas clearly struck a chord with reformers. Harder to know is whether they also appealed to needy parents, whose voice remains obscured or is missing altogether from the archives. When correspondence from the relatives of child migrants does appear in the records, it is usually in cases of disputes, when guardians wrote to find the whereabouts of their children or to object to a proposed emigration. Those who agreed with the policy left less of a trace. A further complication is that it remains unclear whether individual parents understood, when they signed the papers admitting their children to organizations such as Barnardo's, that they were also consenting to the possibility of their son's or daughter's emigration. Many parents were illiterate and could not rely on admitting officers to explain the intricacies of the forms.[115] Even when guardians did grasp the implications of the emigration requirement, they were frequently bullied into signing away their rights. Comments that mothers were subjected to "a little gentle pressure" or "with difficulty [were] induced to yield" their permission appear frequently enough in Barnardo's promotional literature to imply that the practice was widespread.[116] Still, those emigration charities that were more diligent about receiving parental consent, such as the Waifs and Strays Society, did attain relatively high rates of agreement. While the organization did not make parental permission for emigration a prerequisite for admission, it did include a section that asked guardians to consider the option. Only one-third of parents refused to endorse the clause.[117]

What we can know with certainty is that, in an era that lacked many of our modern social safety nets, being a poor mother or father was a precarious and often emotionally exhausting experience. Statistics paint a bleak picture. At the cusp of the twentieth century, 15 percent of all babies born in London died in their first year. Those born to single mothers perished at twice that rate, and on the whole infant mortality levels rose as incomes fell.[118] One 1905 survey showed that, while the death ratio for babies born to households of four rooms or more was 99 per 1,000, it was 219 per 1,000 for families living in one-room tenements.[119] Another study done in North Lambeth between the years 1877 and 1882 indicated that 62 percent of the working-class mothers surveyed had lost two or more children to stillbirth or disease.[120] In a period when the reality of a child's illness or death touched the majority of laboring families, it is likely that the prospect of sending a boy or girl to the empire was a more palatable option than it might appear today. Indeed, the idea that destitution could be temporary, and that the next generation would be less bound by the degradations of poverty, had even more to offer those on the economic margins of society than it did the elite. Undoubtedly, child emigration was a heartrending strategy. But it was not unfathomable, particularly given the fact that it did not always lead to a breakdown of

---

[115] See, for instance, the case of Mary Collard, who in 1886 "signed a paper, not knowing what it contained," which later enabled Barnardo to send her four children to Canada against her wishes, in Parker, *Uprooted*, 246–248.

[116] Thomas Barnardo, *Never Had a Home: A Very Commonplace History* (London: Shaw and Co., 1890), 11; *My Cottage*, 46.

[117] Parker, *Uprooted*, 86.    [118] Ross, *Love and Toil*, 182 and 186.

[119] Anna Davin, *Growing Up Poor: Home, School and Street in London 1870–1914* (London: River Orams Press, 1996), 17.

[120] Ross, *Love and Toil*, 182.

family ties. Parr's study of Barnardo's records found that roughly 70 percent of parents remained in touch with their sons or daughters after their
arrival in Canada. Even more remarkably, nearly one-quarter of those
relatives who had been given no notice of their children's resettlement
managed to reestablish contact later on.[121] Statistics like these bring into
focus the loving attachments and sacrifices that bound poor families of
the era. They also highlight the surprising smallness of the late Victorian
British world, a compactness that allowed Britons of all backgrounds to
imagine that the future of their nation, their families, and their children
lay overseas.

[121] Parr, *Labouring Children*, 72.

## 2    Developing empire, building children

In the summer of 1927, Leo Amery, a Conservative MP and staunch supporter of child emigration, embarked on a tour of the settler empire. The aim of the six-month trip was political. He went in his official capacity as Secretary of State for the Colonies, and his objective was to reaffirm the importance of imperial loyalty across Canada, Australia, New Zealand, South Africa, and Southern Rhodesia, territories that since the Imperial Conference of 1907 were referred to collectively as "the dominions." In the few years since the end of the First World War, Britain's political relationship to its "kith and kin" empire had changed dramatically. In 1923, the dominions gained the right to conduct foreign policy and to sign treaties, a constitutional advance that set them on equal footing with Britain.[1] Two years later, in further recognition of their autonomous status in the empire, the imperial government created a Cabinet post for Dominion Affairs (an appointment also held by Amery), as well as a separate Dominions Office. And, at the watershed 1926 Imperial Conference, Britain formally renounced its right to legislate on their behalf. As the leading voice on empire matters in the government, Amery knew better than anyone else that these developments had reconfigured the political order of the British world. His task on his travels around the globe was thus to remind these progressively sovereign nations that the imperial relationship was worth holding onto.

To spread his message as widely as possible, Amery courted the media at every turn, subjecting his beleaguered wife Florence to an endless

---

[1] The exception was Southern Rhodesia, which remained a Crown colony following a 1922 referendum that rejected union with South Africa in favor of self-governing status in the empire. Although Southern Rhodesia did not have the same foreign policy powers as neighboring South Africa, it did enjoy a high level of political autonomy, and throughout the interwar period the British government effectively treated the colony as if it were a dominion. Donal Lowry, "Rhodesia 1890–1980: 'The Lost Dominion,'" in *Settlers and Expatriates: Britons over the Seas*, ed. Robert Bickers (Oxford University Press, 2010), 112–149, 118–121.

stream of official dinners, state visits, and photo ops.[2] It was no surprise, then, that when the couple arrived in Western Australia in October of 1927, he made sure to schedule a stop at the town of Pinjarra, a sleepy rural backwater that was the site of a new venture run by the London-based Child Emigration Society (CES). Amery's destination was the Fairbridge Farm School, the Society's institution for poor British children. Each year, upwards of a hundred boys and girls aged between five and thirteen arrived at Pinjarra to begin preparing for jobs in the Australian countryside. The scheme suited Amery's purposes perfectly. Trailed by dozens of children and an ever-present photographer, he spent two days strolling the grounds, pointing out the various ways that the school exemplified the continued relevance of the empire. He stressed that Pinjarra was churning out vigorous young settlers who were just the type the dominions needed: "healthy in mind and limb, frank in character, intelligent and trained to country life." Amery also emphasized the scheme's value as a social program, which gave a new chance in life to children who in all likelihood would have ended up "withered, stunted [and] morally warped" had they been left to languish in Britain's slums. Once hopeless, these migrants were now well on their way to becoming "successful farmers" and "valuable additions to the community." Pinjarra was, he concluded, "the finest institution for human regeneration that has ever existed."[3]

This last, striking turn of phrase illuminated Amery's belief that the future of the British people depended on maintaining the close, almost spiritual connection that bound Britain to its settler territories. In his insistence on the restorative power of the rural empire, Amery was echoing the well-established tradition within British social reform circles of extolling the spiritual and physical benefits of pauper emigration. Unlike most Victorian and Edwardian advocates of resettlement, though, when Amery spoke of the regenerative properties of Pinjarra, he was not just calling attention to how the bodies of destitute British children would be mended and soothed, cured and strengthened. Equally important to him was the regeneration of Greater Britain. Like the limbs of a child's body, the various extremities of the empire were being invigorated and repaired through steady infusions of Britannic blood and heritage.

In the aftermath of the First World War, British leaders from across the political spectrum shared Amery's concerns about the health and vitality of the settler empire. At a time when high rates of domestic

---

[2] For an overview of the tour, see Leopold S. Amery, *My Political Life*, vol. II (London: Hutchinson, 1953), 300–474.

[3] CES, Annual Report, 1927, D.296/D1/1/1, ULSCA.

unemployment were adding to anxieties about the war's impact on conventional familial and gender patterns, politicians looked to assisted emigration as a way to stem future political and social unrest. In this respect, as historians have noted, the dominions played an essentially conservative role in the interwar political imagination, enabling officials to envision the stabilization of British society through the resettlement of the poor or the unemployed.[4] Yet this surge of political interest in policies designed to reinforce the British world had even more sweeping consequences. Domestically, it lent support to a new philosophy of child welfare that used the modern science of physiology to update Victorian arguments about young people's responsiveness to their environments. At the same time, it helped transform the ideology and practice of child emigration, replacing the older religious emphasis on cultivating souls with a more secular stress on empire building. Combined, the effect of these developments in the realms of imperial politics and child welfare was to heighten the social and political value of poor boys and girls. By the early 1920s, British politicians and reformers had come to define needy children as essential imperial assets, the bedrock of Greater Britain, and the cornerstone of the worldwide Britannic race.

Across the Atlantic, however, another view of child migrants was taking hold. Just as British political support for the child emigration movement reached new heights, Canadian nationalists mounted a powerful challenge to the view that every British child was worthy of assistance. The resulting public discussion in the dominion about the merits or failings of the initiatives set the stage for a wider debate over the value of Canada's British-centric immigration policies. Although popular support for the empire would remain strong in Canada through the interwar period, the furor over child emigration offered an early sign that popular trust in the ties of "kith and kin" were starting to wane.

### Renewing the bonds of Greater Britain

"Are we on the threshold of a development of our Empire and our trade, or are we about to witness the still-birth or speedy dissolution of our Empire?" asked emigration proponent Thomas Sedgwick at the Royal Colonial Institute in March of 1918. His comment recaptures the apprehension that confronted many empire loyalists in the final days of the

---

[4] Stephen Constantine, ed., *Emigrants and Empire: British Settlement in the Dominions between the Wars* (Manchester University Press, 1990); Kent Fedorowich, *Unfit for Heroes: Reconstruction and Soldier Settlement in the Empire between the Wars* (Manchester University Press, 1995).

First World War. The "Armageddon," as Sedgwick called it, had "shaken up the Empire" in unprecedented ways. Its lasting impact on imperial unity and the global supremacy of the British people was still to be seen.[5]

On the one hand, the war had done much to bring the British world together. The united call to arms and epic character of the struggle had rekindled the old feelings of Britannic pride that so characterized the Victorian era. In the early days of the war, an outpouring of race patriotism stimulated high rates of enlistment from the dominions. Throughout the four years of the conflict, they collectively mobilized over one million soldiers, who fought across a number of theaters and were well respected for their combativeness.[6] In addition to soldiers, the settler territories also sent vital materials and resources, such as wheat and wool from Australia and flour and munitions from Canada. The substantial contributions that the dominions made to the war effort proved their economic and military value to Britain, and positioned the settler empire as a central component of the nation's continued global power.

On the other hand, the strain of total war left its mark on the dominions just as it had in Britain. As early as 1915, the first flood of imperial recruits tapered off to a trickle, leading to divisive political fights over conscription in Canada and Australia. While the Canadian electorate was eventually persuaded to institute a draft two years later, the Australians refused it twice.[7] These "no" votes were never an outright rejection of the cause, but they did signal to British politicians that the war had bolstered the appeal of local attachments throughout the empire, perhaps at the expense of imperial loyalty. "The idea of nationhood has developed wonderfully of late in my own Dominion," the Canadian Prime Minister Sir Robert Borden told his British counterpart, David Lloyd George, as the war neared its conclusion; "I believe the same is true of all the Dominions."[8] In the later stages of the war, when the specter of colonial nationalism combined with newfound pressure for separate dominion

[5] T. E. Sedgwick, "The Imperial Population after the War," March 27, 1918, Migration Correspondence, University of Cambridge, RCS.

[6] Robert Holland, "The British Empire and the Great War, 1914–1918," in *The Oxford History of the British Empire*, vol. IV, ed. Judith Brown and Wm. Roger Louis (Oxford University Press, 1999), 114–137, 128.

[7] Conscription split the Canadian electorate on ethnic lines; Anglophone Canadians were generally for it, while the Quebec-based Francophone population opposed it bitterly. John Herd Thompson, "Canada and the 'Third British Empire,' 1901–1939," in Phillip Buckner, ed., *Canada and the British Empire* (Oxford University Press, 2008), 87–106, 96.

[8] Quoted in Jeffrey Grey, "War and the British World in the Twentieth Century," in *Rediscovering the British World*, ed. Phillip Buckner and R. Douglas Francis (University of Calgary Press, 2005), 233–250, 241.

statehoods, the bonds connecting the settler territories to the mother-land appeared more fragile than they ever had before.

In Westminster, this uncertainty breathed new life into an older polit-ical crusade that sought to use the power of the British state to solidify the unity of the settler empire. Termed the "quest for Greater Britain" by its late Victorian proponents, the campaign's main objective before the war had been to push through a series of constitutional reforms designed to forge the dominions into a vast, transcontinental federation governed by elective parliamentary institutions. As Duncan Bell has commented, this movement for closer union was "one of the most audacious political projects of modern times."[9] It was also poorly suited to the realities of late nineteenth-century international politics, and always remained more of a dream than a practical plan. One of the biggest stumbling blocks was that the goal of locking the dominions into a permanent relationship with the United Kingdom brushed uneasily against the nascent political consciousnesses of the settler territories. The campaign fizzled out by the turn of the century, and, when it was revived during the First World War, the constitutional option had been taken off the table.[10] In its place was an updated version of "imperial preference," which aimed both to anchor the British world in its collective cultural heritage and to tie its separ-ate economies together through protective tariffs and trade incentives. According to this model, Greater Britain was to be a realm of liberty and shared economic interest, not of compulsion.

The driving political force behind the resurrection of these ideas was Amery. Born in India in 1873, where his father was working in the Imperial Forestry Service, he returned with his mother to England as a child, attending Harrow and then Oxford's Balliol College. A voracious reader and independent thinker, Amery developed an eclectic political outlook at Oxford that merged elements of his Conservative upbringing with a newfound attraction to Fabianism as well as to the idealist moral philosophy of T. H. Green. These latter influences led him to view state action as a force for progressive social change. In so doing, they also pushed him to break with the prevailing orthodoxy of free trade, a system he came to understand as profoundly unjust.[11] Already an ardent imperi-alist by the time he left Balliol, Amery strengthened his passion for empire

---

[9] Duncan Bell, *The Idea of Greater Britain: Empire and the Future of the World Order, 1860–1900* (Princeton University Press, 2007), 11.

[10] The exception was the Round Table movement, which continued to advocate federation into the interwar period. See Alex May, "Empire Loyalists and 'Commonwealth Men': The Round Table and the End of Empire," in *British Culture and the End of Empire*, ed. Stuart Ward (Manchester University Press, 2001), 37–56.

[11] Wm. Roger Louis, *In the Name of God, Go! Leo Amery and the British Empire in the Age of Churchill* (New York: W. W. Norton, 1992), 28–74.

while working as a journalist in South Africa, where he covered the Boer War for *The Times*. Lord Milner became a close friend and political mentor during this period, as did Joseph Chamberlain. Amery declared his commitment to imperial protectionism shortly thereafter, and became a leading voice for the cause when he entered Parliament in 1911 as a Conservative. Amiable and well connected, he gained political influence quickly. During the First World War, he secured the plum position of Assistant Secretary to Lloyd George's War Cabinet, and at the beginning of 1919 he followed Milner to the Colonial Office as Undersecretary of State. Although the new assignment moved Amery out of the main currents of European and domestic policymaking, he delighted at the chance to dedicate his full energy to the development of the empire. As he noted in his diary, it was the "work I care most about."[12]

Amery entered the Colonial Office in a period when the problems of reconstruction, particularly the sibling concerns of unemployment and demobilization, dominated the political agenda. The sudden slowdown of the economy at the end of the war had flooded the labor market with jobseekers at the same time that millions of soldiers were returning from the front. In March of 1919, there were already 300,000 veterans on Britain's unemployment rolls, and by the end of the following year 7 percent of the nation's labor force was out of work.[13] Amery was convinced that the solution to these domestic woes lay in a careful redistribution of manpower across the dominions, and he urged his peers to think of Greater Britain as an integrated system, wherein dislocations in one sector could be balanced out by advances in another. To this end, a program of assisted emigration combined with an expansion of British economic investment in the settler territories would boost the dominions' agricultural markets and "reduce the competition for employment, increase wages, and raise the standard of living" across Britain. As he argued in February of 1919, "the key to the problem of post-war reconstruction" was not to be found in domestic initiatives alone, but through the "development of the population and wealth of the whole British Empire."[14]

These ideas struck a chord in the Cabinet, whose members had been eyeing plans for the resettlement of veterans since the later stages of the war. A rushed and clumsily conceived emigration bill had failed to pass in 1918, but Britain's deepening economic problems made the

---

[12] Leopold S. Amery, *The Leo Amery Diaries*, January 10, 1919, vol. I, ed. John Barnes and David Nicholson (London: Hutchinson, 1980), 252.

[13] Fedorowich, *Unfit for Heroes*, 39.

[14] Leopold S. Amery, "Confidential Memorandum on Migration Policy," February 1919, CO721/3, TNA: PRO.

time seem ripe to try again. Amery soon received the go-ahead to found an advisory body, the Oversea Settlement Committee (OSC), which brought together representatives from the Board of Trade; the Ministries of Health, Agriculture, and Labour; the War Office; and related interests such as trade unions and shipping conglomerates. Its first proposal was a free-passage scheme that would provide ex-service personnel and their families with third-class tickets to any of the dominions. Established in April of 1919, the project funded the transportation costs of roughly 86,000 men, women, and children over the next three years. The committee counted this a considerable success, even though the policy never came close to meeting its recruitment goal of 400,000.[15]

The free-passage scheme was an important initial step in Amery's long-term strategy. But the program merely placed Britons overseas and had no mechanisms for guaranteeing that the new arrivals would become "primary producers on the land," as was the hope of the OSC.[16] This emphasis on rural development was essential to retaining the support of the dominions, which were struggling to find employment for their own returning veterans and which contained powerful labor unions that were fiercely protective of urban jobs. As the Australian Minister for Repatriation summarized in a paper that applied equally to Canada and New Zealand, there was "a strong, though not necessarily well-founded, prejudice against bringing people to Australia unless they are likely to become rural settlers or workers." While town populations tended to "view with suspicion ... those who are likely to swell their numbers," they would "heartily approve" any policy that channeled newcomers into agriculture.[17] When the OSC began work in early 1920 on a new set of proposals, it therefore stressed that the forthcoming legislation would center on a "strong policy of land development and land settlement."[18]

The outcome of their planning was the 1922 Empire Settlement Act, which dedicated £3 million annually to any governmental or private

[15] Keith Williams, "'A Way Out of Our Troubles': The Politics of Empire Settlement, 1900–1922," in *Emigrants and Empire*, ed. Constantine, 22–44; Fedorowich, *Unfit for Heroes*, 25–45.

[16] "Record of the Proceedings of a Conference on State-Aided Empire Settlement," March 1921, LAB2/1232/EDO646/1921, TNA: PRO.

[17] Millen to Hughes, January 7, 1919, A3934, SC23 1, ANA. South Africa remained the outlier in these discussions. Although politicians in the dominion favored increasing the White population, they remained wary of any mass immigration schemes that might swell the number of poor Whites, provide competition for African labor, and antagonize the Afrikaner community. Citing the need for a selective immigration policy, the South African government decided not to participate in the empire-settlement legislation. Edna Bradlow, "Empire Settlement and South African Immigration Policy, 1910–1948," in *Emigrants and Empire*, ed. Constantine, 174–202.

[18] Report of the OSC, 1921, *Parliamentary Papers* X, Cmd. 1580, 22.

scheme that increased the number of British settlers in the rural empire. Amery introduced the bill to Parliament in April of that year, and although he was not usually a charismatic speaker – contemporaries sometimes sniped that he might have been Prime Minister had he been half a head taller and his speeches half an hour shorter – he described the legislation with rare eloquence.[19] He began by directing the gaze of his audience away from Europe and toward the "millions of square miles of the richest lands in the world" that lay in the dominions. "We have three-quarters of our people penned, confined, and congested in this little corner of the Empire," while overseas there were "boundless plains, forests without end, water and coal power beyond computation ... waiting for the homesteads and great cities which they could so easily support." Britain, he urged, would never overcome its present difficulties if "our eyes are forever riveted upon this teeming little patch of ground under our feet." Rather, it was essential "to think of our problems in terms of conquest and creation – the creation of new wealth [alongside] the fruitful conquest of Nature." The nation was at the cusp of a new imperial mission, and empire settlement was its sounding bell. The policy was the catalyst that would send a "new vision of Empire pulsing through the veins of this old Mother-country."[20]

As these remarks suggest, the argument for empire settlement encompassed a vivid spatial rhetoric that posed a congested, urban Britain against an expansive, verdant, and largely empty settler world. It is worth noting how closely Amery's imagery lined up with a broader geographic tradition that presented "frontier" spaces as unoccupied territory, a sleight of hand that erased consideration of the dispossession of their Indigenous peoples.[21] His speech also harkened back to the romanticized depictions of the rural empire that had dominated British culture before the war, and which still appeared regularly in the pages of metropolitan newspapers. In the months before Amery's tour de force, *The Times* had described Western Australia as a "settler's El Dorado," a land so fertile that farmers "simply have to scratch the ground and it grows anything."[22] Most striking about the iconography of empire settlement, however, was its natural, even organic quality. Here was a vision of Greater Britain as an interconnected organism, in which British lifeblood coursing out from an industrial heartland nourished new growth in the outer regions

[19] Louis, *In the Name of God, Go!*, 30.
[20] House of Commons, *Debates* 153, 5th series, April 26, 1922, col. 588–591.
[21] Kate Darian-Smith, Liz Gunner, and Sarah Nuttall, eds., *Text, Theory, Space: Land, Literature and History in South Africa and Australia* (London: Routledge, 1996); Anne Godlewska and Neil Smith, eds., *Geography and Empire* (Oxford: Blackwell, 1994).
[22] "White Australia: The Settler's 'El Dorado,'" *The Times*, October 14, 1921, 12.

of the empire. Rich with metaphors of imperial renewal and containing an expectation of continued world dominance, the argument proved irresistible. The Act achieved an "almost universal chorus of generous appreciation," and passed easily.[23]

Yet, as the OSC soon realized, it was simple enough for parliamentarians to envision a "constant stream [of settlers] from this country to the Dominions" but more difficult to make these willing pioneers materialize.[24] In 1921, the Committee was already worried that a British population that was "in the main town-bred and industrial" would find it difficult to assimilate into regions "where the population is largely country-bred and agricultural, and where the principal openings lie in the direction of agricultural development."[25] These fears were backed up by evidence from the dominions. As Canadian authorities pointed out, prewar British immigrants had purchased homesteads at considerably lower rates than their American or continental European counterparts. When given the option, most Britons ended up not on the land but in the country's rapidly growing cities.[26] Coupled with the lower-than-expected turnout for the free-passage scheme, these concerns prompted the OSC to stress that prospective migrants needed to be carefully selected and trained before leaving the United Kingdom. And, although the Committee encouraged an active recruitment campaign, it also held firm that any advanced preparation, persuasion, or incentivizing could only go so far. The policy of empire settlement needed to remain grounded in the ethic of liberty, and in the freedom of choice that purportedly distinguished rational, civilized Britons from the world's subject populations.[27] As Labour's J. R. Clynes argued, "we are seeking the economic development by free men of Empire territory ruled by democracies."[28] In other words, square pegs must not be forced into round holes. Settlers would need to emigrate by their own resolve, driven by a personal desire for farming. Frustratingly for the OSC, that impulse appeared absent in modern Britain. As Amery noted, "even with every training facility ... it is doubtful whether, with

---

[23] Commons, *Debates*, 646.     [24] Ibid, 621.

[25] Report of the OSC, 7.

[26] Between 1897 and 1913, 18 percent of British immigrants had purchased homesteads in Canada in comparison to 33 percent of Americans and 29 percent of continental Europeans. Ninette Kelley and Michael Trebilcock, *The Making of the Mosaic: A History of Canadian Immigration Policy*, 2nd edn. (University of Toronto Press, 2010), 125.

[27] This notion that colonizers were differentiated from the colonized by their ability to enact rational choices was deeply rooted in the British political tradition. Uday Singh Mehta, *Liberalism and Empire: A Study in Nineteenth-Century British Liberal Thought* (University of Chicago Press, 1999).

[28] Empire Settlement and Migration Board, "Report of a Discussion held at the British Empire Exhibition," May 15, 1924, CO 721/97, TNA: PRO.

an adult population of which over ninety percent is industrial, we shall ever get enough men to meet the needs of the Dominions for workers to open up their land."[29]

In essence, this was the same issue of adaptability that had dominated public discussions of the "social question" before the war. Like their late Victorian and Edwardian predecessors, advocates of empire settlement suspected that city living was a powerful determinant of personality and character. The longer individuals spent in an urban environment, working an "industrial" job, getting used to modern conveniences such as corner shops, cinemas, and trams, the less able they became to start over elsewhere. As it had a generation earlier, the need to find a population of Britons who were still capable of changing their ways led policymakers to turn to the potential of children. Winston Churchill, who replaced Milner as Secretary of State for the Colonies in 1921, stressed that child emigration was "most conducive to permanent and successful settlement, because the child migrant when grown up is already accustomed and acclimatized to the conditions of his new home."[30] The OSC was attracted to the schemes less for their humanitarian appeal than for their ability to target Britons who had not yet become "accustomed to industrial city life [or] acquired habits and tastes which increase the difficulty of making a fresh start overseas." It singled out the resettlement of children as the "most valuable" form of emigration, and declared its intent to find between 10,000 and 15,000 boys and girls to sail to the dominions each year.[31]

This escalation of political support for child emigration encouraged many charities to restart their initiatives, the majority of which had been put on hold during the war. Sailing children to Canada had never been formally banned during the conflict, although the reduction of shipping space, alongside the dangers of submarine warfare, had forced an abrupt end to the movement. Barnardo's held out longer than most organizations because of its need to keep beds open in its British branches. It sent a final party of 116 children across the Atlantic in September of 1915, but after that called a halt to the program for five years.[32] When the directors of the charity, together with the Liverpool Sheltering Homes and the Catholic Crusade of Rescue, began indicating their desire to resurrect their programs toward the end of 1919, the OSC jumped at the chance

---

[29] Commons, *Debates*, 580.
[30] Churchill to the Governor-General and Governors of the Commonwealth of Australia, New South Wales, Victoria, Queensland, South Australia, Western Australia and Tasmania, July 22, 1922, CO 886/10/3, TNA: PRO.
[31] Report of the OSC, 8 and 13.
[32] Barnardo's, Council Minutes, September 8, 1915, D.239/B1/2/5, ULSCA.

to champion their efforts. It was soon providing subsidized passage fares and a per capita maintenance grant to help cover the costs of caring for the children in the dominions.[33] The Canadian government offered an additional incentive, providing a subsidy of $1,000 to any agency that resettled a hundred children per year in the dominion, and another $500 bonus for each subsequent hundred.[34]

The strong financial backing that flooded into the movement in the aftermath of the war was an early indication of how the politics of empire settlement had begun to position poor British children as demographic assets who seemed at once adaptable and easily transferable throughout Greater Britain. In their quest to develop the hinterlands of the settler empire, politicians found that the young were some of the most valuable "natural resources" of all; if conserved and managed correctly, needy children promised not only to bring new life into the farmlands of the empire but also to safeguard the strength of the Britannic race.[35] These ideas made the OSC happy to sponsor any initiative that placed boys and girls in the rural dominions. But it reserved its greatest enthusiasm was for a new type of project that was developing not in Canada but in Australia, and that appeared even better positioned than the earlier schemes to affirm the long-term unity of the British world: the Fairbridge Farm School at Pinjarra.

## Empire settlement and the farm school model

Kingsley Fairbridge, the founder of the school that bore his name, was not the typical "child saver." Born in South Africa in 1885 and raised by settler farmers in Rhodesia, he brought to the movement the perspective of a colonist rather than that of a metropolitan social reformer. In fact, he only became aware of the problems of urban destitution in Britain in 1903 when, as a teenager, he visited London for the first time.[36] Writing

---

[33] Ibid, October 15, 1919. The maintenance grants were not extended until after the passage of the Empire Settlement Act. They also varied between the organizations. Most charities received two shillings per child per week, although Barnardo's received a lump sum of £5 for every boy or girl. Bankes Amery to Cuthbertson, June 27, 1924, T161/877, TNA: PRO.

[34] Patricia Rooke and R. L. Schnell, *Discarding the Asylum: From Child Rescue to the Welfare State in English-Canada, 1800–1950* (Lanham: University Press of America, 1983), 251.

[35] This understanding of children as "natural resources" had important precedents in the prewar American pronatalism movement. Laura Lovett, *Conceiving the Future: Pronatalism, Reproduction, and the Family in the United States, 1890–1938* (Chapel Hill: University of North Carolina Press, 2007), especially 109–130.

[36] For a full account of Fairbridge's background and upbringing, see Geoffrey Sherington and Chris Jeffery, *Fairbridge: Empire and Child Migration* (London: Woburn Press, 1998).

of the trip in his memoir, Fairbridge remembered that he had come to the capital expecting a "city of gold and white" and had been disturbed by the poverty and grime that he found there instead. The trip left him with a "keen sense of disappointment," and helped inspire his lifelong commitment to social activism.[37]

These revelations about the scope and nature of urban misery were a common trope in the memoirs of Victorian and Edwardian reformers, as well as in the accounts of the "slummers" who made a pastime of touring London's poorest districts.[38] What set Fairbridge apart from the other activists of his day, however, was that he framed his crusade less in terms of his religious faith or desire for social justice than his deep devotion to the cause of imperialism. As a member of the colonial generation who had experienced the scramble for Africa firsthand, he felt duty-bound from a young age to help retain Britain's hold on its empire. For Fairbridge, that goal would only be accomplished if efforts were first taken to restore the British race in the imperial center. His encounters in London had signaled to him that large sections of the urban population had fallen into a state of moral decay, and he worried that this decline foretold a more general weakening of the imperial spirit. Filling his autobiography with vignettes of slum dwellers' depravity that he found "infinitely repulsive" and reminiscent of "savages," Fairbridge argued that the nation's imperial priorities had been misplaced. Britons were giving too much consideration to the colonized, which distracted them from their own pressing social problems. As he exclaimed after recounting an episode of wife beating he had witnessed on a London street corner, "English women subscribe money to send missionaries to the blacks, while their own sisters are treated thus! Should we not put our own house in order first?"[39]

This desire to protect the sanctity of the imperial ethic was at the heart of Fairbridge's passion for child emigration. Like the Victorian reformers who came before him and the politicians who would later fund his efforts, Fairbridge prized poor children for their malleability and seeming lack of attachments. They were like rough clay made from British soil, waiting to be shaped in the interest of the empire. The idea that deprived boys and girls could be the vanguard of a new imperial mission struck him forcibly on a walk through the Rhodesian bush. As he described his epiphany:

---

[37] Kingsley Fairbridge, *Kingsley Fairbridge: His Life and Verse* (Bulawayo: Rhodesiana Reprint Library, 1974), 30.

[38] Seth Koven, *Slumming: Sexual and Social Politics in Victorian London* (Princeton University Press, 2004).

[39] Fairbridge, *Life and Verse*, 146.

I saw a street in the East End of London. It was a street crowded with children –
dirty children, yet lovable, exhausted with the heat. No decent air, not enough
food. The waste of it all! Children's lives wasting while the Empire cried aloud
for men ... And then I saw it quite clearly: *Train the children to be farmers!* ... Shift
the orphanages of Britain north, south, east, and west to the shores of Greater
Britain, where farmers and farmers' wives are *wanted*, and where no man with
strong arms and a willing heart would ever want for his daily bread. I saw great
Colleges of Agriculture (not workhouses) springing up in every man-hungry corner of the Empire.[40]

Inherent to this vision was a belief that the needs of pauper children
intersected seamlessly with those of the British world. While the youth
of the nation deteriorated amid the filth and the heat of London's slums,
the "man-hungry" empire also suffered, its development stunted from
a dearth of farming families. The answer was to bring these two problems together: to fill the settler territories with pliant British stock, and
to invest the nation's poorest children with a broader social purpose by
sending them where they were "wanted" – a clever turn of phrase that
implied they were *unwanted* by their relations and were therefore expend-
able at home. To Fairbridge, child emigration was no simple act of charity. It was a novel method of imperial social engineering that would turn
"waste ... to providence, the waste of unneeded humanity converted to
the husbandry of unpeopled acres."[41]

Essential to this transformation were the "Colleges of Agriculture"
that Fairbridge imagined spreading throughout the dominions. As he
noted in a 1910 Empire Day editorial in *The Times*, the innovation of
the farm school distinguished his project from the existing schemes in
Canada. While those initiatives aimed just to place boys and girls with
Canadian families, and thus stopped short at resettlement, his would
be more comprehensive, providing "emigration *plus* education."[42] Within
Fairbridge's centralized institutions, child migrants would receive a specialized upbringing to endow them with the skills and character they
would need in their future lives as pioneers. As such, the new model
would serve to counter the more "reckless" forms of emigration that,
in Fairbridge's view, were haphazardly scattering untrained and unloved
pauper children overseas. By failing to ensure child migrants' full reform,
these programs offered little benefit to needy boys and girls. Worse yet,
they placed the sanctity of the empire at risk by threatening to implant
an "incubus of incompetence and wastrelism" in the nascent settler

[40] Ibid, 159–160. Emphasis in the original.
[41] Ibid.
[42] Kingsley Fairbridge, "The Farm School System: A Suggestion," *The Times*, May 24,
1910, 46. Emphasis in the original.

communities of the empire. This gendered imagery was purposeful. By invoking a vivid picture of pure, virginal territory becoming corrupted through the demonic force of pauperism, it presented the farm school as a beacon of salvation in which formerly destitute children would learn both to love the land and to make it bloom.[43]

Fairbridge spent much of his early life in dogged pursuit of his plan. He won one of the first Rhodes Scholarships, and used it to study forestry at Oxford. While in England, he set about publicizing his ideas and building a fundraising network. Having officially established the CES in October of 1909, by 1912 he had convinced the government of Western Australia to give him a plot of land and a small maintenance grant to use in founding the first farm school. Fairbridge and his wife Ruby set sail for Pinjarra in the summer of 1912, and the following year the school was up and running. The couple welcomed the initial class of a dozen boys between ten and twelve years old, most of whom had been selected from Poor Law institutions, although a few came from private homes or charities across Britain. By the end of 1913, the arrival of a second party of boys brought the number of children in residence up to thirty-five.[44]

Fairbridge was truly starting from scratch. Most of the site was forested over when he arrived, and the few farm buildings that were included in the plot were in serious need of repair. Forced to rely on sporadic donations sent from the Society's London committee, Fairbridge and the boys did the bulk of the work by hand. When, in July of 1913, the Western

[43] Ibid. Although Fairbridge became the most prominent proponent of farm school training for child migrants, he was not the first. In 1906, Ellinor Close developed a similar model in New Brunswick, Canada, which took in twelve children aged between five and fourteen. Barnardo's had also briefly operated a farm school for British teenagers in Manitoba, as did Captain Hind in Nova Scotia and Thomas Sedgwick in New Zealand. On these precedents, see "The Farm-Home System: Mrs. Close's Plan," *The Times*, May 24, 1910, 45; T. E. Sedgwick, *Town Lads on Imperial Farms, with Notes on Other Phases of Imperial Migration* (London: P. S. King and Son, 1913); Sherington and Jeffery, *Fairbridge*, 14–15; Marjory Kohli, *The Golden Bridge: Young Immigrants to Canada, 1833–1939* (Toronto: Natural Heritage, 2003). Interestingly, as Fairbridge was conceiving his farm school project, the Scottish missionary John Graham was establishing a strikingly similar scheme for the children of the Eurasian and domiciled European community in India. Graham planned to emigrate his wards to the dominions, where he hoped they would become independent farmers. But dominion concerns over the children's mixed racial descent limited the appeal of his scheme abroad, and by the 1930s only about sixty-five boys had been resettled, the majority in New Zealand. For a full description of Graham's work, see Satoshi Mizutani, *The Meaning of White: Race, Class, and the "Domiciled Community" in British India, 1858–1930* (Oxford University Press, 2011), 137–180.

[44] Although Fairbridge wanted to make his school co-educational, the Western Australian government objected, arguing that the outback was no place for girls. This opposition delayed the arrival of the first party of girls until 1921. On this issue, and for the backgrounds of the boys in the 1913 parties, see Sherington and Jeffery, *Fairbridge*, 32 and 58–60.

Australian Immigration Department sent A. O. Neville, the man who would later achieve fame as the director of the state's Aboriginal child removal policy, to report on the premises, the site was still barely fit for habitation. All of the boys were living in a single "dilapidated cottage" and sharing a bathing facility that consisted of an "iron shed built over an open drain, with no floor." Although the children appeared "in good condition, and seemed to be perfectly happy and contented," they lacked adequate clothing. In the middle of the Australian winter, each boy had "two garments only ... tweed pants, and a sort of khaki or cloth tunic. They wear no hats, boots or stockings, or underclothings." Neville concluded that, while the idea behind the scheme was sound, the setup remained "very primitive, and some of the premises would doubtless be condemned were it a Government institution."[45]

In part, this hardscrabble existence was a product of the Society's meager finances, which kept Fairbridge on a constant search for local donors throughout his years in Western Australia. Yet the roughness was also a reflection of the scheme's underlying ideology. While he found the environment difficult and exhausting, Fairbridge nevertheless acknowledged that it was the ideal setting for the creation of imperial pioneers.[46] He aimed to foster a spirit within the boys of rugged self-reliance and dedication to the empire by having them do as much as possible by themselves, and by enforcing a "Code of Ethics" that was designed to instill the traits of imperial manliness. The rules covered an array of topics, from basic manners ("Avoid spitting, clearing your throat noisily, and making other unpleasant sounds") to lessons in authority ("Learn to obey absolutely and to the letter") to speaking ("You are British boys, and the language that you speak is supposed to be the English language. Do your best always to speak pure English"). Most of all, the code reiterated the children's duty to uphold the mantle of Greater Britain. Each boy was encouraged by "thought and word and deed to make himself of the utmost possible use," and to "train himself to be a faithful servant of God, a loyal subject of the King, and a true soldier of the great Empire." As Fairbridge liked to remind his wards, "Our splendid Mother, the Empire, needs all her children."[47]

By placing the drive for imperial development on equal footing with the humanitarian imperative to reclaim children from poverty, Fairbridge's farm school model marked a significant break with the

---

[45] A. O. Neville, "Report on the Pinjarra Farm School," July 28, 1913, Sherington Papers, Box 1, SLNSW.

[46] CES, 4th Annual Report, September 1913, D.296/D1/2/4, ULSCA.

[47] Kingsley Fairbridge, "Code of the Fairbridge Farm School," *c.* 1915, Sherington Papers, Box 1, SLNSW.

previous philosophy of child emigration. During the Victorian era, the empire had largely appeared as the backdrop for the more compelling story of poor children's redemption. Now, the objective of developing the British world moved front and center, a process that transformed the status of child migrants. No longer simply metaphorical diamonds in the rough waiting to shine, deprived children became political entities that held measurable imperial value. To prove as much, in 1921 Fairbridge invited the director of the local Bureau of Commerce and Industry to visit Pinjarra and evaluate the actuarial potential of his class of child migrants. The assessment came in at £1,000 a head.[48]

This frank quantification of children's worth remains an uncomfortable reminder of the politicizing of child welfare. In an era when many were coming to view the young as emotionally "priceless,"[49] Fairbridge and his supporters continued to appraise needy children's usefulness to the empire in precise economic terms. Back in Britain, the imperial government took notice. After a tough few years of wartime retrenchment, during which he almost closed the school from lack of funding, Fairbridge made a last-ditch attempt to finance his project. He sailed to Britain in June of 1919 pledging to raise at least £10,000 or to "return the money to the donors and not return to Australia."[50] The response he met caught even an idealist like Fairbridge off guard. Within a few months, he had well exceeded his goal, receiving grants of £5,000 from the Red Cross, £2,500 from the Rhodes Trust, and £20,000 from the National Relief Fund.[51] Soon afterward, the OSC agreed to contribute a two-shilling weekly maintenance in support of every child migrant at Pinjarra. This last agreement in particular provided the CES with a stable source of income, and eventually allowed Fairbridge to embark on an ambitious expansion of the school.[52]

Given this sudden outpouring of governmental support, it is tempting to dismiss interwar child emigration as a blatant political project, a welfare initiative in name only. And yet, the movement remained connected to the dominant currents of social reform in the period. Indeed, the ideas that inspired the push for empire settlement found a close corollary in a new vision of child health that was emerging in the field of physiology. Together these trends in imperial politics and child welfare converted

---

[48] Kingsley Fairbridge to the Commonwealth Superintendent for Immigration, October 1, 1921, A436, 46/5/597 Part 1A, ANA.
[49] Viviana Zelizer, *Pricing the Priceless Child: The Changing Social Value of Children* (New York: Basic Books, 1985).
[50] CES, Perth Committee Minutes, June 13, 1919, ACC 3025A/1, SAWA: BL.
[51] CES, 11th Annual Report, 1919–1920, D.296/D1/2/11, ULSCA.
[52] Sherington and Jeffery, *Fairbridge*, 73–88.

interwar child emigration from a philanthropic endeavor into an imperial social policy, one in which the twin aims of reinvigorating the empire and uplifting poor children were closely intertwined.

## An empire of healthy children

"They reckoned I was the skinniest little rat that you ever came across," recalled George Snellin of his arrival at the Fairbridge Farm School in 1921. Diagnosed with tuberculosis as an infant, he remained a "very sick boy" throughout his childhood. Snellin and his three older brothers were members of the CES's first postwar party, having come to the charity through local authorities. The boys' parents had died during the war and, although Snellin's eldest sister tried to keep the family together, the police removed the youngest children from her care. Only six years old at the time of his emigration, Snellin's age exempted him from the more labor-intensive chores at Pinjarra. He also received special treatment on account of his weak constitution. He remembered having to swallow down "raw eggs and vinegar every day" as well as doses of "malt and cod liver oil to build me up." He was kept out of school when it rained, and was never allowed outside if it was wet. And, while the rest of the children went barefoot, he got to keep his boots. Even with these precautions, Snellin continued to suffer bouts of pneumonia through his twenties, and he struggled to convince the Society to grant him permission to marry a fellow child migrant in 1939 after "they said I wasn't strong enough ... to marry and bring up a family and support them." Nevertheless, he built a solid career for himself as a laborer in the farming industries, and together with his wife Lily raised five children. "Proved them wrong there," he noted with pride.[53]

Snellin was born in 1915, at a time of heightened public and governmental concern over the health of Britain's poorest children. A steady decline in the nation's birthrate during the Edwardian years had already raised alarm about the general fitness of the population as well as about the specific issue of infant mortality. The war's disruption of family and community life amplified these anxieties, especially after it was reported that the country's birthrate had fallen by over 25 percent during the conflict. In statistical terms, this signified a net loss of 700,000 potential citizens, a total that roughly equaled the number of British soldiers killed on the battlefield.[54] These sobering figures revived eugenic fears about the

---

[53] Interview with George Snellin, conducted by Chris Jeffery, July 11, 1985, OH 1876, SAWA: BL.

[54] Richard Soloway, *Demography and Degeneration: Eugenics and the Declining Birth Rate in Twentieth-Century Britain* (Chapel Hill: University of North Carolina Press, 1995), 138.

decline of the race, and spurred the state and the voluntary sector into action.[55] The resulting spike of activism in the field of child welfare does much to explain why local authorities judged a thin and sickly boy like George Snellin to be an optimal candidate for emigration. In the aftermath of the war, new developments in the medical study of childhood presented resettlement as one of the most reliable methods for repairing the bodies of ill or malnourished children. Once again, Greater Britain appeared to hold the key to the nation's domestic revival and lasting international power. As the *Daily Chronicle* put it in an article that urged an extension of the emigration movement, "In the battle of life, which is ultimately a battle of nations and races ... it is the child who will win or lose all."[56]

Initially, the increased awareness of infant mortality and childhood disease led to the growth of government funding for pronatalist policies and children's services. During the war, local authorities expanded their existing school meals programs and also became more involved in subsidizing milk for infants and pregnant women. Moreover, even in the face of a large-scale military recruitment of doctors, the rate of British children receiving free medical care rose. By 1919, nearly 700 school clinics across the country were treating some 180,000 boys and girls, while another 400 government-assisted welfare centers were offering medical advice to needy families.[57] Overall, state spending on health provision jumped from 4 percent of the gross national product before the war to around 8 percent afterward.[58] These figures marked impressive advances, but the momentum was short lived. When the unemployment rate began to climb in the early 1920s and the economy slowed to a slump, many of these wartime initiatives fell to the axe of Treasury retrenchment. By 1921, for instance, the Local Government Board (LGB) had limited the distribution of subsidized milk to just the poorest families and to

The infant death rate remained highly differentiated by class; the children of unskilled laboring families died at twice the frequency of their counterparts in the middle and upper classes. Virginia Berridge, "Health and Medicine," in *The Cambridge Social History of Britain, 1750–1950*, vol. III, ed. F. M. L. Thompson (Cambridge University Press, 1990), 171–242, 220.

[55] Jane Lewis, *The Politics of Motherhood: Child and Maternal Welfare in England, 1900–1939* (London: Croom Helm, 1980); Deborah Dwork, *War is Good for Babies and Other Young Children: A History of the Infant and Child Welfare Movement in England, 1898–1918* (New York: Tavistock, 1989); Anna Davin, "Imperialism and Motherhood," in *Tensions of Empire: Colonial Cultures in a Bourgeois World*, ed. Frederick Cooper and Ann Stoler (Berkeley: University of California Press, 1997), 87–151.

[56] "Peopling the Empire: The Children's Chance in a New Land," *Daily Chronicle*, January 24, 1920.

[57] Harry Hendrick, *Child Welfare: Historical Dimensions, Contemporary Debate* (Bristol: Policy Press, 2003), 82; Lewis, *The Politics of Motherhood*, 38.

[58] Lewis, *The Politics of Motherhood*, 18.

pregnant mothers only in their last trimester.[59] These and other cutbacks limited the long-term effectiveness of state programs; as Richard Wall has argued, the improvements in child health registered during the war probably had more to do with the growth of jobs than with government policy.[60]

In the face of the government's economizing, the voluntary sector reasserted its importance in the care of the young. Throughout the interwar period, philanthropic and religious associations remained essential providers of social services. Nationally, they took on pioneering roles in the treatment of childhood disorders and preventative care.[61] Internationally, British charities became major players in the burgeoning movement, based around the League of Nations, to define a universal standard of child protection.[62] The rise of these new philanthropic efforts at home and overseas served both to redefine and to broaden the ideology of European child welfare. Whereas Victorian reformers had concentrated on repairing the subset of children who had been rendered "abnormal" through the forces of neglect, poverty, or delinquency, their interwar counterparts drew their inspiration more from the figure of the "normal" or "whole child."[63] They looked to the latest scientific research on child development, disease prevention, and nutrition in the hopes of designing policies that would optimize the health of all children.[64]

In this endeavor, no field was more influential than the science of physiology, which aims to track the human growth cycle through a close study of the body's organs and systems. Its appeal to interwar reformers was that it offered a neutral, medical model of children's development that broke

---

[59] Ibid, 67.
[60] Richard Wall, "English and German Families and the First World War, 1914–1918," in *The Upheaval of War: Family, Work and Welfare in Europe, 1914–1918*, ed. Richard Wall and Jay Winter (Cambridge University Press, 2005, originally 1988), 43–106.
[61] Geoffrey Finlayson, *Citizen, State, and Social Welfare in Britain, 1830–1990* (Oxford: Clarendon Press, 1994), 218–225.
[62] Dominique Marshall, "The Construction of Children as an Object of International Relations: The Declaration of Children's Rights and the Child Welfare Committee of the League of Nations, 1900–1924," *The International Journal of Children's Rights* 7 (1999): 103–147; Ellen Boucher, "Cultivating Internationalism: The Save the Children Fund, Public Opinion, and the Meaning of Child Relief, 1919–1924," in *Brave New World: Imperial and Democratic Nation-Building in Britain between the Wars*, ed. Laura Beers and Geraint Thomas (London: Institute for Historical Research Press, 2012), 169–188.
[63] Patricia Rooke and R. L. Schnell, "'Uncramping Child Life': International Children's Organisations, 1914–1939," in *International Health Organisations and Movements*, ed. Paul Weindling (Cambridge University Press, 1995), 203–221.
[64] Paul Weindling, "From Sentiment to Science: Children's Relief Organisations and the Problem of Malnutrition in Inter-War Europe," *Disasters* 18, no. 3 (September 1994): 203–212.

free from earlier discussions of class or cultural difference.[65] To the physiologist, all children's development was the same: their bodies were organic entities that advanced through predetermined stages as they learned movement, then speech, and finally high-level thought. This natural progression could be disrupted or slowed if the child's body was starved of food, fresh air, or exercise. But it could also be restored by a close concentration on their physical needs, and on children's relationship to their wider environment. Modern physiology had been around since the seventeenth century, but it only began to shape educational and social policy discussions in the years surrounding the First World War. Its authority grew rapidly because most British reformers were already inclined to believe that the environment had a far greater impact on children's development than heredity. By resurrecting the earlier tenets of the child rescue movement in a more scientific form, physiology added the weight of medical authority to what had previously seemed simple common sense: that three square meals and lots of time outdoors were good for children, and that inadequate food and slum living left them sickly, listless, and wan.

In the early twentieth century, physiology shaped the agendas of a variety of child welfare initiatives. One of its strongest proponents was the Independent Labour Party activist Margaret McMillan, who designed her famous Deptford "camp schools" to invigorate the growth cycles of stunted children by maximizing their exposure to the elements.[66] Physiological principles also underwrote the turn-of-the-century kindergarten and Montessori movements, which prioritized educating the senses over rote learning and focused on stimulating children's autonomous engagement with the world around them.[67] Among children's charities, the science provided new support for the "back to nature" emphasis that had long dominated the work of child rescue. As Barnardo's declared in 1921, "boys and girls can always be better reared in the country than in the crowded cities. Our aim has been succinctly expressed in the phrase: 'Ruralise the child.'"[68] To translate this belief into practice, a few months

[65] Carolyn Steedman, "Bodies, Figures and Physiology: Margaret McMillan and the Late Nineteenth-Century Remaking of Working-Class Childhood," in *In the Name of the Child: Health and Welfare, 1880–1940*, ed. Roger Cooter (New York: Routledge, 1992), 19–44.

[66] Carolyn Steedman, *Childhood, Culture, and Class in Britain: Margaret McMillan, 1860–1931* (London: Virago, 1990).

[67] Kevin Brehony, "English Revisionist Froebelians and the Schooling of the Urban Poor," in *Practical Visionaries: Women, Education and Social Progress, 1790–1930*, ed. Mary Hilton and Pam Hirsch (London: Longman, 2000), 183–199; Peter Cunningham, "The Montessori Phenomenon: Gender and Internationalism in Early Twentieth-Century Innovation," in *Practical Visionaries*, ed. Hilton and Hirsch, 203–220.

[68] Barnardo's 56th Annual Report, 1921, D.239/A3/1/56, ULSCA.

later the society's executive committee replaced their aging Stepney head-quarters in the East End with a new farm property called "Goldings" on the outskirts of London. The organization touted that the move would allow 96 percent of Barnardo wards to be brought up in the "healthier atmosphere of the country," where their bodies could "respond to the natural and spiritual influences around them" and "rapidly improve."[69] One year after the branch opened, the committee could not have been more pleased. The children's physical development was progressing "wonderfully," and they were also "overcoming ... the undesirable habits which had clung to them at Stepney." According to Barnardo's, their connection with nature had proved so enriching that almost none of the children wanted to return to the city, not even "to go in to Hertford to the Cinemas."[70]

Beyond reasserting the basic health benefits of rural living, physiology also sustained reformers' faith in the curative properties of sunshine. The belief took hold in part because the era lacked a more precise, bio-chemical understanding of malnutrition. That knowledge did not begin to emerge until the later years of the Depression, when the spread of persistent hunger beyond the ranks of Europe's very poor prompted a minor boom in nutrition studies.[71] The League of Nations, for instance, did not release recommended calorie or protein guidelines for children until 1935.[72] In contrast, studies seeming to prove the value of sunshine dated as far back as the 1890s, when doctors first used overlaid maps to illustrate that the childhood bone disease rickets occurred at higher rates in neighborhoods where direct sunlight was obstructed.[73] In 1919, Edward Mellanby explained the finding when he discovered that the dis-order was caused by a deficiency of fat-soluble vitamins. Cod liver oil supplements coupled with prolonged sun exposure provided an effect-ive treatment since natural light converts Vitamin D to an active state and improves the absorption of calcium. Charities and local authorities soon embraced "sunshine therapies" not only for the management of rickets but also to fortify "weak" children – although, given the coun-try's unhelpful weather patterns, practitioners often had to resort to the use of solar lamps (Figure 2.1). Violet Coughlin, who was born in 1919

[69] Barnardo's 58th Annual Report, 1923, D.239/A3/1/58, ULSCA.
[70] Barnardo's, Executive Committee Minutes, May 3, 1922, D.239/B3/1/4, ULSCA.
[71] Jay Winter, "Unemployment, Nutrition and Infant Mortality in Britain, 1920–1950" in *The Working Class in Modern British History*, ed. J. M. Winter (Cambridge University Press, 1983), 232–256; James Vernon, *Hunger: A Modern History* (Cambridge: Belknap Press, 2007), 90–117.
[72] Weindling, "From Sentiment to Science," 208.
[73] Chris Otter, *The Victorian Eye: A Political History of Light and Vision in Britain, 1800–1910* (University of Chicago Press, 2008), 65–67.

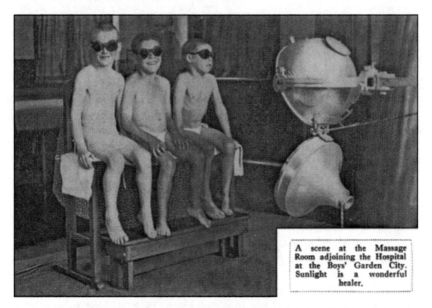

Figure 2.1 "A scene at the Massage Room adjoining the Hospital at the Boys' Garden City. Sunlight is a wonderful healer." Barnardo's 67th Annual Report, 1932, 28, D.239/A3/1/67, ULSCA.

and entered the care of Barnardo's at the age of two, remembered being "constantly sick" as a child. She had difficulty putting on weight – "they called me Skinny Lizzy" – but was never diagnosed with a specific disorder. And so, when she was ten years old, Violet was sent to a specialized clinic called "Sunshine House," which was also run by Barnardo's. As she recalled, the Home provided generalized care "for cripples and people that had a complaint that, like me, [the doctors] couldn't understand what it was." A few years later, Coughlin was included in an emigration party to Australia, no doubt in order to amplify her exposure to sunlight. She remained in the country for the rest of her life.[74]

In addition to sunshine, fresh air and seawater also seemed to offer catch-all cures for lung disorders such as tuberculosis and phthisis as well as for skin diseases such as scrofula. When expanded testing during the war revealed that upwards of one-third of the nation's young were infected with the tuberculosis bacillus, educational authorities launched a campaign to create "open-air schools" wherever possible. By 1937, there were 155 such institutions across the country, with 16,500 children in

[74] Author's interview with Violet Coughlin, May 17, 2006.

attendance.[75] Barnardo's further experimented with seawater spray treatments at its Folkestone Hospital, which it founded in 1920 and located on the coastline of Kent so that children could benefit from ocean breezes. Throughout the interwar years, the organization regularly included pictures and accounts from Folkestone in its promotional literature as a way of illustrating that it traded in the most advanced medical techniques.[76] A typical example from its 1924 report showed a picture of small boys and girls standing outside the hospital in short pants and sleeveless shirts with the caption: "These children (Surgical Cases) are being restored to health and strength by Sunshine and Sea Air at our Folkestone Home."[77]

Through this focused attention on the way children's bodies responded to their environments, physiology sustained reformers' tendency to assess child health in terms of external markers such as height, weight, and musculature, rather than according to internal emotional or psychological criteria.[78] Physiologists held that a child's personality and intellect were determined by their position on the growth cycle.[79] The standard dictum was that a healthy body made for a happy and well-behaved child, while undernourishment or illness clouded the mind and gave rise to apathetic, foul-tempered, or delinquent behaviors. In their more extreme applications, these arguments lent support to models of child welfare that deemphasized or dismissed altogether the importance of emotional ties and parental nurturing. A 1924 Barnardo's promotional booklet on the benefits of sun therapy, for instance, included a photograph of a smiling, rosy-cheeked infant on its back cover alongside a heading that urged readers to "see what sunshine has done for him" (Figure 2.2). The close-up shot and non-descript background stripped the boy of context or case history, making him indistinguishable from any other "normal" baby. This framing quite literally cut the child's parents and family out of the picture. In their place, it positioned sunshine as the dominant force in the boy's transformation into the epitome of health and happiness. The implied context left viewers to imagine for themselves the supposedly bleak and gloomy home from which he had been reclaimed.

[75] Linda Bryder, "Wonderlands of Buttercup, Clover and Daisies: Tuberculosis and the Open-Air School Movement in Britain, 1907–1939," in *In the Name of the Child*, ed. Cooter, 72–95.

[76] For examples see Barnardo's Annual Reports for 1924, 1929, and 1932, D.239/A3/1/59, 64, and 67, ULSCA.

[77] Barnardo's 59th Annual Report, 1924, D.239/A3/1/59, ULSCA.

[78] Nikolas Rose, *The Psychological Complex: Psychology, Politics, and Society in England, 1869–1939* (London: Routledge & Kegan Paul, 1985), 150.

[79] Steedman, *Childhood, Culture, and Class*, 203–214.

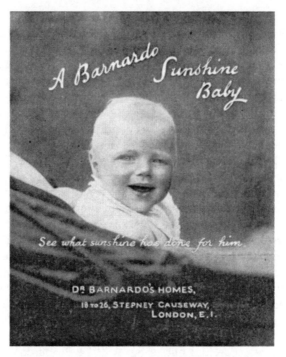

A Barnardo Sunshine Baby

See what sunshine has done for him

DR. BARNARDO'S HOMES,
18 to 26, STEPNEY CAUSEWAY,
LONDON, E.I.

Figure 2.2 "The Gateway to Sunshine." Barnardo's Appeal Booklet, 1924, D.239/A3/17/15, ULSCA.

By reaffirming the power of the environment over the ties of family, and by investing these older ideals with the authority of science, the incorporation of physiological theory into interwar social reform modernized and strengthened the rationale for child emigration. At the same time, the emergence of a universal concept of child rights in the international arena during the early 1920s opened up new rhetorical possibilities for proponents of the movement.[80] It allowed them to argue that every British boy or girl was entitled not simply to the adequate health they could attain at home but also to the optimal fitness they would find in the rural settler empire. "Thousands of our little ones are being deprived of their rightful heritage of clean, fresh air and sunshine," *Woman's World* magazine declared in 1920. But there was no reason for these children to remain

[80] On this larger trend, see Marshall, "The Construction of Children."

"under-fed, poorly clothed, and growing old before their time in over-crowded streets and tenements," when overseas "our Colonies offer them *a clean bill of health and happiness.*"[81] Along the same lines, Arthur Lawley, the London chairman of the CES, stressed that the organization brought children "from slums to sunshine," providing them with a "cleaner, purer, happier life in our spacious Dominions."[82] Lawley was the same man who decades before, when serving as Lieutenant-Governor of the Transvaal, had discouraged Stuart Barnardo from sending boys and girls to South Africa. In the intervening years, the rise of the farm school system, as well as the medicalization of the concept of environmental uplift, had alleviated many of his prior reservations about poor children's capacity to become imperial settlers. He was now one of the movement's strongest backers and a vocal advocate of the idea that transfer to Greater Britain would unlock the latent potential in even the most destitute child. In his eyes, child emigration was a "preventative measure that makes charity unnecessary," for "what is almost a waste product (and even worse) in our great cities is transmuted into sturdy, self-respecting farmers" in the dominions.[83]

As this last comment illustrates, the argument that children's growing bodies responded best to an outdoor lifestyle linked up neatly with the demographic imperatives of empire settlement. The concept of rural development was central both to the interwar ideology of social reform and to the realm of imperial policymaking. Emigration charities were quick to play up these connections in their publicity and appeal literature. The CES conveyed the message visually, filling its leaflets with photographs of children plowing, gardening, or chopping wood at Pinjarra. The intent behind these pictures was to highlight the mutual growth of the empire and of the children. While child migrants' labor cultivated the empty spaces of the British world, the dominions' healthy, country lifestyle invigorated their young bodies and toughened their constitutions. In another version of the theme, one of the Society's 1920 brochures featured a photo of the farm's first class of schoolboys standing beside a group of pines they had planted when they had arrived seven years earlier (Figure 2.3). The comparison cued readers to the interconnected development of the empire and of the young men. Each was essential to the other's future health and prosperity.

---

[81] "From Shadow to Sunshine," *Woman's World*, December 18, 1920. Emphasis in the original.

[82] CES, Arthur Lawley, "From Slums to Sunshine," Annual Report, 1923, 6, D.296/D1/1/1, ULSCA.

[83] CES, Arthur Lawley, "Our Children," Promotional Leaflet, 1922, D.296/F1/2, ULSCA.

Figure 2.3 "A group of Farm School boys, beside a group of pines which they themselves planted seven years previously." CES "A Fair, Sporting Chance," Promotional Appeal Booklet, *c.* 1920, D.296/F1/16, ULSCA.

Capturing the metaphor with typical exuberance, Barnardo's called child emigration a "Divinely-guided method of human afforestation," which would turn "young lives ... bursting with potentialities" into a harvest of "sturdy trees which the Empire may view with pride."[84]

These claims reflected the transformations that had taken place within the child emigration movement in the years following the First World War, as the policy shifted from a primarily evangelical, philanthropic program into a state-funded social and imperial development initiative. While child emigration became overtly politicized in these years, the new emphasis on empire building actually brought its ideology more closely in line with the most up-to-date thinking on matters of child health in Britain. Not only did the physiological vision of welfare sustain metropolitan support for the programs into the interwar period but it also enabled the movement to withstand a new round of criticism that was gaining ground in Canada and that would ultimately redefine the project as a whole.

### Fit for Canada? The Bondfield Commission of 1924

As it had before the war, Canada remained the focus of child resettlement initiatives into the early 1920s. Led by Barnardo's, emigration charities again began placing boys and girls with rural Canadian families in 1920. Although recruitment was slow in the immediate aftermath of the conflict as proponents rebuilt their networks, by 1921 they were

---

[84] Barnardo's 50th Annual Report, 1915, D.239/A3/1/50, ULSCA.

managing to send more than 1,000 children annually across the ocean. Three years later the number exceeded 2,000.[85] The Canadian demand for child migrants also remained high. In 1916, when few children were being sent due to the war, a record 31,000 households had applied for a boy or girl.[86] The fact that reformers had little difficulty in placing children either before or after the First World War can give the impression that the initiatives were broadly popular throughout the dominion. In fact, however, resistance to child emigration arose periodically throughout the policy's more than fifty-year history in Canada. These critiques never seriously questioned the underlying premise of imperial unity that sustained child emigration well into the twentieth century. But they did illustrate that the vision of poor British children's seemingly boundless capacity for transformation in the settler empire always achieved a deeper hold on the metropolitan imagination than it did overseas.

Opposition to the initiatives was slow to develop during the first two decades of the movement's history. Following Confederation in 1867, Canadian authorities were eager to grow the country's agricultural and manufacturing sectors and viewed expanded immigration as an essential part of economic development. Child migrants appeared particularly desirable, not only because the majority went to farms, where the need for labor was the greatest, but also because they tended to remain in the dominion for longer durations than the typical immigrant, who usually continued on to the United States.[87] As early as 1875, the Canadian government had established a $2 per child payment to charities as an incentive to maintain the flow of boys and girls into the country.[88] Back in Britain, although child emigration was widely understood as a humanitarian program that would benefit "hopeless" youth, a short flurry of criticism did arise in 1875, when Andrew Doyle, an inspector sent over by the LGB, wrote a scathing report that characterized the schemes as a form of exploitation. Children, he stated, were being distributed to families without any prior inspection of the households, and once there they were rarely visited or checked up on. Throughout his travels in Canada, Doyle had encountered dissatisfied teenagers who had been "bound to serve without wages, merely for their maintenance and clothing, until they are eighteen."[89] In other words, the system was less an innovative type of social welfare than an outdated

[85] The Canadian government estimated that 1,426 unaccompanied children arrived in Canada in 1920–1921, and 2,080 in 1923–1924. Kohli, *The Golden Bridge*, 376.

[86] Roy Parker, *Uprooted: The Shipment of Poor Children to Canada, 1867–1917* (Vancouver: University of British Columbia Press, 2008), 264.

[87] Of the nearly 1.5 million people who entered Canada between 1867 and 1892, most were in transit to the United States. Kelley and Trebilcock, *The Making of the Mosaic*, 64.

[88] Gillian Wagner, *Children of the Empire* (London: Weidenfeld and Nicolson, 1982), 98.

[89] Andrew Doyle, "Report to the President of the Local Government Board ... as to the Emigration of Pauper Children to Canada," *Parliamentary Papers* LXVII (1875), 20.

method of juvenile labor. Several historians have detailed the fallout from Doyle's report, and a full description here is not necessary.[90] What is important to note is that the consequences of the event were minor; while the LGB temporarily banned the emigration of Poor Law children, no restrictions were imposed on boys and girls recruited through private charities. The expansion of the programs thus continued with little interruption, and, when the Canadian government agreed in 1883 to institute routine inspections of child migrant placements, the LGB again allowed children from workhouses to be included in the parties.

More serious were the critiques about the eugenic quality and "fitness" of child migrants that began to develop around the turn of the century. As Angus McLaren has demonstrated, eugenics emerged as a distinct medical field and reform movement in Canada during the mid 1880s, and its influence, though more pronounced in some provinces such as Alberta and British Columbia than at the national level, lasted until the Second World War.[91] Like their peers in Britain and the United States, Canadian eugenicists were committed to an understanding of social and racial inequality as rooted in heredity, even if they disagreed about the extent to which biology shaped human development relative to the environment. This belief led many to voice concern over the country's immigration policy, which remained unrestricted throughout the nineteenth century. Eugenicists were primarily worried about the increasing proportion of non-British settlers who streamed into Canada in the two decades before the First World War. While more than 60 percent of immigrants to the dominion had arrived from Britain in the late Victorian period, by 1914 their proportion had dropped to 38 percent. Americans made up another 34 percent, and Europeans – particularly those from the most "racially suspect" central, eastern, and southern parts of the continent – were roughly 25 percent.[92] Even more alarming were the estimated 50,000 Chinese, Japanese, and South Asian laborers that entered the country from 1900 to 1915.[93] Given that more than three million immigrants had arrived in the same period, Asians remained a miniscule fraction of the

---

[90] Neil Sutherland, *Children in English-Canadian Society: Framing the Twentieth-Century Consensus* (University of Toronto Press, 1976), 3–34; Wagner, *Children of the Empire*, 81–99; Philip Bean and Joy Melville, *Lost Children of the Empire: The Untold Story of Britain's Child Migrants* (London: Unwin Hyman, 1989), 61–73; Joy Parr, *Labouring Children: British Immigrant Apprentices to Canada, 1869–1924* (University of Toronto Press, 1994, originally 1980), 51–52; Kenneth Bagnell, *The Little Immigrants: The Orphans Who Came to Canada* (Toronto: Dundurn Press, 2001, originally 1980), 37–63; Kohli, *The Golden Bridge*, 21–28; Parker, *Uprooted*, 49–63.

[91] Angus McLaren, *Our Own Master Race: Eugenics in Canada, 1885–1945* (Oxford University Press, 1990).

[92] Kelley and Trebilcock, *The Making of the Mosaic*, 115.

[93] Ibid, 145.

total. Yet their growing numbers raised the frightening prospect of racial miscegenation and generated worries about increased competition for jobs. Unsurprisingly, many of the first provincial and federal restrictions on immigration specifically targeted Asians.[94]

While most anti-immigration activism concentrated on regulating the inward flow of particular ethnicities, there remained a strong current of eugenic philosophy that viewed class distinctions as just as significant as racial differences. To these eugenicists, it mattered little whether migrants were British or not. More essential was whether they had the right hereditary background to integrate into and succeed in Canadian society. In this regard, any form of pauperism was a potential indicator of innate inferiority, regardless of the ethnic "type" in which it was found. In the 1890s, many eugenics proponents had begun warning that poorer immigrants were the bearers of physical disabilities or contagious diseases such as syphilis, which by that time had been linked to a host of conditions such as sterility, miscarriages, neonatal blindness, and insanity. The fact that syphilitic disorders were transmitted congenitally and not genetically was still unrecognized, however, and this ambiguity allowed eugenicists to assert that immorality and sexual impropriety derived from bad breeding.[95] In the early 1900s and into the 1920s, the thrust of the eugenics crusade shifted to a concern with mentality and especially "feeblemindedness."[96] Because psychological conditions also appeared to be associated with high rates of fertility, eugenicists frequently singled out children for special attention, believing that, if insanity or low-grade mentality was detected before young people reached the age of sexual maturity, they could limit the spread of these disorders. In this vein, certain prominent child welfare advocates, such as Charlotte Whitton, a founding member of the Canadian Council of Child Welfare (CCCW), pressed simultaneously for socioeconomic reforms such as child labor legislation and mothers' allowances, as well as for policies that would curb the immigration of young "mental deficients." Defending her position in a 1921 speech, she stressed that the task of "keeping this country strong, virile, healthy, and moral" required ensuring that "the blood that enters its veins is equally pure and free from taint."[97]

---

[94] Marilyn Lake and Henry Reynolds, *Drawing the Global Colour Line: White Men's Countries and the International Challenge of Racial Equality* (Cambridge University Press, 2008), 178–188.

[95] McLaren, *Our Own Master Race*, 72.

[96] Ian Dowbiggin, *Keeping America Sane: Psychiatry and Eugenics in the United States and Canada, 1880–1940* (Ithaca: Cornell University Press, 1997).

[97] Charlotte Whitton, "Mental Deficiency as a Child Welfare Problem," address to the Social Service Council of Canada, *c.* 1921, quoted in Patricia Rooke and R. L. Schnell, *No Bleeding Heart: Charlotte Whitton, a Feminist on the Right* (Vancouver: University of British Columbia Press, 1987), 23.

Whitton's comment illustrates how the same vision of Canada as a young, wholesome, and unadulterated country that so powerfully infused the environmentalist argument for child emigration in Britain could, at the same time, sustain calls overseas for restrictions on the arrival of pauper boys and girls. Starting in the late 1880s, press reports of child migrants who had "failed" or had otherwise run into trouble served as a catalyst for broader discussions on the racial health of British paupers. The horrific 1895 case of George Green, a sixteen-year-old who starved to death in an upstairs room of the farmhouse where he had been placed, is one of the more well-known examples. The coroner's report revealed that Green's body was filthy, emaciated, and covered in bruises and abrasions. Despite this clear evidence of abuse, the trial of his employer, Helen Findlay, concentrated less on her culpability than on Green's supposed deformities. Green was accused of having a severe squint and a hunchback, and of being too frail – mentally and physically – to perform the tasks he was assigned. After weeks of editorials decrying the substandard heredity of child migrants, the trial ended in a hung jury, and all charges against Findlay were dropped.[98] While the coverage of Green's death focused on his alleged physical deficiencies, the press used other cases to highlight the problem of mental disorders among child migrants. In the summer of 1898, for instance, the Manitoba papers carried the story of a thirteen-year-old Barnardo boy, Johnnie Powell, who had shot himself after killing the young son of his employer. Little attention was paid to Powell's living and working conditions, or to his state of mind since arriving in Canada. Rather, the only motive offered for his crime was that his employer had "refused to allow him to go to a picnic."[99] Stories like this one painted a terrifying picture of mentally unstable children, living in the country's heartland, who could erupt into violence at the slightest provocation.[100]

The media attacks against child emigration tended to be stronger in certain provinces, such as Ontario, than others, and they never went unchallenged. Demands for the increased regulation or outright banning of the programs were usually followed by editorials defending the "thousands of [child migrants] ... who turn out good citizens."[101] Nevertheless, the spread of criticism at the local level produced influential results. By the 1890s, a broad cross section of Canadian physicians

[98] For full coverage of the George Green case, see Wagner, *Children of the Empire*, 151–152; Bagnell, *The Little Immigrants*, 63–69.
[99] "A Barnardo Boy Shoots Employer's Son," *Morning Telegram*, June 23, 1898.
[100] For a similar case in Ontario, see "Boy Murderer: Barnardo Youth Slew Benefactor's Daughter and Suicided," *The Comber Herald*, March 25, 1915.
[101] "That Barnardo Boy," *The Windsor Evening Record*, November 28, 1895.

was advocating for more intensive screenings and regular inspections of child migrants.[102] Immigration reform was an issue tailor-made for the nascent medical profession, since it allowed doctors and psychiatrists to assert their unique expertise in deciphering individuals' racial fitness.[103] Most prominently, the psychiatrist C. K. Clarke began a personal crusade to expose what he believed were the "large number of degenerate children" included in child emigration parties. Warning that, if left unchecked, these influxes of inferior-quality boys and girls would sap the strength of the "race as a whole," he repeatedly petitioned the government to hold a national inquiry into child emigration.[104]

Such calls placed politicians in a tight spot. On the one hand, they knew that the most effective way to settle Canada's vast rural hinterland was by allowing unlimited immigration. On the other hand, they could not ignore the increasingly strident public alarm about racial degeneracy and eugenic fitness. In the end, government officials sought a middle ground, gradually implementing new laws designed to standardize the practice of child emigration without overly restricting the movement. In 1893, the Department of the Interior began requiring emigration agencies to medically examine child migrants at the port of embarkation. Four years later, Ontario passed legislation that obliged the charities to maintain complete case records for every boy or girl they sent to Canada, to screen them for illnesses and "vicious tendencies," and to bar any juvenile who had been convicted of a crime in Britain. Similar laws followed in Manitoba, Quebec, and New Brunswick.[105]

The backlash against child emigration was an early reflection of the rise of popular nationalism across Canada, which was manifested in the tendency to contrast the qualities of "home grown" Canadians with the supposed defects of more recent arrivals. Immigration historians have mainly highlighted this trend in relation to the outbursts of xenophobia directed against non-British Europeans and other ethnic minorities. Yet the suspicion of child migrants illustrates that a coherent Anglo-Canadian identity was also developing in opposition to those who were unquestionably of Britannic heritage. Even though Britain remained the dominion's largest single source of immigrants into the 1960s,[106] and even though those who most vocally opposed the schemes, such as Whitton and Clarke, simultaneously

---

[102] Parker, *Uprooted*, 161–166.     [103] McLaren, *Our Own Master Race*, 49.

[104] Clarke to Mrs. Talbot MacBeth, May 2, 1896, quoted in Dowbiggin, *Keeping America Sane*, 140.

[105] Parr, *Labouring Children*, 57; see also Rooke and Schnell, *Discarding the Asylum*, 229–231.

[106] Phillip Buckner, ed., *Canada and the End of Empire* (Vancouver: University of British Columbia Press, 2005), 5.

reaffirmed their faith in the imperial connection, the public protests under-scored the argument that Canadians maintained a standard of physical, mental, and moral fitness that not all Britons possessed. The consequences of this trend were often devastating for individual child migrants, who suf-fered the stigma of being labeled "home children" of questionable stock. Sequestered in remote farming communities where their accents and social backgrounds set them apart, many boys and girls found that they had been judged inferior from the moment they arrived.[107]

The First World War helped to ease these tensions temporarily, both because the flow of children entering the country slowed and because large numbers of former migrants proved their fitness – and patriotism – by enlisting in the Canadian armed forces.[108] By the time the Empire Settlement Act was passed in 1922, the dominion government had again thrown its support behind the movement, agreeing to share with Britain the costs of child migrants' passage fares. Before the arrangement could be implemented, however, two tragic events during the winter of 1923 revived criticism of the policy. Just before Christmas, sixteen-year-old Charles Bulpitt hanged himself in the barn of his employer after having only been in the country for four months. A few weeks later, another teen-ager, Johnny Payne, also committed suicide. Bulpitt's death was linked to ill treatment and overwork, while Payne's seemed to stem from his feelings of isolation and loneliness.[109] The suicides were widely reported on both sides of the Atlantic, and prompted a number of activist organi-zations to renew their scrutiny of the initiatives. In January of 1924, the Social Service Council of Canada argued that the federal supervision of child migrants had been inadequate; the organization was able to show that more than one-third of the children had not received an inspection visit in the previous year.[110] Shortly thereafter, Whitton and the CCCW repeated their calls for a more thorough psychological screening process for prospective migrant boys and girls.[111]

In Britain, the tragedies provoked alarm, mainly in Socialist circles, over the children's work and living conditions. Since the late nineteenth

---

[107] On the prejudices against child migrants in Canada, see Rooke and Schnell, *Discarding the Asylum*, 223–269; Stephen Constantine, "Children as Ancestors: Child Migrants and Identity in Canada," *British Journal of Canadian Studies* 16, no. 1 (2003): 150–159; and the personal narratives collected in Phyllis Harrison, ed., *The Home Children* (Winnipeg: Watson and Dyer, 1979).

[108] Wagner estimated that some 10,000 former child migrant boys enlisted during the war. Wagner, *Children of the Empire*, 218.

[109] Social Service Council of Canada, *Canada's Child Immigrants: Annual Report of the Committee of Immigration and Colonization of the Social Service Council of Canada* (Toronto: Social Service Council of Canada, 1926), i.

[110] Ibid, 26.    [111] Ibid, ii–vi.

century, reformers affiliated with the trade unions had been some of the most active advocates of labor legislation designed to differentiate childhood as a period of play and education, and adulthood as the time for work.[112] This emphasis meant that Socialists had always been somewhat wary of the emigration movement's claims that the children were welcomed into Canadian households as full members of the family, with only nominal work requirements. The suicides seemed to justify their concerns that child migrants were not always treated as well as proponents claimed.[113] In addition, the coverage of the suicides hit Britain just as the nation's first Labour government took office, having campaigned on a pledge to improve the lives of working-class youths. The issue of child migrants' safety offered a perfect opportunity for the fledgling government to back up its election promises. When the Canadian Department of Immigration responded to the public outcry by inviting the OSC to investigate the policy, the new Prime Minister, Ramsay MacDonald, quickly designated a commission to explore all aspects of the child migrant experience in the dominion.

Heading the delegation was Margaret Bondfield, a woman whose lifelong commitment to child protection derived from her own background as a juvenile laborer. She had left home at the age of fourteen to begin an apprenticeship in a draper's shop, and later transitioned into a political career working on behalf of the Independent Labour Party and the Trades Union Congress.[114] Joining Bondfield was another feminist, trade unionist, and member of the OSC, Florence Harrison Bell, as well as the secretary of the OSC, George Plant. No doubt, Bondfield's and Harrison Bell's selection had much to do with their gender. Contemporary assumptions about women's "innate" ability to understand the needs of children would have made an all-male delegation politically untenable. Nevertheless, their credentials as two of the labor movement's most prominent women activists also played an important part in their inclusion. Not only would they be able to evaluate the position of migrant boys and girls *as children* – that is, as members of the population whose welfare required special care – but also as potentially exploited laborers. From the start, it was evident that the prime aim of the Bondfield Commission would be making sure that resettlement did not stifle migrants' entitlement to a childhood free from overwork and strain.

---

[112] Steedman, *Childhood, Culture, and Class*.

[113] Parker, *Uprooted*, 259–260. In Canada, Socialist critiques of the movement tended to focus instead on the risk of falling wages and adult unemployment stemming from the importation of cheap child labor. Parker, *Uprooted*, 152–158.

[114] For an overview of Bondfield's life and career, see her autobiography: Margaret Bondfield, *A Life's Work* (London: Hutchinson, 1948).

As the delegates discovered when they arrived in the dominion in late September of 1924, however, this focus on child protection did not fully address the Canadian reservations about the programs. Bondfield and her peers traveled extensively across the country, holding public meetings; interviewing immigration officials, social workers, and representatives of the voluntary organizations; and visiting child migrants in their new homes. At almost every stop, they were confronted by questions about how the children were being selected. "Social hygiene" was the topic of a meeting between the delegates and the Social Service Council of Vancouver,[115] while in St. John a round of pointed questions led Harrison Bell to assert that "the British government was not dumping its undesirables into Canada." She went on to stress that the selection of child migrants "was wholly in the hands of the Canadian Government," and offered the recent case of 300 children put forward by Barnardo's, of which only thirty-two had been cleared for emigration, as an example that the procedures were sound.[116] In Edmonton, a group of "local leaders" reiterated the need for a "more thorough physical and mental examination before the child leaves England." In response to their grilling, Bondfield felt compelled to refute "the common belief that the Canadian authorities overseas are accepting child immigrants for Canada on a haphazard system." Still, she went on to admit that "generally speaking the mental examination is not sufficiently developed," and expressed her hope "that some agreement [would] be reached as to what constituted an acceptable Canadian standard," which could then "be applied in the old country before the child embarks." "The message we have to take back," she concluded, "is that if we will only keep our people fit and see that our children are developed in the best possible manner, physically, mentally, and morally, a warm welcome awaits them."[117]

Bondfield's statement was a high-profile acknowledgment that the Canadian requirements for child migrants had grown tighter. No longer would any child be accepted into the dominion simply because they were British; now, influential sections of the Canadian public were insisting that only the best of the best were acceptable. The delegation considered these criticisms carefully, yet, to their minds, there was another, more pressing issue with the programs. As they traveled across the country, they conducted surprise inspections of the children's placements and took the chance to chat with boys and girls "individually and privately." Although they reported that the majority of those they visited were

[115] "Child Immigration Under Discussion," *The Gazette*, October 25, 1924.
[116] "British Visitors Have Day in City," *The Evening Times-Star*, October 27, 1924.
[117] "Light Shed Upon Migration Problem," *Edmonton Farm Journal*, October 15, 1924.

"treated with kindness and consideration," and that they had found evidence that the "prospects in Canada for the average [child] are better than they could be in the United Kingdom," they were disquieted to find that the workloads many of the migrants carried were excessive by British standards.[118] They observed that most of the households that took in a child were of a particular size: large enough to need another pair of hands around the farm but too small to afford the wages of an adult worker. In these situations, there was "no doubt" that the boy or girl was "required in the capacity of a help."[119] They also witnessed cases of young children doing chores that seemed too strenuous for their ages, and met migrants who only attended school during the winter months, when their help was less essential to the farm.

This latter situation recalled the "half-time system" in Britain, which had allowed underage boys and girls to divide their days between work and school. Phased out in London by 1900, the practice lingered on in the textile and agricultural industries until finally prohibited by Parliament in 1918.[120] The Commission's finding, just six years later, that children were being sent to Canada "primarily for working purposes" thus occurred at a time when public opinion in the United Kingdom was turning decisively against child labor. This changed climate helps explain why these arguments, which echoed those first put forward by Andrew Doyle nearly fifty years earlier, now achieved a far greater impact. Convinced that child migrants were being denied educational opportunities that they could have if they stayed in Britain, the members concluded that no boy or girl should be permitted to emigrate until they reached the school-leaving age of fourteen. After all, they wrote, if it was generally recognized that the children were sent to the dominion "for working purposes," then it followed that they "should not leave this country until they have arrived at working age."[121] "Let them go to Canada ... by all means if they so wish," Bondfield stated. "But give them some choice in the matter at an age when they are better able to choose."[122]

[118] Margaret Bondfield "Report to the Secretary of State for the Colonies, President of the Oversea Settlement Committee, from the Delegation Appointed to Obtain Information Regarding the System of Child Migration and Settlement in Canada, 1924–1925," *Parliamentary Papers* XV, Cmd. 2285, 1–20, 6, 9, and 18.

[119] Ibid, 7.

[120] Anna Davin, *Growing Up Poor: Home, School and Street in London 1870–1914* (London: River Orams Press, 1996), 98–99; Neil Daglish, "Education Policy and the Question of Child Labour: The Lancashire Cotton Industry and R. D. Denman's Bill of 1914," *History of Education* 30, no. 3 (May 2001): 291–308.

[121] Bondfield "Report to the Secretary of State for the Colonies," 13.

[122] Quoted in G. F. Plant, *Oversea Settlement: Migration from the United Kingdom to the Dominions* (London: Oxford University Press, 1951), 134.

The Commission's critique of the emigration movement was firmly in line with its political philosophy and its delegates' status as Labour representatives. It also, however, provided a convenient means to gloss over the persistent questions about racial fitness that dominated the Canadian discussion of the policy. In their final report, the delegates mentioned the selection concerns only briefly, in a passing statement pointing out that the process was wholly in the hands of the dominion government and that recommended more stringent mental testing.[123] On the whole, though, they ignored the Canadian claims that poor British children were not the right social material for the dominion. Moreover, in emphasizing that emigration to the rural empire still had significant benefits for older youth, they reaffirmed the principle that Britain and Canada were deeply linked through the ties of imperial sentiment and shared racial background. In this respect, a core assumption of the Commission's report was that the same child welfare principles applied universally throughout the British world. As they argued, it was "clear that public opinion in Canada would condemn a system under which a certain number of Canadian householders were provided with unpaid help of this nature."[124] To their mind, child migrants deserved equal treatment because they were identical in body, mind, and spirit with their Canadian kin. In this respect, by recommending a ban on the resettlement of young children, the delegates were seeking to uphold a pan-imperial understanding of child welfare rather than to acknowledge the dominion's national distinctiveness.

The publication of the Bondfield report at the end of 1924 had obvious implications for the emigration charities, which scrambled to control the damage. Nine of the most active societies in the movement, including Barnardo's, the Salvation Army, and the Liverpool Sheltering Homes, met with the OSC in the hopes of enlisting its support. The meeting was cordial, and the committee listened sympathetically as the charities' representatives recited their standard arguments about the physical and spiritual advantages of emigration for slum children and warned that young people with "unsatisfactory" relatives were "liable to be reclaimed by their parents if kept in this country until fourteen years old."[125] But it was already a lost cause. Unbeknownst to the charities, officials in the Colonial Office had decided that, although the investigation had "disclosed the existence of no serious abuse," they would defer to the will of the Canadian government, which in turn bowed to public pressure and

---

[123] Bondfield "Report to the Secretary of State for the Colonies," 13.
[124] Ibid, 12.
[125] British Oversea Settlement Delegation to Canada, Minutes of a Meeting with Representatives of Voluntary Societies, February 10, 1925, CO 721/108, TNA: PRO.

instituted a three-year ban on the immigration of school-aged children effective April 1, 1925.[126]

This temporary measure was not enough for the most vocal opponents of the movement. Even after the new law came into effect, campaigning against the policy continued across the dominion. Most prominently, in early 1925, the ever-vigilant Social Service Council of Canada published a vitriolic screed arguing that child migrants exhibited a "startling ... prevalence of mental defectiveness." In a section titled "The 'Backwash' of Juvenile Immigration," the report maintained that, between 1915 and 1924, Barnardo's had brought to Canada 131 girls who had ended up in the Toronto General Hospital. Of those girls, 7 were reported as insane and 114 mentally defective, leaving only 10 who were designated as "normal." It also noted that these young women had between them produced dozens of illegitimate children.[127] These figures were easily refuted; Barnardo's, after all, had not emigrated any girls to the dominion from 1916 to 1920, and a large number of the women in question were later discovered not to have been child migrants at all. In fact, the statistics were soon found to be so inaccurate that a professor who repeated the claims at the CCCW's annual conference in 1925 was impelled to publish a complete retraction and apology.[128] But this did not stop the Social Service Council from republishing the erroneous information in the second edition of its report, or from using the figures in its crusade against the programs. Its pressure, combined with continued negative press reports in a variety of provincial papers, soon persuaded the Canadian government to make the ban on the immigration of British schoolchildren permanent.

The consequences of the regulation were immediate. Most of the smaller charities wound down their operations and left the emigration business altogether, although some of the larger ones, such as the Salvation Army and the YMCA, were able to keep going by shifting their focus to teenagers. The law created particular problems for Barnardo's, since the organization had long relied on emigration to ease the pressure of overcrowding in its British branches. In a last-ditch attempt to buy time, the executive committee rushed through a final party for Canada made up of "a good number of children under fourteen years of age." The group sailed on March 27, 1925, four days before the ban went into effect.[129] Meanwhile, the organization began redirecting its attention to Australia, where it already had a foothold, having entered into an agreement with

[126] Minutes of the 178th Meeting of the OSC, January 13, 1925, CO 721/97, TNA: PRO.
[127] Social Service Council of Canada, *Canada's Child Immigrants*, 38–43.
[128] Wagner, *Children of the Empire*, 231.
[129] Barnardo's, Executive Committee Minutes, March 4, 1925, D.239/B3/1/7, ULSCA.

the CES two years earlier to accept children at Pinjarra.[130] In addition, local supporters in Sydney had been placing Barnardo's teenagers in positions across New South Wales since 1921.[131] In the aftermath of the Bondfield report, the London directors of the Homes expanded both programs. They wrote to the CES telling them to expect more regular shipments of children, and also encouraged the Sydney group to begin scouting locations for a farm school.[132] These arrangements minimized the loss of Canada and allowed the charity to maintain a steady flow of outmigration throughout the interwar years.[133] Ever scornful of the official interference, Barnardo's executive committee sent a letter to Canadian immigration officials calling their attention to the fact that the children were going to Australia instead of to Canada.[134]

## Conclusion

Barnardo's final snub to the Canadian authorities was a telling indication of the enduring, if largely metropolitan, view of poor British children as highly-sought-after imperial assets. Although reformers such as Kingsley Fairbridge had first started to conceptualize the political value of deprived boys and girls during the Edwardian era, the British government's more recent commitment to empire settlement had reinforced the trend. In the context of the dominions' expanded political sovereignty, the task of preserving the bonds of blood and sentiment that linked Greater Britain appeared more crucial than ever. And, even though the Bondfield report had challenged the structure of Canadian initiatives, it upheld the movement's broader vision of child migrants as the foundation of lasting imperial unity. The sting of the letter was thus its pointed suggestion that overregulation had cost Canada a much-needed commodity and a precious natural resource.

Given the controversy over the policy in the dominion at the time, it is doubtful that Barnardo's rebuke had much of an impact. The nationalist claims that street children from the "old country" were less an asset than a menace to the dominion's future were not the sole cause of the end of child

---

[130] The agreement stated that Barnardo's would pay the CES £15 for every Barnardo's ward educated and trained at Pinjarra. CES, Executive Committee Minutes, July 18, 1923, D.296/B1/2/1, ULSCA.

[131] Barnardo's, Executive Committee Minutes, April 6 and 25, 1921, D.239/B3/1/3, ULSCA.

[132] Barnardo's, Reports by the Chair of the Executive Committee, April 25, 1925 and November 17, 1926, D.239/B3/1/15, ULSCA.

[133] During the later 1920s and 1930s, Barnardo's sent between three and four parties to Australia annually, each averaging around fifty children. For precise yearly figures, see Barnardo's, Annual Reports, D.239/A3/1/60–74, ULSCA; Barnardo's NSW, Executive and Finance Committee Minutes, 1921–1929, Barnardo's Australia, Ultimo.

[134] Barnardo's, Executive Committee Minutes, April 1, 1925, D.239/B3/1/7, ULSCA.

emigration to Canada, but their influence was significant. Having arisen at a time when the British government was more attuned to the problem of unfair child labor practices both at home and throughout Greater Britain, the criticisms emanating from the dominion helped ensure the demise of the Canadian side of the movement. Significantly, a scheme such as the CES's Pinjarra school was immune to the Commission's critique because, although it prioritized the training of boys and girls in agriculture, the children's work on the farm fell into the category of education instead of waged labor. If anything, Fairbridge's technique of grouping children into a centralized institution seemed to protect against the threat of exploitation, since the delegation had warned that the worst abuses were likely to occur in isolated households where migrants would have no recourse to help. Following the Bondfield report, "boarding out" waned throughout the movement as proponents instead aimed to place child migrants in farm schools or orphanages. Ironically, by purging child emigration of methods that had been deemed dangerous or unfair, the delegation's criticisms in the long run brought the policy more closely in line with contemporary, British standards of welfare.

The reconstitution of the child emigration movement in the aftermath of the First World War offers a powerful example of how easily child protection initiatives can become enmeshed with, or even subsumed by, broader ideological currents in the realm of politics. The tendency of interwar British politicians to conceive of the settler empire as a natural whole matched up squarely with the metaphors of organic growth that reformers were using to describe children's development. In this light, the value of the policy was that it provided a means to advance the global power of the Britannic people as it simultaneously improved the lives of individual children. As Barnardo's proclaimed, while it was "impossible to estimate the material and spiritual wealth that has accrued to Great Britain by the rescuing, training, and transplanting of these thousands of young people from the congested areas at home to the open spaces overseas," there remained "not a shadow of doubt that it has been a splendid thing for the child."[135] Yet child emigration also proved valuable to nationalist-minded public figures in Canada, who found a platform for the novel argument that British heritage alone no longer immediately qualified a person for entry into Canadian society. Although programs that resettled children would persist for another four decades, the principle of imperial connectedness that underlay and sustained them had received its first major challenge.

---

[135] Barnardo's 60th Annual Report, 1925, D.239/A3/1/60, ULSCA.

# 3 Upholding the banner of White Australia

Bert Read was not sure where exactly he was born in the summer of 1919, although he assumed it must have been somewhere near Liverpool, since his earliest memories were of growing up in an orphanage in Fazakerley, a suburb just north of the city. He knew his mother, but not well. Read had a serious case of tuberculosis as a child, and his mother, who was unmarried, had trouble coping. By the time he was two, she had placed him in the care of the Fazakerley Cottage Homes, a Poor Law institution run by the city. While she visited from time to time, they never established much of a relationship. His father was even more of a mystery. Later on, when Read was in his early teens and living at the Fairbridge Farm School in Western Australia, he asked his mother who his father had been. "She'd send me photos," he recalled, but "sometimes I don't think they were the same photo." Perhaps she did not know or did not want to tell Read the name. Either way, this lack of family ties never really bothered him. He was a happy, high-spirited child, and felt secure at Fazakerley. He had a lot of chores, but none were strenuous. That said, he remembered the dread that used to come over him whenever he was given the task of polishing boots. "It was *impossible* to put a shine on them," he said. But his cottage mother "growled if you didn't do it properly," so Read found an ingenious solution: "I used to go around when it was my turn and tell the boys to keep out of puddles."

For Read, life at Fazakerley was so routine that those rare times when something unique happened stand out crystal clear in his memory. More than seventy-five years later, he could still feel the thrill of the day when some visitors asked him whether he would like to live in Australia. He was eleven years old at the time and knew nothing about the country, "nothing at all." For a boy who almost never had visitors, though, the attention was exhilarating. He said yes right away and eagerly anticipated the departure. Looking back, when Read described the journey to London to finalize his paperwork at the Australian High Commission, he used the word "excitement" three times in one sentence. There was the excitement of being selected, of the train ride, and of the special trip to see Madame Tussaud's wax works. Smaller sensory details remained vivid. He remembered being given an Australian apple as a taste of his new country, and how his CES uniform felt when he put it on for the first time. He also recalled standing on the docks, watching some of the other boys say goodbye to their relatives. It might have been a bittersweet moment, but, as Read recollected, "no tears were lost because we were excited about the whole business there, and it was better than what we were having." More than anything, Read just wanted to get going, to start this new adventure.

His arrival in Fremantle some six weeks later, in July of 1931, was a different story. "It was a shock," he recalled. "It was so small, and it was winter." The boys were still wearing their summer uniforms from London, but the seasons had reversed, and now they were shivering. Continuing by bus, they got to Pinjarra around noon, and the party huddled together quietly while the staff assigned them to cottages and the other children gathered around to get a look at the new arrivals. The transition was overwhelming. "I was sulky for the first two or three days, there was no question about that," Read remembered, although he stressed that "it wasn't crying for my mum." Rather, it was the palpable feeling of difference in everything, from the daily trek to the dining hall for meals, to the rain that "would just pour down," to the pressures of "fitting in with the kids." The initial strangeness wore off quickly, however. Read kept a journal at the time, and he pointed to it when he said that "within two weeks, according to my diary there, I was one of them." It was as if the atmosphere of the place had just seeped into him by osmosis.

Belying this sense of unconscious assimilation were his memories of the school's calculated attempts to integrate him into the new Australian lifestyle. Still unforgettable were the elocution lessons. "There's so many different dialects of English," he explained, "that they thought ... get the teacher in that was an elocutionist and get us to say A-E-I-O-U, you know, in her style." "It worked," he went on, "only because we all become common at that age. You quickly accept, you know, the local."[1] Indeed, decades later, his speaking voice remained beautiful: a perfect British–Australian hybrid, with long, open vowels and not a trace of his former Scouse accent.

Read's recollections of his early days at Pinjarra offer a tantalizing glimpse at the personal struggles of child migrants to "become common," as he so aptly put it, or to align themselves with a new, and what at first

---

[1] Author's interview with Bert Read, May 28, 2006. Other child migrants to Pinjarra in this period also recalled the elocution lessons; see, for instance, Flo Hickson, *Flo: Child Migrant from Liverpool* (Warwick: Plowright Press, 1998), 30–31.

felt like a foreign, dominion lifestyle. They also shed light on the mechanisms, such as elocution lessons, that were put in place in order to hasten the adjustment process. Throughout the interwar years, child emigration remained an "imperial" project that aimed to strengthen the unity and shared heritage of the British world. As the movement expanded into Australia, however, it intersected with a surge in dominion nationalism that defined the local identity not just in terms of its British past but also through a profound concern with the future racial security of the nation. This new ethic did little to undermine the Australian allegiance to the empire or to weaken the widespread public faith in the value of Greater Britain. Yet it did affect the work of the emigration charities, which designed their initiatives to align with Australia's political mission to protect the homogeneity and "Whiteness" of the country.

Child migrants were by no means the only group of young people whose experiences of childhood were shaped by these racial anxieties. Somewhat better known is the example of the "Stolen Generations" of mixed-race Indigenous children who were forcibly removed from their families and sent to missions, state-run institutions, and foster homes in the nineteenth and twentieth centuries. Bureaucrats justified the policy as a form of welfare that would lead to the children's eventual cultural integration. In reality, the initiatives were an attempt both to create a menial labor pool and, in the interwar period, to control the fertility of the Aboriginal population in order to whiten it out of existence.[2] As Margaret Jacobs has made clear in her comparative history of American Indian and Aboriginal child removal policies in the United States and Australia, the project functioned as a tool of colonial dispossession in multiple respects: it "furthered nation-building aims on one level by trying to erase perceived differences of indigenous peoples and ostensibly to bring them into their nations; at the same time, on another level, it sought to undermine indigenous claims to the land by breaking down indigenous children's intimate affiliations with their kin and country."[3]

---

[2] The literature on the Stolen Generation is now extensive. Important introductions include Russell McGregor, *Imagined Destinies: Aboriginal Australians and the Doomed Race Theory, 1880–1939* (Melbourne University Press, 1997); Quentin Beresford and Paul Omaji, *Our State of Mind: Racial Planning and the Stolen Generations* (Fremantle: Fremantle Arts Centre Press, 1998); Anna Haebich, *Broken Circles: Fragmenting Indigenous Families: 1800–2000* (Fremantle: Fremantle Arts Centre Press, 2000); Fiona Paisley, "Childhood and Race: Growing Up in the Empire," in *Gender and Empire*, ed. Philippa Levine (Oxford University Press, 2004), 240–259; A. Dirk Moses, ed., *Genocide and Settler Society: Frontier Violence and Stolen Indigenous Children in Australian History* (New York: Berghahn Books, 2005).

[3] Margaret Jacobs, *White Mother to a Dark Race: Settler Colonialism, Maternalism, and the Removal of Indigenous Children in the American West and Australia, 1880–1940* (Lincoln: University of Nebraska Press, 2009), 63.

Unlike Aboriginal children, child migrants appeared not as a threat but as an advantage to the Australian nation. Dominion politicians viewed the arriving British boys and girls as Australian citizens in the making, and they were always more generous in their funding for child migrant farm schools than for Indigenous institutions. But, like the Stolen Generations, child migrants grew up in tightly regulated environments designed to make them "useful" to the nation, which meant grooming them for specific niches in Australian society. Significantly, the meaning of utility was defined in distinctly gendered ways in each policy. Throughout the early twentieth century, Australian officials removed Aboriginal girls at higher rates than boys, since they prized young "half-caste" women for their biological ability to reproduce lighter-skinned children.[4] The majority of child migrants in this period, by contrast, were boys, not only because they were more readily available in children's homes in Britain but also because their value was assessed in terms of their capacity to extend the agricultural economy and, with it, White settlement, into the rural hinterlands. In both cases, though, the effort to claim and transform the young in the national interest left child migrants and removed Indigenous children without parental or familial advocates. Ultimately, too, it resulted in restricted educational opportunities and narrowed career choices for both groups. Child emigration, in this regard, further illustrates the impact of what anthropologist Ann Stoler has termed the "intimacies of empire" – or the crucial role played by intimate domains such as child-rearing in the making of colonial racial categories – on both colonized and colonizer alike.[5] As this chapter argues, although child migrants were universally recognized as White, and thus as members of the ruling elite, the racial anxieties inherent to interwar Australian culture nonetheless imposed powerful constraints on their lives.

### Populate or perish

"We have a great undeveloped empty country with millions of acres of Crown land, and we want to people it," declared James Mitchell, the Premier of Western Australia, at a meeting of the Empire Parliamentary Association in London in 1922. A proud empire loyalist, Mitchell's speech was partly motivated by his belief that Britain's imperial mission

[4] Ibid, 72–73.
[5] Ann Stoler, "Tense and Tender Ties: The Politics of Comparison in North American Studies and (Post) Colonial History," *Journal of American History* 88, no. 3 (December 2001): 829–865, 831; see also Ann Stoler, *Carnal Knowledge and Imperial Power: Race and the Intimate in Colonial Rule* (Berkeley: University of California Press, 2010, originally 2002).

would remain unfinished until every inch of Australia had been settled. He was also an ardent nationalist, and, in keeping with the mainstream of political thought in his country, he was equally concerned with the matter of racial pride. Continuing his address, Mitchell noted that Australia was "very near to Japan and to Java, where there are millions of coloured people." Surely, these neighbors were tempted by the richness of the dominion, with its "wonderful climate," productive soils, and lucrative mining industries. If Britons wanted to protect their bastion of European civilization in the Pacific, there was only one solution: "to put British people onto [Australia's] British acres." "I am a 'White' Australian," he concluded, reaching his apex; "I want to go back to the wilds, and I want to take with me just about as many people as you can spare."[6]

 Mitchell was a skillful orator, and his simultaneous suggestion of imminent threat and invocation of imperial and national honor were well tuned to the broader currents of Australian society in the 1920s. Sentiments of White racial superiority had a long track record in the dominion, having dominated the local culture since the arrival of the First Fleet in 1788. During the early part of the nineteenth century, powerful conceptions of difference fueled the brutal frontier violence that nearly annihilated the continent's Indigenous peoples. Aboriginal Australians suffered catastrophic demographic losses stemming from land dispossession, violence, starvation, and disease. Although estimates vary, the standard interpretation suggests that their numbers plummeted from a precontact high of over one million to a low of some 30,000 in the early 1900s.[7] The rise of biological explanations of race during the second half of the nineteenth century also led to a hardening of attitudes toward the Chinese, South Asians, and Pacific Islanders who filled the most backbreaking jobs on the railroads and in the gold mines and sugarcane fields.[8] The separate colonies that made up preunion Australia began restricting non-White immigration in the 1850s, and, by federation in 1901, the nation had become "one of the model countries of racism" in the world.[9] Exclusionary legislation led the agenda of the new Parliament, which

---

[6] "Report of Proceedings at Informal Conference between Members of the Empire Parliamentary Association in the Home and Dominion Parliaments," March 30, 1922, T161/111, TNA: PRO.

[7] Raymond Evans, "'Pigmentia': Racial Fears and White Australia," in *Genocide and Settler Society*, ed. Moses, 103–124, 107.

[8] Ann Curthoys, "Liberalism and Exclusionism: A Prehistory of the White Australia Policy," in *Legacies of White Australia: Race, Culture, and Nation*, ed. Laksiri Jayasuriya, David Walker, and Jan Gothard (Crawley: University of Western Australia Press, 2003), 8–32.

[9] Stefanie Affeldt, "A Paroxysm of Whiteness: 'White' Labor, 'White' Nation, and 'White' Sugar in Australia," in *The Wages of Whiteness and Racist Symbolic Capital*, ed. Wolf D. Hund, Jeremy Krikler, and David Roediger (Berlin: Lit Verlag, 2010), 99–131, 100.

began its first session by deporting nearly every Pacific Islander in the country. Six days later, the passage of the Immigration Restriction Act established the White Australia policy and gave the dominion the ignominious title of being the first modern nation to prohibit the entrance of almost all non-Europeans.[10] These legislative efforts marked the beginning of Australia's larger mission to protect the sanctity of the White race. As the historian Charles Pearson declared in his bestselling 1893 treatise *National Character and National Life: A Forecast*, Australians were "guarding the last part of the world, in which the higher races can live and increase freely, for the higher civilization."[11]

The racial nationalism of the 1920s, then, had deep foundations. In the years surrounding the war, however, these attitudes gained a new valence as they merged with more recent anxiety about the rise of Asia. Although Australia was one of the largest countries in the world, with a landmass of some seven million square miles, its population was tiny: only about five million by the First World War. In comparison, neighboring Japan was one-twentieth the size of Australia but had more than ten times the population. China dwarfed them both with an estimated populace of more than 400 million.[12] By the early twentieth century, fears about the country's seeming emptiness in comparison to the overfilled lands of its neighbors had come dominate the political discourse.[13] As Prime Minister William Hughes put it, Australia was "a tiny patch of white in a great sea of colour," and, with its small population and military isolation from Europe, the young nation was at particular risk of foreign invasion.[14] "While Australia is doing little to develop her huge resources ... Asiatics are endeavouring to find an outlet for their teeming millions," thundered

[10] Evans, "Pigmentia," 114.

[11] Charles Pearson, *National Life and Character: A Forecast* (London: Macmillan, 1893), 17, quoted in David Walker, "Race Building and the Disciplining of White Australia," in *Legacies of White Australia*, ed. Jayasuriya et al., 33–50; 42. On the international reception of Pearson's book, see Marilyn Lake and Henry Reynolds, *Drawing the Global Colour Line: White Men's Countries and the International Challenge of Racial Equality* (Cambridge University Press, 2008), 75–94.

[12] Population statistics from this period are notoriously slippery. *The Statesman's Yearbook* for 1920 listed the population of China at 320 million but acknowledged that the Chinese government abided the much higher figure of 439 million. John Scott Keltie and M. Epstein, eds., *The Statesman's Year-book* (London: Macmillan and Co., 1920), 737. More recent estimates place China's population at 426 million in 1901 and 475 million in 1928. Gregory Veeck, Clifton Pannell, Christopher Smith, and Youqin Huang, *China's Geography: Globalization and the Dynamics of Political, Economic, and Social Change* (Lanham: Rowman and Littlefield, 2007), 103.

[13] David Walker, *Anxious Nation: Australia and the Rise of Asia, 1850–1939* (Brisbane: University of Queensland Press, 1999).

[14] W. M. Hughes, *The Splendid Adventure: A Review of Empire Relations within and without the Commonwealth of Britannic Nations* (London: Ernest Benn, 1929), quoted in Lake and Reynolds, *Drawing the Global Colour Line*, 295.

the Millions Club, a conservative pro-immigration group whose name signaled its goal to increase the White population of Sydney to one million.[15] This ethic was widespread across the political spectrum. Although Labor representatives remained cautious of large-scale immigration projects because of their potential to create competition for jobs in cities, they too agreed that the best way to fortify the dominion was to fill its vacant land with settlers. As Hughes argued in 1921, the country would only be safe when it had a "population sufficiently large to combat any force that may be brought against us." He insisted that "if we are to maintain the White Australia Policy we must be ready and able to defend it. If we are to hold Australia, we must be prepared to people and develop it. Unless we do these things, we ... shall surely lose it."[16]

Getting more people was the first imperative; ensuring that they were British was the second. In the years after the First World War, the "kith and kin" connection remained empowering. The global span of the empire was at its height, and Australians were happy to bask in the vicarious glow of their racial brethren's might. Dominion officials liked to point out that the imperial relationship offered their nation more than a trading partner or military alliance. It also gave them access to some of the "best citizens of the world – Anglo-Saxons, men of our own race and blood."[17] At the same time, therefore, that British politicians were championing empire settlement as an effective way to stimulate the imperial economy, their Australian counterparts were also embracing the policy, although their motives stemmed more from a concern with racial security than from economics. Hughes, who was in power from 1915 through 1923, and who himself came from a migrant background – he had been born in London and only moved south during his twenties – became an enthusiastic advocate. Under his direction, the Commonwealth government began expanding its authority over the work of assisted migration, a realm that had previously been left to the states.[18] By 1920, federal authorities had taken over the tasks of recruiting and transporting Britons to Australia, leaving state officials in charge

---

[15] "Keeping Australia White," *Millions Magazine* 1, no. 5 (November 1919): 1.
[16] "Resolution Passed at the Imperial Conference," 1921, CP 103/12, Bundle 25, ANA.
[17] Ibid.
[18] The early 1920s marked a shift in political attitudes toward assisted immigration in Australia. Whereas in the Edwardian period many state officials had resisted cooperating with voluntary organizations because they viewed the charitable sector as unmethodical, in the aftermath of the First World War, they were more prepared to follow the lead of the federal government in encouraging any form of immigration from Britain. Michele Langfield, "Voluntarism, Salvation, and Rescue: British Juvenile Migration to Australia and Canada, 1890–1939," *Journal of Imperial and Commonwealth History* 32, no. 2 (May 2004): 86–114.

of placing the new arrivals on the land. Hughes' successor, Stanley Bruce, was even more dedicated to the project. Having campaigned on the slogan "Men, Money, and Markets," Bruce was the driving force behind a new development deal with Britain in 1925 that gained the dominion £34 million of low-interest loans for rural public works and agricultural projects. The agreement was explicit that the intent of the funding was to populate Australia's open spaces. It stipulated that every £75 of loan money would introduce at least one new migrant, and aimed to transplant 450,000 Britons by 1930.[19]

Despite this groundswell of political support and financing, the results of Australia's postwar immigration push were meager. As early as January of 1922, Hughes was grumbling that his government's efforts were not living up to expectations. A recruitment drive had been running at full speed for some eighteen months, yet fewer than 20,000 migrants had arrived. "We have a great machine, and the overhead expenses are considerable, but it grinds out a very small quantity of corn," he sighed; "the fruits of the tree of immigration … are merely a barren crop."[20] The core of the problem was the old difficulty of convincing a population of British urbanites that their destiny lay on the land. The dominion's explicit focus on extending settlement into unpopulated areas complicated the matter further, since migrants would have to be true pioneers, able to put down roots in the country's most isolated rural backwaters. Many Australians doubted that adults could commit themselves to such a profound life change. In 1923, Melbourne's *The Age* newspaper warned readers not to trust the intentions of the "ordinary clerk and city laborer, who has never seen a growing crop" but who suddenly declared a desire to farm. The hoped-for immigrant would likely become a social menace, for "when he arrives in Australia he has no desire to go on the land, and so he stays in the city and helps to flood the already glutted labor market."[21]

In response to these concerns, politicians tried various techniques to stem the much-lamented "urban drift." Most notable was the creation of group-settlement schemes that attempted to ease migrants' transition by clumping them together. Expensive and difficult to manage, the majority

---

[19] "Report of the Oversea Settlement Committee," 1926, *Parliamentary Papers* XI, Cmd. 2640, 8. See also Michael Roe, *Australia, Britain, and Migration, 1915–1940: A Study of Desperate Hopes* (Cambridge University Press, 1995), 9–29; William Lines, *Taming the Great South Land: A History of the Conquest of Nature in Australia* (Athens: University of Georgia Press, 1999), 163–194.

[20] Hughes speaking at a conference between Commonwealth and state ministers, January 1922, A458, G154/7 Part I, ANA.

[21] "Peopling Australia: Existing Methods Fail," *The Age*, August 30, 1923. On the wider Australian hostility to urban migrants, see Geoffrey Sherington, *Australia's Immigrants, 1788–1988* (Sydney: Allen and Unwin, 1990), 110–111.

were catastrophic failures. One initiative in Victoria, for instance, sought to establish a community of at least 2,000 families but because of a lack of interest only placed some 400 migrants. Less than a decade later, the state had received more than 300 complaints from the settlers about issues ranging from the unsuitability of the land to having received misinformation and inadequate training. Aware of the scheme's impending collapse, the government offered new holdings to any of the migrants who wanted to stay on the land or £500 compensation for those who did not. After an investment of over £500,000, eighteen settlers chose to continue farming.[22] Similar problems plagued the £34 million agreement, which fell well short of its targets and was called off early in May of 1932. Only £7.8 million was advanced to fund the settlement of roughly 4,000 migrants. Of these, it was estimated that no more than 12 percent would succeed as independent farmers.[23]

As it had in Britain, the trouble of adapting adults to the narrow political agenda of empire settlement led Australian officials to refocus their sights on children. Shortly after the war, Hughes lauded the "plastic state" of young people, arguing that those "on the threshold of life" could most easily be "moulded to the circumstances of Australia."[24] The younger the better was the opinion of many other commentators. On the extreme end of the spectrum was the Queensland-based journalist Joice Nankivell's suggestion of a state-funded "baby ship" that would bring out from Britain regular parties of "say, 300 attractive children" to be "raised in an Australian environment, and with an Australian outlook and education." Nankivell's plan was motivated by a sense of urgency. She stressed that families in the United States had already made offers to take in war orphans, and the thought that "British blood should pass outside the Empire" alarmed her. If Australia could just get hold of them, these infants could be "turned into the citizens of the future."[25] With its combination of sentimentality, emphasis on children's malleability, and insistence on racial unity, Nankivell's proposal struck all the right notes. The Prime Minister's office found it appealing enough to send to the states for consideration, and only dropped it after the directors of each

---

[22] "Report of the Victoria Land Settlement Scheme," 1936, DO57/102, TNA: PRO. See also Note by Terrance Macnaghten, April 6, 1929, DO 57/103, TNA: PRO; Marilyn Lake, *The Limits of Hope: Soldier Settlements in Victoria, 1905–1938* (Oxford University Press, 1987); Sandra Rennie McDonald, "Victoria's Immigration Scandal of the Thirties," *Victorian Historical Journal* 4, no. 4 (1978): 229–237.

[23] Oversea Settlement Board Memo, Government Assisted Migration, 1936, DO 57/102, TNA: PRO.

[24] Hughes speaking in the Australian House of Representatives, September 17, 1920, A458, G154/7 Part I, ANA.

[25] Joice Nankivell, "Emigrate the Babies," *British-Australian*, May 1922.

local Children's Department reported that implementing the plan would require more resources than they had at hand.[26]

Whereas the "baby ship" proposal turned out to be ill conceived and overly idealistic, child emigration appeared to offer a tried-and-tested solution to Australia's immigration dilemma. By the early 1920s, both the CES and Barnardo's had resumed operations in the dominion. As of 1921, the Fairbridge Farm School was again receiving regular parties of boys at Pinjarra and had expanded its work to accept girls as well. The same year, the Barnardo's local committee in New South Wales welcomed its first group of 47 boys, and was soon placing between 100 and 150 children annually in private homes throughout the state. In 1923, it also agreed to begin sending regular shipments of boys and girls to the Pinjarra farm school.[27] Local politicians greeted these developments as hopeful signs, although many remained wary of the high price tag. The CES initiative was particularly expensive, given the length of time needed to shuffle children through the farm school system. As immigration officials noted, while it cost an average of £250 to support a boy of eight or nine at Pinjarra until he was ready for his first job, the same amount could finance the settlement expenses of five adults. The situation boiled down to a question of quantity versus quality. "Putting it in a nutshell," the Secretary of the OSC commented, "the Australian government say that for £50 they can get an immigrant to-day, for £250 they can get a better one six years hence."[28]

Throughout the interwar period, these concerns about expense, or what the Australian Minister for Immigration termed "the business angle of migration," continued to shape the government's interactions with child emigration charities.[29] When approached with requests for funding, dominion authorities made clear that, although they were interested in promoting the settlement of British children, their motives were not philanthropic. Rather, the Commonwealth was only prepared to sponsor schemes of "sound immigration ... controlled by limitations of finance" that would help meet the country's urgent need for a larger rural population.[30] Proponents of the movement learned quickly that their older

---

[26] The correspondence took place from June through October of 1922, and can be found in A457, X400/5, ANA.

[27] Barnardo's NSW, Executive and Finance Committee Minutes, 1921–1929, Barnardo's Australia, Ultimo.

[28] George Plant, Minutes of a Meeting at the Australia House, January 12, 1922, CO 721/45, TNA: PRO. On this point, see also Geoffrey Sherington and Chris Jeffery, *Fairbridge: Empire and Child Migration* (London: Woburn Press, 1998), 100–105.

[29] Memo No. 447, Commonwealth Development and Migration Commission to the Minister of Immigration, June 6, 1928, A461, I349/1/7, ANA.

[30] Gullett to Fairbridge, December 29, 1921, A436, 46/5/597 Part 1 A, ANA.

arguments about giving slum children a fresh start in the land of sunshine carried less weight in Australia than they had in Britain. In response, both Barnardo's and the CES began to play up the political advantages of the programs in their fundraising literature and press advertisements. The strategy of the Barnardo's 1924 Australian appeal campaign, for instance, was to send donors an official letter from the Governor that detailed the scheme's "necessity from an <u>Imperial</u> and <u>White Australia</u> standpoint."[31] The CES also adopted a new focus on race. Enumerating the benefits of its work in a 1921 brochure that it sent to the Prime Minister's Office and published in regional newspapers, the organization noted that its farm school "steadily increases our population, brings in new money, provides employment, helps the helpless, contributes to revenue, develops our back-country, deprives no one of his job, and is one of the best guarantees of the White Australia policy." The social welfare aspect of the movement was still included in this pitch, but its importance had diminished, displaced by a new focus on racial security. "The only real safeguard to a policy of White Australia is a country well populated with people of British stock," the brochure concluded. "If we are to have the exclusive rights to Australia for another generation we must fill up the empty spaces with our own people. This is what the Farm School is doing."[32]

The heightened emphasis on population politics crept into the British side of the work as well. By 1927, the Barnardo's London branch was stressing the urgent "necessity for sending our fit and able citizens of the Motherland to the sparsely-occupied spaces of our great Dominions." It followed up this claim with a full description of child emigration's effectiveness in producing permanent settlers.[33] The CES chose to represent the idea visually, through a map of Western Australia that appeared in its British and Australian literature throughout the interwar years, and which reached its biggest audience in a 1934 full-page advertisement in *The Times* (Figure 3.1). Superimposed on the empty map of the state were a series of lines connecting the organization's base at Pinjarra to the farms and homesteads where "Old Fairbridgians" had settled. The Society also included a scaled representation of England and Wales within the outline of the larger map as a way of reiterating its message. It was an elegant technique that immediately drew the viewer's attention

[31] Barnardo's NSW, Treasurer's Report, December 15, 1924, Barnardo's Australia, Ultimo. Emphasis in the original.
[32] CES, "What the Farm School Has Done for Australia," A461, C349/1/7 Part I, ANA. See also "Fairbridge Farm School," *Western Mail*, September 8, 1921; "Immigration Problem: Placing Children on the Land," *The Age*, September 27, 1921.
[33] Barnardo's 62nd Annual Report, 1927, D.239/A3/1/62, ULSCA.

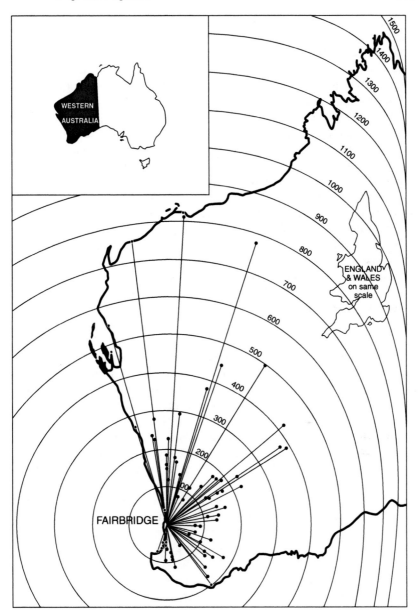

Figure 3.1 Map of Old Fairbridgians. Fairbridge Promotional Appeal Booklet, 1934, D.296/D1/1/1, ULSCA. Reprinted in *The Times*, June 21, 1934.

to the massive emptiness of the dominion while also affirming the organization's ability to fill the outback with fresh generations of Britons. A smaller map of the continent in the upper left corner drove the theme home: the work of populating the dominion had begun, but, until every vacant acre was filled, child emigration would remain an essential part of the drive to create a White Australia.

Beyond the shift in rhetoric, the charities also reconfigured their day-to-day operations in order to prioritize the dominion's settlement aims. In 1921, Kingsley Fairbridge agreed to raise the average age of the children at Pinjarra to eleven, a move that reduced the school's maintenance and education costs and increased the number of boys and girls the organization placed out each year. The change helped win the Society a grant from the Commonwealth government that paid four shillings weekly for every child at the school.[34] Five years later, when the agreement was up for renewal, the charity further sought to cement its relationship with the government by guaranteeing that it would educate, train, and place at least seventy boys and girls in rural positions every year.[35]

Deals like this one provided the charities with stable financing but also locked them into policies that often contradicted their broader philanthropic objectives. Meeting the new quota required the CES to recruit children of specific ages so that the right number would be ready to graduate each year. The organization quickly discovered that this task was easier said than done. In 1928, it became apparent that there were too many young children at Pinjarra and not enough teenagers ready for employment. The Society's Perth committee sent an urgent request to its London headquarters for a party of eighty-eight older boys who could move swiftly through the farm school and into their first jobs.[36] The London directors scrambled to fill the requisition, but the affair left them uneasy. Arthur Lawley, still the chair of the board, reminded Perth that the new stipulation was "rather in conflict" with the organization's aim "to catch them young." He worried that it would be "extraordinarily difficult to get the material morally and physically to come up to the standard demanded" in the short amount of time available.[37] This was less a comment about child welfare than about overall strategy. Longer training made for better settlers, and it would hurt the movement as a whole if the farm school started churning out badly trained or homesick youths. Others on the board did express concern that the new system

[34] Fairbridge to Gullett, October 7, 1921; Hughes to Colebatch, July 10, 1922, A436, 46/5/597, Part 1A, ANA.
[35] CES, Perth Committee Minutes, June 19, 1929, ACC 3025A/3, SAWA: BL.
[36] CES, Executive Committee Minutes, September 23, 1928, D.296/B1/2/2, ULSCA.
[37] CES, Council Minutes, September 13, 1928, in ibid.

would hinder the children's education by pulling boys or girls out of school early to start readying them for employment. When one member, William Sandover, brought the issue to the Perth committee's attention, however, he received the curt reply that maintaining a "certain output" was necessary "in order to prove the scheme a practicable one from the immigration point of view."[38]

The imperative to remain in Australia's good financial graces was amplified by the onset of the Depression. On the eve of the stock market crash in 1929, Australia's economy was already stagnant, with a jobless rate of 10 percent. The downturn had fueled the election of the protectionist Labor leader James Scullin, who had long opposed assisted immigration on the grounds that it led to unemployment. Predictably, when the crash hit at the end of his first week in office, Scullin pledged to pull all state funding for immigration. The new policy had serious implications for child emigration charities, which had been receiving grants from the government for almost ten years and had grown dependent on the steady infusions of state aid. Both Barnardo's and the CES entered into months of negotiations with dominion officials that ultimately resulted in an exception for child migrants. The government agreed to continue its maintenance payments to the charities, albeit at a reduced rate. It also sanctioned the arrival of further children, although only "on the strict understanding that no publicity whatever" would be given to their movements.[39]

The continued Australian support for child emigration through the worst years of the Depression was an indication of dominion officials' abiding belief that the policy offered an effective way to preserve the racial purity of their nation. Not only did state funding keep the societies afloat throughout the 1930s but it also enabled both charities to expand their initiatives. The original farm school at Pinjarra ballooned from roughly eighty children in residence in the years after the war to over 350 by the mid 1930s. The government also approved the creation of four new projects across the continent. By 1938, there were two new farm schools in New South Wales run by Barnardo's and the CES, as well as two more in Victoria and Western Australia operated by the Northcote Children's Trust and the Catholic Christian Brothers order, both newcomers to the movement.[40] These institutions stood as a testament to the interwar faith in social engineering. Although the routines and communal traditions

---

[38] CES, Perth Committee Minutes, September 13, 1927, ACC 3025A/2, SAWA: BL.

[39] Perth Committee Minutes, September 26, 1933, ACC 3025A/4, SAWA: BL.

[40] On these developments, see Barry Coldrey, *Child Migration to Catholic Institutions in Australia: Objectives, Policies, Realities, 1926–1966* (Como, WA: Tamanaraik Publishing, 1995); Sherington and Jeffery, *Fairbridge*, 152–196.

varied somewhat from place to place, all were designed to produce a particular type of settler for White Australia: a well-trained, rural-minded worker who was prepared to live permanently in the country's most isolated regions. As an exploration of the culture of the leading farm school of the period (the CES's Fairbridge Farm School at Pinjarra) demonstrates, reformers tailored child migrants' upbringing in an effort to endow them with the skills, values, and spirits of modern Australian pioneers.

### Crafting Australians

In many respects, John Hay's experience was typical of the interwar generation of child migrants at Pinjarra. Born in London in 1915, by the age of three he was living in an orphanage run by the Anglican Church. He never knew his parents and never discovered the circumstances that led to his placement in the Home, although it is probable that a wartime death or illness played a role. This total break with family was common, even if it happened earlier in Hay's life than was customary for other child migrants. Throughout the 1920s and 1930s, the CES did the bulk of its recruiting through local authorities and children's charities, which meant that most of the boys and girls at Pinjarra were already acquainted with institutional care. Close to one-third were defined as "orphans," having lost contact with both parents through death or "desertion." Nearly half had one parent who was known to be alive, and just over one-sixth were in touch with both parents at the time of their emigration.[41] Life for Hay at the Anglican orphanage was spare. The sisters provided for their wards by begging for food in Covent Garden. But, on the whole, Hay remembered the conditions as "very, very good." He did not fit in perfectly, though. "I was short, fat, untidy, lazy, [and] I used to read a lot, always wanted to read," Hay said. Tired of being teased, and less than thrilled about the prospect of joining the Navy, which was where most of the boys ended up, he decided instead to accept the head sister's offer of a new life in Australia. It was 1926. Hay had just turned eleven years old.

Once he had been nominated for emigration, the arrangements came together quickly. He was taken into central London for a medical inspection and given a small suitcase of clothes for the journey. Before he knew it, Hay was on the boat, traveling third class with an austere matron and thirteen other boys of roughly the same age. The party made the customary stop at Cape Town for lunch and a trip to the zoo, and Hay also recalled an excursion to a park in Fremantle once the group landed in Australia. Beyond those flashes, he remembered little else of the trip or,

---

[41] Sherington and Jeffery, *Fairbridge*, 92–93 and 132–133.

for that matter, of his first days in Pinjarra. His years of growing up in an orphanage had prepared him for the regimented existence of a children's institution, and he slid easily into the rhythm of school, chores, group activities, and set mealtimes. In fact, his life would have transitioned seamlessly from Britain to Australia were it not for his difficulty in getting used to the new custom of going without shoes:

In England we had worn boots and socks and even shoes, but at Fairbridge the first thing that happened, we had no boots, no shoes, no socks. We were immediately in bare feet and so you could imagine that our first trip on the gravel road ... was a very, very short one and it took us some time before we could get used to walking in the gravel. That is probably my first impression of Fairbridge, of walking in bare feet on gravel, a most uncomfortable process [laughs].[42]

It is significant that Hay remembered his transition as having required an act of toughening, a literal hardening of his body to a more demanding imperial lifestyle. Going without shoes was the first of several adjustments Hay would make in preparation for his assimilation into Australian society.

Echoes of these recollections, from the loss of family connections to the sore feet, appear throughout the memoirs and oral histories that have been collected from some of the more than 1,100 child migrants who passed through Pinjarra in the interwar years.[43] The similarities in theme, tone, and content that emerge from these interviews offer a powerful illustration of the uniformity of experience for children at the farm school. In spite of the Society's claim that it offered boys and girls a "natural" upbringing that meant the "difference between mass production and individual treatment," the truth of the matter was that the culture of Pinjarra was highly structured, varying only slightly by gender and age.[44] Nevertheless, there was one important way in which Hay's life was distinct. He was the only child in his class to receive a secondary education. While the rest of his peers went from primary school into farm training, Hay won a rare scholarship to Bunbury High School, and later became a teacher. This trajectory stood in such stark contrast to the norm for Pinjarra that, sixty years

[42] Interview with John (Julian) Hay, conducted by Chris Jeffery, July 10, 1985, OH 1884, SAWA: BL.
[43] Other examples of the tendency to describe the difficulty of adjustment through the trope of tender feet being hardened include: Interview with Queenie Walsh, conducted by Chris Jeffery, February 27 and March 7, 14, and 21, 1986, OH 1878, SAWA: BL; Interview with David Buck, conducted by Chris Jeffery, April 14, 1986, OH 1879, SAWA: BL; Hickson, *Flo*, 25; Lionel Pearce, *Feathers of the Snow Angel: Memories of a Child in Exile* (Fremantle: Fremantle Arts Centre Press, 2002), 94; Author's interview with John Cooper, May 28, 2006; Read interview. Sherington and Jeffery, *Fairbridge*, 264, place the number of children who attended the school in these decades at 1,140.
[44] CES, Annual Report, 1926, D.296/D1/1/1, ULSCA.

on, other migrants could still name him as one of the dozen or so children who were "exceptionally talented ... the cream of the brains."[45]

For the majority of interwar child migrants, the possibility of a life outside agriculture or service was slight. This was an intentional product of the school's efforts to meet Australia's demographic needs, or, as Kingsley Fairbridge put it, to make child migrants "so interested in farm life that they have no hankering after the towns."[46] Like all child welfare initiatives past and present, the scheme was motivated not only by reformers' understanding of children's developmental requirements but also by an idealized vision of the adults these boys and girls would become. The Society's directors imagined child migrants growing into independent producers, and they configured the school in an attempt to bring these self-sufficient farmers into being. They also acknowledged that, before the children would be able to establish their own homesteads, they would first have to work their way up the ladder, beginning by doing backbreaking labor on distant wheat farms and sheep stations. This reality was especially apparent during the early 1930s, when upwards of one-third of Australia's labor force was out of work and when competition was intense for even the most poorly paid jobs.[47] The curriculum of the school was thus designed with both of these futures – the long and the short term – in mind. Staff members sought to endow child migrants with the rugged individualism they deemed fitting for Australian pioneers. At the same time, they strove to instill character traits that were prized in farm hands and domestic servants, such as a ready compliance with orders and deference to authority.

Writ large, this desire to shape the right kind of settler for Australia led the Society to conceive of child migrants less as distinct individuals than as standardized units with identical needs and matching life trajectories. These assumptions found support from the theory of child development that continued to guide British child welfare during the interwar decades: namely, the antihereditarian, environmentalist notion that, once children's links to their pasts had been severed, they were available to be recast in a new mold. In accordance with this belief, throughout the period both the CES and Barnardo's sent boys and girls to Australia without case histories. The charities' directing boards accepted that

[45] Interview with Jack Maude, conducted by Chris Jeffery, September 13, 1985, OH 1875, SAWA: BL.

[46] Fairbridge to the Governor General, December 7, 1921, A461, C349/1/7 Part I, ANA.

[47] Western Australia's agricultural industries were some of the hardest hit by the economic crisis. By 1933, popular dissatisfaction with the government's response had grown so intense that the local electorate voted in a two-thirds majority to secede from the Commonwealth. For an overview, see Geoffrey Bolton, *A Fine Country to Starve In* (Nedlands: Western Australia University Press, 1994, originally 1972).

all reclaimed children came from similar backgrounds and so viewed any information about their prior lives as irrelevant to their care. When Henry Wheeler was sent to Barnardo's Mowbray Park farm school outside Sydney in 1930 at the age of ten, he was given no information about his family's whereabouts. Seventy-five years later, he asked for his file and received just an admittance form that (incorrectly) listed his birth city and included the names and addresses of his mother and grandfather, nothing else.[48] The one late exception to this rule related to religion. In 1937, Barnardo's began providing short descriptions of each child's family history after its executive committee realized that a group of boys and girls who came from Nonconformist families had been baptized as Anglicans after they had arrived in Australia.[49] The nondenominational CES did not begin to keep case files for its migrants until after the Second World War.

This lack of individuation had serious consequences for child migrants' connections to their families. Boys and girls were never formally barred from corresponding with their relatives back in Britain, and some of the children who arrived able to read and write did manage to keep in contact. Charles McKay, who was eight years old when he was included in the first postwar party to Pinjarra in 1921, wrote letters to his mother for close to twenty years before they lost touch. He assumed she had died, and was surprised to find her "within a stone's throw almost of where we used to live" when he returned to Britain on vacation in 1977.[50] In the main, however, the dismissive attitudes toward poor parents that had typified the child rescue movement before the war carried over. Most staff members viewed child migrants' links to their families as a nuisance, and did little to encourage them. "Please send double orphans," requested the CES's Perth committee of its London branch in 1932, as "there is great pressure placed on those children who have 'belongings' to send money home when they begin to earn."[51] The Society also relied on other methods to keep relatives from "interfering and claiming the boys and girls."[52] In 1925, its executive board inserted a paragraph into the application form stating that, if a family member wanted a child returned, he would be liable for all the costs

---

[48] Henry Wheeler, "My Story, in Short," in *With the Best of Intentions: Stories from Dr. Barnardo's Farm School at Mowbray Park near the Oaks, NSW, 1929–1959*, ed. Doreen Lyon (The Oaks: The Oaks Historical Society, 2010), 9–11.

[49] Barnardo's, Executive Committee Minutes, October 13, 1937, D.239/B3/1/11, ULSCA.

[50] Interview with Charles Alexander McKay, conducted by Chris Jeffery, October 8, 1986, OH 1886, SAWA: BL.

[51] CES, Executive Committee Minutes, October 17, 1932, D.296/B1/2/3, ULSCA.

[52] CES, Executive Committee Minutes, November 5, 1925, in ibid.

that the charity had expended on the child's behalf.[53] Given that the legal guardianship of child migrants remained vested with their parents, the stipulation was nonbinding and would not hold up in court. But the rule exploited parents' uncertainty about their rights, and the Society used the clause repeatedly to refuse requests for children's repatriation. In 1938, the father of a boy at Pinjarra reported to the Perth committee that his situation had improved and he could now pay £50 to bring his son home. The members responded that they "sympathized" with his appeal but could not "take steps under any circumstances to countenance the return of such boys and girls." With a final reminder that "parents or relatives desiring the return of any [child] under the age of 21 ... must make themselves responsible to the Society not only for the return fare but for the total amount incurred on maintenance during residence and training," they denied his request.[54]

This disregard for the bonds of family applied equally to siblings who had migrated together. George Snellin, the boy whose weak lungs and frequent bouts of illness kept him inside for much of his early childhood at Pinjarra, grew up to watch each of his three older brothers disappear to separate farms when they reached their teenage years. "We were split up," he said; "One was sent to one place, the other was sent to another place, never together. They all went out at different times, different years." The school's tendency to place child migrants on remote farms cemented the divide, and the brothers soon fell out of touch. "I wouldn't know if they were alive or dead," Snellin commented in 1985. "Since that day to this, I've never seen them. Never heard of them."[55]

Snellin's experience was a typical by-product of Pinjarra's standardized culture, wherein all children were treated alike, without regard for their preexisting attachments or distinct personalities. As in other children's institutions of its size, the daily regimen of the farm school was tightly controlled, so much so that, decades later, former migrants could recall the precise times that each of the day's activities had begun. David Buck was born in London in 1927 and lived with his mother for five years before she placed him in an orphanage. He arrived at Pinjarra in 1933, when he was six years old. As he remembered:

We were out of bed at 6 am usually to the call of the reveille on the bugle blown by one of the older boys. We removed our pajamas, wrapped a towel round our middles and queued up for a cold shower or a cold plunge bath ... After you

[53] Ibid.
[54] CES, Western Australia Subcommittee Minutes, March 15, 1938, D.296/B5/2, ULSCA.
[55] Interview with George Snellin, conducted by Chris Jeffery, July 11, 1985, OH 1876, SAWA: BL.

showered, you dressed, you made your bed, you did your before-breakfast cottage duties … [Breakfast] was in the community dining hall at 7 am except on Sundays when you had it in the cottage. After the washing up was completed, usually done by the school-age boys on rotation, you went back to the cottage and then you dressed for school. School was virtually, a few minutes either way it may have been, but virtually 9 till 3:30 and for the lunch break we all went to the community dining hall … After school you went back to the cottage where there was usually some refreshment for you. The cottage mother may have made some cocoa or there may be milk to drink or there might have been a biscuit, a piece of bread and jam, but something to keep the wolf from a very large door. Then you had your afternoon chores to do … After tea and after everyone had had our baths we had our relaxation time. Each boy had his own private locker storage space for the personal goods that boys, and the girls did the same, collect – your bag of marbles, your comics books, your games and things of this sort. And you would play games. You would read. In winter time there was a fire. If the cottage mother had a wireless this would be put on.[56]

Bedtimes were between 7 and 8 pm depending on age, and the day officially ended at 10:30 pm, when the power was shut down for the night.

Buck's recollection conveys the strong sense of order that permeated Pinjarra in these decades. This almost military style of organization was to some extent a consequence of the appointment of a British Lieutenant-Colonel and First World War veteran, S. J. Heath, as principal in 1928.[57] But it was equally the result of the emphasis the school placed on children's responsibility, which required boys and girls to know where they had to be and what they had to be doing at each moment of the day. Tellingly, adults factor minimally in Buck's description, appearing in the background as providers of snacks or of the occasional entertainment, such as the radio. The children, on the other hand, are depicted as self-reliant actors, whose independence Buck stressed through his unconscious use of the first and second person: "We removed our pajamas"; "After you showered, you dressed, you made your bed, you did your before-breakfast cottage duties."

This propensity to underscore child migrants' autonomy was common across the oral histories. While many interviewees remembered instances of kindness from the staff, in general they presented the relationships between adults and children as detached. Bert Read noted that his cottage mother sometimes read to him in the evening, and that Heath, who had lost an arm in the war, chose him to tie up his shoelaces in the mornings. "He picked me of all the … kids. He picked me … So a little bit of connection I got with him there," Read said, illustrating how small moments of individualized attention could make a child feel honored

[56] Buck interview.     [57] Sherington and Jeffery, *Fairbridge*, 123.

and special.[58] Yet Read went on to describe that such occasions were few and far between. Even the cottage mothers, who lived with up to fourteen boys or girls in single-sex residences and thus had the most sustained contact with the children, tended to be ephemeral presences in former migrants' memories. As John Hay put it, although the cottage was frequently described "as a large family," it was "too large to be considered a family unit. We were an ordered group and in the main an orderly group. We were a happy group, a friendly group ... [But] we were still a group and not a family."[59] This sense of personal isolation could extend to the relationships between the children as well. "I don't think I've really ever made any particular friend any time at the school," Jack Maude commented. "I had several I liked but I never, never hooked on to one individual, not a particular one."[60] For many child migrants, the school's aim of encouraging self-sufficiency translated into a lack of personal affection and love, the emotional effects of which often remained with them into adulthood.

The one area of farm school life in which interviewees remembered staff members prominently was discipline. Having grown up in an era when corporal punishment was widely accepted, most former migrants had vivid recollections of being caned for violations of the rules. John Cooper spent his earliest years in the care of Barnardo's and migrated to Pinjarra in 1934 at the age of nine. Looking back, he commented that at times the punishments felt "over-severe," and he shared stories of receiving multiple canings for minor infractions. "I'll tell you an incident," he said:

The teacher's name was Miss Silk. She was a lovely person and a good teacher. And I was a bit of a rebel of course. And we were having a discussion in the classroom about the pronunciation of the word "often." And it led, you know, one thing led to another and [she] felt that I was out of order ... So she took me into the cloakroom to give me the cane.

Still defiant, Cooper refused to offer up his hand for the punishment, pulling it out of reach just before the blow fell.

So in desperation she started whacking me with the cane around the legs and the back and that. So I took the cane off her and I gave her a few. And then went to bolt straight out the door ... and straight into the headmaster's arms, more or less. He was just about to walk in and there he was. He didn't mess around. He took me straight up to his office and gave me five more.

Cooper emphasized that, both then and now, he believed this particular punishment was merited. He told the story less to illustrate the harshness

---

[58] Read interview.    [59] Hay interview.    [60] Maude interview.

of the discipline than to underscore the fact that he had been a scally-
wag. "I deserved it," he concluded, adding that he regretted the memory
"because she was a lovely person and she was a good teacher. I just got
too smart for my own good."[61] Still, his recollection highlights the staff's
tendency to resort to the cane in order to keep children in line, and
also illustrates the potential for such situations to escalate. "Punishment
loomed large in our lives," remembered Flo Hickson, who arrived at
Pinjarra in 1928 at the age of seven; "always somewhere in the cottage
somebody was being thrashed with a strap."[62] The point of corporal
punishment was to instill in the migrants a respect for authority and
a willingness to submit themselves to the demands of superiors. These
were the qualities of "good children" everywhere, but at Pinjarra they
appeared even more essential, since they would prepare boys and girls
for their future jobs as farmhands or servants.

Chores offered another method for teaching these lessons. Encouraged
to be self-reliant, boys and girls of all ages were given demanding workloads. In the mornings, their tasks included making beds, sweeping the
dormitory, scrubbing tables and chairs, washing plates and cutlery, and
dusting. Afternoons were usually dedicated to outdoor work, such as
weeding the gardens, collecting fertilizer, building the kitchen fire, and
carrying water in from the pump for the evening baths. "I always had
other jobs to do ... right from the word go," noted Queenie Malpass,
who was ten years old when she arrived at the school in 1922.[63] The staff
stressed the importance of performing each job systematically, with the
cottage mothers keeping a close watch to make sure that children stuck
to the procedure. John Lane, who was ten years old when he migrated to
Pinjarra in 1933, remembered learning to scrub a floor:

With me on my knees and Miss standing over me, the instruction began. "Start
from a corner and use the cloth to wet a patch of floor." From then on the orders
came thick and fast. "Don't try to do too much at a time. Put a little more water
on the floor, only half wring out the cloth ... no, that's not the way to wring out
a cloth" ... It took five minutes to do just one small patch. There was the whole
floor to do.[64]

Lane's account underscores the methodical nature of the work, whereby
every facet of the chore, even the wringing of the cloth, was done with
precision. This meticulousness was meant to convey to the migrants
that cleaning was a skill, even an art, that demanded their full attention

---

[61] Cooper interview.    [62] Hickson, *Flo*, 91.
[63] Interview with Queenie Malpass, conducted by Chris Jeffery, December 11, 1986, OH
1885, SAWA: BL.
[64] John Lane, *Fairbridge Kid* (Pinjarra: Fairbridge Western Australia, 2000), 158.

Figure 3.2 Kingsley Fairbridge teaching boxing at Pinjarra in the early 1920s. Fairbridge Annual Report, 1930, D.296/D1/1/1, ULSCA.

and respect. Just as essential, though, were the lessons in diligence that these chores conveyed. The staff was endeavoring to create not only well-behaved children but also attentive workers who would comply fully and without question with any task they were given.

Although boys and girls shared the daily chores equally, other aspects of farm school life were strictly gendered. In keeping with Australian ideals of masculinity and "mateship," boys were encouraged to participate in "manly" group activities such as scouting, military drills, and team sports.[65] Boxing received a particular emphasis during the interwar years both at Pinjarra and across the broader child emigration movement. To

[65] On the culture of "mateship," see Russel Ward, *The Australian Legend* (Melbourne: Oxford University Press, 1958); Richard White, *Inventing Australia: Images and Identity, 1688–1980* (Sydney: George Allen & Unwin, 1981). Much has been written on the ideology of scouting as an imperial character-building activity; see especially Allen Warren, "Popular Manliness: Baden Powell, Scouting, and the Development of Manly Character," in *Manliness and Morality: Middle-Class Masculinity in Britain and America*, ed. J. A. Mangin and James Wolvin (Manchester University Press, 1987), 199–217.

Figure 3.3 "The critics view the contest." Children boxing at Northcote Children's Farm in Victoria in the late 1930s. Fairbridge Annual Report, 1937, D.296/D1/1/1, ULSCA.

some degree, this focus derived from the fact that the school's founder, Kingsley Fairbridge, was himself an accomplished boxer, having won a blue at Oxford before the war. Yet the sport persisted well after Fairbridge's premature death from lymphoma in 1924 because proponents viewed it as a means both to improve physical strength and to bolster feelings of self-worth.[66] Boys were instructed in boxing from their first days at the school, and it was common to see children as young as five or six sparring in practice bouts around the grounds (Figures 3.2 and 3.3).

Girls also played sports, but in general they dedicated their leisure time to quieter, indoor pursuits, such as sewing. Rough-and-tumble behaviors or any indications of a "tomboy" nature were discouraged. As the Society stressed, a main goal of the school was to transform needy girls into confident young ladies who could fend for themselves while remaining "thoroughly domesticated" (Figure 3.4).

The pressure to adhere to traditional gender roles extended to sexuality as well. David Buck felt the atmosphere of Pinjarra was one of "good Christian Puritanism" sustained through regular doses of religion.[67] Although technically nondenominational, the CES, like most other charities of the period, continued to abide by the philosophy that

[66] For Fairbridge's views on the relationship between boxing and character development, see Kingsley Fairbridge, "Code of the Fairbridge Farm School," *c.* 1915, Sherington Papers, Box 1, State Library of New South Wales.
[67] Buck interview.

Figure 3.4 "Thoroughly domesticated." Fairbridge Annual Report, 1930, D.296/D1/1/1, ULSCA.

teaching children the tenets and practice of Christianity was essential to the reformation process. The construction of an Anglican chapel on the grounds in 1931 allowed the school to step up the frequency of church services, and child migrants from that period onward recall attending some form of religious observance, from morning worship to evensong, up to nine times a week.[68] Moreover, neither boys nor girls received sexual education, although this type of silence around the issue was common for the era. As Simon Szreter and Kate Fisher point out in their fascinating oral history of mid-twentieth-century British sexual attitudes, remaining ignorant about sex was crucial to upholding a "respectable" social identity, especially for women. Reliable information was thus hard to come by throughout the interwar years, as schools, parents, neighbors, and doctors all enforced the rule that sexuality should never be addressed openly.[69] Some young people of course knew more than they let on. But in general this information was communicated privately, through family networks to which child migrants no longer had access.[70] For uninformed

[68] Ibid; Cooper interview.
[69] Simon Szreter and Kate Fisher, *Sex before the Sexual Revolution: Intimate Life in England, 1918–1963* (Cambridge University Press, 2010), 63–112.
[70] Kate Fisher, *Birth Control, Sex and Marriage in Britain 1918–60* (Oxford University Press, 2006).

adolescents, Pinjarra's "hush hush program," as Queenie Malpass called it, could have serious consequences. At the age of seventeen Malpass still "had no idea the method that was used to have babies or where they came from." She had also received almost no information about menstruation. "We were given the little towels, you know, to hem and fix up," but beyond that the matter was never mentioned.[71] Without any foreknowledge of what was happening to her body, the onset of a girl's first menstrual cycle could be a frightening and traumatic experience.[72]

Learning not to talk about sex was one facet of a larger, imperial code of respectability that designated certain behaviors as appropriate for "civilized" Whites and others fitting only for "lesser" races. Although these dictates were more pronounced in the African and Asian colonies, where the presence of large colonized populations heightened the need to maintain the cultural divide between the races, they were not absent from a settler territory like Australia.[73] Indeed they grew more prevalent across the dominion in the interwar period amid the rising fears of an Asian threat to the global supremacy of the White race. At Pinjarra, the culture of respectability mandated that all interactions between the genders be kept strictly formal. For John Hay, the social rules came through most memorably in the school's occasional afternoon dance classes. He recalled that the girls and boys lined up on either end of the dining hall. One cottage mother played the piano and another taught the steps. The waltz was mandatory, "of course," as was the two-step, although more ambitious routines such as the schottische and the Gay Gordons sometimes made an appearance. "We didn't know one foot from another," he noted, but "we carried out the instructions":

You see, you would walk across and you would have to bow and say, "May I have the pleasure of this dance?" And the girl, although she hated the sight of you and you didn't think much of her ... would have to get up gracefully and take your arm, and you would have to escort her when the music finished back to her form and bow and say, "Thank you very much," although she'd trodden all over your toes or you'd trodden all over hers.

The classes were followed by an evening dance, during which boys and girls awkwardly shuffled around polished hardwood floors in their bare feet. No one seems to have had much fun, but, as Hay stressed, pleasure

---

[71] Malpass interview.

[72] Szreter and Fisher, *Sex before the Sexual Revolution*, 78–80; for a personal account of the fear associated with menstruation, see Hickson, *Flo*, 112–113.

[73] For an overview, see Philippa Levine, "Sexuality, Gender, and Empire," in *Gender and Empire*, ed. Philippa Levine (Oxford University Press, 2004), 134–155. For Australia, see Marilyn Lake, "The Politics of Respectability: Identifying the Masculinist Context," *Historical Studies* 22, no. 18 (1986): 116–131.

was not really the point. Instead, the enforced sociability was all "part of the training."[74] It was a way of introducing child migrants to the strictures governing White comportment in the empire.

This social education carried over into mealtimes. Throughout Britain and the empire, communal dining was widely accepted as a means to teach children social values. James Vernon has demonstrated that school lunch programs appealed to reformers not only because they nourished children's bodies but also because they provided a venue for the production of "civil and sociable subjects." They offered opportunities to coach children on etiquette and comportment, and as such formed part of the larger democratic mission to "enshrine a new model of society based on the principles of community, solidarity, civility, and efficiency."[75] Meals at Pinjarra served a similar function, allowing the staff to communicate to child migrants the ideals and expectations of White Australia. Breakfast and lunch were taken in a central dining hall, with children seated around long tables with their matron at the head. Supper was designed to provide more of a family atmosphere. It was prepared by the cottage mother and eaten "at home." Regardless of where they took place, meals were by all accounts restrained affairs. Stress was placed on politeness and self-control, traits that appeared as outward markers of one's membership in an advanced White culture. As John Lane remembered, the cottage mother "presided over our table manners, correcting any faults in our eating habits. Elbows had to be kept off the table at all times, and each slice of bread cut into quarters." Maintaining personal composure was vital. "Talking had to be restricted to necessary conversation only," although he acknowledged that many boys and girls "were adept at speaking out of the corner of their mouth."[76] In addition to teaching the White imperial habits of self-regulation, mealtimes were calculated to impart the more local, settler values of egalitarianism and mutual respect. For Bert Read, these lessons came through in the exacting way that food was shared. Each table was given a pound of butter in the morning, "and it was someone's job to cut up the butter. And it had to go to fourteen. You had to make sure it was exactly fourteen pieces of the butter, which wasn't easy to do." Ensuring that each child got his fair share "used to worry me," Read continued, for this small gesture signified the larger ethic of commonality and evenhandedness that lay at the idealized core of the White Australian identity.[77]

---

[74] Hay interview.

[75] James Vernon, "The Ethics of Hunger and the Assembly of Society: The Techno-Politics of the School Meal in Modern Britain," *American Historical Review* 110, no. 3 (2005): 693–725, 713 and 711.

[76] Lane, *Fairbridge Kid*, 109–110.    [77] Read interview.

The most formal attempt to "Australianize" child migrants occurred in the classroom. Until they reached the school-leaving age of fourteen, boys and girls were educated together at a primary school located on site and run by the Education Department. They received the customary Australian education, which emphasized basic reading and math skills, as well as local geography and culture within an imperial framework. "The rest of the world," laughed John Hay, "really didn't exist":

It was the British empire. There was a place called America but we knew nothing at all about that. South America we'd heard they had pampas and cattle were run there. Russia was one of the unknown countries. China had the Yellow River and that was about all as far as we knew. South East Asia, well, jungle country ... Europe – [we did] only the big countries; the smaller ones, even Spain ... got [barely] a mention.[78]

This cursory world tour encouraged child migrants to think of themselves as members of both the Australian nation and of a wider Britannic community, the superiority of which was made clear by the amount of time spent on the other regions of the world. Within the hierarchy of nations, the countries of Greater Britain ranked highest and received the most attention. Australia got a full year, while another year was dedicated to Canada, South Africa, New Zealand, India, and Ceylon. The children inferred that the territories located outside this British world were of little importance. They were consigned to the realm of the "unknown" or dismissed as backward and inconsequential, mere "jungle countries."

These lessons expressed the broader aims of the Pinjarra curriculum perfectly, at once conveying a sense of Britannic racial solidarity while also underscoring to child migrants that their new lives were part of a grander imperial project. Despite the potency of this message, the children's formal schooling remained of secondary importance. Many former migrants agreed with Bert Read that class work had always seemed "a really casual sort of [thing]. No one pushed you at doing anything."[79] Charles McKay, who arrived at Pinjarra in 1921 as a nine-year-old, could not remember ever being given a textbook. All of the subjects were taught from the board, and the children "had to try and remember what the school teacher said."[80] Instead, the true focus of the education was the postprimary training period, which was geared to provide boys and girls with the practical knowledge they would need to enter the agrarian economy. First conceived as a one-year vocational course, in 1935 the training was extended to up to two years. Boys entered a rotation of jobs,

[78] Hay interview.      [79] Read interview.
[80] Interview with Charles Alexander McKay, conducted by Chris Jeffery, October 8, 1986, OH 1886, SAWA: BL.

spending some two months each in the dairy, stables, butchery, kitchen, and fields, as well as an additional month each in the laundry and the poultry house. If the school had already reached its yearly placement quota by the time a boy had finished this schedule, he might be kept on for a further few months of "general duties," which could include working in the store, repairing buildings, stocking firewood, maintaining the sanitation system, and cleaning the outhouses.[81] Girls' training was less varied, consisting mainly of washing, ironing, and mending clothes in the laundry. Having demonstrated an early proficiency in these tasks, a girl might then be selected as a maid of all work in the principal's house, a job that was seen as a special honor. Lily Snellin, the wife of George Snellin and the only child from a family of nine sent to Pinjarra in 1929, reflected that "if you were picked to be the principal's maid ... you were superior and treated as such, as I was."[82] These training routines changed little throughout the interwar period, although the opening of a domestic science center on the grounds in 1935 did broaden the girls' curriculum to include advanced lessons in cooking, sewing, and housecleaning techniques.[83]

The intent of the training program was to introduce child migrants to the duties they would be called on to perform as farmhands and rural servants, as well as to inure them to the rigorous workloads that these jobs carried. The school justified the training period as a character-building experience that prepared every migrant to face the "problems that would confront him later when he set out for the Bush."[84] This argument was uncontroversial at the time, since it was in line with the widely held Australian belief that outdoor chores were good for young people, in that they instilled a strong work ethic.[85] Technically, these duties did not constitute child labor, since the trainees were no longer children, having already reached the school-leaving age. At Pinjarra, their symbolic entry into adulthood was marked through the acquisition of boots and shoes, which separated the trainees from the mass of barefoot children. Nevertheless, the reality remained that the teenagers provided a pool of unpaid workers who were essential to the daily functioning of the farm. At times the distinction between labor and education grew so fine as to become indistinguishable.

[81] CES, Perth Committee Minutes, June 26, 1935, ACC, 3025A/4, SAWA: BL.
[82] Interview with Lily Snellin, conducted by Chris Jeffery, July 11, 1985, OH 1876, SAWA: BL.
[83] CES, Executive Committee Minutes, May 8, 1935, D.296/B1/2/4, ULSCA.
[84] "John Immigrant: The Big Adventure," *Manchester Guardian*, January 15, 1931.
[85] Dorothy Scott and Shurlee Swain, *Confronting Cruelty: Historical Perspectives on Child Protection in Australia* (Melbourne University Press, 2002), 66–69.

The working day of a trainee was long and intense. The boys typically got up at 4:30 in the morning to milk the cows and then moved from one heavy, manual task to the next through the late afternoon. "We made the drains ... we made the roads, like, we carted gravel, we planted the paddocks too," noted Henry Hawkesford, who arrived at Pinjarra in 1924 at the age of thirteen and so received less than six months of schooling before beginning his training. "Even before Christmas I was working on the farm," he explained, since "they were short of labor in that time."[86] The girls' schedule was no less strenuous. In 1936, Colonel Heath wrote to the Society's London committee to argue that the "burden imposed upon our children in the laundry, particularly the girls, is too great ... For girls from 14–15 years of age to stand at the washtub or iron at the ironing table for seven or eight hours a day, five days a week, in the heat of an Australian summer, is detrimental to their health." Heath maintained that the system was both exploitative and counterproductive. Given the monotonous nature of the chores, the girls were likely to develop a "distaste for this type of work in the future" that would defeat the organization's goal of producing enthusiastic rural helpers.[87] The London board was persuaded, but it was still another year before the money was found to supply the farm with up-to-date laundry equipment.

Reforms like this one were rare. More often, the Society's governing boards accepted that child migrants needed to get used to a tough schedule, and they contended that it was better to train boys and girls to keep pace than to see them fail in their first jobs. An extreme version of this argument was voiced in 1932 by one of the Perth committee's most active members, Colonel J. Waley Cohen, a former soldier in the Queen's Westminster Rifles and a veteran of both the South African War and the First World War. "Our justification is that we fill ... a _want_ in the back blocks," he began, adding that the Society's popularity stemmed from its ability to fill Australia's "'out-back' requirements with our orphans." Speaking at the height of the Depression, when even the most unattractive jobs were scarce, he noted that the continued success of the project depended on the school's ability to "keep up the discipline side of our children." To this end, he recommended changing the regimen at Pinjarra to ensure that boys and girls did not get used to "amenities which will not be available in the back blocks." His suggestions included doing away with the school's electric lights and running water, and cancelling all group activities, like the yearly holiday camp, weekly films,

---

[86] Interview with Henry Hawkesford, conducted by Chris Jeffery, February 4, 1986, OH 1889, SAWA: BL.

[87] CES, Executive Committee Minutes, February 25, 1936, D.296/B1/2/4, ULSCA.

and team sports competitions. These pastimes might be "all very nice at Fairbridge" but were damaging indulgences in the long run, for as he pointed out, "when [the children] go out on an isolated farm there is no one to play games with."[88]

This proposal to turn Pinjarra into a quasi-survivalist boot camp was too radical for the Society's directors. It was dropped without serious consideration. Yet the episode remains a stark illustration of how the political drive to populate Australia's hinterlands with British stock defined the experience of interwar child migrants. Waley Cohen's larger point – that needy children could and should be engineered to achieve the dominion's settlement aims – persisted unchallenged. Throughout the period, the only real debate was about whether this goal required boys and girls to forgo the standard touchstones of a happy childhood. Touted as the best and brightest of the empire, in practice child migrants were often treated as second-class citizens. They were slotted into badly paid, menial positions in regions where many Australians refused to live. This treatment had little to do with any purported "outsider" status. While sometimes razzed as "Pommies," on the whole former migrants did not report feeling looked down on for their recent British origins, which in any event placed them in the mainstream of Australian society. Instead, child migrants' relative powerlessness was a function of their unattached status: their lack of connection to families who could advocate on their behalf.[89] Waley Cohen expressed the point with characteristic bluntness, declaring that "we must be careful not to increase the unemployment troubles of [Western Australia] by competing for the near city or in the city jobs for which the children with parents are eligible and suitable." The best positions for child migrants were in those places where Australians were "not inclined to send their own children." Parents, he clarified, without a hint of irony, "naturally wish to keep in touch with their children and, therefore, hesitate to let children go."[90]

These restrictions applied equally to child migrants' education. Throughout the 1930s, the Society's London and Perth committees repeatedly discussed whether children who performed well should be allowed to compete for places at local high schools. In Britain at the time, there had been a slow but steady growth in the number of working-class children pursuing secondary education. By 1927, the proportion of

---

[88] CES, Executive Committee Minutes, October 17, 1932, D.296/B1/2/3, ULSCA. Emphasis in the original.

[89] Indeed, when former migrants reported feeling stigmatized by the community, it was because they were perceived to be orphans rather than because they were "British." See for instance, George Snellin interview; Walsh interview.

[90] CES, Executive Committee Minutes, October 17, 1932.

non-fee-paying spots at grammar schools had increased to 40 percent.[91] There was also the precedent of the handful of children at Pinjarra, like John Hay, who had won state bursaries to local high schools during the 1920s. Together, these trends seemed to imply a need for expanding the opportunities offered to child migrants. Yet the Perth committee worried that any move in that direction would detract from the Society's mission to provide Australia with well-trained rural settlers. The organization's local reputation factored into their decision-making, and they questioned whether it was "right to enter children raised in England in competition with Australian children for scholarships." The issue proved too complicated for them to settle alone. Declaring that they were "opposed to secondary and University education of Fairbridge children," the board opted to leave the final verdict to London.[92]

The Society's executive committee discussed the matter throughout the later months of 1932 and into 1933. Its membership split evenly between those who felt that secondary education worked against the organization's objectives and those who interpreted the scheme's purpose more widely as the creation of "good and useful Australian citizens."[93] In the end, the problem boiled down to a question of finance: would the Society channel money away from farm training in order to pay the living expenses and fees of children attending school in Perth? After months of debate, the committee reached a compromise. In April of 1933, it resolved that, while the board would not "object to any individual or organisation providing funds for the higher education of a child who shows very extra-ordinary promise," they could "under no circumstances provide out of this Society's funds for such cases."[94] Although this stipulation opened the door for some children to pursue nonagrarian careers, the number who actually attained these scholarships remained miniscule, probably no more than a dozen throughout the interwar period.[95] Settlement, rather than education, remained the priority.

## Conclusion

The culture of Pinjarra during the 1920s and 1930s was one of order, obedience, and control. The school's driving intent was to transform the erstwhile street child into a civilized imperial laborer, one who had the

[91] Harry Hendrick, *Children, Childhood and English Society, 1880–1990* (Cambridge University Press, 1997), 68.
[92] CES, Perth Committee Minutes, January 25, 1933, ACC 3025A/3, SAWA: BL.
[93] CES, Executive Committee Minutes, November 16, 1932, D.296/B1/2/3, ULSCA.
[94] Ibid, April 5, 1933.
[95] Heath to Stowe, February 1, 1933, ACC 3026A/35, SAWA: BL.

skills and character to safeguard White Australia. In a period of rising anxiety about the security of the British race in the Pacific, the child emigration movement adapted to reflect the imperatives of dominion nationalism. The effect was a rising tendency to treat child migrants as undifferentiated political units that could be mass-produced to fit the demographic needs of their adoptive homeland. While earlier proponents had enthused that resettlement in the empire broadened the life paths of needy children, even allowing some boys and girls to enter the professional classes, during the interwar period this idealism faded from view. The Victorian vision of child migrants becoming doctors, lawyers, or ladies was no longer compatible with the political demands of the project. Instead, those sent to Australia were limited to manual work in farming and service.

More than anything else about their childhood, it was this aspect of the interwar farm school upbringing that most troubled former migrants in later life. Jack Maude remembered bitterly that school authorities had denied him the chance to take a position in a drapery store in town because he was slated to work as a farmhand. One of his friends, a boy who had been involved in an accident chopping wood and was missing three and a half fingers on one hand, was also sent to a farm, a decision Maude felt was "ridiculous." "A lot of children weren't meant to be farmers," but the "pattern was ... irrespective of who you were or what your inclination was or what you liked, you went on a farm. You had no option."[96] David Buck was one of the lucky few; he won a scholarship, attended high school and university, and became a math teacher. Yet he never understood why "I was sort of touted as being one of ... the bright children of Fairbridge," when there were "a lot of other children who were as equally able, for whom an opportunity was denied." In hindsight he believed the unfairness was "just entrenched into the Fairbridge system," which was "meant to provide ... an agricultural foundation for a colony."[97]

This emphasis was not unique to Pinjarra. It was also shared by the four other farm schools that were established in the dominion during the interwar years, and that together with Pinjarra placed more than 3,000 boys and girls in the dominion by the eve of the Second World War. Proponents of the movement continued to insist that these schemes would eventually allow child migrants to own their own farms, but these claims rang hollow as alumni started to report back on their work experiences. Assessing statistics provided by the CES in 1937, George Plant of

---

[96] Maude interview.     [97] Buck interview.

Britain's OSC noted that, of the boys who had passed through Pinjarra to that point, 56 percent were agricultural laborers, 30 percent were casual workers, 14 percent had "drifted to Perth or the coal fields," and none was "in possession of a farm of his own." Plant concluded that "almost all these old Fairbridge boys have been condemned to low wages and unstable conditions." Instead of providing a leg up in life, the scheme had led them to "a dead end as agricultural labourers ... with little chance of advancement or settled family life."[98] Gordon Green, the organizing secretary of the Society, acknowledged as much when he wrote that the "Old Fairbridgian cannot, with his own small resources, establish himself [as a farmer]. On the other hand, as a farm labourer he is not likely to find himself with sufficient wages or independence ... to warrant marriage and the establishment of a home and rearing of a family." There existed a "rapidly increasing number of Old Fairbridgians over twenty-one and indeed over twenty-five, for whom there is no advancement except in rare cases."[99]

Figures such as these challenged the movement's status as a form of social welfare. They also called into question proponents' assumptions about the adaptability of children. It was obvious to all involved that, while the migrants may have assimilated into their new environments, few had become successful pioneers or independent settlers. This awareness, however, did not lead reformers to reevaluate the aims and methods of the child emigration movement. Rather, supported by the growth of new psychological assessments of children's development within the fields of social welfare and education, their concern instead began to focus on the children themselves.

[98] G. F. Plant, "Progress and Present Situation of Migrants Assisted under Government Schemes," c. 1937, DO 35/667, TNA: PRO.
[99] Green to Plant, February 8, 1937, DO 35/708/4, TNA: PRO.

# 4 "Defective" boys and "problem" girls: selection standards in 1930s Australia and Southern Rhodesia

Queenie Malpass always viewed her selection for emigration to the Fairbridge Farm School as an honor. Born in Winchester, England, in 1912, she lost her mother soon after the First World War to what was probably a case of blood poisoning. The death left her father with two young children and, while he felt that he could continue to care for one, the strain of both was too much. He sent Queenie to Barnardo's but kept her brother at home. "He thought the boy could handle things," she explained, and "he thought that I'd have a better chance if I went to Barnardo's." According to Malpass, her father applied the same logic when it came time to consent to her emigration. In those days, "there was not very many chosen, you know, from Barnardo's. They were very select. And my father said yes, she could go [because it] would probably give me a better chance in life to come." Malpass left for Pinjarra in the early months of 1922, and as an adult she remained proud at having made the cut. The school only accepted the brightest and most capable children, she noted. All others were vetted out in Britain. Or they were sent back after they had arrived. Of the fourteen girls in her cottage, two had been returned: one for being "mentally deficient" and the other because of an illness that required hospitalization. Several more children had been repatriated during her three years at the farm, primarily for what Malpass believed were mental disorders. "I don't know how they got through," she said. The Australian authorities "were pretty thorough with us. They went through us with the third and fourth degree, mentality, everything. Even though we'd been selected, they still went through us."[1]

Throughout the 1920s and 1930s, many child migrants shared Malpass' experience of being grilled by dominion representatives. While Canadian officials had been subjecting arriving boys and girls to medical examinations since the 1890s, interwar Australian immigration authorities took the quest to weed out "inferior-quality" children to new levels.

[1] Interview with Queenie Malpass, conducted by Chris Jeffery, December 11, 1986, OH 1885, SAWA: BL.

126

Like their Canadian counterparts, Australian agents strove to restrict the entry of any child who might have a physical disability or contagious disease. Yet their central concern was with the children's mental health. Relying on the emerging medical expertise of child psychology, as well as on the novel technique of IQ testing, Australian immigration officials set higher entrance requirements for child migrants than had their Canadian predecessors. They also regularly repatriated "problem" children, defined as any boy or girl who seemed uncontrollable, unemployable, or simply lacking in potential.

This growing selectivity was another product of the rise of racialized forms of nationalism across Greater Britain in the aftermath of the First World War. The same anxieties about the vulnerability of the White race that had renewed a political drive to fill the dominions' empty spaces with British stock in the early 1920s also impelled a closer scrutiny of the foundations of "Whiteness" within national populations throughout the settler empire. This chapter charts the impact of those fears through a comparison of the selection standards for child migrants in Australia and Southern Rhodesia, two of the most homogeneous and racially aware regions of the British world at the time. Both territories contained European populations that were 95 percent British – the result of restrictive immigration policies that had been put in place at the turn of the century – and local politicians were eager to keep it that way.[2] While they continued to prioritize the settlement of Britons above all other nationalities, however, officials in both countries espoused distinct interpretations of White racial fitness that tended, over time, to tear away at the older ideal of a united Britannic race. Present throughout the interwar period, these tensions became more pronounced during the Depression, when high rates of unemployment across the empire caused a virtual standstill in transimperial migration. The sudden downturn encouraged immigration authorities to apply stricter admissions criteria, which assessed prospective migrants in terms of their projected economic capacity as well as their ability to uphold the nation's racial agenda. By the eve of the Second World War, the local priorities of Australia and Southern Rhodesia had begun to overshadow Britain's imperial settlement objectives. Although new settlers continued to be welcomed in each of the dominions, it was clear that only the "highest quality" migrants from the United Kingdom need apply.

Within the child emigration movement, these heightened selection standards had the effect of diminishing reformers' optimism about the

[2] A. S. Mlambo, *White Immigration into Rhodesia: From Occupation to Federation* (Harare: University of Zimbabwe, 2002), 11; Derick Schreuder and Stuart Ward, eds., *Australia's Empire* (Oxford University Press, 2008), 10.

potential of youth. Under the growing pressure of dominion nationalism, both Barnardo's and the CES moved away from their earlier emphases on children's adaptability toward more restricted developmental models that centered on notions of "inherent" or fixed defects. The precise articulation of these ideas differed in the two territories. Australian authorities tended to rely on biological or hereditarian arguments, while their Rhodesian counterparts prioritized the role played by culture in defining a child's personality and abilities. But the results were alike in both cases. By the late 1930s, the same needy boys and girls who had long been praised for their malleability and capacity to uphold the imperial mission had been reconfigured as a potential racial threat, a danger to the purity of the "White dominions."

## Mental testing and repatriation from Australia

Although Queenie Malpass first witnessed the rise of official concern about child migrants' "mentality" in the mid 1920s, the repatriations of the interwar period were the product of cultural forces that stretched back much further in Australian society. Like Britain's, the country's birthrate had declined steadily throughout the later Victorian and Edwardian periods. And, as it had in the imperial center, the trend raised the specter of urban degeneracy and provoked widespread alarm about the deterioration of the race. By the turn of the century, a loose coalition of Australian doctors, philanthropists, feminists, and bureaucrats had begun to tackle the problem by campaigning for improvements to maternal and child health. Many of their policy proposals echoed those being put forth in Europe and North America: the expansion of infant welfare centers, free kindergartens, school medical inspections, the improvement of physical education, and the creation of state-funded family allowances and child endowments. Crucially, however, in Australia the growth of maternalist activism took place within a national culture that was already dominated by fears of White racial vulnerability. The anxieties that sustained the White Australia policy equally shaped the ways that local reformers understood questions of population health and national welfare.[3] As a result, during the early decades of the twentieth century Australian doctors and public health

---

[3] Marilyn Lake, "A Revolution in the Family: The Challenge and Contradictions of Maternal Citizenship in Australia," in *Mothers of a New World: Maternalist Politics and the Origins of Welfare States*, ed. Seth Koven and Sonya Michel (New York: Routledge, 1993), 378–395; Shurlee Swain, Patricia Grimshaw, and Ellen Warne, "Whiteness, Maternal Feminism, and the Working Mother, 1900–1960," in *Creating White Australia*, ed. Jane Carey and Claire McLisky (Sydney University Press, 2009), 214–227.

crusaders were more inclined than their European counterparts to view the problems of poor health and urban poverty through the lens of heredity. Environmentalist notions about the importance of proper nutrition and clean living remained a prominent part of the discourse about racial fitness in the dominion. Yet these concepts sat side by side with harder, Social Darwinist attitudes that emphasized the need to isolate and weed out the population's "inferior" elements.[4]

This ideology laid the foundations for a bifurcated social policy agenda that aimed to improve the wellbeing of the racially "desirable" while restricting the reproduction of the "unfit." The 1912 Maternity Allowance Act, for instance, provided a £5 payment to new mothers to help ease the costs of raising a family. But it deliberately excluded Aboriginal and Asian women on the principle that their fertility was to be discouraged rather than promoted.[5] The "yellow peril" scares of the 1920s and 1930s only strengthened this eugenic impulse. Throughout the period medical authorities extended their surveillance of Australian society in a number of new ways. State officials stepped up their efforts to remove mixed-race Indigenous boys and girls to charitable and government-run institutions, believing that by rearing these children as White, and by only allowing them to marry lighter "castes," they could eliminate all trace of Aboriginality in the national population.[6] Racial hygienists increased their policing of poorer White communities as well, with a particular focus on slum children. The hope was that, by targeting the young, they could prevent the spread of any unsanitary or "degenerate" traits among the urban working classes as a whole.[7]

Before any potential contagion could be stopped, it had to be identified. As a result, the interwar years witnessed a boom in biometrics, as public health officials compiled statistics on the heights, weights, chest dimensions, and disease rates of schoolchildren across the country.[8] Alongside these physical indicators of health, they also sought to inspect the hidden recesses of children's minds, an objective that led

---

[4] Rob Watts, "Beyond Nature and Nurture: Eugenics in Twentieth Century Australian History," *Australian Journal of Politics and History* 40, no. 3 (September 1994): 318–334; Stephen Garton, "Sound Minds and Healthy Bodies: Re-considering Eugenics in Australia, 1914–1940," *Australian Historical Studies* 26, no. 103 (November 1995): 163–181; Warwick Anderson, *The Cultivation of Whiteness: Science, Health and Racial Destiny in Australia* (New York: Basic Books, 2003), 165–188.

[5] Lake, "A Revolution in the Family," 379–380.

[6] Anna Haebich, *Broken Circles: Fragmenting Indigenous Families, 1800–2000* (Fremantle: Fremantle Arts Centre Press, 2000), 272–274.

[7] David Kirk and Karen Twigg, "Regulating Australian Bodies: Eugenics, Anthropometrics and School Medical Inspection in Victoria, 1900–1940," *History of Education Review, ANZHES* 23, no. 1 (1994): 19–37.

[8] Anderson, *The Cultivation of Whiteness*, 169–171.

many to embrace the new phenomenon of the IQ test. Intelligence testing had originated in France at the start of the twentieth century. It was adopted for use in Britain by Cyril Burt shortly thereafter and started being used in Australia and Canada around the time of the First World War.[9] From the beginning, policymakers' enthusiasm for the method was more pronounced in the dominions than in Britain. While IQ scores were widely taken up by British doctors in the 1920s to diagnose mental deficiency, most providers remained skeptical of claims that the tests offered an objective assessment of a child's innate cognitive abilities, and the technique was never fully incorporated into the selection procedures for secondary education.[10] The stronger hereditarian leanings of the medical profession in Australia, however, prepared the way for a broad acceptance of the test's rationale. To immigration officers eager to protect the racial health of the nation, intelligence quotients offered a simple assessment of the mental viability of children. They provided a quick, readily understandable, and seemingly scientific means to classify and segregate out the "subnormals" and "feebleminded" from the rest of the nation's White population.

Because of the small scale of the prewar child emigration movement to Australia, the Commonwealth government only became involved in regulating the schemes in 1921, when it made "the right of free selection" a condition of state funding.[11] Before this time, child migrants to the dominion had not been subject to any formal inspection process. The new stipulation meant that children arriving from the early 1920s onward would receive two screenings before they were cleared for entry. The first consisted of a physical and IQ test administered at the dominion's consulate, Australia House, in London. The second was a follow-up medical inspection designed to catch any contagious diseases that had manifested on the journey over.[12] Because this second evaluation, which was usually performed at the dockside, was much less rigorous than the first, the doctors at Australia House tried to be as thorough as possible,

---

[9] For an overview of this background, see Adrian Wooldridge, *Measuring the Mind: Education and Psychology in England, 1860–1990* (Cambridge University Press, 1994), 73–110.

[10] Gillian Sutherland, *Ability, Merit and Measurement: Mental Testing and English Education, 1880–1940* (Oxford: Clarendon Press, 1984), 191–270; Mathew Thomson, *Psychological Subjects: Identity, Culture and Health in Twentieth-Century Britain* (Oxford University Press, 2006), 110–113.

[11] Gullett to Rickard, December 21, 1921, A1, 1936/3667, ANA.

[12] It is unclear when the dominion began requiring IQ tests for child migrants, although the CES's annual report for 1925 featured a picture of young boys undergoing intelligence testing in its London offices, indicating that they had become a routine feature of the predeparture selection process by that time. CES, Annual Report, 1925, D.296/D1/1/1, ULSCA.

pulling out before boarding any child who would not meet the dominion's criteria.

Emigration charities felt the repercussions of the new inspection system immediately. As early as the summer of 1922, Barnardo's executive
committee worried that Australian authorities were setting the bar too
high. The board had been eager to extend its operations throughout the
dominion and had investigated the possibility of establishing schemes in
the states of Victoria and Queensland along the lines of its New South
Wales operations. Yet it quickly became apparent that the requirements
for admission into the country had grown "so stringent" that the organization would have difficulty finding "sufficient boys and girls [who
were] physically and mentally fit to pass through the emigration sieve."[13]
Concerned that it would not be able to sustain the additional obligations,
the committee called off its planned expansion. Five years on, the situation had worsened. Out of a party of fifty-six children selected from its
branches around Liverpool, Australian officials had rejected nineteen,
even though the association "felt that they were all satisfactory" and
"suitable for migration."[14]

These rejections were an early sign that British welfare providers
and Australian immigration authorities were using different methods
to evaluate the fitness of needy children. As they had for decades, the
charity's doctors and branch managers in the United Kingdom relied on
an arsenal of visual cues to judge whether children were strong enough
for resettlement. They would assess their height, weight, and complex-
ion, test their reflexes, and peer into their eyes for signs of discoloration.
To dominion medical officials, these external markers appeared woe-
fully insufficient for measuring the qualities of the mind. A visit by the
chairman of Australia's Development and Migration Commission, H. W.
Gepp, to Pinjarra in 1929 underscored the difficulty. Having received
word that four children at the farm school were "definitely imbecile,"
Gepp arrived at the school accompanied by his vice chair and two members of the CES's Perth Committee. When one of the suspect children,
a girl of fourteen, was brought forward for examination, Gepp noted
that the "child was very attractive and of good physique." Disturbingly,
though, this outward appearance of health masked what the investigators
judged to be a severely underdeveloped mind. As Gepp remarked, "a few
minutes conversation with her revealed that she was incapable of doing
anything without continuous guidance and direction." He concluded

[13] Barnardo's, Executive Committee Minutes, June 28, 1922, D.239/B3/1/6, ULSCA.
[14] Memo for the Director of Migration and Settlement Office on the Migration of Barnardo
Children, December 12, 1927, A1, 1936/3667, ANA.

that the government should deport the girl, and insisted that the case be brought to the attention of the Australian Director of Migration in London "with a view to doing everything possible to eliminat[e] the risk of such consequences in future."[15]

Throughout the period, definitions of mental deficiency remained fluid. Terms such as "subnormal," "backward," "feebleminded," and "dull" were used interchangeably, often without reference to set guidelines. In this light, it is revealing that Gepp did not administer an IQ test to the girl. Rather, he deemed "a few minutes conversation with her" enough to evaluate her intelligence, and never paused to consider that a young woman who had grown up in institutional care might find it difficult to express herself to a government delegation composed of four older men. During the 1920s and into the 1930s, child psychology remained a nascent discipline across Britain and the settler empire. Although the field provoked considerable intellectual and popular excitement, it was slow to receive full acceptance and accreditation by the medical profession.[16] Ironically, this marginal status often served to strengthen the applied power of psychological concepts, since they provided officials and reformers with a "scientific" language that could be flexibly deployed. For a bureaucrat like Gepp, whose background was in mining, such rhetoric allowed him to assume the mantle of psychological expertise, empowering him to make decisions about the fitness of individual children without any formal medical training or experience in the subject.[17]

The same was true for the staff and board members of the dominion's farm schools, who found that a diagnosis of a mental disorder offered a straightforward method for dealing with difficult children. Colonel Heath, the principal of Pinjarra from 1928 to 1936, was a particularly strong advocate of repatriation, viewing the policy as a necessary safeguard of the Society's reputation. Having come to his position with firm ideas about mental deficiency, he was quick to designate boys and girls who failed to conform to his expectations as "sub-par," and to nominate them for deportation. One of his first acts as principal was to notify the

[15] Gepp to the Secretary of the Development and Migration Commission, July 19, 1929, A436, 46/5/597 Part 2, ANA.

[16] Thomson, *Psychological Subjects* offers an overview of the reception of psychological ideas in Britain during this period. On the particular impact of child psychology, see Cathy Urwin and Elaine Sharland, "From Bodies to Minds in Childcare Literature: Advice to Parents in Inter-War Britain," in *In the Name of the Child: Health and Welfare, 1880–1940*, ed. Roger Cooter (New York: Routledge, 1992), 174–199.

[17] Before entering the government, Gepp had worked as a metallurgical engineer and plant manager. Michael Roe, *Australia, Britain, and Migration, 1915–1940: A Study of Desperate Hopes* (Cambridge University Press, 1995), 69.

organization's Perth Committee that a boy at the farm school "appeared to be somewhat mental" and required repatriation.[18]

Significantly, under Heath's tenure, the practice of repatriation was often shaped by gender considerations. In 1934, he wrote to the Society's local board to recommend the return of two boys and two girls. All were graduates of the school and had been working in farm positions throughout the state for a number of years. But, because child migrants remained under the authority of the emigration charities until the age of twenty-one, Heath was still in a position to make decisions about their future. Each case revolved around the issue of sexual impropriety. One of the boys had "been in trouble constantly since leaving" and had recently "attempted misconduct with one of our old girls." Although the youth had been "thwarted in this," Heath argued that he was still a "definite menace to the Society and a disgrace to the School." The two girls, who were nineteen and twenty at the time, were targets for repatriation because they were unmarried and pregnant. Both had accused their employers of fathering the children, although Heath doubted their claims. As he pointed out, one "was always considered below normal" while at Pinjarra, and the other was of "a particularly low grade ... it would have surprised me very much if she had not got into trouble." He considered it "most likely" that, if the girls were allowed to remain in the country, they would "get into trouble again," and he stressed that it would be "best for the Society and for the State" to send them back with the boys.[19] Two months later, Heath changed course. He reported that the two teenage boys had "approached me recently and said they would mend their ways ... and I think it most likely that the scare they have received will bring about the desired result." Although he was willing to give leeway to the youths, he remained uncompromising about the two young women, stating that "it would be quite wrong to retain these girls here and at the first available opportunity I will have them returned to England."[20] Unable to mask their pregnancies, they could not simply offer to reform their ways. All four had been nominated for repatriation for what amounted to sexual indiscretions, but in the end only the girls bore the punishment.

It was not an isolated incident. Barnardo's also returned girls more consistently than boys. In 1927, for instance, the charity shipped back five girls at one time after its welfare officer found them to be "incorrigible."[21] And,

---

[18] CES, Perth Committee Minutes, September 4, 1928, ACC 3025A/3, SAWA: BL. The Committee returned the boy the following month.

[19] Heath to Stowe, December 20, 1934, ACC 3026/8, SAWA: BL.

[20] Heath to Green, February 21, 1935, ACC 3026/9, SAWA: BL.

[21] Barnardo's NSW, Executive Committee Minutes, July 26, 1927, Barnardo's Australia, Ultimo.

of the twenty-five children and juveniles that the CES repatriated between 1934 and 1938, sixteen were girls, even though during the same period the organization had sent more than twice as many boys to Australia.[22] Overwhelmingly, both genders were more often repatriated on account of their minds and morals than for any purported physical disabilities. Nine girls were returned for being "subnormal," "backward," or "mentally unstable," three for unwed pregnancies, two more for "moral weakness," one for a diagnosis of noncontagious syphilis, and the last for being "childish." Of the nine boys, four were returned for being "subnormal," one for "mental trouble," another for suicidal tendencies and for being "sexually unbalanced," two for epilepsy, and only one for being physically unfit.[23] In addition, the young men tended to remain in the country for an average of twenty-one months longer than the women. One youth repatriated for epilepsy had lived in Australia for over thirteen years before his departure. These differences in the length of stay suggest that boys were given more chances to reform after a behavioral lapse than were girls, for whom the consequences tended to be immediate. The gender imbalance of repatriation appears, in this respect, as another by-product of interwar Australia's masculine-dominated culture, which held men and women to distinct standards of sexuality and comportment.[24] While a degree of "larrikinism" was celebrated as a sign of manliness, women were valued for their purity and passivity.[25] Excluded from the Australian ethic of mateship because of their gender, child migrant girls who did not fit the country's normative definition of White femininity found themselves literally expelled from the nation as well.

The message behind these deportations was that British children who "failed" did not deserve a place in the Australian collective. Certainly, diagnoses of mental deficiency were not unique to child migrants. Australian public health authorities were just as concerned about the

---

[22] In total, the Society repatriated at least forty-one children during the interwar years; throughout the period, girls constituted only about one-third of CES migrants. Geoffrey Sherington and Chris Jeffery, *Fairbridge: Empire and Child Migration* (London: Woburn Press, 1998), 146–147.

[23] CES, "Children Repatriated from the Fairbridge Farm School," January 28, 1938, ACC 3026A/41, SAWA: BL.

[24] The literature on the gendered dimensions of Australian nationalism is vast. For an overview, see Angela Woollacott, "Gender and Sexuality," in *Australia's Empire*, ed. Schreuder and Ward, 312–335.

[25] Present since the nineteenth century, this gendered dichotomy was reemphasized in the mythology of the First World War, which portrayed Australian men as protective warriors and Australian women as innocent victims of fate. Carmel Shute, "Heroines and Heroes: Sexual Mythology in Australia, 1914–1918," in *Gender and War: Australians at War in the Twentieth Century*, ed. Joy Damousi and Marilyn Lake (Cambridge University Press, 1995), 23–42.

spread of degeneracy among local White children, especially after a 1925 study estimated that at least 1 percent of schoolchildren across the state of Victoria were so feebleminded that they required segregation.[26] While Australian-born "deficients" were also subject to invasive treatment and discrimination, they remained part of the national community. They could not be sent back. Through the policy of repatriation, interwar dominion authorities were beginning to articulate a local identity that was distinct from the claim of shared British ancestry. Although the Australian government would not define a separate citizenship for the country until 1948, immigration officials were already drawing a line between the baseline characteristics that defined a person as a member of the global Britannic race and the more specific traits that qualified them to become Australian.

This process of differentiation intensified during the Depression. In the face of spiraling unemployment, dominion authorities stepped up their efforts to ensure that the trickle of new arrivals they were letting into the country would make healthy and productive citizens. The increased scrutiny provoked a series of clashes between Australian officials and British emigration charities over the quality and fitness of child migrants, the sharpest of which involved Barnardo's. In the years preceding the dispute, the organization's local committee had steadily expanded its influence throughout New South Wales. It had opened its first Australian farm school, Mowbray Park, in 1929, and four years later succeeded in raising enough donations to convert its reception hostel in Ashfield on the outskirts of Sydney into a new Home for migrant girls aged between six and thirteen. This latter development prompted the association to do a general stocktake of their provisions for young women in the dominion, the conclusions of which were alarming. As the London executive reported, the number of "moral failures" (a euphemism for unwed pregnancies) among Barnardo's wards in Australia was considerably higher than in the other regions where the society worked. In Canada, the rate was 4 percent, while in Britain it was 6 percent. But in New South Wales, the territory that contained the lowest total population of Barnardo girls in the empire, it was 13 percent.[27] To the charity's directing board, the statistic implied that there were flaws in the local committee's operating procedures, and it called on the Australian

---

[26] Anderson, *The Cultivation of Whiteness*, 166. Indeed, a 1928 survey found rates of feeblemindedness at even higher proportions, with an average rate of nearly 3 percent across the nation's schools. Ross Jones, "Removing Some of the Dust from the Wheels of Civilization: William Ernest Jones and the 1928 Commonwealth Survey of Mental Deficiency," *Australian Historical Studies* 40, no. 1 (March 2009): 63–78, 71.

[27] Barnardo's, Executive Committee Minutes, March 7, 1934, D.239/B3/1/10, ULSCA.

branch to improve its safeguards for girls. When Australia House caught wind of the matter, though, dominion officials interpreted the findings less as a breakdown in the systems of training and placement than as a sign that the society was trading in poor-quality migrants. By the end of the year, the question of "illegitimate" pregnancies had provoked a wider selection crisis that embroiled Barnardo's in a two-year debate with the Australian government over criteria of fitness.

First to draw attention to the issue was W. J. Stables, a migration representative at Australia House. In September of 1934, he notified the Commonwealth government that Barnardo's had been "much concerned over the large number of their girls who are in Sydney at the present time with babies." The situation suggested to Stables that the charity was importing "subnormal children of dull intellect," since it was, as he put it, a "well known fact that this type of individual breeds more readily than the normal human being." Usually, such cases would be identified through an IQ test and removed from consideration in London. These examinations had been a provision of Australian state funding, which, as Stables pointed out, the government had rescinded in 1930 on account of the Depression. Since that time, as long as Barnardo's paid the full passage fare and did not apply for a free or subsidized passage, the organization could resettle boys and girls "without reference to [Australia House], and there is no check on the type or physical fitness of the children."[28] Convinced "that the general policy of Barnardo's is only to send overseas those children who are unsuitable for placing in [Britain]," Stables had taken it upon himself to examine the most recent group of boys bound for Mowbray Park. His investigation uncovered the "rather astonishing" fact that Australian authorities had already rejected fifteen of the children in the party.[29]

On receipt of Stables' report, the Australian government sprang into action. Citing concerns about inferior heredity, the Prime Minister's Department called for a full inspection of every child at Mowbray Park. As one official noted, it was a matter of national security: "In the interests of building up good stock in Australia, we should not mince matters

[28] Stables to Farrands, September 20, 1934, A436, 1945/5/168 Part I, ANA. The CES's Fairbridge Farm School continued to receive assisted passages as a special arrangement with the Commonwealth, largely because the CES was a smaller organization and more dependent on governmental funding. Every child going to Pinjarra throughout the 1930s continued to receive medical examinations from Australia House.

[29] Ibid. Barnardo's sent a percentage of their children through the CES to the Fairbridge Farm School. These fifteen boys would have originally been bound for Pinjarra, and thus inspected by immigration authorities in Australia House; after rejection, they returned to the care of Barnardo's, where they were apparently reselected for emigration to Mowbray Park.

when there is a risk of physically and mentally unsuitable children coming to this country as prospective citizens and as prospective fathers and mothers, who themselves may possibly add still more degenerates to our population."[30] These fears of a spreading genetic contamination pushed the process ahead quickly. In early 1935, investigators from the New South Wales Education department went to the farm school to perform physical inspections of all ninety-five boys in residence. They also gave thirty-seven of the more "questionable" children a full mental and psychological workup. Underscoring that their findings revealed "a very serious state of affairs," they reported that three boys were "cases of definite or borderline feeblemindedness, and probably not able to be trained to be self-supporting in the outside world," four were "of a very dull type, possibly able to be trained to be self-supporting in manual occupations," and ten were "of a dull type capable of being trained to be self-supporting in manual occupations." They recommended a general purge of the system. All seventeen of the "misfit children should be returned to Great Britain, and others should not be permitted to emigrate."[31]

The critical element in the investigators' report was their assessment of the boys' capacity for lifelong independence. The testing of IQs seemingly allowed dominion authorities to quantify the potential of individual child migrants in straightforward numerical terms. Even though the majority of the "dull" boys had been judged educable, they remained racially suspect, the likely bearers of tainted genes. The examinations provided proof of one of Australian officials' greatest fears: that Barnardo's was exploiting a "loophole ... to dump 'dud' children within the Commonwealth."[32] Immigration officers soon met with the local committee to demand that they repatriate all seventeen boys, reinstitute the policy of predeparture medical inspections, and submit each party to a second IQ test on arrival in Sydney. They stressed that any boy or girl whose intelligence score was lower than ninety-five would be subject to immediate return to Britain at the association's expense.[33]

The members of the Barnardo's New South Wales committee, many of whom were long-standing supporters of the White Australia policy and advocates of eugenic-based social policy, accepted the new guidelines

---

[30] Farrands to Garrett, October 31, 1934, A436, 1945/5/168 Part I, ANA.
[31] Thomas to Bellemore, May 25, 1935, A436, 1945/5/168 Part I, ANA. Interestingly, this was one of the few disputes about repatriation in which the gender bias went in the opposite direction. In contrast to Stables' fears about unwed pregnancies, all thirty-three of the girls at Ashfield were found to be of normal physical and mental health.
[32] Stables to Farrands.
[33] Bellemore to Brown, May 31, 1935, A436, 1945/5/168 Part I, ANA.

without comment.[34] Back in London, though, the executive board was seething. Its directors argued that returning all seventeen children was excessive. They would sanction the repatriation of the three hopelessly "feebleminded" children but stressed that the other fourteen could be trained and should be given a chance to succeed. They also disputed the "extremely arbitrary" requirement of a ninety-five IQ.[35] The number was much higher than the accepted British cutoff for "subnormal" intelligence, which had been set by the 1929 Mental Deficiency (Wood) Committee at between seventy and eighty points.[36] Moreover, the board noted that the new criteria "would seriously diminish numbers," since few of the more than 5,000 children under the organization's care in Britain now fit the Australian definition of normal racial and mental fitness.[37] The changed conditions had rendered the "migration work of these Homes ... so insecure that its whole future was jeopardised."[38]

In the end, it was the threat of losing the emigration scheme altogether that pushed both sides to a compromise. The charity agreed to repatriate the five boys with the lowest IQ scores and to keep the other twelve under supervision. In exchange, dominion authorities dropped the requirement of retesting on arrival, although they reiterated that any child convicted of a criminal offense or placed in an insane asylum during their first five years in the country would be deported. Yet the minimum IQ standard of ninety-five remained in place, and, true to the executive committee's warning, it produced a stark decline in the number of eligible children. In November of 1936, the organization nominated 199 boys and 68 girls for its fall party, but of these only twenty boys and eighteen girls were cleared for emigration. Sixty-two had been removed from consideration due to parental objections, but the rest had been rejected for medical reasons, including "mental weakness," "not coming up to a reasonable standard of intelligence," a family history of epilepsy, and, in one case, having a stammer.[39] The problem continued through the end of the decade. In January of 1938, a list of 265 boys was whittled down to just 26.[40]

Barnardo's selection crisis highlights the widening gap between the British and Australian views of racial welfare during the interwar years. Although an idealized conception of Whiteness, associated with rationality, liberty, and civilizational advancement, grounded the collective

---

[34] Most notably, the chairman of the committee throughout the interwar period was Sir Arthur Rickard, a vocal proponent of racially based immigration policies.

[35] Barnardo's, Executive Committee Minutes, April 29, 1936, D.239/B3/1/11, ULSCA.

[36] Wooldridge, *Measuring the Mind*, 234.

[37] Barnardo's, Executive Committee Minutes, June 26, 1935.

[38] Ibid, April 29, 1936.

[39] Duffy to Lyons, November 7, 1936, DO35/685/4, TNA: PRO.

[40] Barnardo's, Executive Committee Minutes, January 5, 1938, D.239/B3/1/12, ULSCA.

identity of both countries, in Australia the benchmarks of racial membership were set higher and policed more rigorously than in Britain. Not every shade of White, it seemed, was the same. Of course, since the advent of modern racial science, conceptions of Whiteness had never been hegemonic. Australian politicians decided long before the interwar years that there was a palpable difference between northern and southern Europeans, for instance; they viewed the former as intelligent, efficient workers and dismissed the latter as lazy ne'er-do-wells.[41] What was new to the 1920s and 1930s was the use of this type of thinking to make differentiations *within* the British race. While interwar Australians still championed the superiority of the Britannic people from which they had sprung, this continued racial pride existed alongside a more recent, nationalist assertion that their own country contained a cleaner, fitter, and more efficient blood strain than did anywhere else in the empire.[42] The repatriations of the period were thus a vital part of the dominion's emerging political effort to carve out not only a separate sense of nationhood but also a distinct position of power within the British world and beyond.[43]

Swept up in the midst of this political maneuvering were those boys and girls who found themselves labeled "deficient" and "subnormal" and sent back to Britain. It is impossible to know what happened to them from there. The individual case files remain closed, and the returnees rarely warranted a mention in the official minutes of the emigration agencies. Presumably the younger ones reentered charitable care while the older ones found some form of work or were placed in state-run institutions. But it is easy to imagine the stigma, rejection, and disruption they must have felt from having to start afresh across an ocean twice in their young lives. Initially selected for their pliable constitutions and ability to improve, repatriated child migrants found themselves months

---

[41] Michele Langfield, "'White Aliens': The Control of European Immigration to Australia, 1920–1930," *Journal of Intercultural Studies* 12, no. 2 (1991): 1–14; Anderson, *The Cultivation of Whiteness*, 159.

[42] Notions of the purity and "cleanliness" of the Australian way of life resonated throughout the dominion's popular culture as well. See Richard White, *Inventing Australia: Images and Identity, 1688–1980* (London: Allen & Unwin, 1981), 110–124.

[43] On the simultaneous use of the rhetoric of White racial purity to assert Australian political claims in the international arena, see Marilyn Lake and Henry Reynolds, *Drawing the Global Colour Line: White Men's Countries and the International Challenge of Racial Equality* (Cambridge University Press, 2008). Nor was the increased selectivity unique to Australia. In the later 1930s, the Fairbridge Society encountered similar problems in selecting children for its farm school in Canada. In 1935, only 56 of 176 children put forward to Canada House had been approved, and by 1939 the Society was estimating that it would need to recruit at least 550 boys and girls in order to make its annual target of sending 336 to Canada and Australia. Sherington and Jeffery, *Fairbridge*, 177.

or even years later reclassified as damaged goods, and feared as the carriers of permanent mental or moral defects. This process was not unique to Australia. A similar negotiation over the value and fitness of needy children occurred as the movement extended into Southern Rhodesia, a region of the empire where the local politics of Whiteness took a distinct but no less aggressive form.

### The psychology of Whiteness in Southern Rhodesia

Despite the difficulties of the Depression and the increasing strictness of selection standards, the 1930s were a decade of remarkable growth for the CES. Its flagship Pinjarra farm school maintained an annual enrollment of about 350 children and, with the help of government funding, the site was expanded to include a chapel, several new cottages, an alumni hostel, and updated classrooms. In 1934, the organization received another boost when the Prince of Wales agreed to launch an ambitious fundraising campaign on its behalf. The appeal brought in upwards of £85,000, a figure that was slightly less than the executive committee had hoped for but more than enough to move forward with its plan to create new farm schools.[44] The first opened in British Columbia in late 1935, following the Canadian government's decision to exempt the charity from the ban on the immigration of school-aged children.[45] Two years later, the organization founded a second farm school named Molong in New South Wales, and helped coordinate the establishment of a third in Victoria: the Northcote Children's Farm, which was operated by a separate organization, the Northcote Children's Trust. By the mid 1930s, the movement appeared to be making a full recovery from the setbacks of the Depression. In a gesture designed to mark the revitalization, in 1935 the charity dropped its Edwardian title, the Child Emigration Society, for a simpler and more modern-sounding name, the Fairbridge Society.

It was this general mood of optimism and renewal that prompted the executive committee to revisit the prospect of settling children in southern Africa. The idea was first floated by the Reverend Arthur West, an Anglican minister and dedicated social imperialist who had served on the organization's board for more than a decade. Educated at Oxford in the

---

[44] CES, Executive Committee Minutes, September 25, 1935, D.296/B1/2/4, ULSCA.

[45] For a full discussion of the establishment of the school, see Patrick Dunae, "Waifs: The Fairbridge Society in British Columbia, 1931–1951," *Histoire Sociale – Social History* 21 (1988): 224–250; Sherington and Jeffery, *Fairbridge*, 160–163 and 171–175; Patrick Dunae, "Gender, Generations and Social Class: The Fairbridge Society and British Child Migration to Canada, 1930–1960," in *Child Welfare and Social Action in the Nineteenth and Twentieth Centuries: International Perspectives*, ed. Pat Starkey and Jon Lawrence (Liverpool University Press, 2001), 82–100.

late 1880s, West had come of age at the height of the empire-building fervor of the late Victorian era, and throughout his life he espoused the rugged individualism and Britannic pride that were common to men of his class and generation. After Oxford, he devoted a little over a decade to the Bush Brotherhood, a missionary organization that sent English pastors across the outback of Australia on horseback to preach the gospel. He returned to Britain on the eve of the First World War to take up a position at St. Dunstan's parish in the East End of London, and it was there that he first encountered the realities of slum poverty. Appalled by the desperate conditions in which many of his parishioners lived, and already a firm believer in the redemptive character of the imperial frontier, West was a natural fit for the CES. By the early 1920s, he had become one of the charity's most active champions, donating the collection from every Australia Day service to support its work. He joined the organization's Council in 1924, and five years later became a member of its executive board, a position he kept until his death in 1952.[46]

West had no prior ties to Southern Rhodesia, but he had spent some time vacationing in the region in 1936, when the notion had struck him that an initiative to the country of Kingsley Fairbridge's birth would be a fitting tribute to the charity's founder. It also seemed the next logical step for the movement as a whole. "Being now established in Australia and Canada we should add Africa to our sphere of influence," he urged the other members of the executive committee, noting that the move would allow each of the empire's "three English speaking Continents" to furnish "outlets for our children from the home Island."[47] This labeling of Africa as an "English-speaking continent" was a telling illustration of West's jingoistic brand of imperialism. To his mind, English was the language of power; its authority was so encompassing that, in comparison, Africa's tremendous linguistic diversity paled into nonexistence. The comment also revealed his deep faith in the racial and cultural coherence of Greater Britain. While Canada, Australia, and Southern Rhodesia may have differed in terms of their geography and climate, they remained firmly united in heritage and sense of purpose. According to this view, there was little difference in sending a child to one territory or another, given that all were interchangeably "British" in blood and sentiment.

This trust in the solidity of the settler empire did not blind West to the particularities of Southern Rhodesia. As he detailed in his proposal

---

[46] Interview with Mr. Dunstan A. P. West, conducted by Chris Jeffery, June 25, 1985, OH 1887, SAWA: BL.

[47] A. G. B. West, "Fairbridge Farm Schools Rhodesian Prospects," October 1936, DO 35/697/4, TNA: PRO.

to the committee, a number of factors distinguished the country from the other regions in which the Society operated. The first was that the Rhodesian state was less established than its counterparts in Canada and Australia. The territory had only been incorporated into the empire during the 1890s when the diamond magnate Cecil Rhodes claimed it for the British South Africa Company. Responsible government followed in 1923 after the small White settler community rejected union with South Africa in order to remain independent within the empire. Strictly speaking, Southern Rhodesia was a colony, albeit a self-governing one, and by and large its relations with the imperial government mirrored those of the other dominions. Its state was one of the youngest in the empire, however, and its elite tended to be green and politically insecure. The second, more obvious feature that differentiated Southern Rhodesia from Canada or Australia was its lack of a White majority. In 1936, its European population of some 55,000 ruled a geographical area that was twice the size of Texas and in which Africans outnumbered settlers by over twenty to one.[48] This demographic imbalance, combined with the inexperienced government, produced profound feelings of racial and cultural vulnerability throughout Rhodesian society. As its long-serving Prime Minister Godfrey Huggins described it, the colony was an "island of white within a sea of black," an exposed beacon of British civilization in the vastness of Africa.[49]

Although West conceded that the racial situation presented a "complication of conditions which has to be most firmly faced," he did not think that it was insurmountable.[50] After all, the numerical imbalance only increased the Rhodesian government's enthusiasm for targeted immigration schemes like the one he was proposing. Throughout the early twentieth century, the state had tried to attract settlers using incentives such as free passages and land grants, but the results were always meager. No more than 300 people had arrived under the provisions of the Empire Settlement Act, for instance, a tiny number compared to the hundreds of thousands of men and women who traveled to Canada and Australia in the same period.[51] This slow pace of immigration was intentional. While local politicians liked to envision a dramatically expanded European

---

[48] For population estimates, see Mlambo, *White Immigration*, 69.

[49] Quoted in Dane Kennedy, *Islands of White: Settler Society and Culture in Kenya and Southern Rhodesia, 1890–1939* (Durham: Duke University Press, 1987), 2.

[50] West, "Fairbridge Farm Schools Rhodesian Prospects."

[51] Mlambo, *White Immigration*, 23; approximately 130,000 Britons emigrated to Canada during the 1920s under the provisions of the Empire Settlement Act, and nearly double that number went to Australia. Michele Langfield, "Voluntarism, Salvation, and Rescue: British Juvenile Migration to Australia and Canada, 1890–1939," *Journal of Imperial and Commonwealth History* 32, no. 2 (May 2004): 86–114, 87.

population, they also held firm ideas about the "right type" of migrant for Rhodesia, typically idealized as a hard working, upwardly mobile family man of British stock. And, even as they tried to lure this perfect settler into the country, they took pains to eliminate from contention the myriad people who did not fit the bill. In the years since Rhodesian authorities had started controlling immigration in 1903, a complex system of ethnic and class-based entry requirements had emerged that was designed to exclude non-Europeans and poorer Whites from the country. By the First World War, prospective settlers needed to pass a literacy test in a European language (which during the 1930s was restricted to English) and also to provide proof that they had either a job waiting for them or £50 capital.[52] The bar was set higher for those who hoped to take advantage of the colony's land settlement program, which required applicants to have at least £500 and prior farming experience. The terms were so narrow that, of the 2,000 Britons who expressed interest in the scheme in 1925, only 80 qualified and 40 settled.[53] The state eventually lowered the requirement to between £50 and £200 during the 1930s, but even this new standard remained well out of the reach of the majority of Britain's unskilled or unemployed workers.

The explicit intent behind these regulations was racial. As in other imperial spaces, settler claims to authority in the region relied on the belief that Europeans were distinct from and superior to the African majority.[54] Maintaining the illusion of a firm cultural divide between colonizer and colonized was particularly important in Southern Rhodesia, given that its White population was of lower-middle- and working-class origin and lacked the economic stature of wealthier settler communities such as Kenya.[55] Rhodesian social norms thus enforced a strict, if largely unspoken, code of conduct for settlers that aimed to protect "White prestige" in the colony. Any person who failed to conform to these dictates – by letting Africans get too emotionally close, by living a dirty, lazy, or immoral lifestyle, or by performing tasks that were usually done by servants – threatened to belie the fantasy of European superiority and send the whole system toppling down. With such high stakes at play, the Rhodesian state was aggressive in its policing of incoming migrants. Its goal was to keep out any would-be settlers whose poverty or personality cast doubt on their ability to defend the stature of the European community.

---

[52] Kennedy, *Islands of White*, 82.
[53] Mlambo, *White Immigration*, 23–24.
[54] On this point, see especially Ann Stoler, *Carnal Knowledge and Imperial Power: Race and the Intimate in Colonial Rule* (Berkeley: University of California Press, 2010, originally 2002).
[55] Kennedy, *Islands of White*, 93.

As it had in Australia, the shifting economic tides of the interwar years magnified public concern over the sanctity of White rule. During the 1920s, settlers grew alarmed at the growth of a small class of market-oriented African farmers who seemed poised to challenge Europeans' dominance of the economy. The fears proved unfounded. Protective legislation like the 1930 Land Apportionment Act, which restricted African holdings to poor-quality and overcrowded "Native Areas," ensured that the new agricultural competition never amounted to more than 15 percent of the market.[56] Yet these farmers did project a striking picture of commercial competence that jarred with the usual assumptions about African backwardness.[57] For many Rhodesians, the emerging African middle class raised the frightening prospect that the gap between White and Black was narrowing. More disquieting was the sudden appearance of indigent and unemployed Europeans on the streets of Salisbury and Bulawayo during the Depression. Southern Rhodesia had never had a "poor White" problem like neighboring South Africa, but the mere hint that one might develop was enough to make local officials nervous. The combined effect of these pressures was to reaffirm public support for the colony's restrictive immigration requirements and to strengthen the state's mandate to let in only those who were, in Huggins' words, "independent and self-reliant ... prepared to stand solidly on their own two feet." Southern Rhodesia, as he liked to proclaim, was "no place ... for people who expect to be molly-coddled through life."[58]

This emphasis on self-help, hard work, and personal ambition at the heart of the White Rhodesian identity found a close parallel in the ethic of the child emigration movement. West's proposed focus on children also aligned well with a more recent local obsession with the character – of lack thereof – of young people. Throughout the later 1920s, a chorus of Rhodesian politicians and reformers bemoaned the loss of the pioneering spirit among the colony's children and adolescents. The common complaint was that young Rhodesians were becoming "soft" through the processes of modernization and urbanization and the extension of imperial control. Unlike their parents and grandparents, who had struggled to make ends meet in a hostile land, the generation had grown up in cities and towns, surrounded by modern conveniences and habituated

---

[56] Carol Summers, *From Civilization to Segregation: Social Ideals and Social Control in Southern Rhodesia, 1890–1934* (Athens: Ohio University Press 1994), 236.

[57] Terence Ranger, *Are We Not Also Men? The Samkange Family and African Politics in Zimbabwe, 1920–1964* (London: James Currey, 1995); Michael O. West, *The Rise of an African Middle Class: Colonial Zimbabwe, 1898–1965* (Bloomington: Indiana University Press, 2002).

[58] Huggins, quoted in Public Relations Department of Southern Rhodesia, "Southern Rhodesia: Facts and Figures for the Immigrant," 1946, DO 35/1135, TNA: PRO.

to a cheap and abundant African workforce. As a 1929 investigation into the matter declared, a certain degree of moral decline was the inevitable product of Southern Rhodesia's "mixed society," which encouraged Whites to remain in a childlike state of dependence on servants.[59] The problem was cultural, not biological. As the influential 1932 report of the Carnegie Commission on Poor Whites in South Africa confirmed, there was nothing inherently wrong with the quality of British stock in Africa.[60] The roots of the degeneration were to be found instead in the region's social structures, which eroded the European work ethic, enabled work evasion, and allowed "young life [to] be sapped by debilitating ministrations," as West put it.[61]

The positive side of this tendency to blame young Rhodesians' failings on societal rather than hereditarian forces was that it left open the possibility of reform. On the eve of the Depression, the state embarked on a series of rehabilitation programs intended to strengthen the moral fiber of the White community. Heavy investment in settler education soon produced one of the most advanced educational systems in the empire, which offered free and compulsory schooling until age sixteen, extensive university fellowships, and an array of career and professional training programs.[62] The anxiety about Europeans' overreliance on Africans was also a major influence behind the rise of segregationist legislation. During the general election of 1933, all sides ran on platforms that advocated separate development in one form or another, with Huggins' victorious Reform Party advocating the most exacting proposal of all: a "two pyramids" scheme that promised the near-total segregation of the races.[63]

Picking up on these sentiments, West framed the idea for a new child migrant institution as part of the colony's larger "corporate effort" to affirm the "dignity of all labour" among Rhodesians. "No better boon could be given to this young country," he noted, than the farm school "model of domestic training," which had been proven to endow British children with the skills and determination of independent imperial settlers.[64] His pitch was tailor-made to appeal to the Rhodesian political elite. In early 1937, the government threw its support behind the initiative with

---

[59] *Report of the Education Commission for Southern Rhodesia* (Cape Town: Cape Times, 1929), 14, quoted in Summers, *From Civilization to Segregation*, 248.

[60] Carnegie Commission, *The Poor White Problem in South Africa*, 5 vols. (Stellenbosch: Pro Ecclesia-Drukkery, 1932).

[61] West, "Fairbridge Farm Schools Rhodesian Prospects."

[62] R. J. Challiss, "Education and Southern Rhodesia's Poor Whites, 1890–1930," in *White but Poor: Essays on the History of Poor Whites in Southern Africa, 1880–1940*, ed. Robert Morrell (Pretoria: University of South Africa, 1992), 151–170.

[63] Summers, *From Civilization to Segregation*, 226–293.

[64] West, "Fairbridge Farm Schools Rhodesian Prospects."

a generous offer of land and buildings, a monthly maintenance grant, and full access for Fairbridge children to the colony's educational scholarships.[65] Huggins also set aside time during his next visit to London to attend a "tea-cum-cocktail party" with the Society's executive committee to discuss the plan further. He used the occasion to assure them of the opportunities that awaited needy children in Southern Rhodesia, stressing that there were good jobs for boys in mining, on the railroads, or with the police, and for girls in clerical work, nursing, and sales. Given this range of options, he felt sure that no industrious child migrant "would remain on the lowest rung of the ladder."[66]

Although Huggins emphasized that immigration to Southern Rhodesia "opened up possibilities [for children] which could never exist in any other part of the empire," he made clear that his government's intentions were not philanthropic. Speaking bluntly, he viewed the scheme as "a very necessary adjunct to [the] birth rate" that would help balance out the region's racial demographics. "There was no altruism about the thing," he said. State officials "wanted a larger white population as settlers there, to bring on the natives and to develop the country," and they felt it would be easier to accomplish this goal by importing "pure bred youngsters than by starting a school for 'poor whites.'"[67] As these comments illustrate, the Rhodesian enthusiasm for the plan hinged on ideas about the adaptability of youth. Believing that child migrants would arrive unblemished and ready for reshaping, segregationists such as Huggins argued that, if the boys and girls remained isolated from Africans and other "negative" social forces long enough, they would develop stronger characters than the typical Rhodesian-born child. Such notions reflected the government's growing distrust of the social institution of the family, which in the best cases appeared as a mechanism for reinforcing European rule but in the worst seemed a dangerous center of racial disruption.[68] The most worrisome households were those headed by incompetent or overly lenient parents who failed to draw a clear line for their children between White and Black behavior. Guided by the imperative to keep young Rhodesians from "going native," Huggins was already on record as an advocate for the removal of children from poorer families to better-regulated spaces, such as boarding schools and state-run institutions.[69] The advantage of child emigration was that it targeted "unattached" boys and girls. It simplified the process of creating a White

---

[65] Huggins to Hambro, June 3, 1937, DO 35/697/4, TNA: PRO.
[66] CES, "Notes of a Meeting Held at Mr. Hambro's House," May 26, 1937, D.296/K2/1/2, ULSCA.
[67] Ibid.    [68] Stoler, *Carnal Knowledge*.
[69] Summers, *From Civilization to Segregation*, 237.

elite by eliminating the middleman – the parent – and thus allowed the task of childrearing to be fully subsumed by state interests.

Huggins' focus on children's redemption within institutional settings must have encouraged the executive committee, given how closely it echoed the movement's central tenets. But his comment that the migrants would need to learn how to "bring on the natives" gave them pause. The Society had never attempted a scheme in a region as racially complex as Southern Rhodesia, and the board remained uneasy about how the "peculiar conditions" of Africa would affect the work.[70] Without any precedent, it was unclear what changes would need to be made to the existing model, or even whether it was possible to suit poor children for the burdens of colonial rule. The ever-pessimistic Colonel J. Waley Cohen noted that most of the organization's wards "came from families which had been used to being led and not from those who had been accustomed to leadership." Charles Hambro, the Society's chairman, took up the point, acknowledging that, although "ninety-six percent of the children sent to Western Australia were normal," the majority were "likely to be not as bright as we would desire." Stressing that typical Fairbridge children came from "stock which had not had experience of control," he worried that they might not "be fitted to control natives."[71] The committee decided that, despite Huggins' assurances, it would need to consider the plan further before agreeing to it.

It is worth remembering the context of these discussions. West's proposal came at a time of rising concern among executive committee members about the large number of repatriations from its Australian farm schools and amid a wave of increased scrutiny of the mental fitness of child migrants. The new, eugenics-inspired pressure emanating from the Australian side of the work was beginning to reverberate through the Society's discussions of its other projects, strengthening an undercurrent of hereditarian thinking within the organization as a whole. The trend helps explain why Hambro felt it necessary to bring up the intelligence of Fairbridge children even though the matter was of no obvious concern to Huggins, who, like most Rhodesians, was inclined to view White childrearing in environmental terms. This transference of Australian racial anxieties onto the Rhodesian case, combined with the committee's newfound awareness of the stringent racial hierarchies of the African empire, had important consequences. Before long, the question of whether rescued children were fit to rule a subject, colonized population transformed

---

[70] CES, Minutes of the Southern Rhodesia Committee, September 1, 1938, D.296/K2/1/7, ULSCA.
[71] CES, "Notes of a Meeting Held at Mr. Hambro's House."

what had been a conversation about the uplift of British boys and girls in the African empire into a broader inquiry into the nature of child development and the limits of poor children's potential.

Soon after the meeting with Huggins, the board appointed a sub-committee to delve more deeply into the proposal. Over the next two years, the group read extracts from the Carnegie Commission's report on the poor White problem; consulted with specialists such as Margery Perham, Oxford University's first lecturer in colonial administration; and solicited firsthand accounts from supporters who had spent time in the region. Frustratingly, these investigations produced a wealth of different and often contradictory opinions. On the one hand, the on-the-ground reports were enthusiastic. Many focused on Southern Rhodesia's healthy climate, arguing that it offered the ideal setting for children in need of a fresh start. One long-time supporter, Bertie Heilbron, stated that he had spent "considerable time at a large open-air Swimming Pool" in Bulawayo during a recent vacation, and on the basis of his observations there could happily confirm that Rhodesian children were of "more than average size," had an overall "appearance of good health," and tended not to wear glasses.[72] On the other hand, the testimony of the subcommittee's expert witnesses was more cautious, and raised serious concerns about the long-term stability of the colony. Perham suggested that the region was entering a period of increased racial tension that would make White rule unsustainable. In light of the "problems looming on the horizon," she doubted that young people of any social background would be able to find lasting security in the country, and advised the subcommittee in the strongest terms that "Fairbridge children ought not to be allowed to start life in Southern Africa."[73]

It was not surprising that Perham, a proponent of indirect rule and the gradual devolution of the empire, would oppose a project designed to build up the demographic and political strength of the settler community. Her stature as one of the foremost scholarly authorities on the region made her views difficult to dismiss.[74] But it was the testimony of a different expert witness, Dr. William Moodie, the director of London's Child Guidance Clinic, that decisively shaped the view of the subcommittee. Moodie had been the driving force behind the introduction of

---

[72] CES, "Bertie Heilbron's Report on the Possibility and Desirability of Founding a Fairbridge Farm School in S. Rhodesia," January 1938, D.296/K2/1/5, ULSCA.

[73] CES, Minutes of the Southern Rhodesia Committee, October 27, 1938, D.296/K2/1/12, ULSCA.

[74] On Perham's views and career, see Alison Smith and Mary Bull, eds. *Margery Perham and British Rule in Africa* (London: Frank Cass, 1991); C. Brad Faught, *Into Africa: The Imperial Life of Margery Perham* (London: I. B. Tauris, 2012).

child guidance to Britain in the late 1920s, and had built up a reputation as one of the nation's leading voices on issues related to children's
emotional imbalance. Child guidance, like child psychology more generally, remained an emergent discipline throughout the interwar years,
although, thanks in part to Moodie's advocacy, its popularity was growing. Between 1927 and 1938, forty-six British clinics were founded, and
together they treated between 3,000 and 4,000 children a year.[75] Aptly
described as a "science of social contentment," the object of child guidance was to alleviate moodiness, depression, and delinquent behavior in
the young by aligning their inner drives and instincts to their external
societal environments.[76] Through regular clinic sessions, practitioners
sought to identify points of dissonance in a child's emotional development. They then combined talk therapy with targeted interventions into
the home in an effort to adjust the subject's expectations and perceptions
to the realities of the outside world.[77]

The subcommittee invited Moodie to consider how Southern Rhodesia's
distinct social and racial structures might affect child migrants' mental
wellbeing. Perhaps troubled by Perham's warning of impending political
disruption, they wondered whether the children would be able to accommodate themselves to a fractured society. In his response, Moodie took
the question in another direction. Instead of commenting on the impact
the new atmosphere would have on the children's development, he concentrated on the background of the migrants themselves, noting that
deprived boys and girls typically came from "broken home[s]," where
they had suffered the "violent emotional distress caused by divorce,
insanity, drunkenness, etc." These early, harmful experiences, he felt, had
significant psychological effects. They imprinted on children's minds,
producing a temperament that was "aggressive, hostile to society, easily
upset, touchy, unable to give and take, and not easily educable." Some
of the more resilient boys and girls might escape this fate if they were
removed from their households at a very young age. But Moodie stressed
that these transformations were rare. Pointing out that the majority of
Fairbridge children had "such a background to their lives," he declared
it unlikely that they would "develop into good, just people, who would

[75] Deborah Thom, "Wishes, Anxieties, Play and Gestures: Child Guidance in Inter-War
England," in *In the Name of the Child: Health and Welfare, 1880–1940*, ed. Roger Cooter
(New York: Routledge, 1992), 200–219, 215.
[76] Nikolas Rose, *Governing the Soul: The Shaping of the Private Self* (New York: Free
Association Books, 1999), 158.
[77] Kathleen Jones, *Taming the Troublesome Child: American Families, Child Guidance, and the
Limits of Psychiatric Authority* (Cambridge, MA: Harvard University Press, 1999) offers
a close analysis, drawn from case files, of the work of a leading child guidance clinic in
this period.

command respect." The chances were higher that the young migrants would become "delinquents, who formed gangs with others of their kind, always suspicious and resentful of those outside their set." "Only a small proportion would turn out really well," he concluded.[78]

In retrospect, Moodie's contentions may appear extreme, but in fact his comments resonated with the main currents of British child psychology at the time. As the field expanded during the interwar years, it moved away from an earlier, Freudian-centered focus on innate instincts toward developmental models that incorporated the role of culture, myth, ritual, and societal traditions in the shaping of the mind.[79] The shift reflected the influence of anthropological theory in the broader discipline of psychology, which was a result of the recent extension of psychological clinics throughout the African empire.[80] The association between the two disciplines encouraged practitioners to move away from the concept of essential biological difference toward a new understanding that explained the distinctions between "savage" and "civilized" minds in terms of cultural experience.[81] This mode of thinking raised the prospect that "primitive" mentalities were not exclusive to colonized peoples. Rather, they could arise among European populations who had been reared in degraded or morally corrupt settings. In this respect, Moodie had identified the irrational mental type that lay within the modern British population. Destitute boys and girls were indeed White on the outside, but they bore the hidden weight of early poverty on their minds, which made their mental frameworks akin to those of other "savages" on the inside.

Although this prioritization of culture over biology implied that people were impressionable and had the capacity to change, in practice these ideas tended to reify the distinctions between races and classes.[82] By arguing that every individual was adjusted to fit only his own cultural environment, interwar psychologists implied that reform was impossible

---

[78] CES, Minutes of the Southern Rhodesia Committee, October 27, 1938.

[79] On this transformation in the field of child guidance, see Suzan van Dijken, René van der Veer, Marinus van Ijzendoorn, and Hans-Jan Kuipers, "Bowlby before Bowlby: The Sources of an Intellectual Departure in Psychoanalysis and Psychology," *Journal of the History of Behavioral Sciences* 34, no. 3 (Summer 1998): 247–269.

[80] Jock McCulloch, *Colonial Psychiatry and the African Mind* (New York: Cambridge University Press, 1995); Jonathan Sadowsky, *Imperial Bedlam: Institutions of Madness in Colonial Southwest Nigeria* (Berkeley: University of California Press, 1999); Mathew Thomson, "'Savage Civilisation': Race, Culture, and Mind in Britain, 1898–1939," in *Race, Science and Medicine: Racial Categories and the Production of Medical Knowledge, 1700–1960*, ed. Waltraud Ernst and Bernard Harris (New York: Routledge, 1999), 235–258; Lynette Jackson, *Surfacing Up: Psychiatry and Social Order in Colonial Zimbabwe, 1908–1968* (Ithaca: Cornell University Press, 2005).

[81] Thomson, "Savage Civilisation," 241.

[82] Nancy Stepan, *The Idea of Race in Science: Great Britain, 1800–1960* (London: Macmillan, 1982).

after a person had reached a certain threshold of development. Moodie drew the line in early childhood, and it followed that children deformed by poverty would suffer severe mental stress if they confronted a new social landscape later in life. They would manifest pathologies similar to other "primal" mentalities, and, like colonial subjects, would need to be kept under strict control to keep them from lashing out at a civilization they could not hope to understand.

Moodie's testimony was a serious blow to the project. The subcommittee acknowledged as much in its final report, which asserted that the type of child that the Society sent to Australia or Canada "might prove incapable of assuming the social, political, and economic position necessary for the White man in his relation with the African native." The "extremely important colour problems" in the region placed the idea of opening a farm school on the same lines of those in Canada or Australia out of the question. However, after two years of planning, and with the Rhodesian government's offer of financial support still on the table, the group was loathe to call the plan off entirely. They thus suggested a number of modifications to adapt the proposal for the African context. First and foremost, the school would have to avoid selecting children who had lived in "psychologically and morally disturbed and distressing conditions," such as an urban slum or negligent household, since these settings were liable to produce a "petty minded and aggressive attitude of dominance towards a subordinate, which in this particular instance would be a Native." The scheme needed to be restricted to boys and girls "whose early home life has been reasonably secure and happy ... and who are also sound both in intelligence and temperament."[83] Finding these "children of a different class" would require new methods. Instead of recruiting through local authorities and children's charities, the Rhodesian initiative would have to rely on alternative sources, such as newspaper advertisements and personal referrals.[84]

The final proposal that emerged from the subcommittee was so transformed that, in the end, the executive board decided it would be best administered by a separate organization. By early 1939, a new Council of the Rhodesia Fairbridge Memorial College was formed, although many of its founding members retained close ties to the Fairbridge Society. West, for instance, served on the boards of both organizations, and the Fairbridge executive committee agreed to advise the fledgling charity throughout its early years. Nevertheless, from its beginning the Council

[83] CES, "Report of Southern Rhodesia Committee," February 1939, D.296/ K2/1/10, ULSCA.
[84] CES, Minutes of Southern Rhodesia Committee, October 27, 1938.

took steps to distinguish its work from the rest of the child emigration movement. In a move that seemed calculated to cement its public reputation as a more "elite" organization, it selected a well-known aristocrat, Lord de Saumarez, as its chair. Moreover, its early publicity stressed that, while the scheme would retain aspects of the farm school system, such as the "cottage home" model and a training course "for those whose ultimate aim is farming," on the whole it would more closely resemble a boarding school than a children's institution. The idea was to create a kind of "Fairbridge Scholarship working the opposite way to a Rhodes Scholarship," and one early proposal suggested asking parents or guardians to contribute to the costs of their son's or daughter's emigration.[85] Only children "whose early home life has been reasonably secure and happy (though there may have been poverty in material things), and who are also sound both in intelligence and temperament" would be eligible.[86] To ensure that these guidelines were met, the committee would employ a rigorous selection procedure that required applicants first to pass a health examination by Rhodesian authorities, then a psychological evaluation by a social worker, followed finally by a "written and oral examination before a panel much the same as the entrance interview for Dartmouth," the Royal Navy's officer training college.[87]

These changes represented an obvious shift away from child emigration's philanthropic roots. As a representative in the Dominions Office summarized, the scheme was "mainly a political move" designed to uphold the lasting strength of the White settler community.[88] Unlike other emigration initiatives, its fundamental object was not to rescue Britain's neediest children but to facilitate the settlement of the "secondary school type or ... the children of the 'new poor.'"[89] In this respect, the debates that accompanied the extension of child emigration to Southern Rhodesia – which because of the outbreak of war did not occur until 1946 – revealed the combined impact of local settler politics and the emergence of child psychology on dominant models of children's potential. Throughout the interwar period, Rhodesian immigration policy was governed by one central imperative: that all prospective settlers be equipped to preserve the colony's racial hierarchy. Protecting "White prestige" meant more than simply maintaining a certain economic standing. At the most fundamental level, it meant possessing a certain psychological state that would

---

[85] CES, Minutes of the Rhodesia-Fairbridge Memorial School Council, c. 1939, D.296/ K2/1/11, ULSCA; Sherington and Jeffery, *Fairbridge*, 184.
[86] CES, "Report of the Southern Rhodesia Committee."
[87] CES, Minutes of the Rhodesia-Fairbridge Memorial School Council.
[88] Note by Price, March 13, 1939, DO 35/697/5, TNA: PRO.
[89] Ibid, February 21, 1939.

enable Europeans to assume the "right" attitude toward servants and subordinates, to know instinctively which behaviors were appropriate for Whites and which were not, and to preserve a strict emotional detachment from Africans.[90] As the case of Barnardo's abortive 1902 venture in South Africa (discussed in Chapter 1) illustrated, reformers had long been skeptical of rescued children's ability to attain this ideal. The crucial difference was that, at the turn of the century, the problem had appeared environmental. South Africa did not seem to offer the social and geographic conditions that poor boys and girls needed to climb the ladder to independence. Now, the issue was redefined as an internal pathology that affected the great majority of needy British children. In the face of Southern Rhodesia's strict racial nationalism, poverty had been reconceptualized from an escapable social status into a permanent psychological defect from which even the youngest Britons were not immune.

## Conclusion

In practical terms, the interwar debates over the selection of boys and girls for emigration to Australia and Southern Rhodesia involved only a small proportion of the total number of children in the care of British charities and local authorities. Yet out of this seemingly minor case study several broader, transimperial processes start to emerge. The uptick in concern about the quality and "fitness" of child migrants among dominion officials, particularly those in Australia, helped reveal how the rise of distinct racial nationalisms across the settler empire had already begun to weaken the political faith in the global unity of the British race. Throughout the 1920s and 1930s, politicians in Australia and Southern Rhodesia remained preoccupied by the need to protect the racial integrity of their nascent national communities. Although this effort to police the boundaries of Whiteness was by no means new, its intersection with the interwar science of child psychology did produce unprecedented consequences. Armed with the novel diagnostic tool of the mental test, Australian officials felt empowered to differentiate between British children on the basis of their present viability and future potential to become productive citizens. And, if these seemingly exact, "scientific" assessments appear remarkably subjective in retrospect, that awareness should not lead us to dismiss their power at the time. The growth of IQ testing and other forms of mental evaluation allowed dominion immigration

---

[90] Kennedy, *Islands of White*, especially 153–154; on the psychology of White privilege in Southern Rhodesia during this period, see also Jock McCulloch, *Black Peril, White Virtue: Sexual Crime in Southern Rhodesia, 1902–1935* (Bloomington: University of Indiana Press, 2000).

authorities to delineate where the British heritage ended and their own, distinct national communities began. Even more significantly, these techniques had a powerful impact on the lives of the hundreds of British children who were defined as not quite White enough for the empire, and were either rejected out of hand or sent back "home" to a country most had not seen in years.

The importance of comparing how these developments played out in two parts of the settler world is that it helps tease out the more subtle distinctions within the interwar, transimperial conversation about race and Britishness. The Australian discussion centered on eugenic notions of inherent mental defects and tainted genes, whereas in Southern Rhodesia understandings of Whiteness placed more weight on the importance of cultural experience in determining an individual's personality and character. Of course, the boundaries between these two modes of thinking should not be drawn too starkly. In at least one instance, concepts from one side of the empire were imported into the debates about selection standards in another. Nevertheless, the fact that different interpretations of Whiteness existed even in the seemingly homogenous space of Greater Britain sheds light once again on the deeply situated nature of racial discourse.[91] The qualities that defined someone as "White," and thus as a member of the colonial elite, depended entirely on where that person was at the time; the standards fluctuated across the empire in relation to the varying needs of local politics. This flexibility, combined with the equally pliable concepts of child development coming out of the realm of psychology, made interwar racial and mental science a particularly effective tool in the struggle to define separate dominion identities. As the debates about the selection of child migrants demonstrated, the fracturing of the ideal of pan-Britannic unity across the settler world did not merely result from the political and economic changes of the 1950s and 1960s, as has often been claimed.[92] Rather, the roots of these later shifts can be found in the immigration debates of the interwar period. By the eve of the Second World War, cracks in the shell of Greater Britain had started to appear.

---

[91] Anderson, *The Cultivation of Whiteness*, 3.

[92] See, for instance, the overwhelmingly postwar emphasis of Stuart Ward, *Australia and the British Embrace: The Demise of the Imperial Ideal* (Melbourne University Press, 2001); David Goldsworthy, *Losing the Blanket: Australia and the End of Britain's Empire* (Melbourne University Press, 2002); Phillip Buckner, ed., *Canada and the End of Empire* (Vancouver: University of British Columbia Press, 2005); James Curran and Stuart Ward, *The Unknown Nation: Australia after Empire* (Melbourne University Press, 2010).

For nine-year-old Margaret Clarke, the outbreak of the Second World War
in September of 1939 marked the beginning of a year of near-constant
movement. The youngest of nine children, Clarke was born in 1930 in
Kenya, where her grandparents were missionaries and her father directed
safaris. She returned to Britain with her mother and siblings in 1937, one
year after her father walked out the door, leaving a trail of debt behind
him. Under pressure to raise this large family on her own, her mother
placed the five youngest daughters with the Fairbridge Society. Her plan
was to follow them to Australia when she got back on her feet.

Clarke was thus in Fairbridge care in London when the war broke out,
triggering the first in a series of massive civilian evacuations from cities under
threat of aerial bombardment. Close to 1.5 million people, most of whom
were children, were hustled into the countryside during the first days of the
war.[1] As part of this exodus, Clarke remembered joining a huge "croco-
dile [line] going to the country ... a long line of people." Like most child
evacuees, she and her sisters were placed in separate rural households, first
in Somerset and later in Devon. Flashes of the war intrude on her otherwise
idyllic memories from this period. She recalled walking through fields, watching bombers fly overhead, and swimming among the barbed wire that lined
the coast. "And then suddenly," she explained, "in June of 1940, we were
suddenly told we were going to Australia ... So I had to say goodbye to my
adopted grandfather" – the man with whom she and one of her sisters had
been staying in Devon – and was "suddenly put on a ship." Clarke's frequent
use of the word "suddenly" underscores her childhood sense of dislocation,
a feeling of being swept up in a series of changes beyond her control. "It
was such a rush," she said; "I don't think we were told much at all, actually.
It was all a bit of a shock." She and her sisters joined a party of Fairbridge

[1] For overviews of the evacuation policy and experience, see Ruth Inglis, *The Children's
War: Evacuation, 1939–1945* (London: Collins, 1989); Laura Lee Downs, "'A Very British
Revolution?' L'évacuation des enfants citadins vers les campagnes anglaises, 1939–45,"
*Vingtième siècle* 89 (January–March 2006): 47–60; John Welshman, *Churchill's Children:
The Evacuee Experience in Wartime Britain* (Oxford University Press, 2010).

children bound for Australia by way of Canada, the only route then possible. The group "went up amongst the icebergs" of the north Atlantic, crossed Canada by train, and spent a few weeks at the Fairbridge Farm School in British Columbia. It was "only a short time," but long enough for the other children to paint them terrifying visions of the outback, where poisonous spiders lurked under the toilet seats, bears lived in trees, and bizarre animals hopped about on their hind legs. "It was quite a story they used to kick up," Clarke laughed, "so we didn't want to come to Australia, we wanted to stay in Canada." But on the party went, boarding another ocean liner in July of 1940 and continuing a journey that ultimately led to the Molong farm school in New South Wales. Clarke stayed at Molong until 1946, when her mother succeeded in immigrating to the country and collected Margaret to live with what was left of their scattered family in a small government-sponsored house on the outskirts of Sydney.[2]

Clarke's recollections of being rushed from place to place, across two continents and one hemisphere, provide a vivid impression of the pressures the war placed on the child emigration movement. The Fairbridge Society hoped that Clarke's party would be the first of several to take the overland route to Australia.[3] As it turned out, hers was the last wartime group of child migrants to leave Britain. Just one month after Clarke arrived in Sydney harbor, a U-boat sank the Canada-bound *SS City of Benares*. Among the more than 200 victims were 77 child evacuees who were part of a smaller, but still state-directed, program that sent boys and girls to stay out the war with relatives or friends in the dominions or the United States.[4] Declaring the oceans too dangerous, the government discontinued its overseas evacuation policy, a move that also forced child emigration schemes to grind to a halt. Without new arrivals from Britain, the number of children living in the various farm schools dwindled as those who had arrived before the war grew up, finished their schooling, and went to jobs in the countryside. In 1944, the Northcote Children's Farm in Victoria transferred its remaining school-aged boys and girls to Molong and temporarily shuttered its doors.[5] Eighteen months later, the Barnardo's Mowbray Park farm school closed as well. Its fields were rented out to a local farmer and two of its cottages burned down.[6]

[2] Author's interview with Margaret Clarke, March 22, 2006.
[3] Fairbridge, Executive Committee Minutes, June 11, 1940, D.296/B1/2/5, ULSCA.
[4] More than 11,000 children were privately evacuated abroad between 1939 and 1940, and the government-run Children's Overseas Reception Board facilitated the dispatch of roughly 2,700 more before abandoning the scheme at the end of 1940. Roger Kershaw and Janet Sacks, *New Lives for Old* (Kew: The National Archives, 2008), 170–191.
[5] Fairbridge, Executive Committee Minutes, November 8, 1944.
[6] Barnardo's, Council Minutes, April 17, 1946, B.239/B1/2/9, ULSCA.

As the war ended, many long-standing proponents of child emigration were anxious that the movement might never recover. A lack of shipping space pushed back the prospect of repopulating the farm schools until 1947 at the earliest. There was also the creation of the welfare state to contend with. As one Barnardo's Council member complained, when he had first joined the charity some two decades earlier, the object "had been very simple, viz. to rescue children from bad homes and degrading surroundings and place them in the care of those who would look after both their bodies and their souls." Now, "he felt there was a tendency to ring the children round with every sort of specialist, psychiatrists, educationalists, careers officers, etc." Another member chimed in with his own "haunting fear that the work was becoming an appendage of a Government Department." The state "seemed to be closing in on every side," squeezing the voluntary sector, and forcing philanthropic work to become less flexible and more "inefficient." It was unclear whether child emigration would still have a place in the postwar era of "scientific training" and government-directed welfare.[7]

They need not have worried. The years immediately following the Second World War witnessed not the end but rather the sudden resurgence of the movement, as eight separate organizations either rekindled their interwar initiatives or began new ones.[8] By the mid 1950s, the total number of institutions accepting child migrants in Australia had jumped from seven to almost thirty (Table 5.1). The long-anticipated plan to resettle children in southern Africa came to fruition as well when the Rhodesia Fairbridge Memorial College accepted its first class of eighteen boys between the ages of eight and thirteen in December of 1946. Shortly thereafter, the New Zealand government, a newcomer to the movement, began coordinating the resettlement of child migrants throughout that dominion. All told, nearly 4,000 British child migrants entered these three countries in the twenty years after the war, with Australia taking the lion's share.[9]

---

[7] Ibid, March 20, 1946.

[8] The organizations were: the Australian Catholic Immigration Committee, Barnardo's, the Church of England Advisory Council of Empire Settlement, the Church of Scotland Committee on Social Services, the Fairbridge Society, the National Children's Home, the Northcote Children's Trust, and the Salvation Army. Stephen Constantine, "The British Government, Child Welfare, and Child Migration to Australia after 1945," *Journal of Imperial and Commonwealth History* 30, no. 1 (January 2002): 99–132, 105.

[9] This number combines the roughly 3,000 sent to Australia with the almost 300 sent to Rhodesia and the 550 sent to New Zealand. For detailed estimates, see Kathleen Paul, "Changing Childhoods: Child Emigration Since 1945," in *Child Welfare and Social Action in the Nineteenth and Twentieth Centuries: International Perspectives*, ed. Jon Lawrence and Pat Starkey (Liverpool University Press, 2001), 121–143; Geoffrey Sherington, "'Suffer Little Children': British Child Migration as a Study of Journeying between Centre and Periphery," *History of Education* 32, no. 5 (September 2003): 461–476; Amanda Sircombe, "A Welfare Initiative? The New Zealand Child Migrant Scheme, 1948–1954" (unpublished MA thesis, University of Waikato, 2004).

Table 5.1 Australian child migrant institutions, from largest to smallest, in 1955.

| Name of Institution | State | Capacity | Number of Child Migrant Residents |
|---|---|---|---|
| St. Vincent's Orphanage (Catholic) | Western Australia | 340 | 33 |
| Swan Homes (Anglican) | Western Australia | 253 | 95 |
| St. Joseph's Home (Catholic) | Queensland | 240 | 32 |
| St. Peter's Boys' Town (Catholic) | Western Australia | 220 | 142 |
| Fairbridge Farm School, Pinjarra* | Western Australia | 216 | 180 |
| Fairbridge Farm School, Molong* | New South Wales | 210 | 175 |
| St. Joseph's Farm School (Catholic) | Western Australia | 200 | 114 |
| St. Vincent's Boys' Home (Catholic) | New South Wales | 200 | 4 |
| Nazareth House (Catholic) | Victoria | 150 | 52 |
| Northcote Farm School* | Victoria | 120 | 62 |
| St. Vincent de Paul's Orphanage (Catholic) | South Australia | 120 | 18 |
| St. Vincent Junior Orphanage (Catholic) | Western Australia | 120 | 72 |
| Murray Dwyer Boys' Orphanage (Catholic) | New South Wales | 104 | 23 |
| Peace Memorial Homes (Methodist) | Victoria | 100 | 9 |
| St. John Bosco Boys' Town (Catholic) | Tasmania | 100 | 26 |
| St. John's Orphanage (Catholic) | New South Wales | 96 | 15 |
| St. Bridgid's Orphanage (Catholic) | New South Wales | 92 | 2 |
| St. Mary's Agricultural School (Catholic) | Western Australia | 91 | 60 |
| Barnardo's Homes, Picton* | New South Wales | 80 | 68 |
| Nazareth House (Catholic) | Western Australia | 80 | 46 |
| St. John's Home (Anglican) | Victoria | 80 | 19 |
| St. Joseph's Girls' Orphanage (Catholic) | New South Wales | 68 | 6 |
| Barnardo's Homes, Normanhurst* | New South Wales | 65 | 65 |
| Children's Home (Methodist) | Western Australia | 60 | 3 |
| Clarendon Children's Home (Anglican) | Tasmania | 52 | 9 |
| St. Joseph's Home (Catholic) | Western Australia | 32 | 7 |
| United Protestant Home* | New South Wales | 30 | 22 |

Table 5.1 (*cont.*)

| Name of Institution | State | Capacity | Number of Child Migrant Residents |
|---|---|---|---|
| Dr. Barnardo's, Burwood* | New South Wales | 22 | 15 |
| Burton Hall Training Farm (Anglican)* | Victoria | 10 | 7 |

* Denotes institution that accepted only British child migrants. All others received both child migrants and Australian-born children.
Source: Child Migration to Australia: Report of a Fact-Finding Mission, August 1956, *Parliamentary Papers* XXIII, Cmd.9832.

Various motivations fueled the postwar revival of child emigration. Some of the drive came from religious authorities eager to increase the demographic strength of their local communities in the empire. In particular, the Australian Catholic Church became one of the policy's strongest backers. On the eve of the war, members of the Western Australia-based Christian Brothers order grew concerned that Catholic child migrants were being lost to the faith in the Fairbridge Society's nondenominational farm schools. Eager to maintain pace with the Protestant-affiliated associations that dominated the movement, they started recruiting needy British children for their own Australian orphanages, and managed to place 114 boys before the war intervened. The scheme revived in 1947, and a little more than 1,000 children were sent to Catholic institutions over the next decade, making the church one of the more prominent players in the postwar field.[10] More generally, though, and as in the interwar years, the main impetus behind child emigration was imperial. In the wake of the conflict, child emigration once again became a potent symbol of the strength of the British world concept both in Britain and throughout the dominions. As Geoffrey Shakespeare, the director of the government's overseas child evacuation program, declared while the bombs were still falling, "In a world where chaos may reign round about, the edifice of Empire will stand unassailable, the true Temple of Peace." He predicted that "from this war the Empire will emerge closer knit," its "component parts" bound permanently together through the transfer and cooperative care of British children.[11]

[10] Barry Coldrey, *Child Migration to Catholic Institutions in Australia: Objectives, Policies, Realities, 1926–1966* (Como, WA: Tamanaraik Press, 1995); Barry Coldrey, "'A Charity which Has Outlived Its Usefulness': The Last Phase of Catholic Child Migration, 1947–1956," *History of Education* 25, no. 4 (1996): 373–386; Sherington, "'Suffer Little Children.'"
[11] Geoffrey Shakespeare, "Address to the Victoria League," July 15, 1941, DO 131/28, TNA: PRO.

As it happened, the edifice of empire proved a great deal less secure than Shakespeare imagined. Twenty years on, it had all but crumbled, and not just in terms of Britain's African and Asian colonies but across the dominions as well. The result was a remarkable worldwide revolution in sentiment, as the appeal of Britishness receded throughout the settler territories, clearing space for the emergence of culturally exclusive "new nationalisms" that no longer depended on the Britannic connection.[12] This chapter traces the erosion of the Greater Britain ideal in the two decades following the war, a time when the notion of sending needy British children from one end of the world to another became politically and culturally unthinkable. In part, this fracturing of the settler empire was the product of larger geopolitical and economic changes that slowly weakened the political significance of the British world concept. Historians have focused considerable attention on the period's new military and trade alliances, which shifted dominion politics away from the bonds of empire and toward new strategic positions that no longer centered on Britain. Yet the impact of these high political negotiations on ordinary worldviews was less profound, and understanding how dominion cultures transitioned from ideologies infused by Britannic race patriotism to discrete and less British-centric visions of national belonging requires broadening our gaze to other terrains. The decline of child emigration, in this respect, highlights the less-noted influence of another postwar trend: the growing, if uneven, authority of psychological theory within social policymaking and popular culture throughout the British world. While child emigration initially survived the incorporation of psychology into the early framework of the welfare state, the rise during the 1950s of new ways of conceptualizing children's emotional development undercut the model of transimperial belonging that had long grounded the movement. In its last years, this one-time imperial social policy became an important political mechanism, used by welfarists in Britain to define the boundaries of acceptable practice as well as by dominion authorities to articulate their nation's cultural and political autonomy.

### Fraying imperial ties

The idea of Greater Britain as a global community united by blood, heritage, and shared interests did not just survive the Second World War, it flourished in its wake. Britain's declaration of war in September of 1939

---

[12] Stuart Ward, "The 'New Nationalism' in Australia, Canada and New Zealand: Civic Culture in the Wake of the British World," in *Britishness Abroad: Transnational Movements and Imperial Cultures,* ed. Kate Darian-Smith, Patricia Grimshaw and Stuart Macintyre (Melbourne University Press, 2008), 231–263.

had been the catalyst for a tremendous revival in imperial feeling both at home and in the settler regions. Within a week, each of the dominions had followed the mother country into the conflict, and throughout the six long years of fighting their contribution to the war effort was unparalleled. More than one million Australians, New Zealanders, Canadians, South Africans, and Rhodesians served in the military. Their influence was especially felt within the Royal Air Force, which recruited and trained 169,000 dominions personnel, nearly half of the Bomber Command's total strength in Europe. Equally vital were the steady imports of food, minerals, and armaments that poured into Britain from the Commonwealth countries, sustaining the nation through the nearly two-year period before the American Lend-Lease program came into effect.[13] This valuable economic partnership continued through the later 1940s, when the dominions remained Britain's best customers and critical suppliers of agricultural and material resources. No wonder, then, that well into the 1950s British leaders from across the political spectrum held firm to the belief that the settler empire formed a crucial pillar of the nation's global power. As Clement Attlee succinctly expressed it to the Commons in 1948, "the Commonwealth nations are our closest friends."[14]

The feeling was widely shared overseas. In Australia and New Zealand, where the fighting in the Pacific had been uncomfortably close to home, politicians continued to regard the empire as essential to national security, even as they sought to supplement this traditional relationship with a new defensive alliance with the United States. The Britannic ideal remained central to their domestic policymaking as well. As postwar officials embarked on ambitious reconstruction programs designed to boost their countries' economies, they looked to Britain to supply the migrants and markets that would fuel a rapid industrialization.[15] Similar considerations were at work in Southern Rhodesia, where the war had been at once enormously profitable and profoundly destabilizing. Following the Japanese occupation of many of the empire's Asian colonies in the early years of the conflict, Britain's demand for natural resources from its African territories had intensified dramatically. The result was a sudden

---

[13] Keith Jeffrey, "The Second World War," in *The Oxford History of the British Empire*, vol. IV, ed. Judith Brown and Wm. Roger Louis (Oxford University Press, 1999), 306–328; 310; Ashley Jackson, *The British Empire and the Second World War* (New York: Hambledon Continuum, 2006), 3 and 23–24.

[14] Quoted in John Darwin, *The Empire Project: The Rise and Fall of the British World-System, 1830–1970* (Cambridge University Press, 2009), 548.

[15] James Belich, *Paradise Reforged: A History of the New Zealanders from the 1880s to the Year 2000* (Honolulu: University of Hawaii Press, 2001), 307–316, 531–532, and 538–539; Stuart Ward, *Australia and the British Embrace: The Demise of the Imperial Ideal* (Melbourne University Press, 2001), 13–40.

expansion of the Rhodesian economy that enriched the settler community but that also led to harsh new controls on African workers. While some Africans did experience a modest rise in wages during the war years, the simultaneous decline in imports and sustained high prices left little outlet for their new consumer capacity. Living conditions in the rural locations and in the cities remained poor and overcrowded, and the persistence of these hardships in the midst of an economic boom provoked a wave of labor militancy during the later 1940s. There was a substantial strike in the railway industry in 1945, followed by an even more powerful general strike in 1948.[16] Facing a growing challenge to their authority, many Rhodesian politicians viewed the imperial connection as their best bet for preserving White rule in the colony.

The clearest expression of this resurgent political faith in the British world was the revival of assisted emigration schemes, which together ushered some 1.5 million Britons into the settler territories in the fifteen years after the war. As the hostilities drew to a close, government officials resuscitated the old organic metaphors of empire that had dominated discussions of imperial policy during the 1920s. In 1944, for example, the Dominions Secretary, Lord Cranborne, asserted that the unity of Greater Britain sprung from the very marrow of the Britannic racial heritage. Keeping this connection alive required a strong migration policy that would promote the "interchange of British blood between one part of the Commonwealth and another."[17] These notions resounded throughout the empire. Even though Canada was the first of the dominions to define, in 1946, its own class of citizenship separate from that of Britain, its government reiterated that it would continue to grant British subjects preferred immigration status.[18] New Zealand too remained committed to British immigration before all others, helping to fund the resettlement of roughly 100,000 Britons between 1948 and 1976.[19] But the sentiment particularly hit home in Southern Rhodesia and Australia, where politicians were already devising methods to expand their White populations.

---

[16] Frederick Cooper, *Decolonization and African Society: The Labor Question in French and British Africa* (Cambridge University Press, 1996), 110–140.

[17] Lord Cranborne, speaking at a meeting of Commonwealth Prime Ministers, May 12, 1944, DO 35/1323, TNA: PRO. On the importance of the ideal of racial homogeneity within postwar reconstruction planning, see Kathleen Paul, *Whitewashing Britain: Race and Citizenship in the Postwar Era* (Ithaca: Cornell University Press, 1997), 25–63.

[18] As a concession to the French Canadian population, it also extended the status to French citizens. Ninette Kelley and Michael Trebilcock, *The Making of the Mosaic: A History of Canadian Immigration Policy*, 2nd edn. (University of Toronto Press, 2010), 325–329.

[19] Belich, *Paradise Reforged*, 538. In the same period, more than 200,000 British migrants arrived in New Zealand unassisted. Marjory Harper and Stephen Constantine, *Migration and Empire* (Oxford University Press, 2010), 89.

Soon after Cranborne advocated the renewal of government assistance for empire settlement, the Rhodesian government indicated that it would relax its economic requirements for new migrants so that larger numbers of "people with skill and energy," and not just those few with "capital and education," would be able to enter the country.[20] And, as the war in the Pacific came to a close but as a deep sense of "populate or perish" lingered on, Australia launched a massive recruitment drive. The intent was to increase the population by 2 percent annually, a feat that would require the influx of at least 70,000 migrants every year.[21] Each of these initiatives was grounded in an explicit racial rhetoric that prioritized the settlement of British "stock" above other nationalities. Although the scale of the Australian scheme required casting a wider net throughout Europe, Arthur Calwell, the country's Minister for Immigration, underscored that the government's goal was to enlist ten Britons for every "foreign" migrant it took in.[22] In Southern Rhodesia, where the 1946 Alien Act mandated that non-British migrants could account for no more than 10 percent of the total population, the issue was even more straightforward.[23]

The postwar recovery of the child emigration movement was thus part of a broader commitment to Britishness in the later 1940s. Indeed, the transfer of children to the dominions reflected this enduring confidence in Greater Britain better than did any other policy, for it implied that the bonds of imperial loyalty would persist for generations to come. "Children," noted the Australian Ministry for Post-war Reconstruction in 1944, were essential to the nation's "all-out immigration effort ... because they are most readily assimilable, most adaptable, and have a full working life to give to this country." The Ministry aimed to recruit 50,000 unaccompanied boys and girls by the third anniversary of the armistice, the majority of whom, it hoped, would be British.[24] Projected to cost between £64 and £71 million and to require nearly 16,000 British and Australian staff, the proposal signified a major investment of money

---

[20] Southern Rhodesia, Office of the High Commissioner, "Present Immigration Policy," December 1944, DO 35/1323, TNA: PRO.

[21] A. A. Calwell, "Ministerial Statement," August 2, 1945, DO 35/1135, TNA: PRO.

[22] A. A. Calwell, "Fourth Ministerial Statement," November 22, 1946, DO 35/1135, TNA: PRO. On the political machinations behind the British assisted passage agreement with Australia, see Stephen Constantine, "Waving Goodbye? Australia, Assisted Passages, and the Empire and Commonwealth Settlement Acts, 1945–72," *Journal of Imperial & Commonwealth History* 26 (1998): 176–195.

[23] A. S. Mlambo, *White Immigration into Rhodesia: From Occupation to Federation* (Harare: University of Zimbabwe, 2002), 15.

[24] Ministry of Post-War Reconstruction, "Confidential Memo on Child Migration," *c.* September 1944, A989, 1944/43/554/2/5, ANA; Departments of the Interior and Post-War Reconstruction, "Agenda on Child Migration," approved by the Cabinet on December 6, 1944, A989, 1944/43/554/2/5, ANA.

and resources.[25] It also proved wildly unrealistic, since Britain turned out to have only 3,000 orphans at the end of the war, instead of the tens of thousands that had been predicted. By 1946, Australian officials were forced to scale back the scheme "on account of the exorbitant cost ... and the unlikelihood that children in such numbers could be secured." They resigned themselves to working through the existing child emigration charities instead of taking on a separate recruitment campaign.[26] Despite its failure, the initiative remained an important example of the power of the imperial imagination following the war, a time when the global community of Britons appeared both deeply rooted and resilient.

A similar impulse was at work in New Zealand, where the state began recruiting child migrants in 1948. Although the country had welcomed the arrival of teenaged "youth migrants" in the interwar years, it had never before been a focus of child emigration.[27] The most basic reason was that the Fairbridge Society, which had been at the forefront of the extension of the movement during the 1920s and 1930s, had few connections in New Zealand and little interest in including the dominion in its purview. Equally important, however, was the fact that New Zealand social services had embraced a philosophy of family-based care well before their counterparts in Britain or in the other dominions.[28] Welfare officials in the country began promoting foster placements or the supervision of children in their birth homes as early as the 1910s. In contrast to the Australian government's violent disregard of Indigenous family ties, New Zealand politicians never pursued the removal of children from Maori families or kin groups. And, throughout the interwar years, the state actively promoted the deinstitutionalization of children in care, so that by 1948 there were fewer than 300 children living in government-run homes and their average length of stay was two or three years.[29]

The family-centered nature of New Zealand's social welfare ideology complicated the country's relationship to child emigration. Although postwar officials espoused the demographic benefits of recruiting young Britons, they took pains to adjust the policy so that it might better

[25] Australian Department of Immigration, "Conference of Commonwealth and State Officers," April 3 and 4, 1946, DO 35/1135, TNA: PRO.

[26] Rep. Aust. Tel. No. 288, August 23, 1946, DO 35/1134, TNA: PRO.

[27] Most notable was the Flock House initiative, founded by New Zealand wool growers to assist the immigration of the sons or daughters of British sailors who had been killed or wounded during the First World War. The Church of England and Salvation Army also coordinated the resettlement of teenage farm apprentices to New Zealand during the interwar years. Harper and Constantine, *Migration and Empire*, 88.

[28] Bronwyn Dalley, *Family Matters: Child Welfare in Twentieth-Century New Zealand* (Auckland University Press, 1998).

[29] Ibid, 94.

approximate familial care. Child migrants to the dominion were thus placed not in institutions and farm schools, as was typical elsewhere in the empire, but in foster homes. In addition, the government did more to encourage the subsequent immigration of their parents or relatives, in the hopes that the influx of children would spur a larger wave of Britannic settlement into the country. These modifications made the scheme more bureaucratically cumbersome than the period's other child emigration initiatives, and slowed down the recruitment process significantly. As in Australia, the project never achieved the large numbers that dominion officials hoped for, and in 1954 its directors decided to concentrate only on youths aged seventeen or older, who would not require foster care.[30] New Zealand's postwar foray into child emigration did nevertheless signify the persistent strength of the belief that the ties of Britannic racial heritage and imperial belonging were worth protecting.

Yet, even as metropolitan and dominion politicians confirmed their allegiance to the empire, the threads of the imperial fabric were starting to unravel. Although postwar British leaders struggled to retain the nation's imperial power into the 1960s, by the dawn of that decade it had become clear to all but the hard-liners that the terrain had changed, and there was no going back.[31] Britain's weakened position first became apparent during the austerity years of the late 1940s, when the slow pace of the domestic economic recovery forced the Labour government to increase its dependence on American capital. In 1946, it narrowly avoided bankruptcy by means of a $3.5 billion dollar loan from the United States. Government officials' simultaneous awareness that the military was overextended and that the nation could not afford to suppress a major rebellion in the empire was also an important factor in the decision to retreat from India the following year.[32] During the 1950s,

---

[30] Sircombe, "A Welfare Initiative?," 36. See also Philip Bean and Joy Melville, *Lost Children of the Empire: The Untold Story of Britain's Child Migrants* (London: Unwin Hyman, 1989), 132–133; Heather Wilson, "British Stock for a British Dominion: The New Zealand Government's Child Migration Scheme," (unpublished MA thesis, University of Auckland, 1996); Dugald McDonald and Suzanne de Joux, *British Child Migrants in New Zealand, 1949–1999: Fifty Years of New Stories* (Christchurch: British Child Migrants Society NZ, 2000).

[31] On the narrowed political and economic options available to metropolitan officials in this period, see John Darwin, *Britain and Decolonisation: The Retreat from Empire in the Post-war World* (Basingstoke: Macmillan, 1988); Nicholas White, *Decolonisation: The British Experience since 1945* (New York: Longman, 1999); Kent Fedorowich and Martin Thomas, eds., *International Diplomacy and Colonial Policy* (London: Frank Cass, 2001); Frank Heinlein, *British Government Policy and Decolonisation, 1945–1963: Scrutinising the Official Mind* (London: Routledge, 2002); Ronald Hyam, *Britain's Declining Empire: The Road to Decolonisation, 1918–1968* (Cambridge University Press, 2006).

[32] Wm. Roger Louis, "The Dissolution of the British Empire," in *The Oxford History of the British Empire*, vol. IV, ed. Brown and Louis, 329–355, 331–336.

British policy fluctuated between an intense ambition to hold onto the empire and a growing awareness that the nation's imperial commitments were unsustainable.[33] The Suez Canal Crisis of 1956 was an influential turning point that proved to the world that Britain was no longer capable of acting as a global power without the consent of the United States. In its aftermath, the rising power of anticolonial nationalist movements throughout Africa and Asia, combined with the realization that British trade had become reliant on the European markets, brought about a fundamental reassessment of the value of empire. Two key events of the early 1960s – Macmillan's "Wind of Change" speech in South Africa in February of 1960 and Britain's 1961 application to join the European Economic Community (EEC) – indicated the imperial ideal had lost the salience it once held in the first half of the twentieth century.

Of course, the erosion of the empire was not the product of British calculations alone. In each of the settler territories, the 1950s and 1960s were marked by the emergence of a new cultural politics that slowly weakened the importance of the imperial ethic. The two main centers of the postwar child emigration movement, Australia and Southern Rhodesia, help illustrate the distinct ways that this transition shaped the contours of dominion nationalism in this period. In Australia, as Stuart Ward has argued, the "steady drift from imperial moorings was a gradual, almost imperceptible process" that accompanied the political recognition of Britain's waning power.[34] The rapid development and diversification of the Australian economy in the 1950s provided the initial catalyst. A spike in the worldwide demand for Australian goods, especially for its powerhouse exports of wheat and wool, meant that by the mid 1950s the country was outgrowing the European market. In 1956, the Menzies government took the lead in renegotiating the system of imperial preference in order to loosen the restrictions on Australian commerce. The following year, it entered a new trade treaty with Japan, a critical step that signaled the redirection of the nation's export economy toward East Asia and the Pacific.[35] The decisive shift came, however, in the early 1960s, when Britain's application to join the EEC was broadly interpreted in Australia as a sign that the bonds of Greater Britain were breaking apart. Unsurprisingly, the years following the 1961–1963 EEC crisis witnessed a surge of artistic and literary nationalism that aimed to define Australia's identity in local, rather than imperial, terms. As the Liberal

---

[33] Martin Lynn, ed., *The British Empire in the 1950s: Retreat or Revival?* (New York: Palgrave Macmillan, 2006).
[34] Ward, *Australia and the British Embrace*, 4.
[35] Russel Ward, *The History of Australia: The Twentieth Century* (New York: Harper and Row, 1977), 290–292.

MP William Charles Wentworth remarked in 1966, it was "not so very long ago that most Australians would have thought of themselves primarily as British citizens and, secondarily, as Australian citizens. Today, for most Australians, we are first Australian citizens, and British in some secondary sense."[36]

This marginalization of Britishness in Australian political culture had important implications for the nation's immigration policy, which step by step opened to accept larger numbers of non-British migrants. At the beginning of the 1950s, over 80 percent of Australia's immigrants had come from the United Kingdom. By the end of the decade, the majority were arriving from continental Europe, especially from Italy, Greece, and the Balkans.[37] These changing demographics helped transform urban life across Australia in the 1960s. Melbourne, for instance, developed a rich, European-influenced café culture that reflected both its large population of Italians and its newfound status as the city with the second largest Greek population in the world after Athens.[38] This widening tolerance for non-British, southern European migrants was indicative of the declining political will for the White Australia policy. In 1958, the government quietly discontinued the dictation test requirement, long used to exclude non-Europeans from the country. Eight years later, the Migration Act of 1966 relaxed many of the country's racial quotas and created new provisions for Asian immigration. The remaining restrictions were removed in the early 1970s, and in 1975 the government formally legislated against the use of race as a criterion for admission. This slow reorientation of Australian national identity away from British exclusivity toward a new ethic of multiculturalism not only ushered in a significant rise in non-European immigration but also allowed for the gradual incorporation of the Indigenous population into the citizenry. In 1962, Aboriginal Australians were first granted the right to vote. Five years later, following a national referendum, the federal government extended its legislative power over Indigenous communities, an act that finally accorded Aborigines full citizenship rights.[39]

---

[36] Quoted in Ward, *Australia and the British Embrace*, 240. See also Neville Meaney, "Britishness and Australian Identity: The Problem of Nationalism in Australian History and Historiography," *Australian Historical Studies* 32, no. 116 (April 2001): 76–90; James Curran and Stuart Ward, *The Unknown Nation: Australia after Empire* (Melbourne University Press, 2010).

[37] Andrew Markus, James Jupp, and Peter McDonald, *Australia's Immigration Revolution* (Crows Nest: Allen & Unwin, 2009), 5.

[38] Donald Denoon, Philippa Mein-Smith, and Marivic Wyndham, *A History of Australia, New Zealand, and the Pacific* (Oxford: Blackwell, 2000), 350.

[39] Bain Attwood and Andrew Markus, *The 1967 Referendum: Race, Power, and the Australian Constitution* (Canberra: Aboriginal Studies Press, 1997). These developments reflected

While the Australian turn from empire was a long and piecemeal process, in Southern Rhodesia the break was more sudden. Tensions between the British and Rhodesian governments first arose during the short-lived Central African Federation (CAF), created in 1953 to unite Southern Rhodesia, Northern Rhodesia, and Nyasaland into a political and economic unit. To British officials, combining Southern Rhodesia's industrial power with the mineral wealth of Northern Rhodesia's copper belt and the labor resources of Nyasaland made sound economic sense. It also seemed a hedge against the spread of apartheid-style White supremacy throughout the region, a way of keeping Southern Rhodesia's settlers aligned with the empire rather than with neighboring South Africa. In its early years, the plan appeared to have paid off. Throughout the mid 1950s, the CAF boasted a solidly expanding GDP that jumped from £350 million in 1954 to nearly £450 million two years later.[40] There were also signs of the deepening appeal of political liberalism among the Rhodesian electorate. Most notably, when Godfrey Huggins resigned as Prime Minister of Southern Rhodesia to become the Federation's first leader, the moderately left-leaning Garfield Todd, a former missionary committed to African advancement, succeeded him.[41] One of his first decisions in office was to mandate that government officials and publications begin referring to Africans as "Mister" instead of the customary title of "Native" or "A. M." (African Male).[42] It was a small but significant illustration of the more progressive atmosphere, albeit one that highlighted just how long was the road left to travel.

Despite these positive signs, the basis of the CAF was inherently unstable, with the severest fault lines running along issues of race.[43] Billed as a means of creating multiracial "partnership," the Federation's political system remained palpably unfair. Its constitution stipulated that nine of the Assembly's thirty-five members needed to represent "African interests," but only six of these representatives were Africans; the other three were White settlers. The electorate was also heavily biased toward

the broader postwar drive to assimilate Indigenous peoples into the Australian way of life, a strategy that defined Aboriginal identity as a cultural relic that individuals needed to forego before entering the mainstream of society. On the doctrine and its implementation in this period, see Anna Haebich, *Spinning the Dream: Assimilation in Australia, 1950–1970* (Fremantle: Fremantle Press, 2008).

[40] Robert Blake, *A History of Rhodesia* (New York: Knopf, 1978), 288.

[41] On the spread of political liberalism in this period, see Dickson Mungazi, *The Last British Liberals in Africa: Michael Blundell and Garfield Todd* (London: Praeger, 1999).

[42] Blake, *A History of Rhodesia*, 290.

[43] The best analysis of the growing racial strife within the Federation remains Richard Gray, *The Two Nations: Aspects of the Development of Race Relations in the Rhodesias and Nyasaland* (London: Oxford University Press, 1960).

the White population of Southern Rhodesia. Restrictive franchise qualifi-cations based on literacy and income ensured that, of the approximately 3.5 million Africans in the colony in 1953, no more than 1,000 quali-fied to vote and fewer than 500 were actually on the rolls. In Northern Rhodesia, where nearly all Africans were British protected persons who could not vote, there were ten registered. In Nyasaland, there were none.[44] As local politicians made plain, when they spoke of partnership, they did not mean equality. Rather, according to Huggins' infamous def-inition, the relationship between African and European was akin to that of a horse and its rider.

Even in its less strident forms, the doctrine of partnership remained intensely paternalistic, signifying less the creation of a system of power sharing than the gradual incorporation of the African majority into a White-dominated civil society.[45] Fully aware of these ideological and institutional defects, African political parties throughout the territories opposed the Federation from the start. The later 1950s were punctu-ated by strikes and riots across the CAF, leading to the declaration of a state of emergency in Nyasaland in 1959 and the passage of legislation in Southern Rhodesia allowing the government to detain without charge any African suspected of inciting unrest. As the Federation imploded from within, Rhodesian politics swung to the right. Todd was ousted from power in 1958 when his Cabinet balked at his program of liberal political change and resigned *en masse*.[46] His successor, Edgar Whitehead, fared little better, provoking the simultaneous outrage of Africans by banning the African National Congress and of White settlers by legislating to improve the quality of Indigenous education.

Recognizing that the CAF was unraveling, politicians in Southern Rhodesia began a push for greater independence from Britain as early as 1960.[47] The crux of the matter – apparent to all sides by the start of the decade – was that the settler community's aim of retaining White dominance jarred with the changing framework of the postwar empire. Throughout the last years of the Federation, which finally dissolved at the end of 1963, the majority of Britain's colonies in Africa gained their independence. The collapse of the CAF added two more independ-ent nations, as Nyasaland and Northern Rhodesia became Malawi and Zambia. And, while a series of constitutional negotiations in 1961 granted

[44] Blake, *A History of Rhodesia*, 296.
[45] Michael O. West, *The Rise of an African Middle Class: Colonial Zimbabwe, 1898–1965* (Bloomington: Indiana University Press, 2002), 192–193.
[46] Mungazi, *The Last British Liberals in Africa*, 128–130.
[47] Josiah Brownell, *The Collapse of Rhodesia: Population Demographics and the Politics of Race* (London: I. B. Tauris, 2011), 8–9.

Southern Rhodesia increased control over local affairs in exchange for a limited extension of the African electorate, British officials held firm that they would not consider full independence until a plan for majority rule was in place. The victory of the hardline Rhodesia Front party in December of 1962, followed two years later by its landslide reelection, indicated that settler opposition to multiracialism was intensifying. When, in September of 1965, the Commonwealth Relations Office stated categorically that the end of racial discrimination was the necessary precondition for granting independence, the Rhodesian Prime Minister, Ian Smith, broke off negotiations. Two months later, on November 11, 1965, his Cabinet voted unanimously to proclaim Rhodesia's independence from the empire.[48]

Modeled on its American predecessor, the text of the Rhodesian Declaration of Independence took pains to frame the act of disunion as a political rather than cultural separation.[49] It stressed that the "people of Rhodesia," who had shown "loyalty to the Crown and to their kith and kin in the United Kingdom and elsewhere through two world wars," were determined "to continue exercising ... the same loyalty and devotion" in the future. Underlying these affirmations of lasting Britannic pride, though, an important transformation had occurred. As in Australia, a new collective ethic had emerged, in which local referents and conditions replaced the bonds of empire as the cornerstone of the national identity. Although the rhetoric of shared Britishness lingered on, it paled in importance when compared to White Rhodesians' self-appointed role as the builders of "civilization in a primitive country."[50] That subtle but profound change in attitudes and identifications was not simply the result of the shifts taking place in the arenas of economics and high politics. Just as essential was the expansion of the mental sciences and the building of the welfare state, which together helped broker the creation of separate and explicitly national models of child welfare across the late settler empire.

[48] On these negotiations, see Blake, *A History of Rhodesia*, 363–384. On the broader impact of the UDI during the 1960s and 1970s, see Carl Peter Watts, *Rhodesia's Unilateral Declaration of Independence: International Dimensions* (New York: Palgrave Macmillan, 2012); Luise White, "What Does it Take to Be a State: Sovereignty and Sanctions in Rhodesia, 1965–1980," in *The State of Sovereignty: Territories, Laws, Populations*, ed. Douglas Howland and Luise White (Bloomington: Indiana University Press, 2009), 148–168.

[49] Donal Lowry, "Rhodesia 1890–1980: 'The Lost Dominion,'" in *Settlers and Expatriates: Britons over the Seas*, ed. Robert Bickers (Oxford University Press, 2010), 112–149, 112–118.

[50] Southern Rhodesia, "Unilateral Declaration of Independence," November 11, 1965, in David Armitage, *The Declaration of Independence: A Global History* (Cambridge, MA: Harvard University Press, 2007), 243–245.

## Good homes overseas

In the summer of 1944, a reader browsing the London *Times* would find the front pages dominated by the Allied invasion of Normandy and the Soviet offensive in the east. But, if she turned a bit further to the editorial page, she would encounter a vibrant conversation about a domestic issue that to many commentators appeared just as vital to the future of the British nation: the care of boys and girls in charitable and state-run institutions. The spark that ignited the discussion was an editorial letter written by Lady Allen of Hurtwood, a woman whose prominence in the field of child welfare was growing but who was still better known for her work as a landscape architect than as a reformer. Trained in the belief that material environments had a profound impact on human development, she was horrified by what she considered the cold and austere atmosphere of children's institutions. "Many thousands of [needy] children are being brought up under repressive conditions that are generations out of date," she wrote. Boys and girls were crowded into large Victorian residential homes, in which they received little attention from overworked and untrained staffs. Declaring an urgent need to act, Allen demanded a government commission to "explore this largely uncivilized territory" and to expand state control over the tangled array of charitable and local authority provision for the young.[51]

Published at a time of widespread debate over the direction social policy would take in the postwar years, Allen's letter struck a chord. The Beveridge Report had been submitted to Parliament eighteen months earlier, and by the middle of 1944 it was clear that some large-scale revision to the social insurance system was inevitable, even if the exact content of the changes was still undecided. The importance of Allen's intervention was that she cast light on a subset of the population that was left out of Beveridge's family-centered vision of the welfare state: those neglected or orphaned children who no longer lived with their parents and so would not benefit from the expansion of government services designed to keep families out of poverty.[52] The numbers were substantial. At the end of the war, nearly 125,000 young people in the country fell into this category, of which a little more than 40,000 were receiving care from the largely unregulated voluntary sector.[53]

---

[51] Marjory Allen, "Children in 'Homes': Wards of State or Charity, Inquiry and Reform," *The Times*, July 15, 1944.

[52] On the gendered vision of family located at the ideological center of the welfare state, see Susan Pedersen, *Family, Dependence, and the Origins of the Welfare State: Britain and France, 1914–1945* (Cambridge University Press, 1993).

[53] Myra Curtis, "Report of the Care of Children Committee," *Parliamentary Papers* X, Cmd. 6922, September 1946, 27.

Letters began pouring into the *Times*. By the end of August the paper had broken its editorial record for correspondence about a single issue.[54] While some members of the charitable community wrote in to defend their standards of care, most commentators supported Allen's call for reform. A number contributed sensationalist, firsthand accounts of the "shocking conditions" inside children's homes, where "floggings and beatings were the order of the day" and where helpless boys and girls were treated no better than "inmates."[55] For the most part, though, the conversation centered on more mundane and casual forms of neglect that resulted from poor funding, inadequate staffing, and not enough training. According to the Conservative MP Edward Keeling, the most serious problems stemmed from a simple lack of attention. Keeling described a recent visit to a large group home outside London, during which he had encountered dozens of needy children growing up with "no love and little human sympathy." The emotional consequences of their upbringing had been evident immediately: "They could not talk, because nobody had ever talked to them. They knew one word – 'no' – which they screamed with hard defiant looks, and with hands raised as if to strike. They were anti-social, untrained in any good habits, helpless."[56] The violence committed against these children, Keeling claimed, was not physical but psychological. Abandoned to an institutional environment that lacked opportunities for nurturing, they had become hardened into a state of profound social isolation, unable to understand their own emotions or control their aggressive impulses.

Keeling was not the only correspondent to draw attention to the potential for psychological damage in children's institutions. Numerous child guidance practitioners and local authority officers wrote in to stress the importance of "affection [and] personal interest ... for healthy emotional development," and to voice reservations about whether group homes offered these kinds of experiences to children.[57] George Bernard Shaw, nearly ninety years old and as cantankerous as ever, contributed his observation that, even in highly efficient, medically advanced institutions, boys and girls "died like flies" or "grew up a nervous wreck or disciplinarian

[54] Marjory Allen, *Memoirs of an Uneducated Women: Lady Allen of Hurtwood* (London: Thames and Hudson, 1975), 184.

[55] Alun Price, "Children's Home from Inside. Former Inmate's Experiences. 'Shocking Conditions,'" *The Times*, August 23, 1944.

[56] E. H. Keeling, "Children in Homes. The Institutional System. A War-Time Experiment," *The Times*, July 18, 1944.

[57] Otto Niemeyer, Evelyn Fox, Doris Odlum, R. G. Gordon, and Alan Maberly, "Children in Homes. The Training of Staff. A National Certificate," *The Times*, July 27, 1944. See also John Moss, "Children in Homes. Smaller Units. The Right Kind of Staff," *The Times*, July 24, 1944.

terrorist." Children's wellbeing, he concluded, depended less on whether they were treated according to the most up-to-date, "scientific" methods of physical care than on whether they had mothers who "hugged them, mammocked them, kissed them, smacked them, talked baby talk to them or scolded them."[58] The crucial point to emerge from comments like these was that children possessed an instinctual desire for love, tenderness, and human contact, which Britain's overcrowded and understaffed institutions were doing little to accommodate. In this respect, the transformative effect of the *Times* debate was that it offered a forum for reformers, parliamentarians, and concerned citizens alike to articulate a new model of welfare, one that centered less on children's physiological requirements than on their emotional life and psychological needs.

Although this emphasis on children's psyches had its origins in the interwar expansion of psychoanalysis and child guidance, the massive displacements of the war years did much to push the discussion of young people's emotional health out of the clinic and into the public domain. On the continent, the conflict left an estimated 16 million European children homeless and another 13 million without one or both parents.[59] The losses were considerably less profound in Britain, yet there, too, the war produced broad anxiety about the disruption of households and the destabilization of traditional gender roles.[60] Confronted by the unprecedented upheaval of European family life, leading social workers in Britain and the United States began to reassess their understanding of childhood trauma. As Tara Zahra has argued, while earlier reformers had defined children's suffering in terms of a lack of food, medicine, or moral grounding that seemingly justified a child's removal from the home, their postwar counterparts were more inclined to view any form of family separation as a "humanitarian crisis in its own right."[61] Growing numbers of welfare authorities asserted that the only rightful place to raise a boy or girl was within the realm of the family. It was a vision of children's "best interests" that marked institutions as psychologically harmful.[62]

In Britain, the driving force behind this shift was a series of pioneering wartime studies into the government's evacuation policy. Psychologists had viewed the program, code-named "Operation Pied Piper," as a "great social experiment" that would provide them unparalleled access into the

---

[58] G. B. Shaw, "Bringing Up the Child. A Contrast in Method," *The Times*, July 21, 1944.

[59] Tara Zahra, *The Lost Children: Reconstructing Europe's Families after World War II* (Cambridge, MA: Harvard University Press, 2011), 6.

[60] Sonya Rose, *Which People's War? National Identity and Citizenship in Wartime Britain, 1939–1945* (Oxford University Press, 2003).

[61] Zahra, *The Lost Children*, 64.

[62] Michal Shapira, *The War Inside: Psychoanalysis, Total War and the Making of the Democratic Self in Postwar Britain* (Cambridge University Press, 2013).

private dynamics of family life.[63] By the second year of the war, three major investigations of the project were underway, the most comprehensive and influential of which was the *Cambridge Evacuation Survey*, edited by the educational psychologist Susan Isaacs.[64] The nine-month inquiry followed the progress of two groups of children evacuated from their homes in the London suburbs to private households in Cambridge. Released in 1941, its findings charted a steady deterioration in the children's psychological health, signaled by increased rates of bedwetting, homesickness, and depression. The *Survey* also reported that many parents had recalled their sons and daughters after just a few weeks, despite the government's warning that their lives remained at risk. For Isaacs, such evidence demonstrated that the bond between children and parents was "so deeply rooted ... that it has defied even the law of self-preservation."[65] Concluding that the study had illustrated "first and foremost the strength of family ties," she argued that children who lost the "reassurance provided by the familiar background of their lives" would suffer both present unhappiness and lasting emotional distress.[66]

The significance of the *Cambridge Evacuation Survey* for the wartime critique of children's institutions was its emphasis on nurturing as a basic psychological need. As Isaacs wrote in the *Times* discussion:

It is an established fact, not a matter of sentiment or opinion, that "mothering" and close human contacts are as necessary for full welfare in childhood as are proper diet and medical care. Nor can character, personality and sound social attitudes develop without the experience of personal affection and understanding treatment in the early years.[67]

To Isaacs, the problem with most institutions was their inability to provide a healthy experiential environment in which young people could develop stable attachments to adults. Moreover, by suggesting that

[63] Susan Isaacs, ed., *The Cambridge Evacuation Survey: A Wartime Study in Social Welfare and Education* (London: Methuen and Co., 1941), 2.
[64] The others were Dorothy Burlingham and Anna Freud, *Young Children in War Time* (London: Allen and Unwin, 1942); Women's Group on Public Welfare, *Our Towns – A Close Up: A Study Made in 1939–1942 with Certain Recommendations by the Hygiene Committee of the Women's Group on Public Welfare* (London: Oxford University Press, 1943).
[65] Isaacs, *The Cambridge Evacuation Survey*, 9. Another explanation for this phenomenon is that the first evacuation coincided with the period of "phony war" from the autumn of 1939 through the summer of 1940. When the predicted bombings failed to materialize, many parents decided that it was safe for their children to come back. By January 1940, over two-thirds of the evacuees had returned to their homes. The onset of the Blitz in August of 1940, however, prompted a second evacuation, during which many of the same children went back to the countryside.
[66] Ibid, 154.
[67] Susan Isaacs, "Children in Homes," *The Times*, July 18, 1944.

institutionalized children might prove incapable of developing "sound social attitudes," she raised the frightening prospect that the current welfare system was doing more to detract from than to sustain Britain's vital wartime consensus. It is worth noting that Isaacs did not dismiss the value of group homes completely. After all, her placement of the word "mothering" in quotes implied that caring for the young was an art that could be taught to staff members through "systematic training in all aspects of child development and child welfare."[68] Nevertheless, by defining childrearing as a psychological rather than a purely physiological process, Isaacs and others cast doubt on whether this delicate act could be fully realized outside the sphere of the nuclear family.

Before long, the criticism of the evacuations policy, combined with the publicity generated by Allen's letter in *The Times*, spurred the government to reexamine the conventional practices of child welfare in Britain. In March of 1945, the Home Secretary, Herbert Morrison, appointed a seventeen-member commission to investigate the quality of the nation's state-run and charitable provision for children. Headed by the civil servant Myra Curtis, this Care of Children Committee interviewed 200 witnesses over the next eighteen months, conducted surprise inspections of charity and local authority institutions across forty-one counties, and visited dozens of foster families. All told, its members directly assessed the conditions of some 30,000 boys and girls who lived apart from their families or relatives. These investigations ranked as one of the most extensive government inquiries of the day, and the committee's report, published in September of 1946, has often been seen as a major turning point in the history of British welfarism.[69] Its more than sixty recommendations formed the core of the 1948 Children Act, which provided the Home Office with explicit regulatory powers, bound every local authority to establish a Children's Department, and required the registration of all charities concerned with the young. The commission also presented a strong critique of institutions, and encouraged local authorities to make a "vigorous effort" to increase their use of more family-centered approaches such as adoption or fostering.[70]

---

[68] Ibid.
[69] Jean Packman, *The Child's Generation: Child Care Policy in Britain* (Oxford: Blackwell, 1975); Jean Heywood, *Children in Care: The Development of the Service for the Deprived Child* (London: Routledge & Kegan Paul, 1978, originally 1959), 143–149; Pat Thane, *Foundations of the Welfare State* (New York: Longman, 1996), 243–245; Harry Hendrick, *Child Welfare: Historical Dimensions, Contemporary Debate* (Bristol: Policy Press, 2003), 133–140.
[70] Curtis, "Report of the Care of Children Committee," 179.

Undoubtedly, these proposals represented important transformations in the administration and style of Britain's child welfare system. And yet the theory of child development that underpinned the report remained largely unchanged. Like their interwar predecessors, the committee members continued to understand child health within an environmental framework that focused on the role of external conditions in determining children's overall wellbeing. While the members extended the definition of "normal" development to include a greater stress on emotions, their basic assumption remained that healthy socialization depended to a large degree on the nature of the space in which young people lived. As such, the Care of Children Committee represented less a reversal than an expansion of the established model of childrearing. Its stress on the importance of a "family-like" setting, rather than the *actual* ties of family, ensured the continued viability of various types of care within the burgeoning welfare state, including the emigration of children to farm schools and orphanages throughout the settler empire.

Crucially, the committee restricted its purview to only those children who had already been "deprived of a normal home life." This meant that they did not examine methods of reintegrating boys and girls into their own homes or of preventing family breakdown. Rather, their aim was more generally environmental: to discover the "conditions best calculated to compensate [children] for the lack of parental care."[71] The first step was to take stock of the problems within the existing system. Members devoted the majority of the report to critiquing Britain's children's institutions, with an emphasis on buildings that were too large, overcrowded, or lacked the intimacy of private homes. They expressed particular distain for the thirty-two workhouses they visited, which had become a "dumping ground for children who could not readily be disposed of elsewhere." Designed for adults, none came close to providing a nurturing atmosphere. Instead, they were "large gaunt looking buildings with dark stairways and corridors ... bare boards and draughts, and a continual smell of mass cookings, soft soap and disinfectant."[72] Although most of the other residences the committee viewed were less austere, they too contained serious shortcomings. Members' inspections uncovered "dilapidated furniture," "long narrow dormitories containing rows of iron bedsteads and cots that were formal and ugly," and "either a distressing dearth of pictures or, what was worse, a collection of ugly, uninteresting pictures which appeared to have been thrown out as valueless from other houses."[73]

---

[71] Ibid, 6.     [72] Ibid, 38–39.     [73] Ibid, 63.

Such criticisms presented children's immediate aesthetic environment as a major factor in their emotional development. The cultivation of well-rounded personalities, the committee contended, demanded beautiful surroundings, complete with items such as pictures, flowers, and colored tablecloths that would "delight the eye of any child." But what members usually found on their visits to institutions was "dirt and dreariness, drabness, and over-regimentation."[74] Another problem was that the larger homes tended to be drastically understaffed, with just a few untrained providers on hand to care for dozens of children at a time. The result was a general "lack of interest in and affection for the children" that the committee "found shocking":

The child in these Homes was not recognized as an individual with his own rights and possessions, his own life to live and his own contribution to offer. He was merely one of a large crowd, eating, playing and sleeping with the rest, without any place or possession of his own or any quiet room to which he could retreat.[75]

Again, the essential point was that healthy personalities could only take shape in a certain setting: one that was small enough to ensure that children received individualized attention and would not be simply part of a crowd, but that also contained areas for privacy and reflection, a "quiet room to which he could retreat." As the report observed, "good social habits cannot easily be acquired in crowded, ill-equipped and poorly repaired rooms nor can the child develop the capacity to care for himself in such conditions."[76]

If stark, smelly, and monotonous surroundings were inimical to the production of psychologically sound, democratic individuals, it followed that the ideal sensory environment for children was an intimate, attractive space that contained opportunities for the exercise of free choice alongside sustained, affectionate contact with adults. The committee's recognition that this setting was most easily found within the "free conditions of ordinary family life" underlay their commitment to fostering and adoption.[77] Yet it did not lead members to rule out group homes altogether. On the contrary, the report acknowledged that many private households had drawbacks of their own. They were inherently difficult to regulate, which increased the risk that children would fall through cracks in the system. This point was at the forefront of the committee's discussions, having recently been publicized by the case of Dennis O'Neill, a Welsh boy who had been starved and beaten to death by his foster father

---

[74] Ibid, 74 and 134.     [75] Ibid, 134.
[76] Ibid, 62.     [77] Ibid, 152.

in January of 1945.[78] Moreover, family placements did not guarantee the right material conditions either. In the course of their inspections, members had uncovered a host of inadequate foster homes. They found babies placed in "attics where owing to bomb damage wet dripped in," and children "living at the back of derelict shops" or "playing in garbage heaps amongst dust bins, old tin cans and dirty milk bottles." Noting that these conditions were "often as good as the child's own home," the committee questioned the value of removing boys and girls from one unfit household only to place them in another.[79]

This skepticism about the merits of some foster placements revealed the class biases that underlay the committee's thinking. The "normal home life" that members deemed necessary for children's socialization – with its requirements of a multiroomed, tastefully decorated house and ample leisure time to invest in family togetherness – was impossible to create below a certain income. Like many reformers in the immediate postwar period, the members of the committee continued to assume that responsible parenting had material foundations. This notion had deep roots within British social thought, but it had been revived and strengthened in the public response to the evacuations. As thousands of often ill-clothed, malnourished, and louse-ridden children had entered middle-class homes, commentators had become alarmed by what they perceived as an epidemic of negligent, degenerate, or otherwise "feckless" parenting among the poor.[80] Policymakers' persistent belief, as Richard Titmuss put it in 1950, that "slum mores are consistent with a slum home" strengthened the committee's dedication to ensuring that needy boys and girls would not be fostered in impoverished or otherwise "degraded" households.[81] Although members noted that, when left to their own devices, many parents found excellent placements for their children, they also averred that there remained a subsection of "degenerate and sub-normal mothers [who] usually chose homes in slum areas with poor foster mothers of low mentality from whom it was most difficult to get the child away."[82]

---

[78] On the case and its impact on the Committee, see Heywood, *Children in Care*, 141–143.

[79] Curtis, "Report of the Care of Children Committee," 124.

[80] Jose Harris, "War and Social History: Britain and the Home Front during the Second World War," *Contemporary European History* 1 (1992): 17–35; John Welshman, "Evacuation, Hygiene, and Social Policy: The Our Towns Report of 1943," *The Historical Journal* 42, no. 3 (September 1999): 781–807; Pat Starkey, "The Feckless Mother: Women, Poverty and Social Workers in Wartime and Post-War England," *Women's History Review* 9, no. 3 (September 2000): 539–557.

[81] Richard Titmuss, *Problems of Social Policy* (London: HMSO, 1950), 123.

[82] Curtis, "Report of the Care of Children Committee," 125.

This acknowledgment that despite the benefits of fostering there was still a "risk of acute unhappiness" in private households ensured that institutional care remained a viable option.[83] The Committee remarked that group homes were particularly appropriate for short-term cases, and stressed that a well-run and attractively conceived institution was better than a negligent foster home. For these reasons, members recommended that both the state and charitable organizations be allowed to continue placing children into residential care, provided that the institutional environment mimicked as closely as possible the size and comfort of a "normal home." The 1948 Children Act thus permitted the voluntary sector a large degree of flexibility. While it pushed local authorities to board their wards with families and to try to maintain contact between a child and his or her parents, it did not place the same stipulations on charities.[84] And, by allowing for the transfer of children from state care to voluntary associations, where they were likely to enter institutions, the legislation did little in the short run to reduce rates of institutionalization. In the decades after the war, the proportion of children in the care of local authorities who were in foster placements rose from 35 percent in 1949 to a high of 52 percent in 1963, after which it again declined.[85]

As such, although the Care of Children Committee offered an important critique of the institutional framework of child-centered provision, it did not overturn the long-established philosophy that needy boys and girls would benefit from a move to healthier, more nurturing settings. Emigration proponents were quick to point out that there was nothing in this environmental model of child welfare that could not be recreated within the "sister-nations of the Commonwealth."[86] In fact, the committee's final report had sanctioned the schemes, if tepidly, noting that there was a segment of "children with an unfortunate background" who would do well if given "a fresh start in a new country."[87] To illustrate that the policy remained in line with the new trends in social reform, the existing emigration charities soon incorporated the Committee's language into their publicity materials. The Fairbridge Society's 1948 Annual Report, for instance, offered an "authoritative statement of Fairbridge child care policy" that reflected the recent "progress in child welfare thinking" and "followed closely the provisions of the Curtis Committee." Alongside

---

[83] Ibid, 134.
[84] Constantine, "The British Government"; Julie Grier, "Voluntary Rights and Statutory Wrongs: The Case of Child Migration, 1948–1967," *History of Education* 31, no. 3 (2002): 263–280.
[85] Hendrick, *Child Welfare*, 136.
[86] Barnardo's, Annual Report, 1948, D.239/A3/1/83, ULSCA.
[87] Curtis, "Report of the Care of Children Committee," 177.

the organization's traditional aim of promoting "the settlement within the British Commonwealth of poor boys and girls," it added a new focus on providing "the security and support of home life, and the individual interest in each child which a dutiful parent offers to his own children."[88] In a similar vein, Barnardo's emphasized that the "vital principle" governing its work was the need to maintain "a true family atmosphere." The organization touted that, in the intimate space of a Barnardo's branch home, every child received personalized attention, for "just as the private family is the normal environment for a child, so the Barnardo family is the closest imitation of it."[89]

Underlying these assurances was a vision of a "family" that resembled less a biological entity into which a person was born than a social relationship that could be reproduced within a carefully structured institutional setting. Widely held throughout the voluntary sector, this conception found its clearest expression in the postwar reform project of the National Children's Home (NCH), a Methodist organization whose origins dated back to 1869. With more than 3,000 children receiving care across forty institutions in the United Kingdom, the postwar NCH was one of the period's leading children's charities. Its long-standing director, the Reverend John Litten, was recognized as a modernizer, a reputation that had secured him a spot on the Care of Children Committee, where he both supported the general critique of institutional practices and acted as an advocate for the philanthropic community. Throughout the Committee's investigations, he had maintained that the right kind of residential care offered young people access to resources that were difficult to attain in the "scattered private homes of boarded-out children," such as "progressive education," "proper oversight," "psychological treatment," and "training that will suit [a child's] aptitudes and abilities."[90] The point was not to abandon institutions altogether but to redesign them so that needy children could "be brought up under conditions as like to normal family life as can be."[91]

Putting this ideology into practice, in 1947 Litten launched a major restructuring of NCH care that transformed its large-scale residences into smaller, mixed-gender group homes that catered for eight to ten boys and girls at a time. The aim of these "little houses," as Litten called

[88] Fairbridge, Annual Report, 1948, D.296/D1/1/2, ULSCA; on the changes instituted within the organization following the Care of Children Committee, see Geoffrey Sherington and Chris Jeffery, *Fairbridge: Empire and Child Migration* (London: Woburn Press, 1998), 218–224.

[89] Barnardo's, Annual Report, 1947, D.239/A3/1/82, ULSCA.

[90] "Evidence of the Care of Children Committee," June 12, 1945, MH 102/1451D, TNA: PRO.

[91] NCH, "Work in Progress: Yearbook," 1947, D.541/D1/1/20, ULSCA.

them, was to create an ideal environment for children's emotional growth and individuation. The rooms were divided in order to offer each child "some corner that is his or her very own, a personal cupboard for treasured possessions, and his or her own little bed to sleep in at night." Efforts were also made to create a comfortable, pleasant, and domestic space. "Home, too, must be beautiful," the organization emphasized, for attractive settings were essential to the production of "comfort and good fellowship" as well as "happy memories."[92] All aspects of the décor, from the choice of paintings and curtains to the selection of the "cups and saucers, jugs and bowls," was therefore of "considerable importance," since these smaller touches left "their effect on those who view them day by day."[93] In short, the object of the "little houses" plan was to compensate children for the loss of their natural homes by providing them with the next best thing: an aesthetically stimulating and nurturing atmosphere, in which every boy or girl could develop "the sense of security and well-being which, more than anything else, are the basis of happiness ... and the foundations of true progress."[94]

In its argument that a well-designed physical space could serve as an adequate replacement for the bonds of family, the "little houses" model provided a powerful illustration of the continuities that remained in Britain's postwar child welfare ideology. Despite the rise of psychologically informed understandings of child development during the war years, many providers continued to assess children's needs according to an environmental framework, albeit one that replaced the earlier emphasis on rural settings with a newer stress on the interior design of the home. The result was the persistence throughout the later 1940s and into the 1950s of a vision of deprived children as malleable, individual units who lacked firm attachments to any particular locale or people. In this respect, Barnardo's could continue to style itself as a place "where no child has a 'past,' where every child 'starts level' and where every child finds friends, care, love and a future."[95] Although the organization's directors were more likely to express their "anxiety to avoid breaking up families" in the wake of the Care of Children Committee's report, this stipulation still applied only to those select households they deemed wholesome or morally healthy.[96] For all other children who entered the

---

[92] NCH, "Factors:Yearbook," 1950, D.541/D1/1/20, ULSCA.
[93] NCH, "Home from Home:Yearbook," 1951, D.541/D1/1/20, ULSCA.
[94] NCH, "Factors:Yearbook." On the origins of the "Little Houses" plan, see also NCH, "Blue-Prints: the Reconstruction Plans of the National Children's Home," 1943, D.541/D1/1/20, ULSCA.
[95] Barnardo's, Annual Report, 1947, D.239/A3/1/82, ULSCA.
[96] Barnardo's, Annual Report, 1949, D.239/A3/1/84, ULSCA.

care of Barnardo's with "a story – often a sad one," the charity's primary concern was to perform an act of erasure, "to make this [story] a thing of the past and to turn thoughts and hopes towards the future."[97] Similar notions underwrote the NCH's drive to reenter the child emigration field. The charity had been one of the first to send child migrants to Canada in the 1870s, resettling some 3,000 boys and girls over the next four decades.[98] But it had opted to discontinue the work after the 1924 Canadian ban, and would not have revived the project if not for Litten's advocacy. Working with the Australian Methodist Church, he launched a new scheme to Australia in 1948. The initiative brought the "little houses" concept to the dominion so that, as Litten stressed, the young migrants could retain the "normality and security" of living in "small mixed families."[99]

Litten's status as both a prominent member of the Care of Children Committee and the founder of the NCH's postwar emigration initiative demonstrates the close links that remained between the emigration movement and the wider realm of welfare in the immediate aftermath of the war. In this light, the revival of postwar child emigration offers a reminder of the ideological fluidity of the early years of the welfare state. While some child experts, supported by the psychological critique of institutionalization, stressed the importance of family connections, others argued convincingly that children's healthy emotional development could take place outside their particular family context. Amid the broader renewal of the British world concept of the later 1940s and early 1950s, child emigration remained not simply conceivable but firmly within the realm of acceptable practice. As Litten declared in a 1952 promotional booklet detailing the NCH's resettlement work, while Australia was "as remote from England as geography will permit, and most of its people have never seen – nor ever will – the white cliffs of Dover," Britain remained "their own land." "Going south" was a natural process that implied no loss of connection or culture. Child migrants were merely moving from one side of the Britannic family to the other, joining "a vital portion of the English-speaking race" in a land that espoused an unmatched "loyalty to King and Country."[100]

Yet, even as reformers such as Litten championed the continued glory of Greater Britain, new developments in the field of child psychology were already weakening this vision of imperial child welfare. The rise

---

[97] Barnardo's, Annual Report, 1950, D.239/A3/1/85, ULSCA.

[98] Marjorie Kohli, *The Golden Bridge: Young Immigrants to Canada, 1833–1939* (Toronto: Natural Heritage, 2003), 137–143.

[99] NCH, Minutes of the General Committee, July 29, 1948, D.541/A1/13, ULSCA.

[100] John Litten, "Going South," 1952, D.541/L3/3/9, ULSCA.

during the mid 1950s of an alternate understanding of children's emotional needs, which centered on the psychiatrist John Bowlby's articulation of attachment theory, served to conscribe the boundaries of care in unprecedented ways. These shifts had important consequences beyond the realm of child welfare. As strains began to appear in the political relationship between Britain and the dominions, this new psychological model of child development transformed child emigration into a site of contestation over the limits of imperial power and the meaning of national sovereignty in the late settler empire.

## Forging national childhoods

In 1953, John Bowlby, who was then serving as deputy-director of London's Tavistock Clinic and consulting with the World Health Organization (WHO), released an inexpensive Penguin paperback called *Child Care and the Growth of Love*. The object of the book was to raise awareness about "attachment theory," or, as Bowlby defined it, the need for an "infant and young child [to] experience a warm, intimate, and continuous relationship with his mother (or permanent mother-substitute – one person who steadily 'mothers' him)." Children who did not receive this form of nurturing suffered from "maternal deprivation," a crippling psychological disability that had "far-reaching effects on character."[101] They were insecure, or socially aggressive. They failed to create stable relationships with other people. The most deprived children – those who grew up in overcrowded institutions or austere hospitals – "almost always" suffered development that was "retarded – physically, intellectually, and socially." Hoping to raise awareness about the disorder, Bowlby devoted the majority of the book to chronicling all the "sad results which can follow to babies who are unmothered," a harrowing list that included "persistent stealing, violence, egotism ... sexual misdemeanours," inability to "make true friends, inaccessibility, pointless deceit and evasion," and a lack of "concentration in school."[102]

*Child Care and the Growth of Love* was not the first statement of these ideas. Bowlby had been theorizing along these lines since the late 1930s, when he noticed that many of the juvenile delinquents he was treating at Tavistock shared a common history of early separation from their mothers. He published these findings in 1946 as *Forty-Four Juvenile Thieves: Their Characters and Home-Life*, on the basis of which the WHO invited him to survey the mental health effects of childhood homelessness in

---

[101] John Bowlby, *Child Care and the Growth of Love* (Baltimore: Penguin, 1953), 11–12.
[102] Ibid, 18, 15, and 33.

Europe.[103] By the early 1950s, Bowlby had grown adept at publicizing his research in the media, and was becoming a recognizable presence on the radio and in the pages of newspapers and women's magazines. *Child Care and the Growth of Love* was by far his most successful endeavor, however. It was read by policymakers and the general public alike, went into six reprintings by the end of the 1960s, and ushered the term "Bowlbyism," a shorthand for the notion that children needed to bond with their mothers, into the popular vocabulary.[104]

No doubt, the concept of maternal deprivation caught on quickly because it arrived on the heels of the wartime evacuation studies (in which Bowlby had participated). Yet his theory differed from this earlier understanding of childhood trauma in several key ways. The central players in the evacuation studies, women such as Susan Isaacs, Melanie Klein, and Anna Freud, were all practitioners of Freudian psychoanalysis. Guided by that theoretical framework, they tended to view children's emotional problems in terms of the life of the mind, with its complex impulses, drives, and fantasies.[105] Bowlby, although also profoundly influenced by Freudianism, placed greater weight on the impact of external factors on the psyche.[106] His work aligned more closely with the realm of social psychology, which understood individuals to be "psychologically wedded to the group" and aimed to harmonize a child's inner drives to his external social environment.[107] At heart, then, Bowlby remained in the tradition of environmentalism; it was just that his concept of environment had been severely constricted to include just the mother and her behavior toward her child.[108] In addition, unlike the earlier, Britain-centric surveys of the evacuation policy, Bowlby's approach was explicitly comparative. The backing of the WHO allowed him to draw on wide-ranging, international examples to support his contention that all children, regardless of race, class, or cultural backgrounds, craved maternal affection. Bowlby also used anecdotes from ethology, the study of animal behavior, to drive

---

[103] John Bowlby, *Forty-Four Juvenile Thieves: Their Characters and Home-Life* (London: Bailliere, Tindall & Cox, 1946).

[104] On the popularization of attachment theory in this period, see Denise Riley, *War in the Nursery: Theories of the Child and Mother* (London: Virago, 1983); Nikolas Rose, *Governing the Soul: The Shaping of the Private Self* (New York: Free Association Books, 1999), 166–170.

[105] Shapira, *The War Inside*.

[106] Suzan van Dijken, René van der Veer, Marinus van Ijzendoorn, and Hans-Jan Kuipers, "Bowlby before Bowlby: The sources of an Intellectual Departure in Psychoanalysis and Psychology," *Journal of the History of Behavioral Sciences* 34, no. 3 (Summer 1998): 247–269; Frank C. P. van der Horst and René van der Veer, "The Ontogeny of an Idea: John Bowlby and Contemporaries on Mother–Child Separation," *History of Psychology* 13, no. 1 (2010): 25–45.

[107] Mathew Thomson, *Psychological Subjects: Identity, Culture, and Health in Twentieth-Century Britain* (Oxford University Press, 2006), 226.

[108] Riley, *War in the Nursery*, 94.

home the universal applicability of his theory. One of his more famous examples centered on an experiment with sibling goats, one of which had been separated from its mother. The isolated kid became anxious in the dark, grew solitary, refused to milk, and eventually died. According to Bowlby, the goat's sad fate provided "ample demonstration of the adverse effects of maternal deprivation on the young of mammals."[109] Attachment, in other words, was a fundamental element of existence, a basic biological need shared by species the world over.

Many of these claims were controversial when they first appeared and remain so today. In the decades since the work's publication, psychologists have critiqued Bowlby's work for its haphazard use of evidence, while feminists have charged him with instilling "guilt and suffocation in a generation of mothers" through his insistence that even short-term separations could warp babies' psyches.[110] These criticisms are important, but they should not overshadow the profound impact attachment theory had at the time, or the instrumental role it played in narrowing the ideological parameters of British child welfare in the 1950s. Although Bowlby never claimed that children could only bond with their own, biological mothers, his stress on infancy and early childhood as the critical years for promoting attachment tended, in practice, to reassert the primacy of natal ties. Bowlby's own pronouncements on the subject were ambiguous. While he emphasized that infants could successfully transfer their affections to a "mother-substitute," he also declared that the young were not "slates from which the past can be rubbed by a duster or sponge, but human beings who carry their previous experiences with them," an argument that seemed to underscore the importance of the biological connection.[111] Moreover, in his suggestion that maternally deprived children were liable to become emotionally disturbed adults, Bowlby reconceptualized the figure of the unattached child from an adaptable vessel of potential into a likely bearer of contagion – a "source of social infection as real and serious as are carriers of diphtheria and typhoid."[112] Couched in the language of medical science, these ideas presented the strongest challenge yet to the conventional belief that children could start afresh in a different setting, be it a "family-like" British institution or an imperial farm school. "It must never be forgotten," he contended:

that even the bad parent who neglects her child is nonetheless providing much for him ... [The child] may be ill-fed and ill-sheltered, he may be very dirty and

---

[109] Bowlby, *Child Care*, 22.
[110] Riley, *War in the Nursery*, 100. See also Michael Rutter, *Maternal Deprivation Reassessed* (London: Penguin, 1981, originally 1972); Juliet Mitchell, *Psychoanalysis and Feminism* (New York: Basic Books, 2000, originally 1974).
[111] Bowlby, *Child Care*, 134.    [112] Ibid, 181.

suffering from disease, he may be ill-treated, but, unless his parents have wholly rejected him, he is secure in the knowledge that there is someone to whom he is of value and who will strive, even though inadequately, to provide for him until such time as he can fend for himself.

Reversing the customary dynamic that placed the material wellbeing of the child over the desire to maintain the integrity of the family unit, Bowlby stressed that boys and girls would always "thrive better in bad homes than in good institutions."[113]

The rapid spread of Bowlbyism in the media and popular culture over the middle years of the decade provoked a palpable shift in British welfare practice. As early as 1954, the Ministry of Health began encouraging Children's Officers to expand their use of preventative methods designed to keep families together. Many local authorities were already moving in this direction, both because of Bowlby's influence and because family intervention was cheaper than foster care or institutionalization.[114] The transition was slower in the voluntary sector, but there too, signs of the new thinking started appearing in the later years of the decade. Most prominently, the directors of the Family Service Units, a social work agency established during the war, declared in 1956 that the great majority of children living in "problem families" were not unhappy and should not be removed.[115] The traditional children's charities were less inclined to reject institutionalization completely, although many did begin to integrate family rehabilitation into their services. Even Barnardo's, the organization with the longest record of hostility toward poor parents, established a unit for families at its Barkingside headquarters in 1956.[116] Looking back on the period from the perspective of the 1970s, Eileen Younghusband, a founder of Britain's Children's Department, reflected on how quickly the new philosophy had taken hold. As she recalled, when the Department was first established in 1948, the common assumption had been that the young "must be rescued from inadequate families, the slate wiped clean, and the child given a fresh start." Soon enough, however, "it was realized that the parent lived on inside the child, that his identity was bound up with his origins and hence that everything possible should be done to strengthen home ties."[117] The key part of Younghusband's statement was her use of the word "realized," a term

[113] Ibid, 76.
[114] Pat Starkey, *Families and Social Workers: The Work of Family Service Units, 1940–1985* (Liverpool University Press, 2000), 101 and 85.
[115] Ibid, 56.
[116] For a full description, see Barnardo's, Annual Report, 1958, D.239/A3/1/93, ULSCA.
[117] Eileen Younghusband, *Social Work in Britain: 1950–1975* (London: George Allen & Unwin, 1978), quoted in Rose, *Governing the Soul*, 171.

that accorded attachment theory the status of a self-evident truth, one that had existed throughout time despite its seemingly late discovery by British reformers.

The move toward family rehabilitation had obvious implications for the child emigration movement. Throughout the mid 1950s, emigration charities confronted new opposition from Children's Officers, who made their skepticism known in the dwindling number of local authority children put forward for resettlement.[118] In January of 1954, for instance, W. R. Vaughan, the director of the Fairbridge Society, visited Cornwall on a recruitment drive. The local Children's Officer had been on good terms with the charity in the past, and had frequently proposed boys and girls for its farm schools in Australia. This time, though, Vaughan's reception was noticeably less friendly. The representative told him that local authorities were now "against handing the children over to someone else 12,000 miles away," and – in a clear statement of Bowlbyism – that the "general opinion of most welfare workers was that a bad home was better than any substitute home which could be found for a child."[119] Summarizing the situation the following year, Saville Garner of the Commonwealth Relations Office (CRO) pointed out that, while "it has become the established principle in this country that children deprived of ordinary home life should be placed in another family ... most of the Societies dealing with child migration to Australia place the children on their arrival there in [institutions] of one sort or another." As a result, there was "at least a theoretical inconsistency here in that the Home Office in this country are pursuing one policy," whereas the state-funded emigration charities "are carrying out a different policy."[120]

Amplifying this uncertainty was government officials' lack of detailed evidence as to how child migrants were being provided for overseas. While every institution that accepted British children needed the sanction of the government, the schemes had proliferated so rapidly after the war that the task of inspection and approval had been left entirely in the hands of the Australian welfare authorities. Consequently, even as it funded the movement to the tune of £40,000 a year, the CRO was forced to admit that it had "no very authoritative information as to what happens to the children when they get to Australia," although there was "some suggestion that the care which they receive is not always ... in accordance with up-to-date thought in this country."[121] This sense of a growing divide between the two systems was not far from the mark.

[118] Constantine, "The British Government."
[119] CVOCE, Minutes, January 25, 1954, D.296/H6/1/2/1, ULSCA.
[120] Saville Garner, "Note on Child Migration," August 4, 1955, DO 35/6380, TNA: PRO.
[121] A. P. Morley, "Note on Child Migration," October 1, 1955, DO 35/6380, TNA: PRO.

Although attachment theory was not unheard of in the dominion during the 1950s, it had not penetrated social reform circles as extensively as in Britain. Well into the next decade, the removal of boys and girls to large-scale group homes remained the norm across Australia. In a typical example, a 1961 Australian audit of the state of Victoria found that, out of the 6,918 children in care that year, 847 had been returned to their families and another 967 were with foster parents. The more than 5,000 others were all living in institutions.[122] Of course, owing to a combination of financial stringency and a lack of foster placements, large numbers of children were still in institutional care in Britain as well. Yet the view was that, whereas British local authorities were taking steps to address the issue, Australian providers lacked a similar sense of urgency. Indeed, as early as 1947, the Home Office had begun voicing concern about child emigration on the basis that, while there was a "vigilance and interest, and a reforming spirit" in British welfare policy, the same impulse "probably does not exist in Australia."[123] This perception underlay the renewal of official concern in the mid 1950s that the style of care on offer in the dominion was becoming "totally outmoded and behind the times compared with current thought and practice in the United Kingdom."[124]

Given its cursory understanding of the realities on the ground, the CRO decided to appoint a Fact-Finding Mission to Australia in January of 1956. Headed by John Ross, the former Undersecretary of State for the Home Office and retired director of the Children's Department, the three-person delegation was well equipped to judge whether Australian practices accorded with British ideals. It also included Miss G. M. Wansbrough-Jones, the Children's Officer for the Essex County Council and a strong proponent of Bowlbyism, as well as William Garnett, a member of the High Commissioner's Office, who had conducted a series of informal investigations of child migrant institutions during the war.[125] Over six weeks, the team crisscrossed the country, visiting twenty-six

---

[122] Dorothy Scott and Shurlee Swain, *Confronting Cruelty: Historical Perspectives on Child Protection in Australia* (Melbourne University Press, 2002), 102.

[123] Maxwell to Dixon, August 20, 1947, DO 35/3434, TNA: PRO, quoted in Constantine, "The British Government," 106.

[124] R. E. Armstrong, "Memo of a Meeting with Representatives of the County Councils Association," June 20, 1955, DO 35/10253, TNA: PRO.

[125] In an interview with the Oversea Migration Board in 1955, Wansbrough-Jones argued that "even though the family might not be the ideal permanent surroundings, it was most important not to cut this tie," since a "child separated from his mother and father was likely to build up an entirely distorted and imaginary picture of them in his mind." "Possibility of Increasing the Number of Child Migrants to Australia from the United Kingdom," March 1958, DO 35/10253, TNA: PRO. Garnett's earlier investigations had critiqued child migrants' lack of educational opportunities and general isolation. William Garnett, "Report on Farm Schools in Australia," October 6, 1944, DO 35/1138, TNA: PRO.

group homes, interviewing child migrants, and meeting with immigration officials, child welfare representatives, and the directors of the charities.

The Mission's final report was cordial, emphasizing the "abundant evidence of development and of opportunity" in the country.[126] It left no doubt, however, as to the delegation's serious unease regarding the quality of Australian care. The team reported that, while many providers had expressed a desire to place the young in "circumstances approaching as nearly as possible those enjoyed by a child living in his own home with good parents," little had been done to accomplish this aim. The percentage of children in foster placements varied from state to state, and few of the voluntary organizations had even started the necessary planning to implement a shift to family care. As a result, most child migrants still lived in residential homes that were "institutional in character." The largest ones lacked a "homely atmosphere," "sufficient privacy," and "feminine influence," and so failed to live up to the basic standards set by the Care of Children Committee.[127] While the smaller "cottage homes" at least allowed "children to live in something like family groups," their residents tended to be segregated by age and gender, a practice that made even these more "domestic" environments end up feeling artificial.[128] Another issue was the "fairly isolated situation of a number of the establishments," which meant that the children were unable to "live in close touch with the local community." Child migrants, they worried, remained "to a large extent a community apart, and were not growing up as Australians."[129]

These critiques were proof enough that the institutional care provided to child migrants in the dominion did not fit the postwar British model of "best practice." The delegates' most trenchant criticism, though, related to what they perceived as a widespread ignorance about the recent advances in child psychology. Because formal training programs in child welfare or social work were rare across the country, many Australian providers did not have a "sufficient knowledge of child care methods" to be able to offer the "understanding and care needed to help [child migrants] to adjust themselves to strange surroundings."[130] A substantial proportion of the staff they encountered seemed frankly out of touch. "We heard often," the team noted, the view that "children whom life had treated badly would benefit by transfer to a new country where they could be given a fresh start, away from old scenes and unhappy associations. Few ... seemed to realize that it was precisely such children, already rejected and insecure, who might be ill-equipped to cope with the added strain of migration."

---

[126] "Child Migration to Australia: Report of a Fact-Finding Mission," August 1956, *Parliamentary Papers* XXIII, Cmd. 9832, 5.
[127] Ibid, 4 and 5.    [128] Ibid, 8.
[129] Ibid, 9–10.    [130] Ibid, 8.

The emotional impact of the dislocation was clear to the committee. In their conversations with individual boys and girls, members uncovered many who did not understand why they had been sent to Australia and who were "disturbed by reason of separation from their parents."[131]

In its pointed suggestion that child emigration was doing more psychological harm than good, the Mission's report became the first decisive statement of the postwar period to illustrate just how far the policy had moved away from the British standard of care. The delegation stressed that, if the schemes were allowed to continue, significant changes had to be made in order to bring them in line with the principles governing child welfare in the United Kingdom. Australian institutions would have to hire more staff, especially women, and every person working with children would need to undergo a full course of training. The emigration charities would also have to think more creatively about the question of assimilation, developing new opportunities for child migrants to integrate into their local communities and to forge intimate and personal attachments to adults. Furthermore, to guarantee that charities only selected boys and girls who were psychologically prepared to handle relocation, every case would need the approval of the Secretary of State for the Home Office before emigration. Most importantly, the emigration societies would need to begin the transition away from institutionalization and toward a system of foster care.

What is striking about these conclusions is that, rather than simply renounce the policy, members aimed instead to reform it so that a single (British) conception of welfare might again apply throughout the empire. The basic contention was not that child emigration itself was wrong but that the policy could only work if the transfer of children from one side of the British world to the other did not imply a difference in care. It was an attitude that revealed both the lingering traces of race patriotism and an assumption of imperial authority, most clearly expressed in the view that the British government could dictate the terms of Australian child welfare. As members of the Home Office had already made clear, their opinion was that, for the emigration policy to be revitalized, "means must be found of transmitting the skill and knowledge built up in this country to Commonwealth workers before a start can be made."[132]

The receipt of the Mission's report in June of 1956 triggered a flurry of behind-the-scenes discussions between the CRO and Home Office.[133] It

---

[131] Ibid, 6.
[132] Note by Hill, September 22, 1954, MH 102/2055, TNA: PRO, quoted in Constantine, "The British Government," 110.
[133] Constantine, "The British Government," offers the most comprehensive discussion of these negotiations.

was plain that some action was needed, especially since the British government's funding agreements with the emigration charities were shortly to come up for renewal. Officials remained divided, though, as to the best course to take. The Home Office took the more radical line, proposing a temporary stoppage of all child emigration schemes. Yet CRO representatives worried that such a move would jeopardize its political relationship with Australia at a time when the dominion was in the midst of renegotiating the system of imperial preference. "To take what would appear to be a somewhat high-handed decision to hold up child migration without consulting the Australian Government would appear to be dangerous," recorded one official.[134] Further complicating the situation was a broader sense of uncertainty about whether the British government even had the right to enforce the Mission's recommendations overseas. On the one hand, Australia's 1946 Immigration (Guardianship of Children) Act stipulated that the custody of child migrants transferred to the Australian Department of Immigration on their arrival in the dominion. As a result, conceded John Hope, the Undersecretary of State for the CRO, "once a child was no longer in this country, constitutionally this was nothing to do with the United Kingdom Government." On the other hand, the British state had heavily subsidized the movement, and the children had been born in Britain, which together seemed to imply that "Parliament was entitled to satisfy itself that the children were being maintained in what was here regarded as suitable conditions."[135] Theoretically at least, both governments were entitled to a role in determining the terms of child migrants' upbringing. As children of the empire, the boys and girls could reasonably be assumed to belong equally to Britain and Australia. Nevertheless, in their hesitation to intervene, British officials were acknowledging that their formerly unchallenged claim to the children had come into question. In this respect, the Mission's report had exposed the restricted political space in which imperial authority operated within the late settler empire. When it counted, the old arguments about shared Britishness now rang hollow.

Not wanting to overstep the mark and risk angering the Australians, members of the Home Office and CRO eventually agreed that the best tactic was persuasion. "We are convinced," wrote E. H. Gwynn of the Home Office, "that for cogent practical as well as political reasons it is not possible for us to take any effective responsibility for judging the merits of individual institutions in Australia. This responsibility must rest with the Australian authorities, and the sooner they accept it the better."

---

[134] Costley-White to Shannon, July 3, 1956, DO 35/6382, TNA: PRO.
[135] CVOCE, Minutes of a Meeting with Representatives of the CRO and HO, December 14, 1956, D.296/H6/1/2/2, ULSCA.

To ensure the physical and psychological safety of child migrants, British representatives would need "to come to an agreement with the Australian authorities on the standards that these institutions should be required to reach, and then to leave it to the Australian authorities to enforce them." British experts would "supply the knowledge and experience of child care that the Australians may lack," but ultimately it would be up to the dominion to "apply and adapt [this advice] to their own environment."[136] In the meantime, the British government would play the only card it had, withholding its approval for the further emigration of children until representatives from both sides had settled on a new standard of care.

Although this decision recognized the altered political landscape of the postwar empire, it continued to assume that the principles informing British child welfare should apply throughout the dominions. The representatives of the emigration charities and the Australian government saw the situation differently. To them, the matter was not one of Australian care falling below a universal standard of child welfare. Rather, it was a case of two different, yet equal, conceptions of children's needs. First to present this opinion was the London-based Council of Voluntary Organisations for Child Emigration (CVOCE), a body formed in 1951 to coordinate the work of the charities. Writing to the CRO in late 1956, the CVOCE challenged the Mission's contention that family separation and institutionalization were psychologically harmful in and of themselves. It pointed out that, because the delegation had only examined the present conditions of the children and not their rates of success in later life, it had missed the important fact that the majority of child migrants were not traumatized but instead "became happily and successfully established in the land of their adoption."[137] This point was later taken up by the Australian Minister of Immigration, T. H. E. Heyes, who bristled at the insinuation that dominion authorities had much to learn from their more "progressive" peers in Britain. Even if "it were possible to make valid comparisons in standards of child care in Australia and the United Kingdom" – a stipulation Heyes doubted – then surely Australia should not be judged by an abstract ideal, but by the reality of provision in Britain. What was more important was the fact that the "physical care and general welfare" of child migrants conformed to the "standards set by the Child Welfare Authorities for Australian-born wards of the State." Heyes argued that his government took pains to guarantee that the treatment of British boys and girls was "on the same scale as is applicable

---

[136] Gwynn to Shannon, July 12, 1956, DO 35/6382, TNA: PRO.
[137] CVOCE, "Letter to the Undersecretary of State," CRO, September 13, 1956, D.296/H6/1/2/2, ULSCA.

to Australian children similarly circumstanced."[138] In other words, if child migrants were to be the future citizens of Australia, then their care needed to be consistent with local conditions. It needed to be of the kind that Australians deemed appropriate for their own children.

Heyes' argument was no crude statement of proprietorship, a contention that once the children entered the country they were "owned" solely by the dominion. Instead, his claim rested on a subtler conception of cultural sovereignty. He declared that Australia was a society defined by its unique landscape, climate, and customs. Without a genuine understanding of the country's way of life and cultural identity, the members of the Fact-Finding Mission had been unable to appreciate the distinctiveness of an Australian childhood. He noted that the "mission took the view that migrant children would be more advantageously placed in urban areas" and that locating "children in rural areas appeared ... tantamount to isolating them from the life of the community." According to Heyes, this perspective overlooked the expansiveness of Australian geography, which gave rise to a different form of social interaction than was typical in Britain. Large distances were an accepted part of life in the dominion, and in no way impeded healthy socialization. "Many of Australia's finest citizens were country-bred children reared in the same 'isolation,'" Heyes asserted. In sum, the British view of child welfare was merely that: a *British* model, one that did not necessarily fit outside the United Kingdom. As such, the Australian government concluded that it could "not regard the Report of the Fact Finding Mission as seriously reflecting upon the standard of child care in this country."[139]

The emigration movement had always relied to some degree on the idea that Australian culture and society were distinct from those in Britain. Charities had consistently claimed that the best migrant was a young migrant, since impressionable children were better able to adapt to, and take on the characteristics of, the dominion lifestyle. What was new in this context was the use of this argument to refute, rather than to reinforce, the cultural connections of empire. Previous proponents had assumed that, although the way of life in Australia was in some respects unlike that in the United Kingdom, the dominion remained fundamentally British in heritage and culture. The conflict over child emigration in the later 1950s, however, revealed the extent to which this faith in the essential Britishness of the empire had receded. While the children may have been British in origin, dominion officials argued that they were to become uniquely Australian once resettled, and therefore subject to the

---

[138] Heyes to UK High Commissioner in Australia, January 16, 1957, DO 35/6382, TNA: PRO.

[139] Ibid.

methods and standards of welfare that were specific to the country. Child emigration, a project that had begun as an initiative to cement the bonds of empire, ultimately became a mechanism of asserting the cultural and political sovereignty of the Australian nation.

## Conclusion

In the end, the Australian government's strong response succeeded in pressuring the CRO to stand down. After some cursory improvements were made to the institutions ranked lowest by the delegation, the British government allowed the emigration process to resume. It was clear to officials that these changes had only "served to rectify the faults that the Fact-Finding Mission discovered in regard to the material conditions," without addressing the "other important criticisms ... such as standards of care, quality of staff, selection arrangements, etc."[140] Regardless, British ministers never banned child emigration. On the contrary, the government continued to fund the initiatives through the late 1960s, even though this financial support was less an endorsement of the project than a means of ensuring the maintenance of those children already resettled overseas.[141]

While child emigration persisted with at least tacit government sanction, it never truly recovered from the blow of the Fact-Finding Mission. Shortly after the publication of the report, a number of organizations, including, most prominently, the Catholic Child Welfare Council, opted to close down their initiatives in order to focus on domestic programs.[142] The Fairbridge Society found it increasingly difficult to recruit children, and announced toward the end of 1956 that it would begin a move away from the emigration of unaccompanied boys and girls toward the resettlement of families.[143] The same reason also prompted the Rhodesia Fairbridge Memorial College to begin winding down. In September of 1956, its board decided to send no further children to the colony, and the school officially closed six years later.[144] When the CVOCE held its final meeting in 1959, members conceded that the project had declined to such an extent that child emigration had effectively become "a thing of the past."[145] By the 1960s, the only association that continued to send boys and girls independently of their families was Barnardo's, in large part because it could recruit directly

---

[140] S. Taylor, "Minute on Child Migration," December 12, 1956, DO 35/6382, TNA: PRO. Emphasis in the original.
[141] Constantine, "The British Government," 122–123.
[142] Coldrey, *Child Migration to Catholic Institutions*, 106–110.
[143] CVOCE, Minutes, September 12, 1956; Sherington and Jeffery, *Fairbridge*, 242–244.
[144] Fairbridge, Minutes, September 6, 1956, D.296/B1/2/8, ULSCA.
[145] CVOCE, Minutes, April 28, 1959.

from its branches in the United Kingdom. Even so, the society was only able to find handfuls of children who were orphans or whose parents consented to their resettlement. The frequency of the sailings grew sporadic, and the charity finally abandoned the scheme in 1967.

This slow demise of the child emigration movement casts light on how the rise of new psychological models of child development during the 1950s not only restricted the once fluid boundaries of postwar British welfarism but also reverberated through the realm of imperial politics. Child psychology, with its universal claims about human instincts and behaviors, is often understood as having played a central role in forging greater international consensus about the needs and rights of children during the late twentieth century. Yet the case of child emigration illustrates that it could also fragment earlier, transnational models of belonging, serving as a means for defining the divides *between* different national populations, rather than as a platform for transcending them. In retrospect, it is easy to assume that the vision of children's emotional development that was advocated by Bowlby and his supporters in the Home Office was the sole, correct way to understand child welfare, particularly since family-centered care continues to remain the ideal within social service provision today. That attitude does more to obscure, rather than reveal, however, the fact that attachment theory emerged victorious in this era not because it was the only conceptualization on offer but because it was embraced and touted as universal by an increasingly powerful group of Anglo-American experts at the international level.[146] The historical lesson to take from this case is thus not that the philosophy put forward by British reformers was necessarily "true" but rather that the act of defining the welfare interests of children is always political. To this end, the debate about how best to meet the emotional needs of child migrants became a useful tool for Australian politicians to express their cultural autonomy from Britain and to articulate a distinctly national model of childrearing. Yet this "nationalization" of child welfare occurred on both sides of the divide. While Australian officials came to prioritize local influences over the Britannic heritage, British officials in turn came to view boys and girls as more firmly rooted in their local contexts. The continued spread of Bowlbyism during the 1960s tore away at the earlier "imperial" conception of child welfare that had once portrayed British children as easily transferable within the global community, so that, by the end of that decade, both the child emigration movement and the ideal of Greater Britain had faded from view.

---

[146] On this point, see also Zahra, *The Lost Children*, 88–117.

The first time John Bicknell ever heard of Australia, he was nine years old and living in a Barnardo's branch home in Sussex. As he and a number of other boys played in the common room, a man in military dress entered and asked them to line up in regimented rows. The order was a signal that whatever was going to happen next was important. It bore the weight of authority. The boys quietly fidgeted as the officer gave a speech explaining the Barnardo's emigration program. After twenty minutes or so – a mercilessly long time to a nine-year-old – the man asked whether any of the boys wanted to go to Australia, and dismissed them to think it over. Bicknell was having trouble grasping the situation. "It was all just sort of airy fairy," he recalled. It was only when another boy told him that Australian children rode horses to school and attended classes for just half the day that he began to envision what this novel life might be like for him. A few minutes later, when the group was called back in to give their response, he remembered feeling "overwhelmed," and could only think, "Bloody hell, I'd love a horse to ride to school on. So I immediately put my hand up ... and everything went from there."

The year was 1949, still near the beginning of the postwar child emigration boom. Bicknell's life up to that point had not been easy. Born at the start of the Second World War, he never knew his father, who served in the army throughout his childhood. He and his two brothers were raised by his mother, a strict woman prone to mood swings. According to Bicknell's file, on at least one occasion she was reported to the NSPCC for child neglect; as an adult, Bicknell could still remember spending long hours locked in a backyard shed while she went out. "She wasn't a nice person," he stated simply.[1] When Bicknell was six years old, his parents divorced and his mother placed the boys with Barnardo's. The only other memory he had of her from this time was saying goodbye, three years later, a day or two before he boarded the ship to Australia. By that point the brothers had passed their medical and IQ tests and had been

---

[1] Author's interview with John Bicknell, May 16, 2006.

told that they were on their way to the Mowbray Park Farm School in New South Wales. Bicknell's understanding of what that meant, however, was still hazy. He had the impression that they were going to a place called "Australia House," not "Australia," which was an easy mistake to make, given that all of their pretrip arrangements had been coordinated through that government office in London. This initial confusion aside, Bicknell clearly viewed his emigration as an opportunity to remake his identity. Until that time, he had been known as "Richard," a nickname his mother had given him. He decided "to get rid of Richard once and for all. Once I left ... I determined that I would be called that manly name John, which was my first name anyway, and to do this I simply refused to answer to Richard when called or spoken to. It was amazing how quickly people caught on."[2]

This act of defiant re-creation was the first of many during Bicknell's childhood. As he narrated his life history, he focused on episodes from his past when he had been unfairly categorized or felt out of place. Read together, these moments articulated his lifelong struggle to carve out an identity of his own in active opposition to society's attempts to pigeon-hole him. He spoke of the social stigma of being a Barnardo boy in the years after the war, when so many of the children in charitable care had been "born on the wrong side of the blankets, so to speak. They were bastards." Bicknell's parents had been married when he was born, but still he felt the weight of social opprobrium. The "mere fact that you were put into an institution, people lumped you in with everybody else, whether you were a bastard or not. You became a bastard," and had to prove to the world that the dishonor was unwarranted. He also recounted an early Christmas in Australia when he was riding on a train with one of his brothers. "The whole compartment in the carriage was full of people," he said, "and I just looked up and ... there was my picture up there ... under a caption that said 'Help Barnardo's Help a Child.'" Seeing the fundraising poster was a searing moment: "I didn't think I needed any help at all. I was most incensed. And I tried my hardest not to get near the photo so somebody could compare the photo with me."[3] The anecdote offers a powerful illustration of the ability of oral history to capture past and present simultaneously. The story itself communicates Bicknell's childhood feelings of humiliation, while his choice to retell it demonstrates his continued determination not to be classified as an object of pity.

Bicknell's stress on his ability to set his own terms in life applied equally to his sense of nationhood. Growing up, he often had the sense that he did

---

[2] John Bicknell, *The Dirty Bloody Jizzy* (Gordon, NSW: Mini-Publishing, 2003), 44.
[3] Bicknell interview.

not quite belong in Australia. His outsider status came through in everything from his "Pommy accent," which did not start to fade until he was
in his mid twenties, to his clothes. He pointed out that at Mowbray Park
"we all wore khaki," so that "anybody in the whole area knew a Barnardo
boy straight away. You just had to look at them. They were wearing khaki."
Throughout his youth, he was often concerned that people would not
accept him, and worried that there was something about the way he talked
or looked that would "give him away" in public. Eventually, though, these
feelings diminished, and he began to feel more secure in himself and more
attached to the country. By the time he reached adulthood, there was no
ambiguity about how he identified. He declared that he was "definitely"
an Australian. He might hold dual citizenship and carry a British passport, but there was no doubt about it: Australia had become his home.[4]

This certainty would have pleased the directors of the postwar child
emigration movement, who throughout the 1950s and 1960s employed
a variety of techniques and strategies to promote children's long-term
assimilation into their adoptive countries. They would have been per-
plexed, though, by the way that Bicknell conceptualized his Australian
identity. For he portrayed himself as having become Australian *in spite* of
his British origins. His integration story was woven around the themes of
loss and sacrifice: the loss of his accent, the renunciation of his name. Yet
the underlying principle of child emigration had always been that there
was no divide between the metropolitan conception of British identity
and its settler variants around the world. On the contrary, the assort-
ment of nationalities that made up Greater Britain was understood to fit
within the larger framework of imperial Britishness like a hand within a
glove. This ideal persisted among proponents of the movement into the
1960s, although, as Bicknell's account illustrates, it was growing increasingly tenuous. By the end of that decade, when the last child emigration
scheme drew to a close, the British world concept had been displaced by
more exclusive models of nationhood.

This chapter explores the changing structure of child emigration
throughout this period of imperial decline, paying close attention to

[4] Ibid. Child migrants who arrived prior to the passage of Australia's Nationality and
Citizenship Act of 1948 automatically became Australian citizens (while remaining,
until 1984, British subjects). Those, like Bicknell, who arrived after the act technically
remained British citizens and had to apply for Australian citizenship later in life. Until
1984, Australian passports could be issued both to Australian citizens and to British
residents who were not Australian citizens. This measure allowed many postwar child
migrants to carry both passports. On the complexities of British subjecthood status in
relation to Australian citizenship law, see John Chesterman, "Natural Born Subjects?
Race and British Subjecthood in Australia," *Australian Journal of Politics and History* 51,
no. 1 (2005): 30–39.

how the growing cultural autonomy of Australia and Southern Rhodesia shaped the childhoods and life experiences of migrant boys and girls. It follows the journey of child migrants from their initial selection in Britain to their first jobs in the empire, and merges the archival record with personal stories like Bicknell's to cast light on the broader social forces that shaped their passage into adulthood. Prized for their youthful adaptability, child migrants in both of these countries grew up in "didactic landscapes" that aimed to adjust their characters, personalities, and self-perceptions to the society around them.[5] Their shared institutionalization and separation from family meant that Australian and Rhodesian child migrants had much in common. But their upbringing also diverged in crucial, revealing ways. These distinctions illustrate how settler childhoods in Australia and Southern Rhodesia were gradually coming to appear more dissimilar than alike. In doing so, they also uncover the subtler dimensions of what it meant to be "Australian" or "Rhodesian" during an era when the bonds of imperial sentiment had begun to wane.

### Choosing future citizens

In 1951, Joan Balcombe was a young, single mother working as a teacher in Ramsgate, Kent. Her son John had been born in the early days of the Second World War, just before her husband was sent to Ceylon (now Sri Lanka) with the army. Their marriage did not survive the separation. In 1947, Balcombe divorced John's father and went to live with her sister in a small family home near the coast. Looking back on that time, John described their situation as "not very well off, pretty poor. But everybody was, and I never had any feeling of being deprived in any way." On the whole, he "had a wonderful upbringing," with a mother who adored him and a neighborhood filled with friends.[6]

Everything changed the day Balcombe happened to find a small advertisement for the Rhodesia Fairbridge Memorial College (RFMC) in the *News of the World*. "It went something like this," she remembered: "an

---

[5] Anna Haebich, *Broken Circles: Fragmenting Indigenous Families, 1800–2000* (Fremantle: Fremantle Arts Centre Press, 2000), 379. In this respect, their experiences were in keeping with other groups of institutionalized children of the period, including Indigenous and non-Indigenous Australians and American Indians. The comparison has been explicitly made by the *Forgotten Australians and Former Child Migrants Oral History Project*, 2009–2012, NLA. On the institutional experiences of Indigenous children, see, in addition to Haebich, Brenda Child, *Boarding School Seasons: American Indian Families, 1900–1940* (Lincoln: University of Nebraska Press, 1999); Margaret Jacobs, *White Mother to a Dark Race: Settler Colonialism, Maternalism, and the Removal of Indigenous Children in the American West and Australia, 1880–1940* (Lincoln: University of Nebraska Press, 2009).

[6] Author's interview with John Andrews, December 12, 2005.

opportunity occurs for boys and girls who for one reason or another have been deprived of one or both parents due to the war, to begin a new life in the colonies."[7] Both she and John, who was eleven years old at the time, were intrigued by the idea. For Balcombe, Rhodesia offered a place to start over and the chance of a better life. John's motivations were less coherent but probably had something to do with his avid reading of adventure stories, particularly H. Rider Haggard's tales of Africa. "I think that's what influenced me," he said. "It sounded exciting."[8]

The application process turned out to be more extensive than either of them had expected. The first step was to get references from John's school headmaster and from his minister. Next, John took an aptitude test, the purpose of which was to ensure, in Balcombe's words, that there was "no question of [him] not being normal." Finally, a social worker arrived at the house to interview them:

She came and looked at the main room, which was a nice room but shabby. And she was quite impressed. She said she apologized for coming but she had to know what our home conditions were like ... She said she could tell I was not sending my boy away – this is how she put it – because he was in the way when I wanted to go to the pictures, the cinema. This is how she put it and ... I thought that was silly because if I had gone to the pictures I would have taken John with me! ... [But] she was very pleasant and wished us well.[9]

From the start, Balcombe made clear to the Rhodesian authorities that her intention was to follow John to Southern Rhodesia. She was told that, while they had no objections to her plan, the scheme was solely for children. "They just wanted the cream" – the young, the adaptable – whereas "I was divorced, and not a woman of means." What she did have was a background in nursing and four years of training at a London hospital. She assumed that her own emigration would be easy to arrange.

Even after the months of preparations, the day of John's departure was heart wrenching. There was a small party at Rhodesia House in London for the dozen children in the group as well as for their guardians. As Balcombe recalled it, she was one of only a few parents there. After tea and cakes, the group continued to Waterloo station for the formal goodbyes, which were carefully choreographed to minimize the emotional distress. She remembered that the children, now dressed in gray school uniforms complete with floppy sun hats, "were assembled on the platform and we were just a little higher up." The arrangement was so "we could look down on them and say goodbye ... so as not to see them onto the train and hang all the tears."[10]

---

[7] Author's interview with Joan Balcombe, December 12, 2005.
[8] Andrews interview    [9] Balcombe interview.    [10] Ibid.

Once John had sailed, Balcombe applied for her own entrance visa to the colony. To her surprise, she found that her nursing experience counted for little. Without savings, the Rhodesian authorities would only allow her entry if she could prove she had a job lined up. As the weeks ticked by she began to feel "absolutely desolate." "I had no idea beforehand that they wouldn't accept me as a nurse," but "I knew there had to be a way, because I was so keen." After nine months of inquiring, and when she was "nearly desperate," Balcombe finally found a job as a governess to a young boy whose family was about to move to Bulawayo. It was only then, as she put it, that "the world started to turn again."[11] After her arrival, Balcombe and John continued to live apart for the five years that he attended the RFMC. Indeed, the school's principal made it clear that she should not make a habit of visiting John; she assumed the rule was to avoid upsetting the other children whose mothers had remained in Britain. Ever the problem solver, Balcombe bought her son a bicycle so that he could ride the ten or so miles to visit her every Sunday for dinner.

Balcombe's memories offer a crucial source of information about the reasons why some parents and families opted to participate in postwar child emigration initiatives, as well as the extent to which they were informed of and understood the process. In general, parents' perspectives appear more frequently in the archival record for these decades than for earlier periods, mainly because charities had become more diligent about acquiring the written consent of guardians.[12] Nevertheless, mentions of the wishes and motivations of parents in the official documentation remain cursory at best, and tend to reiterate stock categories that beg more questions than they answer. The Fairbridge Society, for instance, often noted that it had accepted a boy or girl because their "parents were clearly anxious to give their children better opportunities than could be afforded them in their present very undesirable conditions" or because a mother was having "great difficulty in coping with her large family."[13] In these vignettes, poverty was still the most common justification for children's emigration, although illegitimacy and divorce were also regularly cited factors. These asides reveal little, however, about how parents came to make the difficult decision to grant consent or what kind of emotional effects the separation had on them. And, although former migrants were sometimes able to discuss their emigration with their parents later

[11] Ibid.
[12] Barry Coldrey, *Child Migration: Consent of Parents to their Children's Emigration, the Legal and Moral Dimension* (Altrincham: Tamanaraik Press, 1996).
[13] Fairbridge, Care of Children Committee Minutes, June 24, 1954 and June 14, 1955, D.296/B5/3/2, ULSCA.

in life, feelings of guilt and loss often clouded the conversation. Geoff Crimes, who was eight years old when he emigrated to the RFMC with his younger sister in 1952, exchanged regular letters with his mother throughout his time at the school, and returned to live with her ten years later during a trip back to Britain. Even though he carried no bitterness about his mother's decision and was on good terms with her, he found that the subject of his emigration was too sensitive to talk about openly. "She was forever weeping," he explained. The topic would cause her to "get on a down, and she'd always want to know, 'Did I do the wrong thing, did I?'"[14]

Balcombe's account also illustrates the growing trend in the postwar years of parents following their children into the empire. Throughout the 1950s, emigration charities continued to prefer boys and girls who were already living in children's homes in Britain or who had previously lost contact with their relatives, in the belief that these "unattached" youths were most in need of a new start in life and were at less risk of being "unsettled" by parents later on. Yet they were increasingly willing to accept a child whose guardian intended to emigrate separately on one of the era's numerous assisted passage schemes, such as the "Ten Pound Poms" initiative, which brought more than one million Britons to Australia from the late 1940s through the 1970s.[15] Usually, the parent had to agree to wait for a certain period of time before pursuing their own emigration. The typical requirement was two years and, even then, as Balcombe found, mothers and fathers were discouraged from visiting their children.[16] It is clear, though, that a growing minority of parents were willing to accept these conditions if it meant that the family would eventually reunite overseas. Of the thirty-nine applications that the Fairbridge Society's selection committee considered in June of 1951, nineteen were from children who were living with or were actively in touch with their mothers, and most of these women were planning to emigrate as well.[17] For some postwar parents, child emigration was becoming less an option of last resort than a strategy that offered a more cost effective method of relocating the family overseas.

[14] Author's interview with Geoff Crimes, July 18, 2005.

[15] A. James Hammerton and Alistair Thomson, *Ten Pound Poms: Australia's Invisible Migrants* (Manchester University Press, 2005).

[16] See, for instance, the discussions of parental emigration in Fairbridge, Care of Children Committee Minutes, July 13, 1950, April 12, 1951, and June 7, 1951, D.296/B5/3/1, ULSCA.

[17] Ibid, June 7, 1951. The committee rejected five of these candidates outright because their mothers refused to delay their own emigration. But they accepted nine others on the condition that the mothers would wait two years before following their children to Australia.

Most striking, however, is how Balcombe's recollections help shed light on the intricacies of the postwar procedure for selecting child migrants. Her story is particularly valuable given that most of the children who experienced this process firsthand were too young to recall it with any depth later in life. Balcombe's difficulty in securing her own entrance into Southern Rhodesia, coupled with her observation that dominion officials "just wanted the cream," highlights the continued prioritization of children's migration over that of adults, due to persistent assumptions about young people's malleability and capacity to assimilate.[18] At the same time, her description of the long and complicated application procedure demonstrates that the interwar trend toward the increased scrutiny of children's physical and mental fitness lasted well into the postwar period. Throughout the 1950s and 1960s, Australian and Rhodesian authorities maintained a complex bureaucracy that aimed to ensure that prospective child migrants were of "sound stock" and would be capable of becoming productive future members of society.[19] Tellingly, though, they employed markedly different methods for assessing children's capacity to integrate into their new nations.

In both regions, the foremost concern was to ensure child migrants' racial purity. Migration officers made clear that they would not accept any child who exhibited a "coloured strain" and, throughout these decades, the emigration charities carefully reviewed potential migrants' family histories in order to weed out any boy or girl whose Whiteness was suspect.[20] In 1955, when the Fairbridge Society's selection committee "discovered" that one applicant was "a 'coloured' child from Jamaica," they immediately disqualified her, stating simply "she would not be acceptable as a child migrant."[21] The following year, the committee removed a boy from consideration because his parents were "Anglo-Indians, the Indian ancestry going back three generations."[22]

This attention to racial pedigree was in line with the restrictive immigration policies that remained in place through the late 1960s in Australia and even later in Southern Rhodesia. But it put the emigration movement at odds with the broader trends of postwar British welfarism, which was expanding to accommodate growing numbers of non-White children.[23] In an attempt to stay relevant in the era of the welfare state, charities such as

---

[18] Kathleen Paul, "Changing Childhoods: Child Emigration since 1945," in *Child Welfare and Social Action in the Nineteenth and Twentieth Centuries: International Perspectives*, ed. Jon Lawrence and Pat Starkey (Liverpool University Press, 2001), 121–143.

[19] RFMC, "Outline of a Scheme," 1945, D.296/K2/4/2, ULSCA.

[20] Fairbridge, Care of Children Committee Minutes, March 25, 1948, D.296/B5/3/1, ULSCA.

[21] Ibid, August 10, 1955.      [22] Ibid, June 19, 1956.

[23] Pat Starkey, "Can the Piper Call the Tune? Innovation and Experiment with Deprived Families in Britain, 1940–1980s: The Work of Family Service Units," *British Journal*

Barnardo's explicitly tailored their services to meet the needs of boys and girls from immigrant families, and as early as 1952 the organization was providing care for "274 coloured children."[24] While the voluntary sector became more open to providing assistance to multiracial families, dominion officials stubbornly adhered to their long-standing color bar, sometimes disqualifying children just before they were set to sail. Dilys Budd, who was eleven years old in 1947 when she was sent to St. Joseph's Girls' Orphanage in Western Australia, run by the Catholic Sisters of Mercy, remembered boarding the boat in Southampton with a girl named Maureen. As they were finding their cabins, Maureen's "name was called. And we never saw her again ... She was taken off. And the only thing we could think of is she was dark ... She wasn't Black. But she was dark."[25] Over time, dominion requirements that child migrants be unambiguously "White" significantly reduced the number of boys and girls available for emigration. By 1967, the Barnardo's migration department reported that nearly 25 percent of children in the Homes were "coloured" to some degree "and for this reason would be unacceptable in Australia."[26] When the organization formally decided to end its emigration program two years later, its directors cited "the changing scene of child care in this country, which meant there were fewer children suitable for migration," as a main reason.[27]

Within this attention to ancestry, there was some leeway in terms of nationality. As the percentage of British children available for emigration declined, dominion authorities became willing to consider other European children. To this end, Gordon Green, the recently retired Secretary of the Fairbridge Society, traveled across northern Europe in 1947 to survey the prospects of recruiting boys and girls from "Norway, Sweden, Denmark, Holland, Belgium and Germany." Few constructive plans came of the trip, yet it did provide the Society with an opportunity to remind its members that these "Anglo-Saxon" children would also "make first-class citizens for the British Dominions."[28] The charities were less enthusiastic about migrants from southern Europe, although a number of Catholic

of Social Work 32 (2002): 573–587; Jordanna Bailkin, "The Postcolonial Family? West African Children, Private Fostering, and the British State," Journal of Modern History 81, no. 1 (2009): 87–121.

24 Barnardo's, Committee of Management Minutes, December 10, 1952, D.239/B3/2/6, ULSCA.

25 Interview with Dilys Budd, conducted by Ann-Mari Jordens, ORAL TRC 6200/7, Forgotten Australians and Former Child Migrants Oral History Project, March 9, 2010, NLA.

26 Barnardo's, "Report on Migration," May 9, 1967, D.239/C2/6/49, ULSCA.

27 Barnardo's, General Purposes Committee Minutes, September 23, 1969, D.239/B3/3/1, ULSCA.

28 Fairbridge, Minutes of the Annual General Meeting, December 30, 1947, D.296/B1/2/5, ULSCA.

agencies working in Australia did resettle roughly 300 children from the Mediterranean colony of Malta.[29] These attempts to broaden the recruitment of child migrants demonstrate the wider postwar reconceptualizaton of Britishness, which shifted from a primarily ethnic category to a more loosely defined cultural one (even as it remained tethered to the conventional framework of Whiteness).[30] This transition was slow, however, and on the ground in the dominions the older notion that "British was best" remained popular. As a Fairbridge board member found while on a trip to Perth in 1950, there existed "quite a bit of uneasy feeling here about the Balts, Wops and others whom [the Immigration Minister] imported ... All the ordinary Aussies one meets want more British blood."[31]

Although Australian and Rhodesian officials were united in their preoccupation with child migrants' Whiteness, they differed substantially in their interpretation of what constituted racial purity. For Australian officials, a child was "sound" if he was of Anglo-Celtic or European ancestry, free of obvious physical illnesses, had no family history of mental instability, and exhibited an IQ of ninety-five or higher. They sometimes made exceptions if the child's disqualifying condition appeared either temporary or treatable. Barnardo's routinely deferred and later retested children whose IQs registered in the eighties, or who had relatively minor disorders such as tonsillitis or enuresis (bedwetting). And, from the late 1930s onward, the Fairbridge Society operated a pre-emigration hostel, where it placed boys and girls requiring medical attention or who needed some time to adjust to being away from home. There was noticeably less flexibility in the standards for Rhodesia, where immigration authorities continued to subscribe to the view that destitute children from "broken homes" were psychologically unsuited for the African empire.[32] The directors of the RFMC thus required candidates to display the "ability to make good as members of the [settler] community," which meant that, "in addition to being medically fit in every respect, the children selected must be of good intelligence" as well as emotionally stable. "It is no ... benefit to children who do not possess a high standard of intelligence to go out to Africa where, after leaving school, they would not be able to hold their own," a 1954 brochure stressed.[33]

---

[29] Barry Coldrey, *Child Migration from Malta to Australia: 1930s to 1960s* (Como, WA: Tamanaraik Press, 1992).

[30] Kathleen Paul, *Whitewashing Britain: Race and Citizenship in the Postwar Era* (Ithaca: Cornell University Press, 1997).

[31] Wills to Vaughan, January 27, 1950, D.296/H4/1, ULSCA.

[32] Report of the Rhodesia Fairbridge Committee, February 1939, DO 35/697/5, TNA: PRO.

[33] Rhodesia Fairbridge Memorial College brochure, 1954, D.296, K2/4/5, ULSCA. Although the intelligence requirements were never explicitly stated, other charities

Selecting these children required different methods from those typically used by the Australian schemes. Rather than recruit through charities or state agencies, the RFMC relied on newspaper advertisements, personal referrals, and a standing arrangement with the Boy Scouts.[34] Its pre-emigration evaluation of applicants was also more extensive, so much so that, decades later, former migrants to Rhodesia tended to remember the testing more vividly than did those sent to Australia. Stephen Player, who emigrated to the school in 1947 when he was eleven years old, recalled having "quite a long interview" in Rhodesia House in London. The most memorable moment was when he was presented with a sheet of paper depicting shapes of different sizes and asked whether the triangle would fit within the circle, the rectangle in the triangle, and so on. He turned out to be surprisingly good at the task, which perhaps explains why the memory stuck with him.[35] Chris Torpey, on the other hand, remembered the testing because she felt certain she had failed. In the winter of 1955, when she was ten years old, she and two of her sisters traveled to London from Bristol for the initial round of intelligence exams. A few weeks later a woman "came to our house [and] asked me to draw a cat." "To this day," she laughed, "I've got the drawing ability of a two-year-old ... What dyslexia is to reading and writing, well I've that to drawing I'm afraid. And I thought that's it, I'm not going to Rhodesia, I can't draw ... so the lady suggested to me I just do two circles. And that's precisely what I did."[36]

The woman who tested Torpey's artistic skills was most likely a social worker sent to verify her emotional stability. Shortly after the war, the RFMC entered into an arrangement with the British Federation of Social Workers to evaluate the home environment of every candidate. If the inspector reported any misgivings, there followed a "consultation with a child guidance clinic" before final approval.[37] This effort to guarantee the steadiness of family relationships within a program that disrupted them by design may seem ironic, yet it reflected the endurance of older notions of class difference in the postwar Rhodesian understanding of Whiteness. The assumption that the settler population was thoroughly "middle

estimated the minimum qualifying IQ for the RFMC to be 130. Irwin to Hambro, July 8, 1948, D.296/ K2/2/1, ULSCA.

[34] In 1945, Lord Rowallan, the Chief Scout, donated £10,000 to RFMC on the condition that the College accept a set number of scouts annually. "British Share in Fairbridge: Funds for Rhodesian College," *The Times*, October 6, 1945. For details of this cooperation, see the papers of the Boy Scout Association's Migration Committee, 1947–1958, in TC/274, the Boy Scout Archive, Gilwell Park.

[35] Author's interview with Stephen Player, September 25, 2005.

[36] Author's interview with Chris Torpey, October 2, 2005.

[37] Women's Group on Public Welfare, *Child Emigration: A Study Made in 1948–1950 by a Committee of Women's Group on Public Welfare in Association with the National Council of Social Service* (London: National Council of Social Service, 1951), 20.

class" remained central to the Rhodesian claim to racial authority, since it allowed colonial officials to portray White privilege as deriving from supposedly class-specific virtues such as advanced intelligence, rationality, and emotional control. This belief helps clarify the social worker's puzzling comment to Joan Balcombe that it was obvious she was not sending off her child because he was "in the way." The woman's aim was less to evaluate John's emotional preparedness for emigration than Balcombe's standing as a mother. The social worker's polite and respectful demeanor, still memorable more than fifty years later, demonstrates that, despite Balcombe's divorce and John's absent father, the family was assessed to be respectable enough for Rhodesia. It also suggests that not every parent was found to be equally deserving of respect.[38]

In Australia, where the dominance of the European community was more certain, officials were open to the notion that poorer children from disrupted backgrounds could make good. The only Australian-focused organization that appears to have employed a social worker was the Fairbridge Society, which made the appointment in December of 1948, following pressure from the Home Office.[39] When the woman left the association to pursue other employment eighteen months later, the executive committee let the position lapse, arguing that it was not necessary to determine the suitability of children for Australia. The fact that the social work profession joined the movement primarily to meet Rhodesian stipulations about the quality of its migrants, rather than to bring the schemes in line with child welfare standards, indicates the extent to which postwar selection procedures aligned with the distinct national agendas of the late settler empire.

Nevertheless, in a number of small ways, emigration charities did slowly become more attuned to the shifting ideology and standards of postwar British welfarism. Following the 1948 Children Act, some organizations began to heed to the new emphasis on keeping "wholesome" families together. By the late 1940s, the Fairbridge Society's selection committee had begun rejecting otherwise qualified applicants when they felt that there "was not sufficient reason for withdrawing [the child] from an apparently satisfactory home circle," or when they found "good family feeling with no evidence of neglect on the part of the parents."[40] Statements such

---

[38] See, for instance, the comments of one social worker interviewed in the late 1980s, that many of the parents who had applied to send their sons or daughters to the RFMC were "ignorant people, who were very careless about their children," quoted in Philip Bean and Joy Melville, *Lost Children of the Empire: The Untold Story of Britain's Child Migrants* (London: Unwin Hyman, 1989), 100.

[39] Fairbridge, Executive Committee Minutes, April 20, 1948, D.296/B1/2/5, ULSCA.

[40] Fairbridge, Care of Children Committee Minutes, May 10, 1948, D.296/B5/3/1, ULSCA.

as these demonstrated the slow penetration of the era's focus on the role of the family in children's development. At the same time, they belied reformers' continued assumption that they were able and empowered to evaluate the strength or weakness of poor families' emotional ties on the basis of an application file and perhaps a cursory home visit. Usually, the committee's decision that a family should remain together was made in direct contradiction to the guardians' own request that their child be accepted for emigration. As in the cases when a household was deemed "unfit" or "failing," it was the committee's judgment, not that of the parents, that counted most.

In another nod to the changing philosophy of child welfare, charities also made a greater effort to explain the meaning of emigration to the children and to solicit their consent. In a typical example, the NCH instructed its recruitment officers to schedule "preliminary talks" with child migrants to "give all the facts they can about the kind of country Australia really is." The organization suggested that their representatives bring an "array of photographs and pictures" as well as a "good map – or, better still, a big globe" to provide "some idea … of the distances involved." The goal was to illustrate the full range of Australian culture and lifestyle, with topics including:

the climate, the way people dress for workdays and holidays, the kind of homes they live in, and what they have for breakfast, lunch, "afternoon tea," and tea. They should also be told what the Australian towns – little and big – look like, what they sell in their shops, what things cost, and the different Australian money value of the British pound sterling.[41]

Other charities followed suit. Eva Warhurst, the sixth-eldest child in a family of twelve living outside Newcastle, remembered being shown pictorial brochures of Australia before she and four of her siblings were sent to the Fairbridge Molong farm school in 1950.[42] Cliff Remmer, who emigrated to Mowbray Park in 1948 at age twelve, was introduced to the dominion by means of a short documentary movie of "kids riding to school on horses, and picking apples off the side of the road" that the Barnardo's migration officers screened in his branch home.[43]

These gestures notwithstanding, many boys and girls were simply too young to understand the ramifications of the situation. Like Bicknell, few had encountered the idea of the dominions before, either in school

---

[41] John Litten, "Going South," *Child Care*, April 1952, D.541/L3/3/9, ULSCA.

[42] Author's interview with Eva Warhurst, March 30, 2006. After Warhurst's emigration, her mother had six more children, so that the total number in the family eventually grew to eighteen.

[43] Author's interview with Cliff Remmer, May 13, 2006.

or in their daily lives. In part, this reflected the decline of imperial patriotism as a focus of the national curriculum.[44] But it mainly had to do
with the fact that child migrants were usually not old enough to have had
much formal exposure to the idea of empire. Any preconceptions they
had tended to come from the romanticized realm of children's adventure books. This was how Geoff Crimes got the idea that he was going
to "a little ... walled city, ten miles out in the desert. For some reason, I
thought it was desert out in Africa ... As it happened it was nothing like
that whatsoever."[45] Patricia Edwards,[46] who was six years old at the time
of her emigration, remembered having the impression that "I would be
coming back in the evening. Even though ... you know, I had this story
that I had been told that we were going to [Rhodesia]. I had the understanding that that was fine, that was great, it would be very exciting, but
we would also be back in the evening."[47] Former migrants to Australia
shared these memories of confusion. Jean Pringle, who was ten years old
when she arrived at a NCH orphanage in Victoria in 1950, noted that
she and the other children in her party were never given a clear understanding of the distances entailed in their resettlement: "I mean Australia
could've been just around the corner for all we knew ... We didn't know
that it would be thousands of miles away."[48]

This lack of comprehension appears throughout the archival record as
well. In 1968, Miss D. M. Dyson, a long-standing member of Barnardo's,
traveled to Australia to investigate the charity's branch homes. When she
asked a number of current and former child migrants about their pre-
emigration expectations, Dyson found that she had stumbled into a well
of discontent. As she reported to the executive committee: "One boy said
bluntly, 'we were deceived.' Several boys said they expected to ride to
school on horses. Several children spoke of having expected to see kangaroos about ... None seemed to feel they had been given a reasonably
true picture." She reprimanded the charity for being overly aggressive in
its recruitment tactics, and pointed out that the current methods "often

---

[44] This declining influence is illustrated by the fact that most schools had stopped celebrat-
ing Empire Day and other imperial pageants by the mid-1940s. Andrew Thompson, *The
Empire Strikes Back? The Impact of Imperialism on Britain from the Mid-Nineteenth Century*
(New York: Pearson Longman, 2005), 118–122; Andrew Thompson with Meaghan
Kowalsky, "Social Life and Cultural Representation: Empire in the Public Imagination,"
in *Britain's Experience of Empire in the Twentieth Century*, ed. Andrew Thompson (Oxford
University Press, 2012), 251–297, 268–269.

[45] Author's interview with Geoff Crimes, July 18, 2005.

[46] Pseudonym.

[47] Author's interview with Patricia Edwards (pseudonym), July 2005.

[48] Interview with Jean Pringle, conducted by Carolyn Rasmussen, ORAL TRC 6200/103,
Forgotten Australians and Former Child Migrants Oral History Project, November 9,
2011, NLA.

resulted in the migration of a child to his own unhappiness." Dyson pushed the organization to be more straightforward with its boys and girls, taking care not to idealize emigration. There was "no need to mention kangaroos and koala bears, which the school children are unlikely to meet outside Zoos and reserves. But if they must be mentioned, it would be realistic also to mention sharks, snakes, and flies."[49]

This difficulty in fostering realistic expectations was not particular to the child emigration movement. Recent studies of the postwar assisted passage schemes indicate that adults, too, often felt misled, or found that their dreams of life in the dominions did not meet up with the realities they encountered overseas.[50] On the one hand, the problem is inherent to the act of migration. No preparation, no matter how complete, can adequately express the subtler contours of a different culture or capture the complexities of life on the ground. On the other hand, child migrants' feelings of disorientation were a product of the wider fragmentation of the global Britannic identity in a period when the cultural ties of empire were loosening. No doubt, the ideal of the British inheritance continued to inform popular conceptions of nationhood across the dominions into the 1960s and beyond. Increasingly, though, immigration officials were prioritizing distinct, locally based standards of what constituted a person's fitness for assimilation into the national community over older notions of British ethnicity and race patriotism. When child migrants spoke of entering unfamiliar, culturally foreign landscapes, it was because, in many ways, they had.

### Education for socialization

Michael Snell was fourteen years old and living in a NCH orphanage in Painswick, England, when he began keeping a daily diary. Now housed in the National Library of Australia, this small book with its inexpensive black cover is one of the few remaining sources that offer the elusive, in-the-moment perspective of a child migrant. The diary begins on the first of January 1950, a little more than three weeks before Snell would board an ocean liner bound for the Dalmar Methodist Home for Children in New South Wales. The early entries pulse with anticipation as he documented the preparations for the trip. There were several rounds of injections against typhoid fever, a "smashing" farewell party in the orphanage where Snell had lived since the age of five, and a final sightseeing trip to

[49] D. M. Dyson, "Three Weeks with Barnardo's in Australia," March 1968," D.239/B4/13, ULSCA.
[50] James Jupp, *The English in Australia* (Cambridge University Press, 2004), 145–146; Hammerton and Thomson, *Ten Pound Poms*, 40–45.

London.[51] When the day of departure arrived, Snell kept an hour-by-hour account of the occasion: "Started from the branch at 8 o'clock. Got to King George 5th docks at 10 mins to 1 o'clock. Sailed at 4 o'clock. Said good-bye to Sister Maude, Mr. Litten, Mr. Thomas." Three days later, he was reveling in his newfound freedom on the ship, where like most child migrants he was allowed to set his own schedule and to enjoy six weeks without schooling. "I hope [the] boys are enjoying themselves at school doing Arithmetic," he smirked of those back in Painswick. "I['m] just having a nice bar of chocolate at this moment."[52]

The long journey provided Snell with his first fleeting encounters with the empire. He recorded catching sight of the "marvellouse" (sic) Rock of Gibraltar, watching fishing boats "with dark people ... selling baskets and hand bags" at Port Said and Aden, and seeing a "darling" baby elephant at the zoo during an afternoon stop at Colombo.[53] By the beginning of March, the group had reached Melbourne, and the boys spent a few days camping before heading on to Sydney. The day of arrival was a whirlwind. Having awakened early to watch the ship pass under the Harbor Bridge, the party was then whisked to a local hospital for a medical exam. In the late afternoon, Snell arrived at the Dalmar Farm School. Before the day was out, he had received his first lesson in milking cows.

From there, the tone of the diary began to change. Notes of boredom and resentment crept into the pages as Snell detailed his schooling at the local high school. He and the other boys from Dalmar received the conventional Australian curriculum with an added emphasis on agricultural skills. A typical day contained a lesson each in English, math, and science, as well as two periods devoted to agriculture and another three to woodworking. They watched films on famous Australian agriculturalists, such as the wheat breeder William Farrer, and wrote essays on wool production.[54] Overall, the curriculum left Snell unimpressed. "[I] don't learn much at school compared with the English [one]," he noted about a month after he arrived. Some days he just "sat on a wooden stool all day without anything to do."[55] His interest dwindled further in the spring, when he started a period of agricultural training that progressively cut into his school time. For the next few months, he would divide his week between school and the farm, where he sometimes worked ten-hour days in Dalmar's kitchen, dairy, or large commercial garden. The ever longer

---

51  Michael Snell, Diary, January 2, 12, 13, and 23, 1950, MS Acc09/185, NLA.
52  Ibid, January 25 and 27, 1950. Snell wrote in a stream-of-consciousness style with little punctuation. For ease of reading, I have inserted punctuation marks into the quotations taken from the text, but I have been careful not to alter their original intent.
53  Ibid, January 29, 1950, February 3 and 14, 1950.
54  Ibid, March 27, 25, and 30, 1950.    55  Ibid, April 4, 1950; March 10, 1950.

periods spent outside the classroom produced a gradual change in Snell's self-identity, as he began to define himself less as a schoolchild than as a worker. In mid April, he still felt part of the group that attended school, writing that "we go back to school again [today], but I never went because I had to stay home and help in the garden." But, by the end of the month, when his training was leaving only one day for school per week, he had stopped using the term "we," and instead placed himself apart from the "boys" who attended classes regularly.[56] In early June, he recorded his "last day at school ... In the morning I done a English exam for a bit of practice."[57] It was one week before his fifteenth birthday. The next day he was back working in the kitchen.[58]

To some extent, Snell's disappointing experience of Australian schooling can be explained by his advanced age at emigration. Most child migrants were thirteen or younger when they arrived in Australia, guaranteeing them at least two years of education before they reached the school-leaving age of fifteen. Those sent to Southern Rhodesia were younger still, having generally been selected between the ages of six and ten.[59] Arriving at age fourteen, Snell had little time to prove his abilities in school before his training period began. Moreover, being a newcomer to the country, and having grown up in institutional care, it is unlikely that he would have known whom to approach for guidance if he wanted to extend his education. Snell's diary gives the impression of a child going through the motions, growing frustrated and embittered at the course his life was taking but without a clear understanding of the alternatives. It is a sentiment echoed today by many former migrants when they look back at their education in the late empire.[60]

Scholars of childhood have long recognized the classroom to be one of the most important social spaces for the cultivation of the young. While never monolithic, educational systems provide an important "means of cultural transmission," wherein children encounter the collective beliefs, ideals, and identities of the society around them.[61] Of

[56] Ibid, April 12 and 24, 1950.     [57] Ibid, June 6, 1950.

[58] For more on Snell's life and experiences at Dalmar, see also Interview with Michael Snell and Bobbie Snell, conducted by Rob Willis, ORAL TRC 5484/90, Child Migrants Oral History Project, August 25, 2006, NLA; Interview with Michael Snell, conducted by Rob Willis, ORAL TRC 6200/2, Forgotten Australians and Former Child Migrants Oral History Project, November 17, 2009, NLA.

[59] RFMC, Annual General Meeting Minutes, December 12, 1955, courtesy of Catherine Maunder.

[60] See, for instance, the commentaries in David Hill, *The Forgotten Children: Fairbridge Farm School and Its Betrayal of Britain's Child Migrants to Australia* (Sydney: Random House, 2007), 133–157.

[61] J. A. Mangan, ed., *The Imperial Curriculum: Racial Images and Education in the British Colonial Experience* (New York: Routledge, 1993), 2. On the relationship between

course, the matter of whether boys and girls actually accept and take in those messages remains open to debate. It is particularly difficult for historians to answer this question, since they generally lack firsthand accounts written by children and so need to rely on retrospective memories when trying to reconstruct the historical perspectives of young people. My objective here is not, therefore, to demonstrate that the lessons child migrants received in school molded their identities in any definitive way, "forming" them into Australians or Rhodesians. Rather, it is to identify how the national agendas of these two late settler territories defined the opportunities offered to children such as Snell. In both regions, local education authorities worked hand in hand with the emigration charities to tailor the child migrants' curriculum to promote their lasting cultural integration. During the last days of the empire, these formal educational structures aimed to prepare formerly British children for entry into the increasingly sovereign Australian or Rhodesian nations.

In Australia, the system of child migrant schooling came under increased scrutiny during the later 1940s after a series of wartime investigations criticized the farm school curriculum for being too narrow. William Garnett of the High Commissioner's Office, who would later serve as a delegate of the British government's Fact-Finding Mission, reported in 1944 that, although emigration proponents claimed that every boy or girl sent to the dominion would have the "freedom to follow its bent," the truth of the matter was that the institutions were "not equipped to provide training other than in farming and domestic subjects." Like their interwar predecessors, child migrants were still receiving a basic primary education followed by upwards of two years' training for jobs as farm laborers and domestic servants. Less than 10 percent entered occupations outside the rural industries, and only a tiny proportion was able to move beyond low-skilled wage labor.[62] Garnett's report forced the charities to admit that their long-standing vision of emigration as enabling needy children to become independent producers on the land was profoundly unrealistic. There was "little doubt," members of Barnardo's Council noted, "that children migrated to Australia had a

education and socialization, see also J. A. Mangan, ed., *"Benefits Bestowed"? Education and British Imperialism* (New York: Manchester University Press, 1988); Anna Davin, *Growing Up Poor: Home, School and Street in London, 1870–1914* (London: River Orams Press, 1996), 113–153; Harry Hendrick, *Children, Childhood and English Society, 1880–1990* (Cambridge University Press, 1997), 63–78.

[62] William Garnett, "Report on Farm Schools in Australia," October 6, 1944, DO 35/1138, TNA: PRO. For a similar critique by a member of the Australian Interdepartmental Committee on Migration Policy, see Caroline Kelly, "Child Migration: A Survey of the Australian Field," 1944, A436, 1945/5/54, ANA.

hard life, [with] few of them rising to be managers or owners, [and] the majority remaining as farm labourers."[63]

In the interwar years, revelations like these would likely have been explained away as a case of substandard selection procedures and "defective" children. This time, however, they accompanied reports of child migrants testing *higher* on IQ exams after arriving in Australia than they had in Britain.[64] The timing was important as well. Coming at the end of the war, when public hostility toward hereditarian arguments reminiscent of Nazi propaganda was on the rise, the criticisms intersected with a wider intellectual current that presented the cultivation of free-thinking, individual personalities as the cornerstone of postwar stabilization and democratization.[65] This view had already resulted in a major revision of the British educational system under the 1944 Education Act, which attempted to accommodate children's unique aptitudes and abilities by creating three types of secondary schools: grammar, technical, and modern. In Australia, the push to diversify child migrants' schooling also appeared in line with the changing face of the dominion's postwar society, which, as one emigration proponent noted, was becoming "more industrialized" and thus generating jobs "in many vocations other than agriculture."[66] At the end of the war, having petitioned the Ministry of Immigration for approval to broaden their curricula, each of the emigration charities received the Australian government's assurance that any child migrant "of high standard of intelligence and physical fitness" would be "given the opportunity of obtaining higher education and, if they wish, of entering industrial or professional walks of life."[67]

This effort to extend child migrants' education beyond farming and service did open up some new career channels during the early postwar period. The Fairbridge Society was particularly active in reforming its methods. In 1948 it instituted a policy of having every boy or girl turning fourteen meet with the principal or another "vocational training

---

[63] Barnardo's, Council Minutes, April 18, 1945, B.239/B1/2/9, ULSCA; on Garnett's report and the subsequent response, see also Geoffrey Sherington and Chris Jeffery, *Fairbridge: Empire and Child Migration* (London: Woburn Press, 1998), 209–224; Hill, *The Forgotten Children*, 257–263.

[64] Fairbridge, Executive Minutes, July 12, 1944, D.296/B1/2/5, ULSCA.

[65] Mathew Thomson, *Psychological Subjects: Identity, Culture, and Health in Twentieth-Century Britain* (Oxford University Press, 2006), 209–249; Tara Zahra, *The Lost Children: Reconstructing Europe's Families after World War II* (Cambridge, MA: Harvard University Press, 2011); Michal Shapira, *The War Inside: Psychoanalysis, Total War and the Making of the Democratic Self in Postwar Britain* (Cambridge University Press, 2013).

[66] Kirkpatrick to Wiseman, December 17, 1945, DO 35/1138, TNA: PRO.

[67] Calwell to Chief Migration Officer, Australia House, September 26, 1945, A445, 133/2/115, ANA.

expert" to discuss their aspirations and employment prospects.[68] The reports of these conversations reveal a range of ambitions, from nursing and hairdressing for the girls to veterinary surgery and carpentry for the boys. And, although farming remained a popular choice, especially with the boys, those children with especially strong school records were encouraged to pursue a leaving certificate and, more rarely, a university education, instead of entering the agricultural training program.[69] In subsequent years, the Society made strides toward expanding child migrants' career options. In 1955, it reported that, of the ninety-nine Fairbridge boys who had entered employment since the war, roughly 60 percent had taken jobs outside the rural industries.[70]

Despite these attempts to broaden child migrants' career choices, on the whole the educational culture of the Australian movement remained overwhelmingly rural throughout the postwar years. Snell's experience of being shuffled into farm training before reaching the official school-leaving age was by no means unusual. One reason was that child migrants were only encouraged to apply for university if they ranked at the very top of their class, and, for a number of structural reasons, they tended to enter the Australian school system with reading and math skills well below the norms set for local children. A routine examination of ninety boys and girls at Fairbridge Pinjarra and the Church of England Swan Homes in Western Australia, for example, revealed that only thirteen met the educational guidelines for their age while the rest were "scholastically retarded" between one and three years. As the Education Department acknowledged, this trend had little to do with child migrants' actual intellectual abilities. Many had gone through frequent changes of residence in Britain during and after the war, and this disruption to their schooling was further compounded by the extended vacation on the journey to the dominion.[71] To reach parity with Australian children, child migrants required remedial teaching and coaching. Yet, in an institutional setting where the ratio of staff to child ranged from one in twelve to one in fourteen, such personalized attention was rare.

For child migrants to continue their education beyond the minimally required level, they needed to show exceptional promise or determination. John Bicknell always puzzled over the fact that he was the only Barnardo

[68] Fairbridge, Annual General Meeting Minutes, December 30, 1947, D.296/B1/2/5, ULSCA.
[69] A. E. Ball, "Vocational Review Reports," April 28–November 4, 1952, Perth Committee Minutes, AC3025A/5, SAWA: BL.
[70] Fairbridge, Executive Committee Minutes, October 6, 1955, D.296/B1/2/8, ULSCA.
[71] "Report by the Careers Research Branch of the Education Department on Swan Homes, August 1950, and Fairbridge Pinjarra," October 17, 1950, PP6/1, 1950/H/4051, ANA.

boy in his age group allowed to study for his leaving certificate. Looking back, he explained it as a consequence of his stubbornness: "I did put my foot down, I remember, and said, 'I want to go on to fifth year and I want to do my leaving certificate.' And even though my marks were quite low ... I was allowed to."[72] More often, children who seemed to be falling behind at school were dismissed as low achievers and steered toward vocational instruction and agricultural work.[73] Those migrants who were "not able or obviously resistant to further education of the academic kind," explained Frederick Woods, the principal of Fairbridge Molong, "start training as Farm Trainees in the case of the boys, and Domestic and Home science training for the girls."[74] One of the children tapped for a vocational route was Cliff Remmer, who remembered being placed back two years in primary school when he arrived in Australia. He stood out as the oldest and tallest boy in the class, and soon lost interest in the lessons. "I didn't learn a thing. I didn't want to be there," he said. When he turned fourteen, he was placed in an "opportunity class" dedicated to teaching rural skills, and the following year started his farm training.[75] As Remmer's story indicates, although new educational options existed during the postwar years, many child migrants did not receive the encouragement or assistance to pursue them. Raised on remote farm schools and urged to fill their time with rural activities from a young age, the boys and girls had few role models to emulate outside agriculture and little awareness of what alternate futures they might pursue. No wonder, then, that, as Woods noted in 1950, farming remained the "avenue of occupation that most interests the boys," while "marriage seems to be increasingly the chief vocation in which the girls are interested."[76]

The disruptive consequences of emigration and institutional life go some of the way toward explaining why the shift away from agricultural work never fully materialized. Even more central, however, was the persistence of the rural ideal at the core of postwar Australian nationalism. Throughout the 1950s and 1960s, Bush archetypes such as the honest frontiersman, the determined sheep farmer, and the faithful farmwife continued to have a powerful hold on the national imagination, not only because they offered a sense of emotional and spiritual stability in an era of rapid urban and industrial change but also because they remained powerful metaphors for expressing the country's distinctiveness from

[72] Bicknell interview.
[73] Hill, *The Forgotten Children*, 186–207.
[74] Fairbridge, "Report Read to the Executive Committee of the Fairbridge Society," September 19, 1950, D.296/B1/2/6, ULSCA.
[75] Remmer interview.
[76] Fairbridge, "Report Read to the Executive Committee."

Britain.[77] In the aftermath of the war, the Australian government made agricultural expansion a major plank of its reconstruction effort, creating large subsidies for rural technologies and encouraging farming communities to institute new civic celebrations such as agricultural shows and country festivals.[78] The trend recast rural occupations not as "dead-end jobs" but as noble professions that epitomized the best aspects of the national character: independence, rugged efficiency, and classless solidarity.

These notions led postwar emigration proponents to reemphasize country living as the best way to promote a child's lasting assimilation. Even as they touted the importance of offering boys and girls a range of occupational choices, they invested heavily in efforts to modernize the farm training programs and to entice children to select an agrarian career. In 1952, the board of the Fairbridge Society sanctioned the construction of a new agricultural wing at the Pinjarra Farm School, which they saw as a means to help solve the "greatest problem confronting this country today ... the falling off in primary production [and] the drift from rural areas to cities."[79] The local committee of Barnardo's was equally enthusiastic about the need to steer its wards toward agriculture. In 1951, the charity called on "our country supporters" to invite migrant boys and girls to their homes, so that the children could see "the varying types of farms and stations" and "sample real country life." In practice, the aim of presenting postwar child migrants with additional options often boiled down to providing them with "wider opportunities of realising what country occupations have to offer."[80]

Missing from the emigration movement's romanticized vision of the Australian heartland was any acknowledgment of the difficulties child migrants would face when they entered their first jobs on the scattered farms and sheep stations of the countryside. For Richard Stewart, who arrived at Fairbridge Pinjarra in 1949 at the age of twelve, the experience of leaving the school, "getting away from the kids I was used to ... going out into the strange wide world where no one knew me and doing a job that I had never tackled before," was "rather horrifying." Placed on a farm where he was the youngest employee, he found that the only other boy in the district his age was another Pinjarra alum who lived five miles

---

[77] Richard White, *Inventing Australia: Images and Identity, 1688–1980* (London: Allen and Unwin, 1981); Richard Waterhouse, *The Vision Splendid: A Social and Cultural History of Rural Australia* (Fremantle: Curtin University Books, 2005).

[78] Joy McCann, "History and Memory in Australia's Wheatlands," in *Struggle Country: The Rural Ideal in Twentieth Century Australia*, ed. Graeme Davison and Marc Brodie (Melbourne: Monash University ePress, 2005), 1–17.

[79] Fairbridge, Perth Committee Minutes, July 1, 1952, ACC 3025A/5, SAWA: BL.

[80] Barnardo's NSW, Annual Report, 1951, D.239/A3/19/8, ULSCA.

away.[81] Feelings of loneliness also plagued Julia Futcher, who emigrated to Fairbridge Molong in 1954 at the age of twelve. Sent to work as a servant and nanny on a sheep station four years later, Futcher had "really, really hated" the experience. The "people were alright and quite nice," she stressed; "it was just the fact that it was so isolated." Having never learned to drive, she lacked the means to get to the nearest town. And, although her employers had a radio, the house was so remote that the signal would fade in and out. Futcher stayed on the station for four long years before moving to Sydney to get married.[82] For her and for many other child migrants who made the difficult transition from trainee to laborer, rural Australia was less a site of rugged camaraderie and spiritual fulfillment than of harsh solitude and seclusion.

A similar strand of ruralism informed postwar conceptions of Rhodesian nationhood. In a territory where Europeans comprised no more than 5 percent of the population, settlers had long justified their presence as stewards of the land, sent to conserve, enhance, and cultivate Africa's "unused" spaces.[83] This agrarian ideology gained new salience in the years after the war as the colony entered a period of tremendous demographic and economic change. A wave of immigration more than doubled the European population, which rocketed from 84,000 in 1946 to an all-time high of 218,000 in 1959, where it remained through the 1970s.[84] Most of these new arrivals settled in towns and cities, taking jobs in the skilled trades and burgeoning manufacturing sector. Yet, even as this rapid urban and industrial expansion caused the percentage of Europeans employed in agriculture to decline, the ideal of the pioneer farmer remained a mainstay of Rhodesian public culture.[85] This sentimental vision of the imperial heritage enabled White settlers, old and new, to profess an intrinsic connection to the land at a time when the rest of Africa was on the path to decolonization and majority rule.

In line with this postwar rural nostalgia, the initial design of the RFMC incorporated several elements of the conventional farm school model. Its London-based board of directors conceived the institution as a "training

[81] Author's interview with Richard Stewart, July 16, 2006.
[82] Author's interview with Julia Futcher, December 15, 2005.
[83] David McDermott Hughes, *Whiteness in Zimbabwe: Race, Landscape, and the Problem of Belonging* (New York: Palgrave Macmillan, 2010).
[84] Allison Shutt and Tony King, "Imperial Rhodesians: The 1953 Rhodes Centenary Exhibition in Southern Rhodesia," *Journal of Southern African Studies* 31, no. 2 (June 2005): 357–379, 359; Josiah Brownell, *The Collapse of Rhodesia: Population Demographics and the Politics of Race* (London: I. B. Tauris, 2011), 73.
[85] Robin Palmer, *Land and Racial Domination in Rhodesia* (Berkeley: University of California Press, 1977); Donal Lowry, "Rhodesia 1890–1980: 'The Lost Dominion,'" in *Settlers and Expatriates: Britons over the Seas*, ed. Robert Bickers (Oxford University Press, 2010), 112–149.

ground for those whose ultimate aim is farming," where students would follow a curriculum covering "all possible general forms of agriculture."[86] When the school opened in 1946 on a decommissioned airbase on the outskirts of Bulawayo, it contained livestock pens and more than 2,000 acres of fields set aside for cattle, cotton, and mealies. The staff started a chapter of the Young Farmers' Club, which provided tips to the boys and girls on how to plant gardens and encouraged them to take part in local agricultural competitions.[87] They also made efforts to involve the early parties of children directly in the production process. "I feel sure some of the boys will recall," the College's first housemother later wrote, "that we rushed from church on Sunday, got into our leisure clothes and picked the cotton into huge sacks."[88] Several former migrants who arrived in the late 1940s did in fact speak of spending long afternoons in the sun learning how to drive a tractor, feed livestock, or pick cotton.[89]

Agrarian images dominated the scheme's publicity as well. A typical example was the cover of its 1946 promotional brochure, which presented a highly stylized vision of the Rhodesian landscape, with neatly cultivated fields, a lush evergreen forest, and a herd of cattle grazing nearby (Figure 6.1). In the foreground, a migrant boy pointed toward the agrarian scene, mimicking a pioneer pose, while a girl companion knelt adoringly at his feet. Constructed to appeal to British audiences, the image contained little resemblance to Southern Rhodesia's arid topography. Its intent was less to convey the realities of the setting than to project the scheme as part of the larger colonial mission to bring commercial and cultural development to Africa.[90] Moreover, the absence of Africans from the picture papered over the thornier issues of political rule. The brochure's focus on the nonhuman environment, and on child migrants' future mastery of it, portrayed the White presence in Southern Rhodesia as both natural and uncontested.

As the College's administration soon realized, however, these attempts to groom child migrants for a life on the land were deeply

[86] Fairbridge, RFMC Brochure, c. 1939, D.296/K2/1/11, ULSCA.
[87] RFMC, Annual General Meeting Minutes, October 14, 1954, courtesy of Catherine Maunder.
[88] Ann Raitt in *Windows: Rhodesia Fairbridge Memorial College Autobiographies*, ed. Peter Gould (Christchurch: Fairbridge Marketing Board, 2001), 48.
[89] Author's interviews with Fred Gunning, September 24, 2005; Stephen Player; Alistair Marshall, October 10, 2005; John Barton, July 4, 2009; and Peter Robinson, July 4, 2009.
[90] On the concept of development and its relationship to postwar British imperialism in Africa, see Frederick Cooper, "Modernizing Bureaucrats, Backward Africans, and the Development Concept," in *International Development and the Social Sciences: Essays on the History and Politics of Knowledge*, ed. Frederick Cooper and Randall Packard (Berkeley: University of California Press, 1997), 64–92.

Figure 6.1 RFMC, "Outline of the Scheme," Promotional Appeal Booklet, *c.* 1946, D.296/K2/4/2, ULSCA.

out of step with the racial structures of Rhodesian society. In a culture that defined unskilled manual work as demeaning to Europeans, the spectacle of White children picking cotton was a profound affront to the racial hierarchy. The only respectable careers open to settlers in the agricultural economy were as farm managers or owners, yet the start-up funds required for these positions were well beyond the means of child migrants. Indeed, the enormous cost of commercial agriculture was one of the reasons why, despite the settler community's sentimental attachment to farming, the colony never possessed more than a handful of agricultural colleges.[91] Progressively aware of these complications, the school's executive committee backed away from the farm school model by 1948, noting that it was incompatible with the cultural dictates of colonial Africa. Whereas agrarian training was appropriate in dominions such as Australia, where "all work is done by White men," in Southern Rhodesia "all unskilled and a good deal of the semi-skilled work is done by non-Europeans." The board argued that for "the Whites, to hold their own," it was imperative that they were "well-educated, trained efficient."[92] Child migrants sent to Rhodesia would thus receive a broader-based curriculum than was customary in the Australian farm schools. After primary school, every Rhodesian migrant was given a choice of three local secondary schools and also became eligible for university bursaries and scholarships. Although it remained possible for interested boys to become "pupil farmers and ... farm managers in due course," the majority took courses that prepared them for work in industry or the civil service.[93] Furthermore, while Australian child migrants tended to enter the workforce at the age of fifteen, those sent to Rhodesia usually stayed in school until they were seventeen or eighteen, having received their leaving certificate.

These differences in the style and scope of education offered to child migrants help reveal the growing divides between the national cultures of Greater Britain during the postwar era. It is true that, well into the 1960s, Rhodesian political culture upheld a strong reverence for the British heritage, which remained a prominent part of imperial civic celebrations such as the royal tours of 1947 and 1953 or the Rhodes Centenary Exhibition of 1953.[94] Alongside these continued expressions of Britannic sentiment, however, local officials stressed that full integration into Rhodesian society required a specialized form of education that would invest young people with the skills of colonial leadership. As early as 1930, a government-appointed education commission decreed that, in order to "create and maintain a community" that was "in every aspect of its life, characteristically Rhodesian," the school curriculum

[91] R. J. Challiss, *The European Educational System in Southern Rhodesia, 1890–1930* (Salisbury: University of Zimbabwe, 1980), 99–100.
[92] RFMC, Information Sheet, 1948, D.296/K2/3/1, ULSCA.
[93] RFMC, Promotional Brochure, 1954, D.296/K2/4/5, ULSCA.
[94] Shutt and King, "Imperial Rhodesians."

could not be "imported bodily from another country ... It must be home grown."[95] Seen in this light, the early restructuring of the RFMC represented its directors' acknowledgment that the form of education on offer in the other parts of the Angloworld was inadequate for the distinct cultural requirements of southern Africa. Regardless of their collective birthright, child migrants needed more than a British education to ensure that they would "grow up as Rhodesians, calling Rhodesia 'home.'"[96]

By positioning education as a crucial mechanism for socializing the young to the colonial order, Rhodesian authorities ensured that the boys and girls sent to the RFMC received a wider range of school experiences and career choices than did their peers in Australia. In practice, though, child migrants' ability to make the most of those opportunities was still limited by the institutional setting in which they lived. "You went to school and that was it," remembered John Moxham, who emigrated to the College in 1948 at the age of nine. "There was no sort of encouragement to do any better."[97] Ken Pinchess was eight years old in 1949 when he arrived at the RFMC. He detested school and did everything possible to avoid it, noting that "all we were interested in was *not school* ... I mean, I wouldn't learn French. I wouldn't learn Latin. I used to bunk it every time I got to a classroom. I just wouldn't go." Without support from the staff or teachers, he struggled to complete his certificate requirements at the local technical school and gave no thought to attending university.[98] The general lack of guidance continued when child migrants reached the point of entering their first jobs. "If you were academically ... good at all your subjects you probably had a choice of going on to university," explained Alan Buckles, who arrived at the College in 1951 when he was seven years old. "Otherwise, it was 'These are the jobs that are available. Choose one.'" Presented with a range of low-ranking government jobs, Buckles opted for a post in a distant customs office, largely because it was the same path his brother had taken the previous year.[99] As in Australia, the end of child migrants' education was abrupt and perfunctory. "You didn't graduate. You left school," summarized Susan Corrans, who was

[95] Southern Rhodesia, "Report of the Education Commission" (Cape Town, 1929), quoted in Donal Lowry, "'South African without the Afrikaners': The Creation of a Settler Identity in Southern Rhodesia," paper presented at the Biennial South African Historical Association Conference, Rhodes University, 1995. See also Dickson Mungazi, "A Strategy for Power: Commissions of Inquiry into Education and Government Control in Colonial Zimbabwe," *The International Journal of African Historical Studies* 22, no. 2 (1989): 267–285, 276.

[96] RFMC, Information Sheet.

[97] Author's interview with John Moxham, July 6, 2009.

[98] Author's interview with Ken Pinchess, October 1, 2005.

[99] Author's interview with Alan Buckles, October 29, 2005.

nine years old when she came out in the same party as Buckles.[100] In both regions, child migrants' education aimed to invest them with the distinct, local knowledge they required to adapt to their new societies. It stopped short, though, of providing the practical tools and emotional support they needed to launch themselves as autonomous members of the national community.

## Cultivating national character

The first nine years of Gillian Hand's life were spent in a small, rent-controlled row house in a poorer neighborhood of Brighton. Her parents had married at the end of the war, shortly after her mother became pregnant. Thrown together by necessity, the marriage was "doomed from the start." Hand's father exited the scene when she was five and her sister was a newborn. Left without a steady income, their small family soon became "very deprived" and was forced to rely on assistance from social workers. One of these women gave Hand her first Malteser, so that, decades later, the taste of the candy could still recall shadowy memories of unfamiliar visitors and government-issued care packages. In retrospect, Hand acknowledged that these years were probably hardest on her mother, who was "very bright ... and hadn't had the education that she should have had."[101] Hand's description calls to mind Carolyn Steedman's portrait of her own mother in *Landscape for a Good Woman*: an ambitious, working-class woman who felt trapped by motherhood and by the harsh fairness of Britain's postwar austerity years.[102] This sense of wanting more helped explain for Hand why her mother sent her soft-spoken, artistic daughter to the RFMC. The scheme must have appeared as a stepping stone, a way of "giving me what she should have had and never had ... I think she meant well by it."

Hand left for Southern Rhodesia in 1954. Only flashes of the trip out with a party of twelve other children stayed with her. She remembered the neighbors coming over to say goodbye, and how confined and dark it seemed in the bowels of the ship. She could still see African children running alongside the train from Cape Town to Bulawayo, and feel the first blast of "the heat, the *heat*, and the amount of sun and the wide openness of it." Nothing remained of her arrival at the College, but her early memories of the place give a sense of its institutional character and of the difficulties many child migrants experienced in adapting to a new

[100] Author's interview with Susan Corrans, December 7, 2005.
[101] Author's interview with Gillian Hand, January 22, 2006.
[102] Carolyn Steedman, *Landscape for a Good Woman: A Story of Two Lives* (London: Virago, 1986).

environment and routine. Her first housemother was less a maternal figure than an "intimidator … She shouted a lot, she tread very heavily, so
she would come thundering through the wooden floored dormitory, and
you'd just be shaking." Others were gentler. Her second housemother
"still had a strong voice, but she cared about us in a way that we felt –
well, I felt – we mattered." Hand appreciated this kindness, but it was not
enough to make her feel at home. "I never settled in," she remembered;
"I never felt that was where I wanted to be."[103]

Looking back on these years, Hand recalled that one of the hardest parts of the adjustment process was wrapping her mind around the
colonial racial culture. There were bewildering mixed messages. At the
RFMC, the "standard line" about the African population was: "Don't
go near them, they're dangerous." It was an expression of fear that most
likely reflected the broader, imperial response to the Mau Mau uprising
in Kenya, which at the time was feeding lurid images of African violence
throughout the British and imperial press.[104] But, when Hand would visit
Rhodesian households, either for a weekend with a school friend or a
summer holiday, she would find herself surrounded by African servants.
Unable to avoid them, she learned instead to calculate her response. In
these homes, she and her friends "were trained to see … that it was our
right for them to serve us," and that because "we've got White skins, we
are more important than them." While Hand only remained in the colony for six years before her mother remarried and asked her to return
to Britain, this mode of thinking proved difficult to shake off. "It didn't
change until I became a feminist and a therapist and started to really see
people as they are and not through preconceptions," she said. "It was a
long time in the changing."[105]

Hand's reflections cast light on the subtleties of acculturation, or the
tacit, unspoken, and generally undirected ways that children absorb
the norms of their society.[106] While the formal systems of child migrant
schooling steered boys and girls toward particular careers in the social
structure, the informal lessons imparted outside the classroom about
what it meant to be Australian or Rhodesian often left a more profound
impression. Proponents took the task of assimilation seriously, and, as

---

[103] Hand interview.
[104] Joanna Lewis, "'Daddy Wouldn't Buy Me a Mau Mau': The British Popular Press and
the Demoralization of Empire," in *Mau Mau and Nationhood*, ed. E. S. Atieno Odiambo
and John Lonsdale (Oxford: James Currey, 2003), 227–250.
[105] Hand interview.
[106] For a helpful discussion of this concept, see J. A. Mangan, ed., *Making Imperial
Mentalities: Socialisation and British Imperialism* (New York: Manchester University
Press, 1990).

they had in the interwar years, used the controlled setting of child migrant institutions to introduce the boys and girls to the core elements of the national character. The Fairbridge Society defined its task not solely in terms of skills-building: teaching boys and girls "how to read and write, till the soil, or become proficient at some occupation or profession." "Of far greater importance," members stressed, was their responsibility to mold cultural mentalities, to convey broader truths about "the right way to think and live."[107] As Hand's experience illustrates, this process of acculturation could be messy and confusing. During an era in which separate national identities were replacing the ideal of a shared imperial heritage, child migrants were sometimes left without a clear sense of what it took to belong.

Although the schemes to Australia and Southern Rhodesia were organized along different lines, they shared a number of features that were common to postwar children's homes throughout the empire. The first similarity was in their design. The RFMC and the majority of the Australian establishments continued to be run on the "cottage home" or "little house" model, which grouped twelve to fourteen children together in single-sex dorms that also included a small apartment for the "cottage mother" or matron.[108] Pitched as a "growing place for souls" where children could "grow and unfold naturally," cottage homes were in fact institutional spaces that had been constructed on low budgets and with efficiency in mind.[109] Certain money-saving practices, such as having all children take turns using a communal bathing facility, or eat their meals in a central dining hall, added to the artificiality of the setting.[110] So too did the convention of grouping children by sex and age, which meant that brothers and sisters usually lived apart and that children changed dorms every year or two.

The central staff figure in child migrants' lives was the cottage mother, who supervised all aspects of the daily routine, settled minor squabbles, and enforced the rules. It was a taxing and monotonous job. Cottage mothers were unofficially on duty around the clock, received no training and few holidays, and were poorly paid. Unsurprisingly, the turnover rate was high. The RFMC appears to have had somewhat greater stability

---

[107] Fairbridge, Annual Report, 1953, D.296/D1/1/2, ULSCA.
[108] The exception was the Catholic initiatives to Australia, which tended to use extant orphanages. For a full account, see Barry Coldrey, *Child Migration to Catholic Institutions in Australia: Objectives, Policies, Realities, 1926–1966* (Como, WA: Tamanaraik Press, 1995).
[109] "Fairbridge School: An Ideal Realised," *Sydney Morning Herald*, March 24, 1938.
[110] Some institutions, such as Fairbridge Pinjarra, contained bathrooms and kitchens in the cottage homes, although this design was not the norm.

in its staffing, due to its policy of bringing matrons out from Britain on three-year contracts.[111] In Australia, cottage mothers were usually local women, who were more able to leave the job at a moment's notice for work elsewhere. Staffing shortages plagued the Australian farm schools throughout the postwar period, forcing their directors to improvise solutions for sudden vacancies. Richard Stewart, for instance, remembered arriving at Fairbridge Pinjarra to find that the woman employed to run his cottage had just quit. As he was nearly thirteen and the oldest in his party, the principal put him in charge until a replacement could be found.[112]

The lack of continuity among cottage mothers in both Australia and Southern Rhodesia meant that most child migrants did not develop strong relationships with them. Although several former migrants spoke lovingly about their matron's efforts to create small moments of intimacy and individualized attention, the more typical memory was of emotional distance. As Chris Torpey put it, she was "like a mother in that she got impatient with you and all that sort of thing. But I think she purposely didn't get close to anybody ... I mean they cared for our needs ... [But] if you had a problem you wouldn't go to a member of staff. It just didn't appear to be done."[113] Vivian Finn, who was eight years old when he arrived at the RFMC in 1956, stressed that the term "cottage mother" was a misnomer, since it implied an "intimate, affectionate relationship, a caring, concerned relationship," which he never experienced at the College, "not remotely."[114] Indeed, over the nine-month period that Michael Snell recorded his day-to-day experiences at Dalmar, his matron appeared in his diary only once, in a fleeting mention of her treating his mosquito bites.[115] And, as Hand's account underscores, some children viewed their cottage mothers as terrifying, larger-than-life figures, who were quick to take out the frustrations of their difficult jobs on the children in their charge. Despite emigration charities' efforts to portray cottage mothers as the epitome of the nurturing homemaker of the 1950s (Figures 6.2 and 6.3), the structure of the schemes ensured that the care many child migrants received was at best detached and impersonal and at worst abusive and frightening.[116]

---

[111] CVOCE Minutes, March 13, 1953, D.296/H6/1/2/1, ULSCA.
[112] Stewart interview.
[113] Torpey interview.
[114] Author's interview with Vivian Finn, September 22, 2005.
[115] Snell, Diary, April 8, 1950.
[116] For personal commentaries (mainly negative) of child migrants' treatment by staff members, see Bean and Melville, *Lost Children of the Empire*, 82–84 and 110–125; Hill, *The Forgotten Children*, 72–76 and 154–185. For an analysis of the structural forces that could lead to the physical and sexual abuse of children by staff members

Figures 6.2 and 6.3 "A happy home is the basis of a happy Fairbridge."
Fairbridge Pinjarra, Annual Report, 1951, D.296/D1/1/2, ULSCA.

A further similarity linking the Australian and Rhodesian child migrant experience was regimentation. Former migrants to both countries strongly recalled living "by the bell," and could often recite the weekly timetable of their institution down to the hour. There were striking differences, however, in the ways that they described their nonschool hours. Australian migrants overwhelmingly spoke of structured and supervised activities, such as scouting, team sports, and chores. Julia Futcher noted that her afternoons at Fairbridge Molong in the mid 1950s consisted of horseback riding, field hockey, and household labor: "Scrub floors, clean bathrooms. Weed gardens, washing. You name it we did it ... Set the tables, sweep the floor, polish the floors."[117] When June-Marie Reid was ten and traveled to Barnardo's Burwood home for girls near Sydney in 1952, she had already been in the organization's care for five years. That time in the British branches had accustomed her to performing regular chores, but not to the extent that was expected of her in Australia. "We had to work. Work, work, work, the whole time. Oh a whole lot, housework, scrubbing, polishing ... We didn't play very much."[118] Men also remembered childhoods ruled by tightly managed activities and duties, although theirs were more likely to be outdoor tasks. Michael Oldfield recalled that his mornings at Barnardo's Mowbray Park were spent helping in the kitchen or the dairy and his after-school time was dedicated to gardening or feeding livestock. "There was always an adult person or two supervising," he emphasized. "You weren't doing these things on your own."[119]

In contrast, the memories of former migrants to the RFMC evoked notions of unrestricted free time and personal autonomy. As Jimmy Hewitson, who arrived in 1950, having just turned ten, put it, "We were given our own space ... We used to be able to wander off into the bush, either on our own or in the company of other boys, depending on how we felt. You know, wander around without sort of being supervised or anything like that."[120] Men and women alike spoke of spending long hours in the afternoons or on weekends exploring the surrounding area in groups of two or three, going on long picnics in the neighboring hills, or building small shacks out of found bricks and corrugated iron. John Andrews, the son of Joan Balcombe, reminisced in a rush of words about having "the

in postwar Australian institutions, see Barry Coldrey, "'A Strange Mixture of Caring and Corruption': Residential Care in Christian Brothers Orphanages and Industrial Schools during Their Last Phase, 1940s to 1960s," *History of Education* 29, no. 4 (2000): 343–355.

[117] Futcher interview.
[118] Author's interview with June-Marie Reid, May 18, 2006.
[119] Author's interview with Michael Oldfield, February 23, 2006.
[120] Author's interview with Jimmy Hewitson, October 20, 2005.

run of this great big area, or bush ... We were allowed out at weekends, and we could get a packed lunch from the kitchens as well and go off into the bush on our own at weekends, and it was wonderful. That's really when I started to learn about African wildlife and things like that."[121]

Andrews' nostalgic tone highlights the personal and subjective quality of memory, which helps begin to explain the disparity between the Australian and Rhodesian recollections. This is not to say that former migrants' narratives of their childhood are not accurate or "true" but rather to point out that later experiences and adult self-understandings play an important role in defining how people construct their life histories. For former migrants to Australia, descriptions of heavy workloads can serve as a metaphor for overcoming a difficult childhood or as a means to express their respect for the value of hard work. On the other hand, Rhodesian migrants' tales of traveling independently and without fear through the African bush can offer a platform for communicating a less easily expressed sense of mourning for the passing of White Rhodesia. For former migrants such as Andrews, who stayed in the country through the UDI and fought in the guerrilla war of the 1970s, the rural landscape of their youth later transformed into a place of hidden threats and seemingly random acts of violence. In comparison to these subsequent feelings of insecurity, memories of childhood mobility offer a vision of Africa in which settlers could still consider themselves at home.

Undoubtedly, this backward gaze might lead former migrants to emphasize certain elements of their childhood over others. Yet attention to the constructed quality of memory should not obscure the genuine regional differences that these memories reflect. Reviewing children's daily responsibilities in their farm schools in 1950, the Fairbridge Society detailed a long list of chores that in Southern Rhodesia would have been assigned to African servants, including "washing up, sweeping, dusting ... setting the table for dinner, setting fires, collecting chips, or chopping firewood, fetching coke, watering the garden and general tidying up."[122] Put simply, Australian child migrants remember a more controlled and work-filled existence because that was the reality. While the Australian programs aimed to endow boys and girls with the skills and characteristics of an idealized rural Australia, particularly a rugged "can do" spirit and steady work ethic, this practical training would have been perceived as unnecessary, even potentially detrimental, in Southern Rhodesia. There, the object was to foster a proprietary relationship to the land, a sense that the children

---

[121] Andrews interview. See also the testimonies of former Rhodesian child migrants in Bean and Melville, *Lost Children of the Empire*, 103–105; Gould, *Windows*.

[122] Fairbridge, Executive Committee Minutes, September 19, 1950, D.296/B1/2/6, ULSCA.

held mastery over a setting where the settler presence was increasingly questioned.[123] Child migrants' greater freedom to roam and ability to exercise more choice in how they spent their leisure time provided lessons in pioneering, self-governance, and colonial authority. In play as in their formal schooling, Rhodesian migrants learned the privileges of Whiteness in the African empire.

This social education carried over into other aspects of child migrants' institutional life, such as the structures for maintaining order and discipline. Emigration charities had long considered punishments as a tool for readying young people for their entry into society. As the directors of Barnardo's argued, enforcing a disciplinary code encouraged children to see themselves as part of a larger collective, to "learn that they cannot share the privileges of a community unless they share its duties and responsibilities." Punishments designed to humiliate, such as "head cropping, wearing labels," or public canings, did more harm than good, since they stigmatized and marginalized children rather than reinforcing their attachment to others and to the society around them.[124] Viewing discipline as a mechanism to train children for corporate life, proponents attempted to align their punishment systems to the broader values and ethics of the nation. The result was two distinct conceptions of discipline in Australia and Southern Rhodesia, each designed to prepare child migrants for a particular national future.

At a time when corporal punishment remained widely accepted throughout the empire, child migrants, like most institutionalized children, were subject to frequent and sometimes violent physical reprimands for breaking the rules. In both regions, the disciplinary code followed a strict gendered hierarchy. The male principals of the institutions were responsible for caning children for offenses such as disobeying staff, talking back, running away, smoking, or experimenting sexually. Cottage mothers were officially not allowed to use physical punishments, although smacks and other forms of rough handling were common. June-Marie Reid, for instance, remembered that the two older matrons who ran her institution combined humiliation with frequent outbursts of aggression to keep children in line: "If you said you didn't like something, you were made to stand up and eat the rest of your meal standing up with your chair set behind you. I [also] had my face slapped many, many times."[125] Generally though, in Australia the discipline was strictly enforced from

---

[123] On this point, see also Hughes, *Whiteness in Zimbabwe*.

[124] Barnardo's, Miss Martindale, "Instructions on Maintenance of Discipline in Girls' Homes," September 1942; P.T. Kirkpatrick, "Rules as to the Maintenance of Discipline in Homes for Boys," September 1942, B.239/B1/2/9, ULSCA.

[125] Reid interview.

the top down, and most former migrants portrayed canings as a routine part of their upbringing. Margaret Clarke, who described the punishments at Fairbridge Molong as "severe," recalled that the principal once caned her with a hockey stick after her cottage mother accused her of lying.[126] It was not a one-time occurrence. Shortly after she left the school, the Society's local committee instructed the principal to stop using the hockey stick as a disciplinary instrument, noting that, although "corporal punishment was sometimes necessary," the method "sounds repellant."[127] Most punishments were less extreme, yet Clarke's anecdote illustrates the larger point that the pattern of Australian discipline tended to buttress male authority and to underscore the differential power relationship between adults and children.

Canings were a fact of life at the RFMC as well, but there this hierarchical model of punishment was coupled with a horizontal emphasis on students' responsibility to police each other. Early on, the College instituted a prefect system, a common attribute of elite British boarding schools, that allowed designated senior boys to enforce the rules among their peers. Each prefect was also assigned a younger boy, called a "fag," who took over the small number of chores that Rhodesian migrants performed, such as bed-making and polishing shoes. This culture of peer regulation took less formal modes as well, and many former migrants spoke in detail about an institutional culture of bullying and hazing at the RFMC. "If you didn't stand up for yourself, you got put down," remembered Ken Pinchess, who went on to describe a yearly initiation during which junior boys were coerced to "run the gauntlet" through rows of seniors who whipped them with rolled-up towels dipped in soap or saltwater. Gender-specific rituals such as this one used peer violence to enforce a colonial code of manliness that stressed bravery, physical strength, and endurance. "Depending on how you performed in that," noted Geoff Crimes, "your rating [among the boys] was up and down accordingly."[128] It is unclear whether the staff was aware of these specific acts of intimidation and harassment, but a certain degree of bullying does seem to have been condoned as a means of building character. Following an episode when she was caned by a group of older girls, Chris Torpey approached the principal's wife to show her the welts on her legs. The response she received was "learn to fight, mate." The incident

---

[126] Author's interview with Margaret Clarke, March 22, 2006. Other former migrants to the school remember being hit with all manner of items, including wooden spoons, a riding crop, and ironing cords. Hill, *The Forgotten Children*, 154–167.

[127] Fairbridge, Hudson to Hambro, March 16, 1948, D.296/19/25, ULSCA.

[128] Pinchess and Crimes interviews. Other former migrants who spoke of this initiation include John Moxham and Bruce Harris (pseudonym).

taught Torpey that she was expected to maintain an attitude of tough self-assurance. "I realized I'd made a mistake" by reporting the bullying. It "wasn't the thing to do" since "people wouldn't think you'd got a very strong backbone."[129]

These systems of punishments were not unique to Australia and Southern Rhodesia. Both were based on well-established precedents in Britain, where canings had long enforced deference in the classroom and where prefects and hazing were entrenched features of public school life.[130] What is striking about their deployment in the settler empire, however, is how they expose varying assumptions about the qualities British children needed to take on in order to assimilate to their new cultural environments. In Australia, the discipline aimed to steel child migrants to abide the realities of the rural outback – the nation's "struggle country" – where they would be called on to perform difficult and strenuous labor with little reward.[131] As working-class children sent to eke out a living on the soil, they were being trained to submit not only to their employers but also to the requirements of the land. Obedience was central to the Rhodesian system as well, but it was of a different kind. The object there was to reiterate the settler obligation to the White community, reinforcing each individual's need to learn the web of social strictures that upheld the racial hierarchy. Formal and informal modes of disciplinary violence were essential to the process of transforming children into the colonial elite. As the long-serving Prime Minister Godfrey Huggins bluntly put it, the country needed young men who had "fagged at school and have been flogged at school" and who understood how both to command and to obey.[132]

There was only so much of this knowledge that could be gained on school grounds. One of the main obstacles that the RFMC's staff faced was that they too tended to be recent immigrants to the country, with little prior experience of colonial race relations. They were thus in the same position as many of the postwar new arrivals, who were often bewildered by the subtler conventions governing Black–White interactions. As the journalist John Parker recounted of his family's first days in Southern Rhodesia's capital of Salisbury in the mid 1950s, "we had never found ourselves in any situation where race had affected us in any way." He

---

[129] Torpey interview.

[130] Hendrick, *Children, Childhood and English Society*, 73–78; Barry Coldrey, "'The Extreme End of a Spectrum of Violence': Physical Abuse, Hegemony and Resistance in British Residential Care," *Children and Society* 15 (2001): 95–106.

[131] Davison and Brodie, *Struggle Country*.

[132] Quoted in L. H. Gann and M. Gelfand, *Huggins of Rhodesia: The Man and His Country* (London: Allen & Unwin, 1964), 70.

found race relations an uncomfortable subject to talk about, and soon learned to keep quiet about it in polite society.[133] A similar culture of silence permeated the RFMC. Former migrants remembered vague warnings that "if we didn't look smart and, you know, get our education, [the Africans] would take our jobs."[134] But they were given no explicit instructions on how to behave, and instead were expected to acquire the colony's social cues through osmosis. "I think we just picked up on how things were," said Tim Warner, who was almost nine when he arrived at the College in 1947. The message, as he interpreted it, focused less on overt superiority than on simple difference: "Black people did the cooking and the driving and whatever ... They had their station and jobs in life ... They just had different jobs to do ... And to question it at that stage seemed superfluous. It just didn't cross your mind, really. Well, not at that age anyway."[135]

The staff's inability or unwillingness to tackle the question of race led the College to rely on other methods of connecting child migrants with the colony's racial culture. From its inception, the school dedicated a handful of spaces to local Rhodesian children, who attended the on-site primary school and sometimes boarded there as well. It also instituted a policy of sending migrants to spend their school holidays with settler families. Former migrants remembered traveling alone on trains for days at a time to reach destinations scattered throughout the colony, in places such as Gatooma and Que Que in the north, Umtali in the east, or even South Africa. Some of the Australian schemes also created holiday initiatives after the war, but in general they were only sporadically implemented and never became widespread.[136] The greater use of these programs in Southern Rhodesia was tied directly to the imperative of acculturation. As the directors of the RFMC argued, the projects would allow child migrants "to mix with Rhodesian boys and girls of their own age and so start to become young Rhodesian citizens from their earliest days."[137]

In practice, this process of "turning our children into good Rhodesians" often entailed embarrassing lessons in comportment, as migrants learned to modify their conduct toward Africans.[138] The memories of these uncomfortable moments stayed with them decades later. Bruce

---

[133] John Parker, *Rhodesia: Little White Island* (London: Pitman Publishing, 1972), 4.
[134] Torpey interview.
[135] Author's interview with Tim Warner, October 2, 2005.
[136] As a 1952 Home Office inspection of the Australian schemes revealed, while "on paper [the holiday] arrangement was accepted ... in practice very little was done." Fairbridge, Executive Committee Minutes, May 8, 1952, D.296/B1/2/7, ULSCA.
[137] RFMC brochure, 1954, D.296/K2/4/5, ULSCA.
[138] Address by Lord Hawke, Annual General Meeting Minutes, November 26, 1953, DO 35/10278, TNA: PRO.

Harris,[139] for instance, vividly recollected going on a holiday hunting trip with a Rhodesian friend and an African servant when he was ten years old. At the time, he wanted strongly "to be part of the Rhodesian scene," and so began mimicking his friend's behavior, "trying to be as brave as he was." Fitting in meant going without shoes, for his friend had been "brought up so that he could get up in the morning and not even bother about socks and shoes ... just go outside and walk through the bush without problem at all." Yet Harris' feet were still tender and uncalloused, and the walk quickly became painful. "So anyway, here's me," he said, "I'm trying to be brave, and I'm walking across all this parched area, a burnt out area ... And I'm hobbling and I'm trying to get through the bush." Eventually, Harris' pain became so severe that the African servant was forced to carry him on his back. His Rhodesian friend's response was immediate and shaming. "He couldn't stop laughing," Harris recalled. "He just [said], 'this pongo' – that's what we were called – 'pongo can't even walk through the bush.'"[140]

Harris' account provides an intriguing window into child migrants' personal experiences of acculturation during the postwar period. It gives a sense of his strong childhood desire to integrate, to adopt the mannerisms and outlook that would make him "part of the Rhodesian scene." But it also demonstrates the intermediary position that he and other child migrants occupied. Despite his efforts, he was still very much an outsider, a "pongo." As Harris and others found, the path toward "becoming Rhodesian" was more difficult than it first seemed. It was filled with unexpected slip-ups, such as his gaffe of showing dependence on an African. And it was an awkward, frequently humiliating process, which as an adult he still associated with the pain of hardening his feet. His story offers an example of the ambiguities associated with growing up as a child migrant in the late empire, when boys and girls received countless subtle reminders that their acceptance as full-fledged members of the community hinged on their ability to take on the dominant characteristics of the national culture. The difficulties of acculturation that former migrants faced remained one of the many deeply felt consequences of the breakdown of transimperial bonds of belonging in the postwar world.

## Conclusion

During the two decades following the Second World War, the cultural ties that had long bound the British world gradually dissolved under

---

[139] Pseudonym.
[140] Author's interview with Bruce Harris (pseudonym), September 2005.

the forces of ideological change, global political and economic realignment, and the rise of exclusive forms of settler nationalism. In many ways, child migrants' unique social position, located halfway between the British past they had left behind and the Australian or Rhodesian society that was to be their permanent home, amplified their experience of this shift from empire to nationhood. Throughout the period, the emigration movement grew increasingly linked to the distinct national agendas of the late dominions, as the schemes' directors attempted to assimilate child migrants by tailoring their selection, education, and upbringing. In school, at play, and through contact with the local community, child migrants learned the characteristics and skills that would be central to their adult lives. For those sent to Australia, full integration meant acquiring an intrinsic sense of the land and love of the rural lifestyle. In short, they were asked to learn the elements of Australian culture that symbolically distinguished the dominion from Britain. For those sent to Southern Rhodesia, the focus was on internalizing the colony's racial hierarchy and on gaining an awareness of the cultural divide between Europeans and Africans that underwrote settler authority. Through both formal and tacit means, Rhodesian migrants were taught to associate with skin color the privileges that in Britain they would more closely have connected to differences of class.

How effective were these methods of acculturation in the late empire? The answer is difficult to fix with precision. Judging by the submissions to the recent governmental inquiries on child emigration, the majority of those sent to Australia remain in that country today.[141] However, because many child migrants received minimal school qualifications and entered low-paying occupations, this fact may say more about their relative lack of social mobility than the extent of their integration. By contrast, only a handful of those sent to the RFMC have stayed in Zimbabwe, due both to the country's political instability and to the demise of settler dominance. Former migrants appear to have left the region in three main stages: the first in the mid 1960s around the UDI, another wave in the early 1980s during the changeover to majority rule, and the remainder in the early 2000s when the Mugabe government began its seizure of White-owned farms. In an informal survey conducted in 1996, an alum found that only 15 percent of the somewhat fewer than 300 children sent to the RFMC between 1946 and 1957 remained in the country.[142] Doubtless, the number is even lower now.

---

[141] House of Commons, Health Committee, *The Welfare of Former British Child Migrants* (London: HMSO, 1998); Senate Community Affairs Reference Committee, *Lost Innocents: Righting the Record* (Canberra: Commonwealth of Australia, 2001).
[142] Vivian Finn, "Fairbridge Introduction," in Gould, *Windows*, 1–7, 4.

The matter of how former migrants currently choose to identify their nationality is equally tricky. When asked whether they self-identify as British, Australian, Rhodesian, or some other nationality, the answers varied dramatically. Some former migrants retained strong identity links to Britain that persisted throughout their childhoods and into their adult years. "I *never* wanted to be an Australian, ever," noted Julia Futcher. "I was always, always English." By 1966, after a series of jobs as a nanny and shop assistant, she had saved enough money to return to London. "I just had to get back to England," she remembered, "and when I got back ... it was like I was set free."[143] But others clearly rejected a British identity. "I'm Australian through and through," declared Eva Warhurst. As a teenager, she "vowed that I'd never marry a Pommy," and although she kept in touch with her family members back in the United Kingdom, she never felt a strong pull to visit.[144] The issue was especially complex for former migrants to Southern Rhodesia, who generally felt unable to identify either with modern Zimbabwe or with metropolitan Britain. Many fell back on older, hybrid forms of identity, such as "British Rhodesian" or "colonial British." Today, many former child migrants have found it difficult to feel at home either in Britain or in the countries that once constituted the British world. It is to this complicated question of belonging in the postimperial world that the conclusion of this book turns.

[143] Futcher interview.    [144] Warhurst interview.

# Conclusion: the problem of postimperial belonging

"I swear to God ... the fire they had there that night, I'll never forget it," said Alistair Marshall of the blaze that swept through the offices of the RFMC some years after he arrived in the colony from Scotland. He was not sure exactly when it had happened, and guessed that it must have been in the late 1940s, perhaps 1950. But his recollections of the event were still crystal clear. He spoke of being jostled from sleep late at night, and hustling with the other boys from his dorm to a safe distance away from the flames. Given the drama of the fire, it is easy to see why its memory had been imprinted in Marshall's mind. This sudden break from ordinary life would have aroused a powerful emotional response in the children who witnessed it: fear combined with the tingle of adventure. Marshall had another reason for remembering the fire, though, for its legacy continued to affect him long into his adulthood. Like the other children at the school that night, his case file had been destroyed, leaving him without a birth certificate or any official documentation of the decade he spent in Britain before emigrating to the College. Years later, he would discover that many of the basic assumptions he had about himself were, factually speaking, wrong. When he first returned to Britain in the late 1950s and reconnected with his father, for instance, he learned that he had been born in 1936, not in 1934 as he had always thought. And, more recently, when a relative interested in genealogy unearthed a copy of his birth certificate, Marshall discovered that Alistair was not his given name. It must have been a nickname he acquired early on, most likely during the war, when he was evacuated away from his parents and placed with an aunt who raised him until he left for Southern Rhodesia. These subsequent revelations about his identity were jarring. As he noted with an air of understatement, "It's a bit of a shock when you find out these things."

For many years, the cause of the fire had remained a mystery to Marshall. But eventually, an explanation had emerged. "I found out later," he said, that "there was a government directive telling Robbie [the principal, Tom Robinson] to destroy our documents." Marshall acknowledged that he had never learned why it was "that all records had to be destroyed," although he thought that it must have been "something political. Something to do, I don't know, could be Ian Smith's time, you know, that sort of thing."[1] This reference to Smith, the leader of the Rhodesia Front government who ushered the colony through its 1965 Unilateral Declaration of Independence from the empire, was technically inaccurate. While Smith had been active in local politics during the 1950s, he only rose to national prominence in the 1962 elections, more than a decade after Marshall believed the fire had occurred. Objectively, the mention of Smith's involvement did not make sense, yet it did succeed in communicating Marshall's point: the destruction of the case files, and the subsequent distortion of his identity, was directly related to the end of empire. As he saw it, when the fabric of imperial belonging was torn apart, this one-time colonial training school had become a political liability, its alumni transformed from the future leaders of Greater Britain into embarrassing reminders of the imperial past. And so, he believed, the government had attempted to obliterate all traces of their existence.

Marshall was not the only person to mention the fire, or to connect it to a larger political conspiracy. Stephen Player, who arrived at the school a few months after Marshall, also spoke of a fire in which "they burnt all our records, our school records, our history and everything," although he did not specify when it had occurred, or who exactly "they" were.[2] John Moxham emigrated in 1948, and thus overlapped with both men. But he placed the fire much later, around 1956 or 1957, after he had graduated and joined the workforce. "It was just after I left, only a couple of years after I left," he stated, "but what went up in there was all the records, all the school records ... [and] there was a suggestion that there was some skullduggery behind there."[3] Susan Corrans, who arrived in 1951, also dated the fire to this later period. She offered the most comprehensive explanation:

When the child migration stopped, you know, it started slowing down in the mid-fifties, late fifties. And the British government up 'til then, you know, they had been funding it. And they told Mr. Robinson to burn all the children's records ... I don't know whether it was covering their tracks or what, I really don't know. And we didn't know this at the time. And Mr. Robinson refused ... for a long time, and the British government cut off all the funding to him. And for a long time the keeper of Bulawayo, the town, helped fund him in many ways, but he couldn't go on and on, and in the end he did have to ... He had to burn them.[4]

This version contains a number of important nuances. Here, the directive came explicitly from British government operatives interested in

---

[1] Author's interview with Alistair Marshall, October 10, 2005.
[2] Author's interview with Stephen Player, September 25, 2005.
[3] Author's interview with John Moxham, July 6, 2009.
[4] Author's interview with Susan Corrans, December 7, 2005.

"covering their tracks." Meanwhile Robinson, a father figure to many of the College's alumni, is styled as a paternal protector, who struggled to save the children's histories from destruction until he was forced to bow to political and economic pressure. But the gist of the story is the same. During the final days of empire, child emigration, and by extension child migrants, became a shameful embarrassment, something that needed to be covered up, secreted away, and forgotten.

What should we make of these memories that seem at once so hazy – a fire, ordered by unknown officials sometime in the late 1940s or maybe a decade later – but that contain such a consistent message about decolonization and the loss of identity? It might be tempting to dismiss the talk as a childhood rumor that has been exaggerated and embellished over the years. A little digging in the archive, however, reveals that this is no simple case of false memory syndrome. On November 3, 1948, the *Bulawayo Chronicle* carried a small item describing a late-night fire at the RFMC that "completely gutted" the administrative block. The article reported that "all the college records and accounts, all the children's private dossiers, the warden's personal papers, the library books, maps and magazines were lost in the flames." The principal, it turns out, was not the well-loved Robinson but his immediate predecessor, C. J. Edgecombe, who was described as "a heart-broken man ... at the scene of the desolation." Edgecombe was quoted as saying that the school had "suffered a most serious blow, and it would be necessary to start again from the beginning, building up the records and files of the pupils." He admitted that "some of the papers lost were irreplaceable – the early records of the College, Press cuttings of its activities, its visitors' book, and the dossiers containing particulars of the children." And as to the cause of the fire? The paper reported that it was still "unknown" but that it was being attributed "to a 'short' in the electrical wiring system."[5]

As is so often the case, the realities of history turn out to be more innocuous than the stories we tell of the past. It is, of course, possible that British officials did order the destruction of the children's records, or that there were two fires, one in 1948, the other in the mid 1950s. But there is no archival evidence to support the more sinister interpretations, and they seem unlikely given Britain's continued funding of the College until it closed in 1962.[6] Instead, it is more probable that the fire constitutes what oral historian Alessandro Portelli has termed an "event": a

---

[5] "Disaster Strikes at Fairbridge College: Sports Gear and Fire in Flames," *Bulawayo Chronicle*, November 3, 1948.

[6] In 1956, the Commonwealth Relations Office agreed to fund the College (alongside the Rhodesian government) until the last child migrant had graduated. Note by Taylor, September 5, 1956, DO 35/10278, TNA: PRO.

historical moment that later became "the ground upon which collect-ive memory and imagination built a cluster of tales, symbols, legends, and imaginary reconstructions."[7] The story of the fire, in other words, has taken on meanings that resonate powerfully in the lives of former migrants today. It is a way of expressing deeply felt emotions, such as dis-location and alienation, that many might find difficult or even shameful to discuss openly. More broadly, it is an indication that, for some former migrants, the memories of their childhoods continue to be a locus for articulating powerful questions about who they are and where they fit in the modern, postimperial world.

The slow unraveling of the ideal of Greater Britain in the twentieth century not only destroyed the once-potent vision of the settler empire as a coherent whole, united by blood and sentiment, but also eliminated the ideological foundations of the child emigration movement. Once touted as a means to improve both individual lives and the strength of the imperial connection, by the end of the century the transfer of British boys and girls to live among their "kith and kin" overseas had become unthinkable. On the one hand, children had come to be seen as psycho-logically complex beings, bound to their families and their natal homes by intense emotional ties. On the other hand, the larger edifice of empire had crumbled, freeing dominion politicians and populations to define their national interests and cultural identities without reference to their Britannic roots.

What lasting effects did these shifts have for those former child migrants whose lives had been so profoundly shaped by the vision of the British world? Throughout its history, advocates of child emigration had maintained that the empire offered a replacement for what was otherwise lacking in needy children's lives. For boys and girls without families or whose parents had been deemed unworthy of their care, the dominions would provide a substitute home. As the *Daily Chronicle* put it in 1920, the settler territories stood collectively as "a smiling, warm-hearted mother" to the "abandoned, unclaimed, destitute, or orphaned children … of the British Empire."[8] Over time, however, the concepts of mothering and of the family that underwrote such statements had narrowed dramatically. By the late 1960s, when child emigration ended, few would have argued that a political formation, such as the empire, or a spiritual relationship, such as the bonds of Britannic heritage, could adequately compensate

---

[7] Alessandro Portelli, *The Death of Luigi Trastulli and Other Stories: Form and Meaning in Oral History* (Albany: State University of New York Press, 1991), 1.

[8] A. M. Drysdale, "Peopling the Empire: The Children's Chance in a New Land," *Daily Chronicle*, January 24, 1920.

a child for a mother's love. Imperial institutions, once styled as necessary replacements for children "deprived of a normal home life," were similarly critiqued as incapable of providing the personalized affection and familial care that children needed to develop a stable sense of self. Occurring alongside the demise of the older ethic of transimperial unity, these changes placed former migrants in an uncomfortable, liminal position, as the political philosophies and welfare ideals that had structured their childhoods either disappeared or were reconfigured as abusive and damaging. As adults, many have struggled to understand their unconventional childhoods and to deal with their continued and sometimes debilitating feelings of rootlessness and displacement. For them, the eclipse of the British world and the changes of the postimperial era have been experienced as a crisis of belonging. This chapter explores two aspects of former child migrants' recent search for identity, considering first the pull of reuniting with family, which has been emphasized most strongly in the Australian context, and second the pursuit of national belonging, which has been more dominant among former Rhodesian migrants.

### Family and identity in the late twentieth-century critique of child emigration

Child emigration went out with a whimper, not a bang. As the numbers being sent by the British charities dwindled during the late 1950s and 1960s, and as the boys and girls in the Australian and Rhodesian farm schools and orphanages left for their first jobs, the policy quietly faded from public view. Some former migrants made efforts to keep in touch with each other through organizations such as the Old Fairbridgians Association or, more rarely, through newsletters sent out by staff members.[9] But most appear to have let the connection drop as they focused instead on building lives for themselves in their new countries. The process was frequently a difficult one, made harder by the general lack of aftercare services provided by the emigration charities. "In the first two years or so, I moved at least fifteen times," remembered John Bicknell of the period just after he left Mowbray Park in 1958. "I lost count of the doss houses where I stayed and all the rest of it. Couldn't settle at all. And there was no one to fall back on. I was given a set of clothes and £10, which was the first week's lodging … and everything from there on was up to me. There was no aftercare whatsoever." Having been a ward

---

[9] Examples of newsletters and updates sent to alumni of the RFMC between 1950 and 1991 by the principal, Tom Robinson, and his wife, Dot, can be found in Peter Gould, ed., *Windows: Rhodesia Fairbridge Memorial College Autobiographies* (Christchurch: Fairbridge Marketing Board, 2001), 149–196.

of Barnardo's, first in Britain and then in Australia, since the age of six, he was "totally institutionalized" when he embarked on this abrupt transition to the "outside world." Simple tasks were often frightening and upsetting. He recalled his panic at having to make a call from a public telephone box in Sydney: "I'd never used one before, and I was seventeen years of age. And I just, well, I wet my pants. And I had to get someone to show me how to use it. And I hung on like this [clutching the receiver], wondering what the hell I was going to say if someone answered at the other end." Raised to be a farmer, Bicknell felt wholly unprepared for urban life. "Yes, I knew a lot about the bush and all the rest of it, [but] in the city I didn't know what to do with myself," he commented. His narrow upbringing was "one of the reasons, I suppose, why I moved around so often."[10]

Over the decades, Bicknell did not give much thought to the relatives and family he had left behind in Britain. He had been sent to Australia with his two brothers and had mostly negative memories of his mother. Yet he also felt little inclination to establish contact with his wider circle of relatives – his father, his aunts and uncles – and never looked on a map to find the town in which he had been born. In part, this lack of interest was the result of child migrants' training in Australian and Rhodesian institutions, which stressed giving up past attachments in order to focus on forging new lives overseas. Patricia Carlson, who grew up in Catholic orphanages and was sent to Australia as a teenager in 1948, was taught early on to accept that she had no family. Although at times she "wished for a mother … [and] would think about what, if I had a mother, what would she look like," she did not feel able to talk about these yearnings. As she recalled, none of the girls in the home "thought it important to have a mother," since they were not given permission, either formally or informally, to discuss their memories of, or hopes for, a family connection.[11]

Despite the emphasis on starting over, many former migrants still longed for lost relatives. Dilys Budd, whose mother had died a few years before she emigrated to Australia in 1947, had been told that her two older sisters would follow her to the dominion on the next boat. They never arrived. Throughout her teenage years, she wrote regularly to her sisters in an effort to reestablish contact. But no replies came, and Budd believes that the nuns who ran the orphanage to which she was sent in Western Australia held the letters back in order to encourage a "clean break" with her old life. Nevertheless, the ache of the separation did

[10] Author's interview with John Bicknell, May 16, 2006.
[11] Interview with Patricia Carlson, conducted by Susan Marsden, ORAL TRC 6200/23, Forgotten Australians and Former Child Migrants Oral History Project, September 29, 2010, NLA.

not fade, and, when Budd finally found her sisters thirty years later, she thought, "wasted years ... These lovely people and I haven't known them. I wasn't allowed to know them for all these years." It was the "cruelest" part of her emigration experience, and the only aspect of her childhood that still fills her with bitterness.[12] Although many, if not all, former migrants undoubtedly experienced a similar pull of wanting to recover their links to family, for decades few felt able to act on those desires. Throughout their young adulthoods, family remained an unspoken topic, one that was usually cloaked in mystery and quiet pain.

In the 1980s, however, the silence surrounding the subject of lost families started to be broken. The decade witnessed a rapid growth of advocacy groups dedicated to raising awareness about the history of child emigration and to seeking redress for men and women who had been hurt by the policy. One of the first was the Child Migrant Friendship Society of Western Australia, founded in 1982 by a group of former migrants who aimed to relieve the "suffering, helplessness, distress, misfortune, poverty, destitution, and emotional disturbance" that they believed the initiatives had produced.[13] Five years later, Margaret Humphreys, a Nottingham-based social worker, established the Child Migrants Trust, which campaigned to pressure the emigration charities, as well as the British and Australian governments, to acknowledge the trauma endured by former migrants. The Trust actively promoted its work in recovering identity documents and fostering family reunifications in Britain, and demanded that both governments provide compensation. It was instrumental in the release of a 1989 popular history and documentary, *Lost Children of the Empire*, which was followed by Humphreys' widely read 1994 memoir, *Empty Cradles*.[14] Combined, these works revealed harrowing accounts of physical and psychological suffering in child migrant institutions, and emphasized the message that the emigration movement had produced lifelong emotional harm. As Humphreys argued, "To take children from their families and their countries was an abuse; to strip them of their identity was an abuse; to forget them and then deny their loss was an abuse ... Few tragedies can compare."[15]

---

[12] Interview with Dilys Budd, conducted by Ann-Mari Jordens, ORAL TRC 6200/7, Forgotten Australians and Former Child Migrants Oral History Project, March 9, 2010, NLA.

[13] Senate Community Affairs References Committee, *Lost Innocents: Righting the Record-Report on Child Migration* (Canberra: Commonwealth of Australia, 2001), 134.

[14] Philip Bean and Joy Melville, *Lost Children of the Empire: The Untold Story of Britain's Child Migrants* (London: Unwin Hyman, 1989); Joanna Mack and Mike Fox, dirs., *Lost Children of the Empire* (Manchester: Granada Television, 1989); Margaret Humphreys, *Empty Cradles* (London: Doubleday, 1994).

[15] Humphreys, *Empty Cradles*, 373.

This sudden surge of activism took place in, and was fueled by, a context of growing public concern about the past practice of child and family services in Britain and across the former dominions, as well as amid the rise of neoliberal attacks on government-directed welfare provision. In Australia, where the critique was the most influential, the initial discussion centered on the history of the state-sponsored removals of Indigenous children, who were later placed in orphanages or in White adoptive households. Aboriginal activists had steadily campaigned against the programs throughout the twentieth century, but it was only in the 1980s that the "Stolen Generations" emerged as a focus of public attention and regret. In 1982, the organization Link-Up was founded, committed to reuniting Indigenous children with their birth families and communities.[16] Its growing prominence spurred hundreds of individuals to come forward to tell their painful stories of removal and to demand a governmental inquiry.[17] By the 1990s, these testimonies had done much to root the trope of "coming home" within the Australian imagination.[18] In this vein, when the government eventually held a national inquiry into the practice of Aboriginal child removal in 1996, it titled the report *Bringing Them Home*.[19] Although many former migrants today reject the comparison between their own experiences and those of the Stolen Generations, the Indigenous battle for recognition was instrumental in giving prominence to the notion, later espoused by critics of child emi-

[16] Denise Cuthbert and Marian Quartly, "'Forced Adoption' in the Australian Story of National Regret and Apology," *Australian Journal of Politics and History* 58, no. 1 (2012): 82–96, 85.

[17] Many of these testimonies were given prominence in the work of historian Peter Read. See in particular Peter Read, *The Stolen Generations: The Removal of Aboriginal Children in New South Wales, 1833–1969* (Sydney: New South Wales Department of Aboriginal Affairs, 1981); Peter Read, *A Rape of the Soul So Profound: The Return of the Stolen Generations* (Sydney: Allen and Unwin, 1999).

[18] Kate Murphy, Marian Quartly, and Denise Cuthbert, "'In the Best Interests of the Child': Mapping the (Re)emergence of Pro-adoption Politics in Contemporary Australia," *Australian Journal of Politics and History* 55, no. 2 (2009): 201–218, 203. On parallel developments in Canada, New Zealand, and the United States, see Kristen Lovelock, "Intercountry Adoption as a Migratory Practice: A Comparative Analysis of Intercountry Adoption and Immigration Policy and Practice in the United States, Canada, and New Zealand in the Post WWII Period," *International Migration Review* 34, no. 3 (Autumn 2000): 907–949, 921–922. Laura Briggs notes that, although a similar campaign against the placement of American Indian children with non-Native adoptive families achieved some important policy results in the 1970s, the history of Indigenous child removal in the United States never received the same degree of recognition as it has in Australia and Canada. Laura Briggs, *Somebody's Children: The Politics of Transracial and Transnational Adoption* (Durham: Duke University Press, 2012), 59–93.

[19] Human Rights and Equal Opportunity Commission, *Bringing Them Home: Report of the National Inquiry into the Separation of Aboriginal and Torres Strait Islander Children from Their Families* (Canberra: Commonwealth of Australia, 1997).

gration, that separating children from their natal families and cultures was psychologically and emotionally scarring.[20]

Running parallel to the escalation of Aboriginal activism was a powerful international movement to reform domestic adoption laws. Larger social forces tied to the development of second-wave feminism in the later 1960s and 1970s, such as a lessening of the stigma attached to unwed pregnancies and the creation of benefits programs for single mothers, produced a climate in which fewer women in developed countries felt impelled to give their children up for adoption. It also encouraged those who had previously been coerced into relinquishing their sons or daughters to speak out about their experiences.[21] Like their Indigenous counterparts, these testimonies carried enormous emotional force. They helped dismantle the conventional view that adopted boys and girls were "unwanted," and shed light on the lasting effects of family dislocation not only for children but for birth mothers as well.[22] By the 1980s, legislators in Britain, Australia, Canada, and elsewhere had begun to alter domestic adoption laws in order to create greater openness in the process. Prior practices of sealing adoption records were largely abandoned, and new systems were created to facilitate a continuing relationship between birth parents and adopted children. These reforms made domestic adoptions both more difficult to perform and increasingly unattractive to adoptive parents.[23] The numbers started to plummet, to the extent that Australia, which carried out nearly 10,000 adoptions per year in the early 1970s, now has one of the lowest rates of domestic adoption in the world.[24] More broadly, the "openness" trend in late twentieth-century adoption policy provided further reinforcement for the view, again taken up by advocates for child migrants, that it was essential for children to know where they

---

[20] Dilys Budd, for instance, argues that, while there are some similarities between child emigration and the history of Aboriginal child removal, ultimately the two policies differed "because in Australia at least they didn't send them to another country. But they sent us to another country ... We were just shipped out. Exported. We were exported out of the country." Budd interview. Yet such statements ignore the fact that, throughout the history of child emigration, Britain and Australia were commonly perceived as united within a shared Britannic culture whereas Aboriginal children were believed to occupy a separate, and inferior, culture. It is only after the breakdown of the Greater Britain ideal that the claim that child migrants were "exported" has been able to achieve widespread acceptance.

[21] Murphy et al., "'In the Best Interests of the Child,'" 202; Briggs, *Somebody's Children*, 95.

[22] Denise Cuthbert, Ceridwen Spark, and Kate Murphy, "'That Was Then, but This Is Now': Historical Perspectives on Intercountry Adoption and Domestic Child Adoption in Australian Public Policy," *Journal of Historical Sociology* 23, no. 3 (September 2010): 427–452, 438.

[23] Ibid, 431–432.

[24] Murphy et al., "'In the Best Interests of the Child,'" 203.

came from. Indeed, in some cases, the influence was direct; before turning her attention to child emigration, Margaret Humphreys had started her career in Britain counseling adults who had been adopted during the era of sealed records laws.[25]

This confluence of factors had important effects for former migrants who grew up knowing little about their family histories. The changing cultural atmosphere helped some give voice to hurts that had long been silenced; for others, it awakened a curiosity about their roots and a desire to recover family ties. As the British and Australian governments held inquiries into the policy in 1998 and 2001, respectively, hundreds of men and women came forward to submit stories of abuse and institutionalization. A main theme of these submissions was the lasting pain that resulted from having lost a relationship with their families in Britain. As the Australian report summarized, "for many former child migrants the greatest hardship was loss of identity ... The sense of dislocation and not belonging, of loss of family, and of emptiness." Citing the "need to know where they came from, why they were sent to Australia, and to contact surviving relatives in the United Kingdom and elsewhere," both inquiries recommended the establishment of government funds to support records-tracing services and to provide free trips to former migrants seeking to reestablish relationships with family members in Britain.[26]

These efforts have produced countless family reunions, the successes of which have found a prominent place in the current media representation of child emigration. When John Bicknell returned to Britain in the early 2000s on a trip funded by the British government, he discovered that he had an additional four half-brothers and two half-sisters, from his father's second marriage, about whom he had never known. Establishing contact with these family members was a "healing experience." As he put it in his memoir, although "many families drift apart, not many have had the opportunity of a lifetime that we all had, to bind fast those family ties."[27] Yet, for others, the results of reuniting with relatives have been more ambiguous. June-Marie Reid spoke movingly of her fraught relationship with her mother, who had placed her with Barnardo's when she was five years old and who consented to her emigration to Australia when she was almost eleven. Reid reconnected with her mother in the early 1960s, when she first returned to Britain with her Australian fiancé,

[25] Humphreys, *Empty Cradles*, 29.
[26] Senate Community Affairs References Committee, *Lost Innocents*, 137. The report of the British inquiry was published as House of Commons, Health Committee, *The Welfare of Former British Child Migrants* (London: HMSO, 1998).
[27] John Bicknell, *The Dirty Bloody Jizzy: An Autobiography* (Gordon, NSW: Mini-Publishing, 2003), 176.

and again in the late 1970s, when she and her then-husband decided to try living in England for a couple of years. During the latter visit, Reid had a falling out with one of her sisters, after which her mother cut off all contact with her. When she returned in 2005 on a government-funded trip, her mother refused to see her. "I'm still pretty hurt from mum not wanting to have anything to do with me," she said, "because I thought she might make amends and let bygones be bygones ... But she can't be bothered." Although Reid continues to be "homesick" for England, the experience forced her to face again the hard truth of her childhood abandonment. Talking about her initial placement with Barnardo's, Reid stressed that her mother "didn't want me. She definitely didn't want me," even though "I missed her. I loved my mum, and I adored her." Ultimately, the reunion trip was more upsetting than heartwarming, leaving Reid feeling doubly rejected since she again had to acknowledge that her mother "didn't want anything to do with me."[28]

Reid's story casts light on the messier, and deeply personal, experiences of reunification, which have received much less coverage in the public discussion of child emigration in Britain and Australia. The typical media depiction ends at the moment of reconnection, and thus presents the rebuilding of family bonds as a self-evident good in and of itself rather than as the complicated and sometimes upsetting process it often turns out to be.[29] Furthermore, in emphasizing the importance of familial connections, of "coming home," and of knowing where one truly "belongs" for psychological and emotional "wholeness," the cultural discussions surrounding Indigenous child removal, domestic adoption, and child emigration have perpetuated an idealized and normative vision of the biological family, centered especially on the figure of the mother, as the cornerstone of child and adult wellbeing. Sixty years after the rise of Bowlbyism, children are now more deeply "attached" than ever to their natal homes and families, while earlier (and equally idealized) views that emphasized young people's malleability, resilience, and capacity to remake their lives in new settings have been reconstituted as abuse.[30]

Or at least, this is the view that holds sway for Western children. For, while rates of domestic adoption have fallen steadily across the developed world in the postwar period, and as child emigration has been redefined as traumatizing, the proportion of intercountry adoptions has risen

---

[28] Author's interview with June-Marie Reid, May 18, 2006.

[29] See, for instance, the portrayal of family reunions in the recent feature film *Oranges and Sunshine*, based on Humphreys' *Empty Cradles*: Jim Loach, dir., *Oranges and Sunshine* (Screen Australia, 2010).

[30] On this point, see also Tara Zahra, *The Lost Children: Reconstructing Europe's Families after World War II* (Cambridge, MA: Harvard University Press, 2011), 222–245.

dramatically. Between 1990 and 2004, over 45,000 boys and girls were transferred between more than 100 countries every year.[31] The similarities between these transnational movements of children and the history of child emigration are striking. The majority of the boys and girls involved in intercountry adoptions are "social orphans," meaning that they have living parents who relinquished them to charities or to the state, primarily due to poverty.[32] Whereas domestic adoptions stress the value of a continued relationship between birth parents and adopted children, intercountry adoptions have grown popular precisely because geographical distance tends to preclude the same kind of openness, leaving birth families "off-shore, out of sight, and potentially out of mind."[33] Moreover, the rhetoric of intercountry adoption frequently invokes older concepts of providing children with "clean breaks" and "fresh starts," while stressing the program's value in developing the demographic capacity of the nation-state, albeit with multiculturalism and antiracism supplanting the prior ideological emphasis on Britannic racial homogeneity.[34] All told, there are two main distinctions between the history of child emigration and modern-day intercountry adoption: boys and girls are no longer sent to institutions but to families, and overwhelmingly they are placed in settings that bear little resemblance to their natal cultures.

The similarities between the past of child emigration and the present of intercountry adoption should not cause us simply to dismiss the latter as an outmoded form of abuse. But they should compel a closer consideration of the global inequalities that continue to determine children's lives around the world today.[35] Although child emigration is now history, the processes that first brought it into being within the realm of Greater Britain – childhood destitution, the powerlessness of poor parents, the politics of nation-building, the potency of racial hierarchies and class discrimination – still remain within the stratified relationship between the "first" and the "third" worlds. While children in developed countries are now widely accepted as belonging with their biological families, the children of developing nations have come to appear more transferable than ever.

[31] Kate Murphy, Sarah Pinto, and Denise Cuthbert, "'These Infants Are Future Australians': Making the Nation through Intercountry Adoption," *Journal of Australian Studies* 34, no. 2 (June 2010): 141–161, 141.

[32] Laura Briggs and Diana Marre, "The Circulation of Children," in *International Adoption: Global Inequalities and the Circulation of Children*, ed. Laura Briggs and Diana Marre (New York: New York University Press, 2009), 1–28, 12.

[33] Cuthbert et al., "'That Was Then, but This Is Now,'" 434.

[34] Murphy et al., "'These Infants Are Future Australians.'"

[35] Recent work within the history of childhood has begun to draw attention to these issues. See for instance, the special issue of *The Journal of Social History* 38, no. 4 (Summer 2005), edited by Peter Stearns and dedicated to the globalization of childhood.

### Exiled from empire: nationhood after the demise of the British world

The desire to reestablish links to family was not the only search for belonging that former migrants embarked on in the later twentieth century, even if it has garnered by far the most attention. Less noticed, but equally significant, have been the struggles of former Rhodesian migrants to establish a postimperial identity and sense of nationhood following the transformation of the colony into the nation of Zimbabwe. Having spent their formative years in a polity that was fiercely committed to maintaining White-dominated rule, many of these men and women were left feeling untethered by decolonization, no longer "at home" in independent Africa but not comfortable in the self-styled multicultural Britain of the postempire era, either. Raised to think of themselves as British imperial citizens, Rhodesian migrants witnessed the foundations of that identity disintegrate as the world transformed around them. This was a process – the eclipse of the British world – that affected all postwar child migrants; but, for those who had been sent to Southern Rhodesia, its impact was more dramatic and personal than in Australia because it signaled a loss of country.[36] For many, the shifts of the decolonization period forced them to search for new forms of attachment, and new places to call home.

"Exile," wrote Edward Said, "is a condition of terminal loss." More than a political category, it is a psychological state, one that produces a range of emotional responses, from the "crippling sorrow of estrangement" to jealous insecurity. The power of exile lies in its tendency to produce political action. At the individual level, it can manifest as a desperate search for roots, while among collectives it frequently leads to an "exaggerated sense of group solidarity" or the seeking out of "a new world to rule."[37] To Said, exile was one of the most consequential political experiences of the modern era. His definition of the concept, though, was fairly narrow. "True exile," he contended, occurred only among the most disenfranchised and marginalized of peoples, such as the refugees of war, political violence, and humanitarian crises. It was a term that applied to what might be considered the victims of empire, not to the colonizers. As he wrote: "Colonial officials, missionaries, technical experts, mercenaries and military advisers on loan may in a sense live in exile, but they have not been banished. White settlers in Africa, parts of Asia and Australia

---

[36] For insightful reflections on the changing cultural consciousness within postimperial Australia, see James Curran and Stuart Ward, *The Unknown Nation: Australia after Empire* (Melbourne University Press, 2010).

[37] Edward Said, *Reflections on Exile and Other Essays* (Cambridge, MA: Harvard University Press, 2000), 173, 178, and 181.

may once have been exiles, but as pioneers and nation-builders the label 'exile' dropped away from them." In this model, the crucial distinction was a person's relationship with his homeland, as well as to the dominant cultural orthodoxy more generally. The colonial elite did not fit the category because they retained the option of returning to and reintegrating into the metropole, whereas for true exiles "homecoming is out of the question."[38]

When making comparisons, historians must always remain aware of degrees of difference, and Said was right to point out that the emotional consequences suffered by political and economic refugees are of a different order than those experienced by the beneficiaries of imperialism. Nevertheless, our sensitivity to the pathos of the displaced should not obscure the fact that the decolonization forced an estimated three to four million White colonials from countries throughout the European empires to which they had developed a deep attachment, at the same time that it transformed these territories beyond recognition.[39] In drawing attention to this other form of exile, my intent is not to evoke sympathy for those whose power and comfort long depended on the violence of colonial dispossession. Rather, it is to illustrate that, in the postimperial era, many former settlers feel themselves to be exiles from an empire that no longer exists. This self-identification as displaced people, which is perhaps strongest among former Rhodesians but is not exclusive to them, should not be overlooked, for it constitutes an important social force that continues to shape their politics and cultural attitudes into the present.

Chris Torpey eloquently expressed her sense of dislocation. As a child, she had a strong pride in her adoptive country, and would "swell up about three times" whenever her role as one of "Rhodesia's future citizens" was mentioned. She remained at the College until it closed down in 1962, and had "every intention of staying in Rhodesia," but her growing disenchantment with the Smith regime, combined with the death of a boyfriend who was serving in the Rhodesian army during the guerilla war, persuaded her to return to Britain in the mid 1970s. Looking back, she frankly acknowledged the racial inequalities of Rhodesian society, and admitted that White rule in Africa was untenable. Still, she cherished her memories of the colony "as it was," and did not want to tarnish them by traveling back to Zimbabwe, even though one of her sisters continued to live there. While Torpey had requested that her ashes be spread in the country, she had no plans to visit it in life. "It's almost like not

---

[38] Ibid, 181.

[39] The numbers displaced from the British colonies have been estimated at between 380,000 and 500,000. Andrea Smith, ed., *Europe's Invisible Migrants* (Amsterdam University Press, 2003), 32.

wanting to see somebody when they've died [or] when they're very, very ill," she said. "You'd rather remember them as they were."[40] This notion that modern-day Zimbabwe bears no resemblance to Rhodesia "as it was," that the country former migrants once knew has disappeared, was echoed by John Andrews. He described the end of empire as a painful, irreversible process: "It's like losing our country, Rhodesia, that we loved … If you can imagine having to go through that, and losing your country. You've got to look forward. You've got to go forward all the time, and not spend your whole life looking over your shoulders."[41]

Today, although the alumni of the RFMC are scattered throughout the world, the majority have resettled in Britain. Some returned as young adults in the 1950s and 1960s, usually at the behest of family members but sometimes because of simple curiosity about the land of their birth. Others came back around the time of the UDI, during the 1970s, as the fighting turned against the Rhodesian forces, or in the early 1980s amid the transition to majority rule. On the whole, their migration was voluntary, a point that distinguished their experience from those of other displaced settler colonials, such as the Japanese repatriated from Manchuria or the Germans expelled from Eastern Europe at the end of the Second World War.[42] Additionally, unlike "true exiles," former child migrants to Southern Rhodesia were automatically considered full British citizens. They had little trouble applying for British passports or establishing residency, and, with some petitioning, they could usually receive pension benefits. Their White skins also exempted them from the more blatant forms of racism and prejudice that many non-White colonial migrants faced in this period. At the political level, then, former Rhodesian migrants' transition "home" was straightforward. Strikingly, though, no matter when they went back, former migrants emphasized that their return was more culturally difficult than they had expected. Brought up to consider themselves Britons overseas, many were disturbed by the realities of British life they encountered when on the ground. In a sense, these difficulties of reassimilation should not be surprising. Even during the high imperial era, settlers from the dominions frequently reported unease when their journeys to Britain exposed the disjuncture between their colonial, national, and imperial identities.[43] The difference, however, is that, in

---

[40] Author's interview with Chris Torpey, October 2, 2005.

[41] Author's interview with John Andrews, December 12, 2005.

[42] Lori Watt, "Imperial Remnants: The Repatriates in Postwar Japan," in *Settler Colonialism in the Twentieth Century*, ed. Caroline Elkins and Susan Pedersen (New York: Routledge, 2005), 243–255; R. M. Douglas, *Orderly and Humane: The Expulsion of Germans after the Second World War* (New Haven: Yale University Press, 2012).

[43] On this point, see especially Angela Woollacott, *To Try Her Fortune in London: Australian Women, Colonialism, and Modernity* (Oxford University Press, 2001), 139–180.

the postimperial world, Rhodesian migrants who realized that they "fit" more easily in the empire than in the metropole lacked an alternative home to go back to.

Vivian Finn, who returned to Liverpool at the age of fifteen after four years in Southern Rhodesia and eighteen months in Singapore, remembered feeling "out of kilter" when he arrived back in 1962. "It was a dump," he noted with characteristic bluntness. "We disgorged in the station in London and took the train to Liverpool ... I remember walking down Queens Drive, looking for ... a shop that would sell me cigarettes. Picked up that habit in Rhodesia. And yeah, it was cold. It was horrible. It was really very alien. It was crowded. It seemed poor."[44] In a previous interview, Finn had compared his reactions to those of postwar Caribbean immigrants to the country, pointing out that they shared "this idea of Britain as being something out of Evelyn Waugh, or Jane Austen, you know, the upper class, plenty of space, and all this sort [of thing]. And when you come, and when you come in the winter, it's bloody awful."[45] Stephen Player had a similar response when he returned to visit his dying father in the early 1950s. Although he had only left the country four years previously, he arrived in Britain "completely a stranger to it," his foreignness made evident by the fact that he was the one person at the docks wearing "khaki shorts in January." He recalled being "absolutely staggered" by the poverty he saw in London, since he had "assumed that every European country was well-off." After his father's death, Player stayed in Britain for another fifteen years, but he never fully adjusted to being back. When a job came up in the mid 1960s working with an airline in Kenya, he jumped at the opportunity. He only returned to the country permanently when he retired some three decades later, and today he still thinks of himself as "a stranger in England ... I don't quite understand the people here." Like Finn, who spoke of lacking a clear "geographic identity," Player felt that he had never reestablished an emotional connection to the mother country.[46] Ultimately, he concluded, "you end up not belonging anywhere."[47]

Rhodesian migrants were not the only former colonials who felt apart from the mainstream of British culture in the postwar period. As A. James Hammerton and Alistair Thomson have shown, a significant minority of the "Ten Pound Poms" who emigrated to Australia in the 1950s and 1960s felt "unsettled" and "disillusioned" when they returned to the United Kingdom later in life. Many regretted their decision to relocate

[44]  Author's interview with Vivian Finn, May 20, 2009.
[45]  Author's interview with Vivian Finn, September 22, 2005.
[46]  Finn interview, May 20, 2009.
[47]  Player interview.

back, and those who had the ability settled in Australia a second time as soon as they had saved the money.[48] Elizabeth Buettner's research on Anglo-Indians going home after service in the Raj also highlighted that many felt "estranged from British society" when they returned, due both to their long absences from the country and to the distinct cultural mentalities they had developed in the empire.[49]

These examples help point out that the study of late imperial and postcolonial immigration into Britain, which has overwhelmingly concentrated on the creation of non-White Caribbean, African, and South Asian Diasporas in British cities, is too narrow.[50] Throughout the postwar years, there were sizable groups of White colonials settling back in Britain. A 1965 parliamentary report on immigration indicated that, during the previous year alone, officials had admitted close to 213,000 men and women from Australia, New Zealand, and Canada, a figure that exceeded the 194,000 people admitted from all of the other Commonwealth and dependent territories combined.[51] By overlooking the experiences of White colonial migrants, scholars have perpetuated the tendency – first established with the growth of "race relations" scholarship in the 1950s – to define Black, Colored, and Asian immigration as problematic and disorderly while assuming that White migrants assimilated easily and painlessly.[52] The effect has been to reify the myths that the British nation was monolithically White in these decades, that British definitions of what it meant to be White were all the same, and that White

---

[48] A. James Hammerton and Alistair Thomson, *Ten Pound Poms: Australia's Invisible Migrants* (New York: Manchester University Press, 2005), 308–312.

[49] Elizabeth Buettner, "From Somebodies to Nobodies: Britons Returning Home from India," in *Meanings of Modernity: Britain from the Late-Victorian Era to World War II*, ed. Martin Daunton and Bernhard Rieger (New York: Berg, 2001), 221–240, 222; Elizabeth Buettner, *Empire Families: Britons and Late Imperial India* (Oxford University Press, 2004), 188–251; Elizabeth Buettner, "'We Don't Grow Coffee and Bananas in Clapham Junction You Know!': Imperial Britons Back Home," in *Settlers and Expatriates: Britons over the Seas*, ed. Robert Bickers (Oxford University Press, 2010), 302–328.

[50] For instance: Winston James and Clive Harris, *Inside Babylon: The Caribbean Diaspora in Britain* (New York: Versa, 1993); Mike Phillips and Trevor Phillips, *Windrush: The Irresistible Rise of Multi-racial Britain* (New York: Harper Collins, 1998); Wendy Webster, *Imagining Home: Gender, "Race" and National Identity, 1954–1964* (New York: Routledge, 1998); Nasreen Ali, Virinder S. Kalra, and Salman Sayyid, *A Postcolonial People: South Asians in Britain* (London: C. Hurst and Co., 2006); Wai-ki Luk, *Chinatown in Britain: Diffusions and Concentrations of the British New Wave Immigration* (London: Cambria Press, 2008).

[51] "Immigration from the Commonwealth," *Parliamentary Papers*, Cmd. 2739 (London: HMSO, 1965), 4.

[52] Chris Waters, "'Dark Strangers' in Our Midst: Discourses of Race and Nation in Britain, 1947–1963," *Journal of British Studies* 36 (April 1997): 207–238; Michael Rowe, *The Racialisation of Disorder in Twentieth Century Britain* (Aldershot: Ashgate, 1998).

colonials somehow "belonged" in postwar Britain in a way that other imperial subjects did not.[53]

In fact, many Rhodesian returnees soon discovered that their entrenched assumptions about how White men and women should comport themselves were at odds with the standards held by their British family members, friends, and neighbors. Alistair Marshall recalled his shock when he first "saw a Black man and a White man" together on a street in Edinburgh:

> I said, "They can't walk with him!" That was my attitude. Because, you know, coming from over there ... And when I saw me sister – me stepmother had a café, and apparently when [my sister] finished her work, she used to go to the café and scrub the floors on her hands and knees and things like that ... Well I said, "What the hell are you doing? That's kaffirs' work!" You know, to me, what I would say is "That's kaffirs' work. You stop it!" And I made her stop.[54]

Patricia Edwards[55] remembered feeling the same kind of outrage in the early 1960s when, as a teenager just back in London after nine years in Southern Rhodesia, a Black man sat next to her at a restaurant. Unable to handle her discomfort, she slammed her lunch tray on the table and walked out.[56] Edwards was open about her struggle as a young woman to unlearn the racial attitudes she had assimilated in the colony, and emphasized that the task was made harder because the "expectations of what we were being expected to conform to were so unknown ... English attitudes were so different to the attitudes we'd grown up in."[57] In the postwar period, divergent interpretations of Whiteness brought to the surface the ideological differences that had long lay beneath the imperial myth of a united, global Britannic people.

This is not to imply that Britain in the 1960s or 1970s was a society universally dedicated to diversity and multiculturalism. It was not. These were the decades of the "new racism," marked by the growing popularity of Enoch Powell and the rise of anti-immigration groups such as the "White Defence League."[58] And, although several former migrants reported encountering hostility at their Rhodesian accents post-UDI, and sensing that they "weren't that welcome" because in Britain "the

---

[53] On this last point, see also James Hampshire, *Citizenship and Belonging: Immigration and the Politics of Demographic Governance in Postwar Britain* (New York: Palgrave Macmillan, 2005).

[54] Marshall interview.

[55] Pseudonym.

[56] Author's interview with Patricia Edwards (pseudonym), September 2005.

[57] Author's interview with Patricia Edwards (pseudonym), July 2005.

[58] Paul Gilroy, *There Ain't No Black in the Union Jack: The Cultural Politics of Race and Nation* (University of Chicago Press, 1991).

White in Africa was a dirty word," there remained a strong current of popular sympathy toward Rhodesian independence that lasted through the 1960s.[59] Even so, former migrants such as Edwards and Marshall had grown up in a segregated society, where the color line was both more explicit and more uniformly enforced. Whiteness to them meant conforming to a code of conduct that most Britons appeared not to understand. As John Moxham put it, "a lot of them ... weren't that loyal in the way we thought they should be loyal," which made him feel that "going back there, you weren't a Brit in Britain."[60]

This sense of being out of place, of living in a country that should have been familiar but was not, led former migrants to carve out social spaces in which they could commune with fellow colonials and reaffirm their cultural attitudes. In London, the place was Earls Court, west of the city center, which housed the Overseas Visitors Club (OVC), a meeting ground for travelers from the dominions. Peter Gould, who arrived in London in 1958 at the age of twenty-one following eleven years in Southern Rhodesia, nostalgically remembered how "thousands of 'colonials' like myself were converging on the OVC all hell-bent on having a great time." He and the friends he met there called themselves the "Globe Trotters," a name that differentiated their own cosmopolitan status from what they perceived to be the more "domesticated" personalities of the British.[61] Patricia Edwards and her brother Ray,[62] who moved to Earls Court in the early 1960s – and who have a habit of finishing each other's sentences – felt drawn to the neighborhood because "it was an area where there were more people like us":

PATRICIA: That was so much better, being in Earls Court. Because it was all ...
RAY: ... like-minded people.
PATRICIA: All Rhodesians, you know, Australians.
RAY: South Africans, Australians.
PATRICIA: You know, all similar, similar approaches to us.
RAY: They were all very much like us.[63]

Much like the neighborhood of Bayswater, which had become a refuge for returning Anglo-Indians earlier in the century, Earls Court offered dominion migrants emotional ballast and a cultural connection to their

---

[59] Moxham interview. On British attitudes toward the UDI, see Alice Ritscherle, "Disturbing the People's Peace: Patriotism and 'Respectable' Racism in British Responses to Rhodesian Independence," in *Gender, Labour, War and Empire: Essays on Modern Britain*, ed. Philippa Levine and Susan R. Grayzel (London: Palgrave Macmillan, 2009), 197–218.
[60] Moxham interview.    [61] Gould, *Windows*, 252.    [62] Pseudonyms.
[63] Author's interview with Patricia and Ray Edwards (pseudonyms), July 2005.

colonial pasts. As Jimmy Hewitson remarked, Britain was an "alien culture, completely" when he returned in 1966. The "only reason it wasn't too alien, was the fact that I went to Earls Court, which is where all the colonials go ... So it was just a sort of home from home as it were, you know, and the sort of English you used to ... mix with."[64]

Hewitson's use of the term "English," rather than British, reveals the continued ambiguity of postimperial settler identity. At base level, it echoes the earlier belief in Greater Britain as a worldwide community held together by a shared ethnicity. Although the colonials at Earls Court came from the various dominions, they remained "English" at their core, rooted at least in part to the land of their or their ancestors' birth. His larger point, however, is that there was a palpable difference between the "sort of English" whose true "home" was in the empire, and their metropolitan counterparts. His message is that the bonds of empire had been fundamentally redefined, creating two distinct English communities: the domestic and the imperial. This notion of separateness was reiterated by John Moxham, who spoke of falling in with a group of White colonials from east and southern Africa on his arrival in London. "We were practically different from everybody else," he said, noting that "although we came from vast distances in Africa, we could all identify with each other."[65] Such experiences support Wendy Webster's contention that the British cultural landscape was redefined in the later 1950s and 1960s to emphasize domestic over imperial themes.[66] As these oral histories indicate, this rise of "Little Englandism" was perceptible at the time to former colonials, who discerned a widening cultural divide between metropolitan Britain and the settler world. More subtly, they also suggest that this drawing back from empire in the postwar period not only excluded non-White Commonwealth immigrants from popular conceptions of British nationhood but also excluded their White colonial counterparts.

For a sizable minority of Rhodesian migrants, the solution to these feelings of dislocation was to migrate again to one of the other former dominions. South Africa and Australia were the most popular choices since, until recently, these countries had shared a similar ethos of White racial superiority that was familiar to men and women who had grown up in Southern Rhodesia. John Barton, one of the youngest members of the first class of the RFMC that arrived in 1946, stayed in the colony until Robert Mugabe came to power in 1980. Having spent most of

[64] Author's interview with Jimmy Hewitson, October 20, 2005.
[65] Moxham interview.
[66] Wendy Webster, *Englishness and Empire, 1939–1965* (Oxford University Press, 2007).

his adulthood working for the Rhodesian government, he decided that
it was time to leave. Returning to Britain, though, was out of the question. His career in advertising had occasionally taken him to London
during the 1970s, where he had witnessed demonstrations against the
Rhodesian regime that often turned personal: "we used to get kicked out
of places because they wouldn't accept us." Instead, he opted to move
his young family to South Africa, the country that he felt "was the closest
to our lifestyle."[67] Similar reasons impelled James Gunning to relocate
to Australia in the early 1990s following a career in the army and some
years working across southern Africa and Asia. "I couldn't go back to
South Africa, obviously," he said, which was then in the last days of the
apartheid regime, "and Australia seemed to be the closest replica."[68]
Others, however, met unexpected obstacles when trying to move on. John
Andrews, who had served in the Rhodesian police throughout the 1960s,
decided in 1977 that it was time to take his family out of the country.
"We tried to get into Australia," he noted, "but we couldn't because they
only wanted at that time bricklayers and school teachers or something.
We tried to get into New Zealand but ... we had three children and they
would only take you if you had two, no more than two at that time. So
it was back to England. With our tails – well, I always felt, with my tail
between my legs."[69]

This phenomenon of onward migration remains understudied by historians, but is in itself an important legacy of the imperial era. It indicates that, for former migrants such as Barton, Gunning, and Andrews,
the ideal of Greater Britain still holds meaning, even after it has long
since faded from view across the United Kingdom. Moreover, the strategy of onward migration, like the act of self-segregating in areas such as
Earls Court, offered a way to avoid adapting to the challenges of multiculturalism. It enabled former migrants to maintain the attitudes and
beliefs they had forged in the empire, and also encouraged a culture of
victimhood among that segment of the migrant population who felt displaced from postimperial Britain. Whether or not one agrees that these

---

[67] Author's interview with John Barton, July 4, 2009. By the late 1960s, Rhodesia House in
    London was the site of frequent antiapartheid and anti-UDI protests. A common tactic
    was the replace with Rhodesian flag with the Union Jack, a symbolic act that would have
    strengthened Rhodesian migrants' perception that they were unwanted in Britain. On
    these protests, which continued throughout the 1970s, see Josiah Brownell, *The Collapse
    of Rhodesia: Population Demographics and the Politics of Race* (London: I. B. Tauris, 2011),
    99; on the broader phenomenon of postwar White colonial returnees representing the
    positive and negative connotations of imperial Britishness within metropolitan society,
    see Buettner, "'We Don't Grow Coffee and Bananas.'"
[68] Author's interview with James Gunning, February 4, 2006.
[69] Andrews interview.

claims are legitimate, the identity itself is an important political reality, for it continues to inform postcolonial settlers' vision of modern Britain, of the imperial past, and of the project of cultural integration. It helps these former beneficiaries of colonial rule to reposition themselves as the casualties of decolonization, allowing them to present the demise of their political and economic power in terms that are more palatable to current, mainstream sensibilities. They can solicit sympathy for their loss of homeland, nationhood, and sense of belonging rather than for their loss of overt racial authority – although the two are very much connected. And in this respect, these sentiments of exile remain one of the most lasting and politically significant echoes of the British world in the postimperial age.

# Appendix: oral histories

This appendix lists the names of the men and women interviewed for this book, including their gender, the farm school or institution they attended, and the date and location of the interview. Three interviewees, all of whom attended the Rhodesia Fairbridge Memorial College, wished to remain anonymous. In the text, I have given them the pseudonyms Patricia Edwards, Ray Edwards, and Bruce Harris.

| Name of Interviewee | Gender | Institution Attended | Date of Interview | Location of Interview |
|---|---|---|---|---|
| Bill Anderson | M | RFMC | November 9, 2005 | Dudley, UK |
| John Andrews | M | RFMC | December 12, 2005 | Pershore, UK |
| Jim Arthur | M | Fairbridge Pinjarra | February 4, 2006 | Safety Beach, AUS |
| Lynne Babbington | F | RFMC | July 19, 2005; September 25, 2005; May 24, 2009 | London, UK |
| Joan Balcombe | F | RFMC (mother) | December 12, 2005 | Pershore, UK |
| John Barton | M | RFMC | July 4, 2009 | Johannesburg, RSA |
| Ian Bayliff | M | Fairbridge Molong | April 3, 2006 | Ambarvale, AUS |
| Peter Bennett | M | Fairbridge Molong | March 13, 2006 | Sydney, AUS |
| John Bicknell | M | Barnardo's Mowbray Park | May 16, 2006 | Lakesland, AUS |
| Mike Blair | M | Murray Dwyer Orphanage | April 7, 2006 | Parramatta, AUS |
| Alan Buckles | M | RFMC | October 29, 2005 | Milton Keynes, UK |
| Margaret Clarke | F | Fairbridge Molong | March 20, 2006; June 11, 2009 | Sydney, AUS |

| Name of Interviewee | Gender | Institution Attended | Date of Interview | Location of Interview |
|---|---|---|---|---|
| John Cooper | M | Fairbridge Pinjarra | May 28, 2006 | Pinjarra, AUS |
| Susan Corrans (née Stokes) | F | RFMC | December 7, 2005 | Peterborough, UK |
| Violet Couglin | F | Barnardo's | May 17, 2006 | St. Mary's, AUS |
| Geoff Crimes | M | RFMC | July 19, 2005; May 24, 2009 | London, UK |
| Lady Aileen Dodds-Parker | F | Fairbridge Board Member | June 26, 2005 | London, UK |
| Malcomb Field | M | Fairbridge Molong | March 4, 2005 | Orange, AUS |
| Vivian Finn | M | RFMC | September 22, 2005; May 20, 2009 | St. Helens, UK |
| Julia Futcher | F | Fairbridge Molong | December 15, 2005; May 22, 2009 | Sittingbourne, UK |
| Fred Gunning | M | RFMC | September 24, 2005 | Brentwood, UK |
| James Gunning | M | RFMC | February 4, 2006 | Frankston, AUS |
| Bill Hall | M | Fairbridge Molong | March 5, 2006 | Uranquinty, AUS |
| Gillian Hand | F | RFMC | February 9, 2006 | Wentworth Falls, AUS |
| Jimmy Hewitson | M | RFMC | October 20, 2005 | Rossendale, UK |
| John Lane | M | Fairbridge Pinjarra | May 28, 2006 | Pinjarra, AUS |
| Alistair Marshall | M | RFMC | October 10, 2005 | St. Anne's, UK |
| John Moxham | M | RFMC | July 6, 2009 | Johannesburg, RSA |
| John Neil | M | RFMC | December 6, 2005 | Croydon, UK |
| Michael Oldfield | M | Barnardo's Mowbray Park | February 23, 2006; March 2, 2006 | Petersham, AUS |
| Frank Pearce | M | RFMC | June 4, 2009 | Sydney, AUS |
| Ken Pinchess | M | RFMC | October 1, 2005 | Leicester, UK |
| Stephen Player | M | RFMC | September 25, 2005 | Winchester, UK |
| Bert Read | M | Fairbridge Pinjarra | May 28, 2006 | Pinjarra, AUS |
| June-Marie Reid | F | Barnardo's Burwood | May 18, 2006 | South Windsor, AUS |
| Cliff Remmer | M | Barnardo's Mowbray Park | May 13, 2006 | Busby, AUS |

| Name of Interviewee | Gender | Institution Attended | Date of Interview | Location of Interview |
| --- | --- | --- | --- | --- |
| Peter Robinson | M | RFMC | July 4, 2009 | Johannesburg, RSA |
| Dick Shepherd | M | RFMC | October 29, 2005 | Newport, UK |
| Richard Stewart | M | Fairbridge Pinjarra | May 28, 2006 | Pinjarra, AUS |
| Chris Torpey | F | RFMC | October 2, 2005 | Bristol, UK |
| Eva Warhurst | F | Fairbridge Pinjarra | March 30, 2006 | Wentworthville, AUS |

# Bibliography

ARCHIVAL COLLECTIONS

UNITED KINGDOM

Boy Scouts Association Archive, Gilwell Park
  *Papers of the Emigration Department*
Cambridge University Library, Royal Commonwealth Society, Cambridge
  (CUL: RCS)
  *Papers of the Royal Colonial Institute Emigration Committee*
The National Archives, Public Record Office, Kew (TNA: PRO)
  *Cabinet (CAB)*
  *Colonial Office (CO)*
  *Dominions Office (DO)*
  *Home Office (HO)*
  *Law Officers (LO)*
  *Ministry of Labour (LAB)*
  *Ministry of Health (MH)*
  *Ministry of the Treasury (T)*
  *Registrar General's Office (RG)*
University of Liverpool, Special Collections and Archives, Liverpool (ULSCA)
  *Barnardo's Homes Archive*
  *Child Emigration (Fairbridge) Society Archive*
  *National Children's Home Archive*
  *Papers of the Council of Voluntary Organisations for Child Emigration*
University of Oxford, Bodleian Library, Oxford
  *Rhodes Trust Archive*


AUSTRALIA

Australian National Archives, Canberra (ANA)
  *Development and Migration*
  *Home and Territories*
  *Immigration and Lands*
  *Interior*
  *Post-war Reconstruction*
  *Prime Minister's Department*
  *Transport*

Barnardo's New South Wales Archives, Ultima
*Executive and Finance Committees*
National Library of Australia, Canberra
*Forgotten Children and Former Child Migrants Oral History Collection*
State Archives of Western Australia, Battye Library, Perth (SAWA: BL)
*Fairbridge Oral History Collection*
*Papers of the Western Australian Fairbridge Society*
State Library of New South Wales, Mitchell Library, Sydney (SLNSW)
*Papers of the New South Wales Fairbridge Society*
*Sherington Papers*


UNITED STATES

Vassar College, Special Collections and Archives
*Margaret Bondfield Papers*


PUBLISHED SOURCES

"A Barnardo Boy Shoots Employer's Son." *Morning Telegram*, June 23, 1898.
Adams, Mark, ed. *The Wellborn Science: Eugenics in Germany, France, Brazil and Russia*. New York: Oxford University Press, 1990.
Affeldt, Stefanie. "A Paroxysm of Whiteness: 'White' Labor, 'White' Nation, and 'White' Sugar in Australia." In *The Wages of Whiteness and Racist Symbolic Capital*, ed. Wolf D. Hund, Jeremy Krikler, and David Roediger, 99–131. Berlin: Lit Verlag, 2010.
Ali, Nasreen, Virinder S. Kalra, and Salman Sayyid. *A Postcolonial People: South Asians in Britain*. London: C. Hurst and Co., 2006.
Allen, Marjory. "Children in 'Homes': Wards of State or Charity, Inquiry and Reform." *The Times*, July 15, 1944.
*Memoirs of an Uneducated Woman: Lady Allen of Hurtwood*. London: Thames and Hudson, 1975.
Alpen, John. *From Millions to Sydney*. Sydney: The Sydney Club Limited, 1988.
Amery, Julian. "Introduction." In *The Leo Amery Diaries*, ed. John Barnes and David Nicholson, 11–22. London: Hutchinson, 1980.
Amery, Leopold S. *The Leo Amery Diaries*, 2 vols., ed. John Barnes and David Nicholson. London: Hutchinson, 1980.
*My Political Life*, 2 vols. London: Hutchinson, 1953.
Anderson, Warwick. *The Cultivation of Whiteness: Science, Health and Racial Destiny in Australia*. New York: Basic Books, 2003.
Armitage, David. *The Declaration of Independence: A Global History*. Cambridge, MA: Harvard University Press, 2007.
Arnold, David. *The Problem of Nature: Environment, Culture and European Expansion*. Oxford: Blackwell, 1996.
Attwood, Bain. "'Learning about the Truth': The Stolen Generations Narrative." In *Telling Stories: Indigenous History and Memory in Australia and New Zealand*, ed. B. Attwood and F. Magowan, 182–212. Sydney: Allen and Unwin, 2001.
Attwood, Bain and Andrew Markus. *The 1967 Referendum: Race, Power and the Australian Constitution*. Canberra: Aboriginal Studies Press, 1997.
eds. *The Struggle for Aboriginal Rights*. Sydney: Allen & Unwin, 1999.

Bagnell, Kenneth. *The Little Immigrants: The Orphans Who Came to Canada.* Toronto: Dundurn Press, 2001, originally 1980.

Bailkin, Jordanna. "The Postcolonial Family? West African Children, Private Fostering, and the British State." *Journal of Modern History* 81, no. 1 (2009): 87–121.

Ballantyne, Robert. *Dusty Diamonds: Cut and Polished.* London: James Nisbet and Co., 1884.

Ballantyne, Tony. *Orientalism and Race: Aryanism in the British Empire.* New York: Palgrave, 2002.

Barnardo, Thomas. "Is Philanthropic Abduction Ever Justifiable?" *Night and Day* (November 1885): 149–150.

*Never Had a Home: A Very Commonplace History.* London: Shaw and Co., 1890.

Barnardo's. "A Gilt-Edged Investment." *Night and Day* 29 (December 1906): 7.

Bean, Philip and Joy Melville. *Lost Children of the Empire: The Untold Story of Britain's Child Migrants.* London: Unwin Hyman, 1989.

Behlmer, George. *Child Abuse and Moral Reform in England, 1870–1908.* Stanford University Press, 1982.

*Friends of the Family: The English Home and Its Guardians, 1850–1940.* Stanford University Press, 1998.

Behlmer, George and Fred Leventhal, eds. *Singular Continuities: Tradition, Nostalgia, and Identity in Modern British Culture.* Stanford University Press, 2000.

Belich, James. *Paradise Reforged: A History of the New Zealanders from the 1880s to the Year 2000.* Honolulu: University of Hawaii Press, 2001.

*Replenishing the Earth: The Settler Revolution and the Rise of the Angloworld, 1783–1939.* Oxford University Press, 2009.

Bell, Duncan. *The Idea of Greater Britain: Empire and the Future of the World Order, 1860–1900.* Princeton University Press, 2007.

Beresford, Quentin and Paul Omaji. *Our State of Mind: Racial Planning and the Stolen Generations.* Fremantle: Fremantle Arts Centre Press, 1998.

Berridge, Virginia. "Health and Medicine." In *The Cambridge Social History of Britain, 1750–1950*, vol. III, ed. F. M. L. Thompson, 171–242. Cambridge University Press, 1990.

Bickford-Smith, Vivian. "Revisiting Anglicisation in the Nineteenth Century Cape Colony." In *The British World: Diaspora, Culture and Identity*, ed. Carl Bridge and Kent Fedorowich, 82–95. London: Frank Cass, 2003.

Bicknell, John. *The Dirty Bloody Jizzy: An Autobiography.* Gordon, NSW: Mini-Publishing, 2003.

Blackbourn, Geoff. *The Children's Friend Society: Juvenile Emigrants to Western Australia, South Africa and Canada, 1834–1842.* Northbridge: Access Press, 1993.

Blake, Robert. *A History of Rhodesia.* New York: Knopf, 1978.

Bland, Lucy and Lesley Hall. "Eugenics in Britain: The View from the Metropole." In *The Oxford Handbook of the History of Eugenics*, ed. Alison Bashford and Philippa Levine, 213–227. Oxford University Press, 2010.

Bolton, Geoffrey. *A Fine Country to Starve In.* Nedlands: Western Australia University Press, 1994, originally 1972.

*Spoils and Spoilers: Australians Make Their Environment, 1788–1980*. Sydney: Allen and Unwin, 1981.

Bondfield, Margaret. *A Life's Work*. London: Hutchinson, 1948.

Report to the Secretary of State for the Colonies, President of the Oversea Settlement Committee, from the Delegation Appointed to Obtain Information Regarding the System of Child Migration and Settlement in Canada. *Parliamentary Papers*, vol. XV. Cmd. 2285. 1924–1925.

Booth, Charles. *Life and Labour of the People in London*, 17 vols. London: Macmillan, 1889–1903.

Booth, William. *In Darkest England and the Way Out*. London: Salvation Army, 1890.

Boucher, Ellen. "Cultivating Internationalism: The Save the Children Fund, Public Opinion, and the Meaning of Child Relief, 1919–1924." In *Brave New World: Imperial and Democratic Nation-Building in Britain between the Wars*, ed. Laura Beers and Geraint Thomas, 169–188. London: Institute for Historical Research Press, 2012.

"The Limits of Potential: Race, Welfare, and the Interwar Extension of Child Emigration to Southern Rhodesia," *Journal of British Studies* 48 (October 2009): 914–934.

Bowlby, John. *Child Care and the Growth of Love*. Baltimore: Penguin, 1953.

*Fourty-Four Juvenile Thieves: Their Characters and Home-Life*. London: Bailliere, Tindall & Cox, 1946.

"Boy Murderer: Barnardo Youth Slew Benefactor's Daughter and Suicided." *The Comber Herald*, March 25, 1915.

Bradlow, Edna. "The Children's Friend Society at the Cape of Good Hope." *Victorian Studies* 27, no. 2 (Winter 1984): 155–179.

"Empire Settlement and South African Immigration Policy, 1910–1948." In *Emigrants and Empire: British Settlement in the Dominions between the Wars*, ed. Stephen Constantine, 174–202. Manchester University Press, 1990.

Brehony, Kevin. "English Revisionist Froebelians and the Schooling of the Urban Poor." In *Practical Visionaries: Women, Education and Social Progress, 1790–1930*, ed. Mary Hilton and Pam Hirsch, 183–199. London: Longman, 2000.

Bridge, Carl and Kent Fedorowich, eds. *The British World: Diaspora, Culture, and Identity*. London: Frank Cass, 2003.

Briggs, Laura. *Somebody's Children: The Politics of Transracial and Transnational Adoption*. Durham: Duke University Press, 2012.

Briggs, Laura and Diana Marre. "The Circulation of Children." In *International Adoption: Global Inequalities and the Circulation of Children*, ed. Laura Briggs and Diana Marre, 1–28. New York: New York University Press, 2009.

"British Share in Fairbridge: Funds for Rhodesian College." *The Times*, October 6, 1945.

"British Visitors Have Day in City." *The Evening Times-Star*, October 27, 1924.

Broome, Richard. *Aboriginal Australians: Black Responses to White Dominance, 1788–2001*. Crows Nest: Allen & Unwin, 2002.

Brownell, Josiah. *The Collapse of Rhodesia: Population Demographics and the Politics of Race*. London: I. B. Tauris, 2011.

Bryder, Linda. "Wonderlands of Buttercup, Clover and Daisies: Tuberculosis and the Open-Air School Movement in Britain, 1907–1939." In *In the Name of the Child: Health and Welfare, 1880–1940*, ed. Roger Cooter, 72–95. New York: Routledge, 1992.

Buckner, Phillip, ed. *Canada and the End of Empire*. Vancouver: University of British Columbia Press, 2005.

"Canada and the End of Empire, 1939–1982." In *Canada and the British Empire*, ed. Phillip Buckner, 107–126. Oxford University Press, 2008.

"The Creation of the Dominion of Canada, 1860–1901." In *Canada and the British Empire*, ed. Phillip Buckner, 66–86. Oxford University Press, 2008.

Buckner, Phillip and R. Douglas Francis, eds. *Rediscovering the British World*. University of Calgary Press, 2005.

Buettner, Elizabeth. *Empire Families: Britons and Late Imperial India*. Oxford University Press, 2004.

"From Somebodies to Nobodies: Britons Returning Home from India." In *Meanings of Modernity: Britain from the Late-Victorian Era to World War II*, ed. Martin Daunton and Bernhard Rieger, 221–240. New York: Berg, 2001.

"'We Don't Grow Coffee and Bananas in Clapham Junction You Know!': Imperial Britons Back Home." In *Settlers and Expatriates: Britons over the Seas*, ed. Robert Bickers, 302–328. Oxford University Press, 2010.

Burlingham, Dorothy and Anna Freud. *Young Children in War Time*. London: Allen and Unwin, 1942.

Burton, Antoinette. "India, Inc? Nostalgia, Memory, and the Empire of Things." In *British Culture and the End of Empire*, ed. Stuart Ward, 217–232. New York: Manchester University Press, 2001.

ed. *After the Imperial Turn: Thinking With and Through the Nation*. Durham: Duke University Press, 2003.

Buti, Antonio. "British Child Migration to Australia: History, Senate Inquiry, and Responsibilities." *Murdoch University Electronic Journal of Law* 9, no. 4 (December 2002).

Carey, Hilary. *God's Empire: Religion and Colonialism in the British World, 1801–1908*. Cambridge University Press, 2011.

Carnegie Commission. *The Poor White Problem in South Africa*, 5 vols. Stellenbosch: Pro Ecclesia-Drukkery, 1932.

Carter, Sarah. "Aboriginal People of Canada and the British Empire." In *Canada and the British Empire*, ed. Phillip Buckner, 200–219. Oxford University Press, 2008.

Casey, Michael. *The Rhetoric of Garfield Todd: Christian Imagination and the Dream of an African Democracy*. Waco: Baylor University Press, 2007.

Castree, Noel. "Socializing Nature: Theory, Practice, and Politics." In *Social Nature: Theory, Practice and Politics*, ed. Noel Castree and B. Braun, 1–21. Oxford: Blackwell, 2001.

Challiss, R. J. "Education and Southern Rhodesia's Poor Whites, 1890–1930." In *White but Poor: Essays on the History of Poor Whites in Southern Africa, 1880–1940*, ed. Robert Morrell, 151–170. Pretoria: University of South Africa, 1992.

*The European Educational System in Southern Rhodesia, 1890–1930*. Salisbury: University of Zimbabwe, 1980.

Chen, Xiaobei. *Tending the Gardens of Citizenship: Child Saving in Toronto, 1880s–1920s.* University of Toronto Press, 2005.

Chesterman, John. "Natural Born Subjects? Race and British Subjecthood in Australia." *Australian Journal of Politics and History* 51, no. 1 (2005): 30–39.

Chesterman, John and Brian Galligan. *Citizens without Rights: Aborigines and Australian Citizenship.* New York: Cambridge University Press, 1997.

Child, Brenda. *Boarding School Seasons: American Indian Families, 1900–1940.* Lincoln: University of Nebraska Press, 1999.

"Child Immigration Under Discussion." *The Gazette,* October 25, 1924.

Chilton, Lisa. *Agents of Empire: British Female Migration to Canada and Australia, 1860s–1930.* University of Toronto Press, 2007.

Colby, Frank Moore. *The New International Year Book for the Year 1914.* New York: Dodd, Mead, and Co., 1915.

Coldrey, Barry. "'A Charity which Has Outlived Its Usefulness': The Last Phase of Catholic Child Migration, 1947–1956." *History of Education* 25, no. 4 (1996): 373–386.

*Child Migration: Consent of Parents to their Children's Emigration, the Legal and Moral Dimension.* Altrincham: Tamanaraik Press, 1996.

*Child Migration from Malta to Australia: 1930s to 1960s.* Como, WA: Tamanaraik Press, 1992.

*Child Migration to Catholic Institutions in Australia: Objectives, Policies, Realities, 1926–1966.* Como, WA: Tamanaraik Press, 1995.

"'The Extreme End of a Spectrum of Violence': Physical Abuse, Hegemony and Resistance in British Residential Care." *Children and Society* 15 (2001): 95–106.

*The Scheme: The Christian Brothers and Childcare in Western Australia.* O'Connor, WA: Argyle-Pacific Publishers, 1993.

"'A Strange Mixture of Caring and Corruption': Residential Care in Christian Brothers Orphanages and Industrial Schools during their Last Phase, 1940s to 1960s." *History of Education* 29, no. 4 (2000): 343–355.

"'A Thriving and Ugly Trade': The First Phase of Child Migration, 1617–1757." *History of Education Society Bulletin* 58 (Autumn 1996): 4–14.

Cole, Douglas. "The Problem of 'Nationalism' and 'Imperialism' in British Settlement Colonies." *Journal of British Studies* 10, no. 2 (May 1971): 160–182.

Colley, Linda. *Britons: Forging the Nation, 1707–1837.* New Haven: Yale University Press, 1992.

Collini, Stefan. *Public Moralists: Political Thought and Intellectual Life in Britain, 1850–1930.* Oxford: Clarendon Press, 1991.

Constantine, Stephen. "British Emigration to the Empire-Commonwealth since 1880: From Overseas Settlement to Diaspora?" In *The British World: Diaspora, Culture and Identity,* ed. Carl Bridge and Kent Fedorowich, 16–35. London: Frank Cass, 2003.

"The British Government, Child Welfare, and Child Migration to Australia after 1945." *Journal of Imperial and Commonwealth History* 30, no. 1 (January 2002): 99–132.

"Children as Ancestors: Child Migrants and Identity in Canada." *British Journal of Canadian Studies* 16, no. 1 (2003): 150–159.

*The Making of British Colonial Development Policy: 1914–1940.* London: Frank Cass and Co., 1984.

"Waving Goodbye? Australia, Assisted Passages, and the Empire and Commonwealth Settlement Acts, 1945–72." *Journal of Imperial & Commonwealth History* 26 (1998): 176–195.

ed. *Emigrants and Empire: British Settlement in the Dominions between the Wars.* Manchester University Press, 1990.

Cook, Jeanne F. "A History of Placing-Out: The Orphan Trains." *Child Welfare* 74, no. 1 (January–February 1995): 181–197.

Cooper, Frederick. *Africa since 1940:The Past of the Present.* Cambridge University Press, 2002.

*Decolonization and African Society: The Labor Question in French and British Africa.* Cambridge University Press, 1996.

"Modernizing Bureaucrats, Backward Africans, and the Development Concept." In *International Development and the Social Sciences: Essays on the History and Politics of Knowledge*, ed. Frederick Cooper and Randall Packard, 64–92. Berkeley: University of California Press, 1997.

Cooper, Frederick and Ann Stoler, eds. *Tensions of Empire: Colonial Cultures in a Bourgeois World.* Berkeley: University of California Press, 1997.

Cooter, Roger, ed. *In the Name of the Child: Health and Welfare, 1880–1940.* New York: Roultedge, 1992.

Crawford, John and Ian McGibbon, eds. *One Flag, One Queen, One Tongue: New Zealand and the South African War.* Auckland University Press, 2003.

Cunningham, Hugh. *Children and Childhood in Western Society since 1500.* New York: Longman, 1995.

*Children of the Poor: Representations of Childhood since the Seventeenth Century.* London: Blackwell, 1992.

Cunningham, Peter. "The Montessori Phenomenon: Gender and Internationalism in Early Twentieth-Century Innovation." In *Practical Visionaries: Women, Education and Social Progress, 1790–1930*, ed. Mary Hilton and Pam Hirsch, 203–220. London: Longman, 2000.

Curran, James and Stuart Ward. *The Unknown Nation: Australia after Empire.* Melbourne University Press, 2010.

Curthoys, Ann. "Liberalism and Exclusionism: A Prehistory of the White Australia Policy." In *Legacies of White Australia: Race, Culture, and Nation*, ed. Laksiri Jayasuriya, David Walker, and Jan Gothard, 8–32. Crawley: University of Western Australia Press, 2003.

Curthoys, Ann and Marilyn Lake, eds. *Connected Worlds: History in Transnational Perspective.* Canberra: ANU E-Press, 2005.

Curtis, Myra. Report of the Care of Children Committee. *Parliamentary Papers*, vol. X. Cmd. 6922. 1945–1946.

Cuthbert, Denise and Marian Quartly. "'Forced Adoption' in the Australian Story of National Regret and Apology." *Australian Journal of Politics and History* 58, no. 1 (2012): 82–96.

Cuthbert, Denise, Ceridwen Spark, and Kate Murphy. "'That Was Then, but This Is Now': Historical Perspectives on Intercountry Adoption and Domestic Child Adoption in Australian Public Policy." *Journal of Historical Sociology* 23, no. 3 (September 2010): 427–452.

Daglish, Neil. "Education Policy and the Question of Child Labour: The Lancashire Cotton Industry and R. D. Denman's Bill of 1914." *History of Education* 30, no. 3 (May 2001): 291–308.

Dalley, Bronwyn. *Family Matters: Child Welfare in Twentieth-Century New Zealand.* Auckland University Press, 1998.

Darian-Smith, Kate, Patricia Grimshaw, and Stuart Macintyre, eds. *Britishness Abroad: Transnational Movements and Imperial Cultures.* Melbourne University Press, 2008.

Darian-Smith, Kate, Liz Gunner, and Sarah Nuttall, eds. *Text, Theory, Space: Land, Literature and History in South Africa and Australia.* London: Routledge, 1996.

Darwin, John. *Britain and Decolonisation: The Retreat from Empire in the Post-war World.* Basingstoke: Macmillan, 1988.

*The Empire Project: The Rise and Fall of the British World-System, 1830–1970.* Cambridge University Press, 2009.

"A Third British Empire? The Dominion Ideal in British Politics." In *The Oxford History of the British Empire,* vol. IV, ed. Judith Brown and Wm. Roger Lewis, 64–87. Oxford University Press, 1999.

Davenport Hill, Florence. "Emigration of Children." *The Times,* December 27, 1886, 6.

Davidson, Jenny. *Breeding: A Partial History of the Eighteenth Century.* New York: Columbia University Press, 2009.

Davidson, Jim. "The De-dominionisation of Australia." *Meanjin* 38, no. 2 (July 1979): 139–153.

"De-dominionisation Revisited," *Australian Journal of Politics and History* 51, no. 1 (March 2005): 108–113.

Davin, Anna. *Growing Up Poor: Home, School and Street in London, 1870–1914.* London: River Orams Press, 1996.

"Imperialism and Motherhood." In *Tensions of Empire: Colonial Cultures in a Bourgeois World,* ed. Frederick Cooper and Ann Stoler, 87–151. Berkeley: University of California Press, 1997.

Davison, Graeme and Marc Brodie, eds. *Struggle Country: The Rural Ideal in Twentieth Century Australia.* Melbourne: Monash University ePress, 2005.

Denoon, Donald, Philippa Mein-Smith, and Marivic Wyndham. *A History of Australia, New Zealand, and the Pacific.* Oxford: Blackwell, 2000.

Diamond, Marion. *Emigration and Empire: The Life of Maria S. Rye.* New York: Garland, 1999.

Dilke, Charles. *Greater Britain: A Record of Travel in the English-Speaking Countries during 1866 and 1867,* 2 vols. London: Macmillan, 1868.

"Disaster Strikes at Fairbridge College: Sports Gear and Fire in Flames." *Bulawayo Chronicle,* November 3, 1948.

Douglas, R. M. *Orderly and Humane: The Expulsion of Germans after the Second World War.* New Haven: Yale University Press, 2012.

Dowbiggin, Ian. *Keeping America Sane: Psychiatry and Eugenics in the United States and Canada, 1880–1940.* Ithaca: Cornell University Press, 1997.

Downs, Laura Lee. *Childhood in the Promised Land: Working-Class Movements and the Colonies de Vacances in France, 1880–1960.* Durham: Duke University Press, 2002.

"'A Very British Revolution?' L'évacuation des enfants citadins vers les campagnes anglaises, 1939–45," *Vingtième siècle* 89 (January–March 2006): 47–60.

Doyle, Andrew. Report to the President of the Local Government Board, by Andrew Doyle, Local Government Inspector, as to the Emigration of Pauper Children to Canada. *Parliamentary Papers,* vol. LXIII. 1875.

Driver, Felix. *Geography Militant: Cultures of Exploration and Empire.* Oxford: Blackwell, 2001.

"Moral Geographies: Social Science and the Urban Environment in Mid-Nineteenth Century England." *Transactions of the Institute of British Geographers, New Series,* 13, no. 3 (1988): 275–287.

Drysdale, A. M. "Peopling the Empire: The Children's Chance in a New Land." *Daily Chronicle,* January 24, 1920.

Dubow, Saul. "Colonial Nationalism, the Milner Kindergarten, and the Rise of 'South Africanism,' 1902–1910." *History Workshop Journal* 43 (Spring 1997): 53–85.

"How British Was the British World? The Case of South Africa." *Journal of Imperial and Commonwealth History* 37, no. 1 (March 2009): 1–27.

Duke of Argyll. "Planting Out State Children in South Africa." *Nineteenth Century* 47, no. 278 (April 1900): 609–611.

Dunae, Patrick. "Gender, Generations and Social Class: The Fairbridge Society and British Child Migration to Canada, 1930–1960." In *Child Welfare and Social Action in the Nineteenth and Twentieth Centuries: International Perspectives,* ed. Pat Starkey and Jon Lawrence, 82–100. Liverpool University Press, 2001.

"Waifs: The Fairbridge Society in British Columbia, 1931–1951." *Histoire Sociale – Social History* 21 (1988): 224–250.

Dwork, Deborah. *War is Good for Babies and Other Young Children: A History of the Infant and Child Welfare Movement in England, 1898–1918.* New York: Tavistock, 1989.

Eddy, John and Derek Schreuder, eds. *The Rise of Colonial Nationalism: Australia, New Zealand, Canada and South Africa First Assert Their Nationalities, 1880–1914.* Sydney and Boston: Allen and Unwin, 1988.

"The Emigration of Pauper Children." *The Times,* June 11, 1875.

Evans, Raymond. "'Pigmentia': Racial Fears and White Australia." In *Genocide and Settler Society: Frontier Violence and Stolen Indigenous Children in Australian History,* ed. A. Dirk Moses, 103–124. New York: Berghahn Books, 2005.

Fairbridge, Kingsley. "The Farm School System: A Suggestion." *The Times,* May 24, 1910, 46.

*Kingsley Fairbridge: His Life and Verse.* Bulawayo: Rhodesiana Reprint Library, 1974.

"Fairbridge Farm School." *Western Mail,* September 8, 1921.

"Fairbridge School: An Ideal Realised." *Sydney Morning Herald,* March 24, 1938.

"The Farm-Home System: Mrs. Close's Plan." *The Times,* May 24, 1910, 45.

Faught, C. Brad. *Into Africa: The Imperial Life of Margery Perham*. London: I. B. Tauris, 2012.

Fedorowich, Kent. *Unfit for Heroes: Reconstruction and Soldier Settlement in the Empire between the Wars*. Manchester University Press, 1995.

Fedorowich, Kent and Martin Thomas, eds. *International Diplomacy and Colonial Policy*. London: Frank Cass, 2001.

Fink, Janet. "Children of Empire: The Alignments of Church, State, and Family in the Creation of Mobile Children." *Cultural Studies* 21, no. 6 (November 2007): 847–865.

Finlayson, Geoffrey. *Citizen, State and Social Welfare in Britain, 1830–1990*. Oxford: Clarendon Press, 1994.

Fisher, Kate. *Birth Control, Sex and Marriage in Britain 1918–60*. Oxford University Press, 2006.

Forbes, Urquhart A. "Overcrowding and Emigration." *London Quarterly Review* 8, no. 2 (October 1902): 236–252.

Forsyth, W. D. *The Myth of Open Spaces: Australian, British and World Trends of Population and Migration*. Melbourne University Press, 1942.

"From Shadow to Sunshine." *Woman's World*, December 18, 1920.

Frost, Nick and Mike Stein. *The Politics of Child Welfare: Inequality, Power and Change*. New York: Harvester Wheatsheaf, 1989.

Fuchs, Rachel. *Abandoned Children: Foundlings and Child Welfare in Nineteenth Century France*. Albany: State University of New York Press, 1984.

Gann, L. H. *A History of Southern Rhodesia: Early Days to 1934*. London: Chatto & Windus, 1965.

Gann, L. H. and M. Gelfand. *Huggins of Rhodesia: The Man and His Country*. London: Allen and Unwin, 1964.

Garton, Stephen. "Sound Minds and Healthy Bodies: Re-considering Eugenics in Australia, 1914–1940." *Australian Historical Studies* 26, no. 103 (November 1995): 163–181.

Gilbert, William. "Maria S. Rye." *Good Words* 12 (January 1871): 573–577.

Gill, Alan. *Orphans of the Empire: The Shocking Story of Child Migration to Australia*. Sydney: Millennium Books, 1997.

Gilroy, Paul. *There Ain't No Black in the Union Jack: The Cultural Politics of Race and Nation*. University of Chicago Press, 1991.

Glynn, Desmond. "'Exporting Outcast London': Assisted Emigration to Canada, 1886–1914." *Histoire Sociale: Social History* 15, no. 29 (May 1982): 209–238.

Godlewska, Anne and Neil Smith, eds., *Geography and Empire*. Oxford: Blackwell, 1994.

Goldsworthy, David. *Losing the Blanket: Australia and the End of Britain's Empire*. Melbourne University Press, 2002.

Gordon, Avery. *Ghostly Matters: Haunting and the Sociological Imagination*. Minneapolis: University of Minnesota Press, 2008.

Gordon, Linda. *The Great Arizona Orphan Abduction*. Cambridge, MA: Harvard University Press, 1999.

Gorman, Daniel. *Imperial Citizenship: Empire and the Question of Belonging*. Manchester University Press, 2006.

Gould, Peter, ed. *Windows: Rhodesia Fairbridge Memorial College Autobiographies.* Christchurch: Fairbridge Marketing Board, 2001.

Grant, Kevin, Philippa Levine, and Frank Trentmann, eds. *Beyond Sovereignty: Britain, Empire and Transnationalism, 1880–1950.* New York: Palgrave Macmillan, 2007.

Gray, Richard. *The Two Nations: Aspects of the Development of Race Relations in the Rhodesias and Nyasaland.* London: Oxford University Press, 1960.

Grey, Jeffrey. "War and the British World in the Twentieth Century." In *Rediscovering the British World,* ed. Phillip Buckner and R. Douglas Francis, 233–250. University of Calgary Press, 2005.

Grier, Julie. "Voluntary Rights and Statutory Wrongs: The Case of Child Migration, 1948–1967." *History of Education* 31, no. 3 (2002): 263–280.

Grimshaw, Patricia, Marilyn Lake, Ann McGrath, and Marian Quartly. *Creating a Nation.* Ringwood: McPhee Gribble, 1994.

Hadley, Elaine. "Natives in a Strange Land: The Philanthropic Discourse of Juvenile Emigration in Mid-Nineteenth-Century England." *Victorian Studies* 33, no. 3 (Spring 1990): 411–439.

Haebich, Anna. *Broken Circles: Fragmenting Indigenous Families, 1800–2000.* Fremantle: Fremantle Arts Centre Press, 2000.

*Spinning the Dream: Assimilation in Australia, 1950–1970.* Fremantle: Fremantle Press, 2008.

Hall, Catherine. *Civilising Subjects: Metropole and Colony in the English Imagination, 1830–1867.* University of Chicago Press, 2002.

ed. *Cultures of Empire, a Reader: Colonizers in Britain and the Empire in the Nineteenth and Twentieth Centuries.* Manchester University Press, 2000.

Hall, Catherine and Sonya Rose, eds. *At Home with the Empire: Metropolitan Culture and the Imperial World.* Cambridge University Press, 2006.

Hamer, David. *New Towns in the New World: Images and Perceptions of the Nineteenth Century Urban Frontier.* Columbia University Press, 1990.

Hamilton, Paula and Linda Shopes, eds. *Oral History and Public Memory.* Philadelphia: Temple University Press, 2008.

Hammerton, A. James and Alistair Thomson. *Ten Pound Poms: Australia's Invisible Migrants.* New York: Manchester University Press, 2005.

Hampshire, James. *Citizenship and Belonging: Immigration and the Politics of Demographic Governance in Postwar Britain.* New York: Palgrave Macmillan, 2005.

Harper, Marjory, ed. *Emigrant Homecomings: The Return Movement of Emigrants, 1600–2000.* Manchester University Press, 2005.

Harper, Marjory and Stephen Constantine. *Migration and Empire.* Oxford University Press, 2010.

Harris, Bernard. *The Health of the Schoolchild: A History of School Medical Service in England and Wales.* Buckingham: Open University Press, 1995.

Harris, Jose. "Between Civic Virtue and Social Darwinism: The Concept of the Residuum." In *Retrieved Riches: Social Investigation in Britain, 1840–1914,* ed. David Englander and Rosemary O'Day, 67–87. Aldershot: Scolar Press, 1995.

*Private Lives and Public Spirit: A Social History of Britain, 1870–1914.* Oxford University Press, 1993.

"War and Social History: Britain and the Home Front during the Second World War." *Contemporary European History* 1 (1992): 17–35.

Harrison, Phyllis, ed. *The Home Children*. Winnipeg: Watson and Dyer, 1979.

Haultain, Arnold. "Who Should Emigrate to Canada?" *Monthly Review* 11, no. 33 (June 1903): 91–108.

Heinlein, Frank. *British Government Policy and Decolonisation, 1945–1963: Scrutinising the Official Mind*. London: Routledge, 2002.

Hendrick, Harry. *Children, Childhood and English Society, 1880–1990*. Cambridge University Press, 1997.

*Child Welfare: Historical Dimensions, Contemporary Debate*. Bristol: Policy Press, 2003.

Heywood, Jean. *Children in Care: The Development of the Service for the Deprived Child*. London: Routledge & Kegan Paul, 1978, originally 1959.

Hickson, Flo. *Flo: Child Migrant from Liverpool*. Warwick, Plowright Press, 1998.

Hill, David. *The Forgotten Children: Fairbridge Farm School and Its Betrayal of Britain's Child Migrants to Australia*. Sydney: Random House, 2007.

Hilton, Boyd. *Age of Atonement: The Influence of Evangelicalism on Social and Economic Thought, 1796–1865*. New York: Clarendon Press, 1988.

Holland, Robert. "The British Empire and the Great War, 1914–1918." In *The Oxford History of the British Empire*, vol. IV, ed. Judith Brown and Wm. Roger Louis, 114–137. Oxford University Press, 1999.

Holt, Marilyn. *The Orphan Trains: Placing Out in America*. Lincoln: University of Nebraska Press, 1992.

Hopkins, A. G. "Rethinking Decolonization," *Past and Present* 200 (August 2008): 211–247.

Hopkins, Eric. *Childhood Transformed: Working-Class Children in Nineteenth Century England*. Manchester University Press, 1994.

House of Commons, Health Committee. *The Welfare of Former British Child Migrants*. London: HMSO, 1998.

Hughes, David McDermott. *Whiteness in Zimbabwe: Race, Landscape, and the Problem of Belonging*. New York: Palgrave Macmillan, 2010.

Hughes, W. M. *The Splendid Adventure: A Review of Empire Relations within and without the Commonwealth of Britannic Nations*. London: Ernest Benn, 1929.

Human Rights and Equal Opportunity Commission. *Bringing Them Home: Report of the National Inquiry into the Separation of Aboriginal and Torres Strait Islander Children from Their Families*. Canberra: Commonwealth of Australia, 1997.

Humphreys, Margaret. *Empty Cradles*. London: Doubleday, 1994.

Hyam, Ronald. *Britain's Declining Empire: The Road to Decolonisation, 1918–1968*. Cambridge University Press, 2006.

Igartua, José. *The Other Quiet Revolution: National Identities in English Canada, 1945–1971*. Vancouver: University of British Columbia Press, 2006.

"Immigration Problem: Placing Children on the Land." *The Age*, September 27, 1921.

Inglis, Ruth. *The Children's War: Evacuation, 1939–1945*. London: Collins, 1989.

Isaacs, Susan. "Children in Homes." *The Times*, July 18, 1944.

ed. *The Cambridge Evacuation Survey: A Wartime Study in Social Welfare and Education*. London: Methuen and Co., 1941.

Jackson, Ashley. *The British Empire and the Second World War*. New York: Hambledon Continuum, 2006.

Jackson, Lynette. *Surfacing Up: Psychiatry and Social Order in Colonial Zimbabwe, 1908–1968*. Ithaca: Cornell University Press, 2005.

Jacobs, Margaret. *White Mother to a Dark Race: Settler Colonialism, Maternalism, and the Removal of Indigenous Children in the American West and Australia, 1880–1940*. Lincoln: University of Nebraska Press, 2009.

James, Winston and Clive Harris. *Inside Babylon: The Caribbean Diaspora in Britain*. New York: Versa, 1993.

Jeffrey, Keith. "The Second World War." In *The Oxford History of the British Empire*, vol. IV, ed. Judith Brown and Wm. Roger Lewis, 306–328. Oxford University Press, 1999.

"John Immigrant: The Big Adventure." *Manchester Guardian*, January 15, 1931.

Jones, Kathleen. *Taming the Troublesome Child: American Families, Child Guidance, and the Limits of Psychiatric Authority*. Cambridge, MA: Harvard University Press, 1999.

Jones, Ross. "Removing Some of the Dust from the Wheels of Civilization: William Ernest Jones and the 1928 Commonwealth Survey of Mental Deficiency." *Australian Historical Studies* 40, no. 1 (March 2009): 63–78.

Jordan, Thomas. *The Degeneracy Crisis and Victorian Youth*. Albany: State University of New York Press, 1993.

Joyce, Patrick. *Visions of the People: Industrial England and the Question of Class, 1848–1914*. New York: Cambridge University Press, 1991.

Jupp, James. *The English in Australia*. Cambridge University Press, 2004.

Keeling, E. H. "Children in Homes. The Institutional System. A War-Time Experiment." *The Times*, July 18, 1944.

"Keeping Australia White." *Millions Magazine* 1, no. 5 (November 1919): 1.

Kelley, Ninette and Michael Trebilcock. *The Making of the Mosaic: A History of Canadian Immigration Policy*, 2nd edn. University of Toronto Press, 2010.

Keltie John Scott and M. Epstein, eds. *The Statesman's Year-book*. London: Macmillan and Co., 1920.

Kennedy, Dane. *Islands of White: Settler Society and Culture in Kenya and Southern Rhodesia, 1890–1939*. Durham: Duke University Press, 1987.

Kennedy, Roseanne. "Stolen Generations Testimony: Trauma, Historiography, and the Question of 'Truth.'" In *The Oral History Reader*, ed. Robert Perks and Alistair Thomson, 506–520. New York: Routledge, 2006.

Kershaw, Roger and Janet Sacks. *New Lives for Old*. Kew: The National Archives, 2008.

Kevles, Daniel. *In the Name of Eugenics: Genetics and the Uses of Human Heredity*. New York: Knopf, 1985.

Kirk, David and Karen Twigg. "Regulating Australian Bodies: Eugenics, Anthropometrics and School Medical Inspection in Victoria, 1900–1940." *History of Education Review, ANZHES* 23, no. 1 (1994): 19–37.

Kohli, Marjorie. *The Golden Bridge: Young Immigrants to Canada, 1833–1939*. Toronto: Natural Heritage, 2003.

Koven, Seth. "Remembering and Dismemberment: Crippled Children, Wounded Soldiers, and the Great War in Britain." *American Historical Review* 99, no. 4 (October 1994): 1167–1202.

*Slumming: Sexual and Social Politics in Victorian London.* Princeton University Press, 2004.

Lake, Marilyn. *The Limits of Hope: Soldier Settlements in Victoria, 1905–1938.* Oxford University Press, 1987.

"The Politics of Respectability: Identifying the Masculinist Context." *Historical Studies* 22, no. 18 (1986): 116–131.

"A Revolution in the Family: The Challenge and Contradictions of Maternal Citizenship in Australia." In *Mothers of a New World: Maternalist Politics and the Origins of Welfare States,* ed. Seth Koven and Sonya Michel, 378–395. New York: Routledge, 1993.

Lake, Marilyn and Henry Reynolds. *Drawing the Global Colour Line: White Men's Countries and the International Challenge of Racial Equality.* Cambridge University Press, 2008.

Lane, John. *Fairbridge Kid.* Pinjarra: Fairbridge Western Australia, 2000.

Langfield, Michele. *More People Imperative: Immigration to Australia, 1900–1939.* Canberra: Australian National Archives, 1999.

"Voluntarism, Salvation, and Rescue: British Juvenile Migration to Australia and Canada, 1890–1939." *Journal of Imperial and Commonwealth History* 32, no. 2 (May 2004): 86–114.

"'White Aliens': The Control of European Immigration to Australia, 1920–1930." *Journal of Intercultural Studies* 12, no. 2 (1991): 1–14.

Lees, Lynn. *The Solidarity of Strangers: The English Poor Laws and the People, 1700–1948.* Cambridge University Press, 1998.

Levine, Philippa. "Sexuality, Gender, and Empire." In *Gender and Empire,* ed. Philippa Levine, 134–155. Oxford University Press, 2004.

Lewis, Jane. *The Politics of Motherhood: Child and Maternal Welfare in England, 1900–1939.* London: Croom Helm, 1980.

*The Voluntary Sector, the State and Social Work in Britain: The Charity Organisation Society/Family Welfare Association since 1869.* Aldershot: Edward Elgar, 1995.

Lewis, Joanna. "'Daddy Wouldn't Buy Me a Mau Mau': The British Popular Press and the Demoralization of Empire." In *Mau Mau and Nationhood,* ed. E. S. Atieno Odiambo and John Lonsdale, 227–250. Oxford: James Currey, 2003.

"Light Shed Upon Migration Problem." *Edmonton Farm Journal,* October 15, 1924.

Lines, William. *Taming the Great South Land: A History of the Conquest of Nature in Australia.* Athens: University of Georgia Press, 1999.

Livingstone, David. "Climate's Moral Economy: Science, Race and Place in Post-Darwinian British and American Geography." In *Geography and Empire,* ed. Neil Smith and Anna Godlewska, 132–154. Oxford: Blackwell, 1994.

Loach, Jim, dir. *Oranges and Sunshine.* Screen Australia, 2010.

Lord Bishop of Glasgow and Galloway. "The Cyanide Process." *Night and Day* 33, no. 252 (1910).

Lorimer, Douglas. "From Victorian Values to White Virtues: Assimilation and Exclusion in British Racial Discourse, 1870–1914." In *Rediscovering the British World,* ed. Phillip Buckner and R. Douglas Francis, 109–134. University of Calgary Press, 2005.

Louis, Wm. Roger. "The Dissolution of the British Empire." In *The Oxford History of the British Empire*, vol. IV, ed. Judith Brown and Wm. Roger Lewis, 329–355. Oxford University Press, 1999.

    *In the Name of God, Go! Leo Amery and the British Empire in the Age of Churchill.* New York: W. W. Norton, 1992.

Lovelock, Kristen. "Intercountry Adoption as a Migratory Practice: A Comparative Analysis of Intercountry Adoption and Immigration Policy and Practice in the United States, Canada, and New Zealand in the Post WWII Period." *International Migration Review* 34, no. 3 (Autumn 2000): 907–949.

Lovett, Laura. *Conceiving the Future: Pronatalism, Reproduction, and the Family in the United States, 1890–1938.* Chapel Hill: University of North Carolina Press, 2007.

Lowry, Donal. "Not Just a Teatime War." In *The South African War Reappraised*, ed. Donal Lowry, 1–22. Manchester University Press, 2000.

    "Rhodesia 1890–1980: 'The Lost Dominion.'" In *Settlers and Expatriates: Britons over the Seas*, ed. Robert Bickers, 112–149. Oxford University Press, 2010.

    "'South African without the Afrikaners': The Creation of a Settler Identity in Southern Rhodesia." Paper presented at the Biennial South African Historical Association Conference, Rhodes University, 1995.

Luk, Wai-ki. *Chinatown in Britain: Diffusions and Concentrations of the British New Wave Immigration.* London: Cambria Press, 2008.

Lynn, Martin, ed. *The British Empire in the 1950s: Retreat or Revival?* New York: Palgrave Macmillan, 2006.

Macintyre, Stuart. *A Concise History of Australia.* Cambridge University Press, 1999.

Mack, Joanna and Mike Fox, dirs. *Lost Children of the Empire.* Manchester: Granada Television, 1989.

Macnicol, John. "The Effect of the Evacuation of Schoolchildren on Official Attitudes to State Intervention." In *War and Social Change: British Society in the Second World War*, ed. Harold L. Smith, 3–31. Manchester University Press, 1986.

Mandler, Peter. "Against 'Englishness': English Culture and the Limits to Rural Nostalgia, 1850–1940," *Transactions of the Royal Historical Society* 7 (1996): 155–175.

Mangan, J. A., ed. *"Benefits Bestowed"? Education and British Imperialism.* New York: Manchester University Press, 1988.

    ed. *The Imperial Curriculum: Racial Images and Education in the British Colonial Experience.* New York: Routledge, 1993.

    ed. *Making Imperial Mentalities: Socialisation and British Imperialism.* New York: Manchester University Press, 1990.

Manne, Robert. "Aboriginal Child Removal and the Question of Genocide, 1900–1940." In *Genocide and Settler Society: Frontier Violence and Stolen Indigenous Children in Australian History*, ed. A. Dirk Moses, 217–243. New York: Berghan Books, 2004.

Marks, Shula and Stanley Trapido. "Lord Milner and the South African State," *History Workshop* 8 (October 1979): 50–80.

Markus, Andrew. *Race: John Howard and the Remaking of Australia.* Sydney: Allen & Unwin, 2001.

Markus, Andrew, James Jupp, and Peter McDonald. *Australia's Immigration Revolution*. Crows Nest: Allen & Unwin, 2009.

Marsh, Jan. *Back to the Land: The Pastoral Impulse in England from 1880 to 1914.* New York: Quartet Books, 1982.

Marshall, Dominique. "The Construction of Children as an Object of International Relations: The Declaration of Children's Rights and the Child Welfare Committee of the League of Nations, 1900–1924." *The International Journal of Children's Rights* 7 (1999): 103–147.

Martin, Ged. "Canada from 1815." In *The Oxford History of the British Empire*, vol. III, ed. Andrew Porter, 522–545. Oxford University Press, 1999.

May, Alex. "Empire Loyalists and 'Commonwealth Men': The Round Table and the End of Empire." In *British Culture and the End of Empire*, ed. Stuart Ward, 37–56. Manchester University Press, 2001.

Mazower, Mark. *Dark Continent: Europe's Twentieth Century.* New York: Vintage, 1998.

McCann, Joy. "History and Memory in Australia's Wheatlands." In *Struggle Country: The Rural Ideal in Twentieth Century Australia*, ed. Graeme Davison and Marc Brodie, 1–17. Melbourne: Monash University ePress, 2005.

McCulloch, Jock. *Black Peril, White Virtue: Sexual Crime in Southern Rhodesia, 1902–1935.* Bloomington: University of Indiana Press, 2000.

*Colonial Psychiatry and the African Mind.* New York: Cambridge University Press, 1995.

McDonald, Dugald and Suzanne de Joux. *British Child Migrants in New Zealand, 1949–1999: Fifty Years of New Stories.* Christchurch: British Child Migrants Society NZ, 2000.

McDonald, Sandra Rennie. "Victoria's Immigration Scandal of the Thirties." *Victorian Historical Journal* 4, no. 4 (1978): 229–237.

McGregor, Russell. *Imagined Destinies: Aboriginal Australians and the Doomed Race Theory, 1880–1939.* Melbourne University Press, 1997.

McLaren, Angus. *Our Own Master Race: Eugenics in Canada, 1885–1945.* Oxford University Press, 1990.

Meaney, Neville. "Britishness and Australian Identity: The Problem of Nationalism in Australian History and Historiography." *Australian Historical Studies* 32, no. 116 (April 2001): 76–90.

"Britishness and Australia: Some Reflections." *Journal of Imperial and Commonwealth History* 31, no. 2 (May 2003): 121–135.

Mehta, Uday Singh. *Liberalism and Empire: A Study in Nineteenth-Century British Liberal Thought.* University of Chicago Press, 1999.

Miller, Carman. *Painting the Map Red: Canada and the South African War, 1899–1902.* Montreal: McGill-Queen's University Press, 1992.

Mitchell, Juliet. *Psychoanalysis and Feminism.* New York: Basic Books, 2000, originally 1974.

Mitchell, Margaret. "The Effects of Unemployment on the Social Condition of Women and Children in the 1930s." *History Workshop Journal* 19 (1985): 105–127.

Mizutani, Satoshi. *The Meaning of White: Race, Class, and the "Domiciled Community" in British India, 1858–1930.* Oxford University Press, 2011.

Mlambo, A. S. *White Immigration into Rhodesia: From Occupation to Federation.* Harare: University of Zimbabwe, 2002.

Monet, Jacques. "Canadians, Canadiens, and Colonial Nationalism, 1896–1914: The Thorn in the Lion's Paw." In *The Rise of Colonial Nationalism: Australia, New Zealand, Canada and South Africa First Assert Their Nationalities, 1880–1914*, ed. John Eddy and Derek Schreuder, 160–191. Sydney and Boston: Allen and Unwin, 1988.

Morrell, Robert, ed. *White but Poor: Essays on the History of Poor Whites in Southern Africa, 1880–1940*. Pretoria: University of South Africa, 1992.

Moses, A. Dirk, ed. *Genocide and Settler Society: Frontier Violence and Stolen Indigenous Children in Australian History*. New York: Berghahn Books, 2005.

Moss, John. "Children in Homes. Smaller Units. The Right Kind of Staff." *The Times*, July 24, 1944.

Moyles, R. G. and Doug Owram. *Imperial Dreams and Colonial Realities: British Views of Canada, 1880–1914*. University of Toronto Press, 1988.

Mrs. Meredith, "Juvenile Emigration." *Sunday at Home* 1369 (July 24, 1880): 477–478.

Mungazi, Dickson. *The Last British Liberals in Africa: Michael Blundell and Garfield Todd*. London: Praeger, 1999.

"A Strategy for Power: Commissions of Inquiry into Education and Government Control in Colonial Zimbabwe." *The International Journal of African Historical Studies* 22, no. 2 (1989): 267–285.

Murdoch, Lydia. *Imagined Orphans: Poor Families, Child Welfare, and Contested Citizenship in London*. New Brunswick: Rutgers University Press, 2006.

Murphy, Kate, Sarah Pinto, and Denise Cuthbert. "'These Infants Are Future Australians': Making the Nation through Intercountry Adoption." *Journal of Australian Studies* 34, no. 2 (June 2010): 141–161.

Murphy, Kate, Marian Quartly, and Denise Cuthbert. "'In the Best Interests of the Child': Mapping the (Re)emergence of Pro-adoption Politics in Contemporary Australia." *Australian Journal of Politics and History* 55, no. 2 (2009): 201–218.

*My Cottage: A Story of Dr. Barnardo's Village Home for Orphan and Destitute Girls* (London: Shaw and Co., 1885).

Nankivell, Joice. "Emigrate the Babies." *British-Australian*, May 1922.

Natural Resources, Trade, and Legislation of Certain Portions of His Majesty's Dominions: Final Report. *Parliamentary Papers*, vol. X. Cmd. 8462. 1917–1918.

Niemeyer, Otto, Evelyn Fox, Doris Odlum, R. G. Gordon, and Alan Maberly, "Children in Homes. The Training of Staff. A National Certificate." *The Times*, July 27, 1944.

Nord, Deborah Epstein. "The Social Explorer as Anthropologist: Victorian Travelers among the Urban Poor." In *Visions of the Modern City: Essays in History, Art, and Literature*, ed. William Sharpe and Leonard Wallock, 122–134. Baltimore: Johns Hopkins University Press, 1987.

O'Connor, Stephen. *Orphan Trains: The Story of Charles Loring Brace and the Children He Saved and Failed*. New York: Houghton Mifflin, 2001.

Otter, Chris. *The Victorian Eye: A Political History of Light and Vision in Britain, 1800–1910*. University of Chicago Press, 2008.

Packman, Jean. *The Child's Generation: Child Care Policy in Britain*. Oxford: Blackwell, 1975.

Paisley, Fiona. "Childhood and Race: Growing Up in the Empire." In *Gender and Empire*, ed. Philippa Levine, 240–259. Oxford University Press, 2004.

Palmer, Howard. "Reluctant Hosts: Anglo-Canadian Views of Multiculturalism in the Twentieth Century." In *Immigration in Canada: Historical Perspectives*, ed. Gerald Tulchinsky, 297–333. Toronto: Copp Clark Longman, 1994.

Palmer, Robin. *Land and Racial Domination in Rhodesia*. Berkeley: University of California Press, 1977.

Parker, John. *Rhodesia: Little White Island*. London: Pitman Publishing, 1972.

Parker, Roy. *Uprooted: The Shipment of Poor Children to Canada, 1867–1917*. Vancouver: University of British Columbia Press, 2008.

Parr, Joy. *Labouring Children: British Immigrant Apprentices to Canada, 1869–1924*. University of Toronto Press, 1994, originally 1980.

Parry, Suzanne. "Identifying the Process: The Removal of 'Half-Caste' Children from Aboriginal Mothers." *Aboriginal History* 19, no. 2 (1995): 141–153.

Paul, Kathleen. "Changing Childhoods: Child Emigration since 1945." In *Child Welfare and Social Action in the Nineteenth and Twentieth Centuries: International Perspectives*, ed. Jon Lawrence and Pat Starkey, 121–143. Liverpool University Press, 2001.

*Whitewashing Britain: Race and Citizenship in the Postwar Era*. Ithaca: Cornell University Press, 1997.

Pearce, Lionel. *Feathers of the Snow Angel: Memories of a Child in Exile*. Fremantle: Fremantle Arts Centre Press, 2002.

Pearson, Charles. *National Life and Character: A Forecast*. London: Macmillan, 1893.

Pedersen, Susan. *Family, Dependence, and the Origins of the Welfare State: Britain and France, 1914–1945*. Cambridge University Press, 1993.

Pelham, W. H. W. "Emigration of Pauper Children." *The Times*, January 22, 1877, 4.

"Peopling Australia: Existing Methods Fail." *The Age*, August 30, 1923.

"Peopling the Empire: The Children's Chance in a New Land." *Daily Chronicle*, January 24, 1920.

Peters, Laura. *Orphan Texts: Victorian Orphans, Culture, and Empire*. Manchester University Press, 2000.

Phillips, Mike and Trevor Phillips. *Windrush: The Irresistible Rise of Multi-racial Britain*. New York: Harper Collins, 1998.

Philpot, Terry. *Action for Children: The Story of Britain's Foremost Children's Charity*. Oxford: Lion Publishing, 1994.

Plant, G. F. *Oversea Settlement: Migration from the United Kingdom to the Dominions*. London: Oxford University Press, 1951.

Portelli, Alessando. *The Death of Luigi Trastulli and Other Stories: Form and Meaning in Oral History*. Albany: State University of New York Press, 1991.

Potter, Simon. "Communication and Integration: The British and Dominions Press and the British World, 1876–1914." In *The British World: Diaspora, Culture and Identity*, ed. Carl Bridge and Kent Fedorowich, 190–206. London: Frank Cass, 2003.

*News and the British World: The Emergence of an Imperial Press System, 1876–1922*. New York: Oxford University Press, 2003.

Price, Alun. "Children's Home from Inside. Former Inmate's Experiences. 'Shocking Conditions.'" *The Times*, August 23, 1944.

Price, Richard. *Making Empire: Colonial Encounters and the Making of Imperial Rule in Nineteenth-Century Africa.* Cambridge University Press, 2008.

Prochaska, Frank. *Christianity and Social Service in Modern Britain: The Disinherited Spirit.* Oxford University Press, 2006.

*The Voluntary Impulse: Philanthropy in Modern Britain.* London: Faber, 1988.

Ranger, Terence. *Are We Not Also Men? The Samkange Family and African Politics in Zimbabwe, 1920–1964.* London: James Currey, 1995.

Read, Peter. *A Rape of the Soul So Profound: The Return of the Stolen Generations.* Sydney: Allen and Unwin, 1999.

*The Stolen Generations: The Removal of Aboriginal Children in New South Wales, 1833–1969.* Sydney: New South Wales Department of Aboriginal Affairs, 1981.

Report of the Inter-Departmental Committee on Migration Policy. *Parliamentary Papers*, vol. X. Cmd. 4689. 1934.

Report of the Inter-Departmental Committee on Physical Deterioration. *Parliamentary Papers*, vol. XXXII. Cmd. 2175. 1904.

Report of the Oversea Settlement Committee. *Parliamentary Papers*, vols. XXII–XIV. Cmds. 573, 1134, 1580, 1804, 2107, 2383, 2640, 2847, 3088, 3308, 3589, 3887, 4143, 4391, 4687, 4993, 5200, 5314, 5766. 1919–1938.

Rich, Paul. *Race and Empire in British Politics*, 2nd edn. New York: Cambridge University Press, 1990.

Richards, Eric. *Britannia's Children: Emigration from England, Scotland, Wales and Ireland since 1600.* London: Hambledon and London, 2004.

Riley, Denise. *War in the Nursery: Theories of the Child and Mother.* London: Virago, 1983.

Ritscherle, Alice. "Disturbing the People's Peace: Patriotism and 'Respectable' Racism in British Responses to Rhodesian Independence." In *Gender, Labour, War and Empire: Essays on Modern Britain*, ed. Philippa Levine and Susan R. Grayzel, 197–218. London: Palgrave Macmillan, 2009.

Roberts, Barbara. *Whence They Came: Deportation from Canada, 1900–1935.* University of Ottawa Press, 1988.

Roe, Michael. *Australia, Britain, and Migration, 1915–1940: A Study of Desperate Hopes.* Cambridge University Press, 1995.

Rooke, Patricia and R. L. Schnell. *Discarding the Asylum: From Child Rescue to the Welfare State in English-Canada, 1800–1950.* Lanham: University Press of America, 1983.

*No Bleeding Heart: Charlotte Whitton, a Feminist on the Right.* Vancouver: University of British Columbia Press, 1987.

"'Uncramping Child Life': International Children's Organisations, 1914–1939." In *International Health Organisations and Movements*, ed. Paul Weindling, 203–221. Cambridge University Press, 1995.

Rose, Lionel. *The Erosion of Childhood: Child Oppression in Britain, 1860–1918.* New York: Routledge, 1991.

Rose, Nikolas. *Governing the Soul: The Shaping of the Private Self.* New York: Free Association Books, 1999.

*The Psychological Complex: Psychology, Politics and Society in England, 1869–1939.*
London: Routledge & Kegan Paul, 1985.

Rose, Sonya. *Which People's War? National Identity and Citizenship in Wartime Britain, 1939–1945.* Oxford University Press, 2003.

Ross, Ellen. *Love and Toil: Motherhood in Outcast London, 1870–1918.* Oxford University Press, 1993.

Ross, John. Child Migration to Australia: Report of a Fact-Finding Mission. *Parliamentary Papers*, vol. XXIII. Cmd. 9832. 1955–1956.

Rowe, Michael. *The Racialisation of Disorder in Twentieth Century Britain.* Aldershot: Ashgate, 1998.

Rowntree, Seebohm. *Poverty: A Study of Town Life.* London: Macmillan, 1901.

Rutherdale, Myra. "Scrutinizing the 'Submerged Tenth': Salvation Army Immigrants and Their Reception in Canada." In *Canada and the British World: Culture, Migration, and Identity*, ed. Phillip Buckner and R. Douglas Francis, 174–198. Vancouver: University of British Columbia Press, 2006.

Rutter, Michael. *Maternal Deprivation Reassessed.* London: Penguin, 1981, originally 1972.

Rye, Maria S. Letter Addressed by Miss Rye to the President of the Local Government Board. *Parliamentary Papers*, vol. LXXI. 1877.

"Our Gutter Children." *The Times*, March 29, 1869, 8.

Sadowsky, Jonathan. *Imperial Bedlam: Institutions of Madness in Colonial Southwest Nigeria.* Berkeley: University of California Press, 1999.

Said, Edward. *Reflections on Exile and Other Essays.* Cambridge, MA: Harvard University Press, 2000.

Schreuder, Derick and Stuart Ward, eds. *Australia's Empire.* Oxford University Press, 2008.

Scott, Dorothy and Shurlee Swain. *Confronting Cruelty: Historical Perspectives on Child Protection in Australia.* Melbourne University Press, 2002.

Searle, Geoffrey. *Eugenics and Politics in Britain, 1900–1914.* Leyden: Noordhoff Publishing, 1976.

*The Quest for National Efficiency: A Study in British Politics and Political Thought, 1899–1914.* Berkeley: University of California Press, 1971.

Sedgwick, T. E. *Town Lads on Imperial Farms, with Notes on Other Phases of Imperial Migration.* London: P. S. King and Son, 1913.

Seeley, J. R. *The Expansion of England: Two Courses of Lectures.* London: Macmillan, 1883.

Senate Community Affairs References Committee. *Lost Innocents: Righting the Record – Report on Child Migration.* Canberra: Commonwealth of Australia, 2001.

Shapira, Michal. *The War Inside: Psychoanalysis, Total War and the Making of the Democratic Self in Postwar Britain.* Cambridge University Press, 2013.

Shaw, G. B. "Bringing Up the Child. A Contrast in Method." *The Times*, July 21, 1944.

Sherington, Geoffrey. *Australia's Immigrants, 1788–1988.* Sydney: Allen and Unwin, 1990.

"Fairbridge Child Migrants." In *Child Welfare and Social Action in the Nineteenth and Twentieth Centuries: International Perspectives*, ed. Jon Lawrence and Pat Starkey, 53–81. Liverpool University Press, 2001.

"'Suffer Little Children': British Child Migration as a Study of Journeying between Centre and Periphery." *History of Education* 32, no. 5 (September 2003): 461–476.

Sherington, Geoffrey and Chris Jeffery. *Fairbridge: Empire and Child Migration.* London: Woburn Press, 1998.

Shute, Carmel. "Heroines and Heroes: Sexual Mythology in Australia, 1914–1918." In *Gender and War: Australians at War in the Twentieth Century*, ed. Joy Damousi and Marilyn Lake, 23–42. Cambridge University Press, 1995.

Shutt, Allison and Tony King. "Imperial Rhodesians: The 1953 Rhodes Centenary Exhibition in Southern Rhodesia." *Journal of Southern African Studies* 31, no. 2 (June 2005): 357–379.

Sinha, Mrinalini. *Specters of Mother India: The Global Restructuring of an Empire.* Durham: Duke University Press, 2006.

Sircombe, Amanda. "A Welfare Initiative? The New Zealand Child Migrant Scheme, 1948–1954." Unpublished MA thesis, University of Waikato, 2004.

Smith, Alison and Mary Bull, eds. *Margery Perham and British Rule in Africa.* London: Frank Cass, 1991.

Smith, Andrea, ed. *Europe's Invisible Migrants.* Amsterdam: Amsterdam University Press, 2003.

Social Service Council of Canada. *Canada's Child Immigrants: Annual Report of the Committee of Immigration and Colonization of the Social Service Council of Canada.* Toronto: Social Service Council of Canada, 1926.

Soloway, Richard. *Demography and Degeneration: Eugenics and the Declining Birthrate in Twentieth-Century Britain.* Chapel Hill: University of North Carolina Press, 1995.

Spencer, Ian. *British Immigration Policy since 1939: The Making of Multi-racial Britain.* New York: Routledge, 1997.

Starkey, Pat. "Can the Piper Call the Tune? Innovation and Experiment with Deprived Families in Britain, 1940–1980s: The Work of Family Service Units." *British Journal of Social Work* 32 (2002): 573–587.

*Families and Social Workers: The Work of the Family Service Units, 1940–1985.* Liverpool University Press, 2000.

"The Feckless Mother: Women, Poverty and Social Workers in Wartime and Post-war England." *Women's History Review* 9, no. 3 (September 2000): 539–557.

Stead, W. T. "For All Those Who Love Their Fellow-Men." *Review of Reviews* (December 1901): 670–678.

Stedman Jones, Gareth. *Outcast London: A Study in the Relationship between Classes in Victorian Society.* Oxford: Clarendon Press, 1971.

Steedman, Carolyn. "Bodies, Figures and Physiology: Margaret McMillan and the Late Nineteenth-Century Remaking of Working-Class Childhood." In *In the Name of the Child: Health and Welfare, 1880–1940*, ed. Roger Cooter, 19–44. New York: Routledge, 1992.

*Childhood, Culture and Class in Britain: Margaret McMillan, 1860–1931.* London: Virago, 1990.

*Landscape for a Good Woman: A Story of Two Lives.* London: Virago, 1986.

*Strange Dislocations: Childhood and the Idea of Human Interiority, 1780–1930.* Cambridge, MA: Harvard University Press, 1995.

Stepan, Nancy. *The Idea of Race in Science: Great Britain, 1800–1960.* London: Macmillan, 1982.

Stevenson, Francis. "Child-Settlers for South Africa." *Nineteenth Century* 50, no. 298 (December 1901): 1020–1029.

Stoler, Ann. *Carnal Knowledge and Imperial Power: Race and the Intimate in Colonial Rule.* Berkeley: University of California Press, 2010, originally 2002.

*Race and the Education of Desire: Foucault's History of Sexuality and the Colonial Order of Things.* Durham: Duke University Press, 1995.

"Tense and Tender Ties: The Politics of Comparison in North American Studies and (Post) Colonial History." *Journal of American History* 88, no. 3 (December 2001): 829–865.

Summers, Carol. *From Civilization to Segregation: Social Ideals and Social Control in Southern Rhodesia, 1890–1934.* Athens: Ohio University Press, 1994.

Sutherland, Gillian. *Ability, Merit and Measurement: Mental Testing and English Education, 1880–1940.* Oxford: Clarendon Press, 1984.

Sutherland, Neil. *Children in English-Canadian Society: Framing the Twentieth-Century Consensus.* University of Toronto Press, 1976.

Swain, Shurlee. "'Brighter Britain': Images of Empire in the International Child Rescue Movement, 1850–1914." In *Empires of Religion*, ed. Hilary Carey, 161–176. New York: Palgrave Macmillan, 2008.

"Child Rescue: The Emigration of an Idea." In *Child Welfare and Social Action in the Nineteenth and Twentieth Centuries: International Perspectives*, ed. Pat Starkey and Jon Lawrence, 101–120. Liverpool University Press, 2001.

Swain, Shurlee, Patricia Grimshaw, and Ellen Warne. "Whiteness, Maternal Feminism, and the Working Mother, 1900–1960." In *Creating White Australia*, ed. Jane Carey and Claire McLisky, 214–227. Sydney University Press, 2009.

Swain, Shurlee and Margot Hillel. *Child, Nation, Race and Empire: Child Rescue Discourse, England, Canada, and Australia, 1850–1915.* Manchester University Press, 2010.

Szreter, Simon and Kate Fisher. *Sex before the Sexual Revolution: Intimate Life in England, 1918–1963.* Cambridge University Press, 2010.

Tallack, William. "The Emigration of Children." *The Times*, November 26, 1886, 4.

Thane, Pat. *Foundations of the Welfare State.* New York: Longman, 1996.

"That Barnardo Boy." *The Windsor Evening Record*, November 28, 1895.

Thom, Deborah. "Wishes, Anxieties, Play and Gestures: Child Guidance in Inter-War England." In *In the Name of the Child: Health and Welfare, 1880–1940*, ed. Roger Cooter, 200–219. New York: Routledge, 1992.

Thompson, Andrew. *The Empire Strikes Back? The Impact of Imperialism on Britain from the Mid-Nineteenth Century.* New York: Pearson Longman, 2005.

Thompson, Andrew with Meaghan Kowalsky. "Social Life and Cultural Representation: Empire in the Public Imagination." In *Britain's Experience of Empire in the Twentieth Century*, ed. Andrew Thompson, 251–297. Oxford University Press, 2012.

Thompson, John Herd. "Canada and the 'Third British Empire,' 1901–1939." In Phillip Buckner, ed., *Canada and the British Empire*, 87–106. Oxford University Press, 2008.

Thomson, Mathew. *Psychological Subjects: Identity, Culture and Health in Twentieth-Century Britain*. Oxford University Press, 2006.

"'Savage Civilisation': Race, Culture, and Mind in Britain, 1898–1939." In *Race, Science and Medicine: Racial Categories and the Production of Medical Knowledge, 1700–1960*, ed. Waltraud Ernst and Bernard Harris, 235–258. New York: Routledge, 1999.

Titmuss, Richard. *Problems of Social Policy* (London: HMSO, 1950), 123.

United Kingdom. Parliamentary Debates, Commons. 5th series, 1918–1939.

Urwin, Cathy and Elaine Sharland. "From Bodies to Minds in Childcare Literature: Advice to Parents in Inter-War Britain." In *In the Name of the Child: Health and Welfare, 1880–1940*, ed. Roger Cooter, 174–199. New York: Routledge, 1992.

van der Horst, Frank C. P. and René van der Veer. "The Ontogeny of an Idea: John Bowlby and Contemporaries on Mother–Child Separation." *History of Psychology* 13, no. 1 (2010): 25–45.

van Dijken, Suzan, René van der Veer, Marinus van Ijzendoorn, and Hans-Jan Kuipers. "Bowlby before Bowlby: The Sources of an Intellectual Departure in Psychoanalysis and Psychology." *Journal of the History of Behavioral Sciences* 34, no. 3 (Summer 1998): 247–269.

Veeck, Gregory, Clifton Pannell, Christopher Smith, and Youqin Huang. *China's Geography: Globalization and the Dynamics of Political, Economic, and Social Change*. Lanham: Rowman and Littlefield, 2007.

Vernon, James. "The Ethics of Hunger and the Assembly of Society: The Techno-Politics of the School Meal in Modern Britain." *American Historical Review* 110, no. 3 (2005): 693–725.

*Hunger: A Modern History*. Cambridge: Belknap Press, 2007.

Wagner, Gillian. *Barnardo*. London: Weidenfeld and Nicolson, 1979.

*Children of the Empire*. London: Weidenfeld and Nicolson, 1982.

Walker, David. *Anxious Nation: Australia and the Rise of Asia, 1850–1939*. Brisbane: University of Queensland Press, 1999.

"Race Building and the Disciplining of White Australia." In *Legacies of White Australia: Race, Culture, and Nation*, ed. Laksiri Jayasuriya, David Walker, and Jan Gothard, 33–50. Crawley: University of Western Australia Press, 2003.

Walkowitz, Judith. *City of Dreadful Delight: Narratives of Sexual Danger in Late Victorian London*. Chicago: Chicago University Press, 1992.

Wall, Richard. "English and German Families and the First World War, 1914–1918." In *The Upheaval of War: Family, Work and Welfare in Europe, 1914–1918*, ed. Richard Wall and Jay Winter, 43–106. Cambridge University Press, 2005, originally 1988.

Ward, Russel. *The Australian Legend*. Melbourne: Oxford University Press, 1958.

*The History of Australia: The Twentieth Century*. New York: Harper and Row, 1977.

Ward, Stuart. *Australia and the British Embrace: The Demise of the Imperial Ideal*. Melbourne University Press, 2001.

"Echoes of Empire." *History Workshop Journal* 62, no. 1 (October 2006): 264–278.

"The End of Empire and the Fate of Britishness." In *History, Nationhood, and the Question of Britain*, ed. Helen Brocklehurst and Robert Phillips, 242–258. New York: Palgrave, 2004.

"Imperial Identities Abroad." In *The British Empire: Themes and Perspectives*, ed. Sarah Stockwell, 219–245. Oxford: Blackwell, 2008.

"The 'New Nationalism' in Australia, Canada and New Zealand: Civic Culture in the Wake of the British World." In *Britishness Abroad: Transnational Movements and Imperial Cultures*, ed. Kate Darian-Smith, Patricia Grimshaw, and Stuart Macintyre, 231–263. Melbourne University Press, 2008.

ed. *British Culture and the End of Empire*. New York: Manchester University Press, 2001.

Warren, Allen. "Popular Manliness: Baden Powell, Scouting, and the Development of Manly Character." In *Manliness and Morality: Middle-Class Masculinity in Britain and America*, ed. J. A. Mangin and James Wolvin, 199–217. Manchester University Press, 1987.

Waterhouse, Richard. *The Vision Splendid: A Social and Cultural History of Rural Australia*. Fremantle: Curtin University Books, 2005.

Waters, Chris. "'Dark Strangers' in Our Midst: Discourses of Race and Nation in Britain, 1947–1963." *Journal of British Studies* 36 (April 1997): 207–238.

Watt, Lori. "Imperial Remnants: The Repatriates in Postwar Japan." In *Settler Colonialism in the Twentieth Century*, ed. Caroline Elkins and Susan Pedersen, 243–255. New York: Routledge, 2005.

Watts, Carl Peter. *Rhodesia's Unilateral Declaration of Independence: International Dimensions*. New York: Palgrave Macmillan, 2012.

Watts, Rob. "Beyond Nature and Nurture: Eugenics in Twentieth Century Australian History." *Australian Journal of Politics and History* 40, no. 3 (September 1994): 318–334.

Webster, Charles. "Health, Welfare and Unemployment during the Depression." *Past and Present* 109 (1985): 204–230.

Webster, Wendy. *Englishness and Empire, 1939–1965*. Oxford University Press, 2007.

*Imagining Home: Gender, "Race" and National Identity, 1954–1964*. New York: Routledge, 1998.

Weindling, Paul. "From Sentiment to Science: Children's Relief Organisations and the Problem of Malnutrition in Inter-War Europe," *Disasters* 18, no. 3 (September 1994): 203–212.

Welshman, John. *Churchill's Children: The Evacuee Experience in Wartime Britain*. Oxford University Press, 2010.

"Evacuation, Hygiene and Social Policy: The Our Towns Report of 1943." *The Historical Journal* 42, no. 3 (September 1999): 781–807.

West, Michael O. *The Rise of an African Middle Class: Colonial Zimbabwe, 1898–1965*. Bloomington: Indiana University Press, 2002.

Wheeler, Henry, "My Story, in Short." In *With the Best of Intentions: Stories from Dr. Barnardo's Farm School at Mowbray Park near the Oaks, NSW, 1929–1959*, ed. Doreen Lyon, 9–11. The Oaks: The Oaks Historical Society, 2010.

White, Luise. "What Does it Take to Be a State: Sovereignty and Sanctions in Rhodesia, 1965–1980." In *The State of Sovereignty: Territories, Laws, Populations*, ed. Douglas Howland and Luise White, 148–168. Bloomington: Indiana University Press, 2009.

White, Nicholas. *Decolonisation: The British Experience since 1945*. New York: Longman, 1999.

White, Richard. *Inventing Australia: Images and Identity, 1688–1980*. London: Allen and Unwin, 1981.

"White Australia: The Settler's 'El Dorado,'" *The Times*, October 14, 1921, 12.

Wilcox, Craig. *Australia's Boer War: The War in South Africa, 1899–1902*. Oxford University Press, 2002.

Williams, Keith. "'A Way Out of Our Troubles': The Politics of Empire Settlement, 1900–1922." In *Emigrants and Empire: British Settlement in the Dominions between the Wars*, ed. Stephen Constantine, 22–44. Manchester University Press, 1990.

Wilson, Heather. "British Stock for a British Dominion: The New Zealand Government's Child Migration Scheme." Unpublished MA thesis, University of Auckland, 1996.

Wilson, Kathleen, ed. *A New Imperial History: Culture, Identity and Modernity in Britain and the Empire, 1660–1840*. Cambridge University Press, 2004.

Winter, Jay. "Unemployment, Nutrition and Infant Mortality in Britain, 1920–1950." In *The Working Class in Modern British History*, ed. J. M. Winter, 232–256. Cambridge University Press, 1983.

Women's Group on Public Welfare. *Child Emigration: A Study Made in 1948–1950 by a Committee of Women's Group on Public Welfare in Association with the National Council of Social Service*. London: National Council of Social Service, 1951.

　　*Our Towns – A Close Up: A Study Made in 1939–1942 with Certain Recommendations by the Hygiene Committee of the Women's Group on Public Welfare*. London: Oxford University Press, 1943.

Wooldridge, Adrian. *Measuring the Mind: Education and Psychology in England, 1860–1990*. Cambridge University Press, 1994.

Woollacott, Angela. "Gender and Sexuality." In *Australia's Empire*, ed. Derick Schreuder and Stuart Ward, 312–335. Oxford University Press, 2008.

　　*To Try Her Fortune in London: Australian Women, Colonialism, and Modernity*. Oxford University Press, 2001.

Woolmer, D. L. "Up the Ladder." *Quiver* 985 (January 1903): 881–887.

Zahra, Tara. *Kidnapped Souls: National Indifference and the Battle for Children in the Bohemian Lands, 1900–1948*. Ithaca: Cornell University Press, 2008.

　　*The Lost Children: Reconstructing Europe's Families after World War II*. Cambridge, MA: Harvard University Press, 2011.

Zelizer, Viviana. *Pricing the Priceless Child: The Changing Social Value of Children*. New York: Basic Books, 1985.

# Index

CPSIA information can be obtained
at www.ICGtesting.com
Printed in the USA
LVOW10s1926141217
559744LV00014B/239/P

9 781316 620304